The American
Military Tradition

The American Military Tradition

From Colonial Times to the Present

SECOND EDITION

**Edited by John M. Carroll
and Colin F. Baxter**

ROWMAN & LITTLEFIELD PUBLISHERS, INC.

Lanham • Boulder • New York • Toronto • Oxford

IAN & LITTLEFIELD PUBLISHERS, INC.

ublished in the United States of America
by Rowman & Littlefield Publishers, Inc.
A wholly owned subsidary of The Rowman & Littlefield Publishing Group, Inc.
4501 Forbes Boulevard, Suite 200, Lanham, Maryland 20706
www.rowmanlittlefield.com

PO Box 317
Oxford
OX2 9RU, UK

British Library Cataloguing in Publication Information Available

Library of Congress Cataloging-in-Publication Data

The American military tradition : from colonial times to the present /
edited by John M. Carroll and Colin F. Baxter.— 2nd ed.
p. cm.
Includes bibliographical references and index.
ISBN-13: 978-0-7425-4427-7 (cloth : alk. paper)
ISBN-10: 0-7425-4427-3 (cloth : alk. paper)
ISBN-13: 978-0-7425-4428-4 (pbk. : alk. paper)
ISBN-10: 0-7425-4428-1 (pbk. : alk. paper)
1. United States—History, Military. I. Carroll, John M. (John Martin),
1943– II. Baxter, Colin F., 1942–
E181.A445 2007
355'.00973—dc22   2006008393

Printed in the United States of America

©™ The paper used in this publication meets the minimum requirements of
American National Standard for Information Sciences—Permanence of Paper
for Printed Library Materials, ANSI/NISO Z39.48-1992.

Contents

Preface

THIS BOOK contains twelve original chapters on major issues and events in American military history. Although the authors are dealing with complex material and an extended time span ranging from the colonial era to the present, they have attempted to make their chapters meaningful, challenging, and enjoyable for the undergraduate student and the general reader by focusing on a number of central themes in the U.S. military experience. Designed to complement a standard textbook for courses in U.S. military history or to supplement other reading material, the book presents interpretive material from new viewpoints, as well as traditional ones, and should assist in stimulating class discussion and instigating debate. The authors, both teachers and researchers, have not hesitated to express opinions or take stands on critical issues and have tried to produce an exciting, readable, and thought-provoking study rather than a mere collection of facts.

The American Military Tradition includes a general introduction and an afterword and focuses on central questions about the nation's military heritage: Who fought America's wars, and how did they fight them? The chapters trace the evolution of America's military tradition from reliance on the citizen-soldier, the Minuteman of the Revolution, to a mixed force including a growing number of professional soldiers, to an era of mainly all-professional armed forces. In accounting for this gradual transition, the authors examine the shifting position of the United States in international affairs, changes in technology and weaponry, new military strategies, and battlefield events that contribute to America's evolving military posture. Beyond this, the chapters provide readers with a sample of what commanders and common soldiers faced in combat by examining specific battles from our more than two centuries of military history. While the authors do not intend this volume to be a comprehensive account of America's wars or military tradition, they do hope to provide a useful commentary and analysis concerning some of the most pressing questions and issues in the nation's martial experience.

The initial idea for this book resulted from the experiences and friendships that many of the authors gained while attending the U.S. Army Training and Doctrine Command ROTC Workshop in military history at the United States Military Academy in the mid-1980s. Many of us concluded at the time that we lacked an adequate, succinct text for our military history courses. We found that the book helped fill that void and was also of interest to a larger public audience. This revised and expanded edition of *The American Military Tradition* includes both revised chapters and new chapters written by specialists from a variety of different backgrounds. We believe that these new chapters, as well as the revised ones, enhance the quality of the volume and keep it abreast of new interpretations and the challenging events of the twenty-first century.

We would like to acknowledge the numerous people who contributed to the completion of this book. Many friends offered suggestions; colleagues read parts of the manuscript. To all our friends and colleagues, our thanks. We would like to thank the officers who were especially helpful in guiding many of us through the summer workshop at West Point many years ago. Also, we are extremely pleased that a number of internationally recognized military scholars agreed to contribute new chapters to this revised edition. All of the scholars who contributed to the book gave generously of their time and talents and accepted our editorial revisions with remarkable forbearance. Special thanks go to Matt Hershey, who got this project underway, and especially to Laura Gottlieb and her staff at Rowman & Littlefield who brought it to fruition.

Introduction

WITH THE FIRST successful English settlements in the New World during the early seventeenth century, colonists gave considerable attention to military matters. Contrary to the popular image of devout Pilgrims feasting with peaceable Indians in Plymouth during the 1620s, most British colonials were acutely aware of the perils that they faced in their tenuous settlements on the edge of a vast continent. It was no accident that one of the first heroes of the colonial era was Capt. John Smith, a military veteran of many European wars, who was employed by the Virginia Company to teach the military art to settlers in Jamestown. Even the pious Pilgrims in Massachusetts to the north retained Capt. Myles Standish, a veteran of the Dutch wars for independence, to help protect them. Lesser-known military leaders were hired by other colonies as more English settlements dotted the Atlantic coast during the 1600s. One of the priorities in these settlements was to establish a plan of defense to protect British colonials from raids by hostile Indians, pillaging from seaborne buccaneers and pirates, or attacks by the French or Spaniards.

Whether they came to North America for religious or economic reasons or a combination of the two, most colonials were a product of English tradition and history. In the military sphere, British settlers shared a fear of a professional standing army and would rely on the long-established institution of the militia for their defense. Standing armies had been a recent development in Europe, and many citizens came to distrust and even despise the king's forces. Recruited mainly from the lower ranks of society, the standing army served the king and the elite class. Citizens paid taxes to support this professional force and the wars that it waged in the name of the monarch.

The standing army was also used to expand the king's dominance over his realm, to impose more centralized control, and to collect taxes and put down urban demonstrations and riots. In Britain, many citizens believed that such an army was a threat to their basic rights as Englishmen. The militia, a citizen force dating back to feudal times, was locally controlled and seen as a bulwark against centralized authority. In every colony, the militia would develop into the primary military institution.

The early English settlers in America were fortunate to have landed in an area where Indian tribes had experienced a drastic decline in population. But the colonials would discover that the Indians could be a formidable foe. To protect themselves, they constructed forts and defense perimeters and organized militias. The nature of the militia varied from colony to colony and evolved over time. Colonial laws decreed that all able-bodied men belonged to the militia. They supplied and maintained their own weapons and were compelled to attend periodic musters. These musters were frequent during the early stages of colonization, when danger was acute, but became less frequent by the early 1700s. The weaponry of the militiaman evolved over time. At first, the colonial soldier, like his European counterpart, wore armor and carried a pike or a matchlock musket, and usually a sword. Neither the armor nor the pike was effective in fighting Indians in the rugged North American forests. The matchlock musket was superior to the Indian bow and arrow, but it was slow to load and often misfired, especially in inclement weather. Indians seldom stood and fought in massed formations, and militiamen found their weapons cumbersome in tracking tribesmen through the dense forests. By the 1600s the militiamen were armed with flintlock muskets that could be loaded in thirty seconds and were less apt to misfire than the old matchlocks. Both weapons were muzzle-loading smoothbores best suited for firing in volleys.

The militia was a distinctly local institution, and its men seldom fought far from home. Its officers came from the upper stratum of colonial society and usually participated in political affairs as well. Despite the irregular style of combat required in fighting Indians in rugged terrain, militia units were trained for the more open, massed style of combat common in Europe. They drilled on town or village greens in lines in accordance with British military manuals and discharged volleys against the imagined enemy. Militiamen were slow in mastering the art of Indian-style irregular combat.

By the 1700s many militia regiments, especially in coastal areas, declined in efficiency as the Indian menace lessened. During the long series of wars against France and its Indian allies in North America (Imperial Wars, 1689–1763), the real fighting was not done by the militia but rather by British regulars and provincial forces recruited by colonial governments for a single campaign. Only occasionally did militia regiments take the field. The militia, however, remained as an infrastructure that supported provincial forces and was ably suited to defend the home colony, as British regulars would discover during the American Revolution.

During the Imperial Wars, provincial forces fought alongside British regulars in many campaigns. British officers were almost unanimous in their criticism. According to them, the Americans were lazy, ill-disciplined, slovenly, and ineffective; they had mastered neither the irregular Indian-style combat nor the European method of open-field fighting. Many redcoats confused the provincial forces with the militia that they would confront in the mid-1770s. Most provincials came to despise their British superiors. They regarded the majority of British professionals as haughty, merciless, cruel, and godless. The Americans also exaggerated their own military contributions to the final defeat of New France (formalized by the Treaty of Paris, 1763) and minimized the role of the British professional forces. This helps account for the confidence with which many Americans protested British policies after the Treaty of Paris and went to war against the mother country in 1775. The 1763 treaty, which should have fostered closer bonds between Britain and America, left a legacy of estrangement and bitterness for many colonials.

The dispute between Britain and America, which led to the Revolution, began immediately after the Treaty of Paris. The Proclamation of 1763, issued by King George III, which forbade colonial migration beyond the Appalachian Mountains, together with the stationing of British forces in coastal cities, caused some colonial leaders to become suspicious of British policies and intentions. While the main focus of American discontent centered on the political principle that Parliament had no right to tax the colonies without their consent (a process that began with the Sugar Act of 1764), the presence of British land and naval power to enforce these and other restraining laws contributed to American resentment of British hegemony.

In the first chapter, David Overy and Kevin Gannon provide an overview of what historian Francis Parkman described as a half century of conflict for the mastery of North America. During the Imperial Wars, American volunteers and British professionals fought side by side against the French, but the experience mainly demonstrated their differing views on how warfare should be conducted and exposed a cultural gap between the two societies. The conclusion of the French and Indian War led only to a deepening division between the two peoples, which resulted in open rebellion by the colonials in 1775. Despite the confidence that many Americans had in their military abilities, the rebellious colonies faced a difficult challenge in confronting one of the most powerful nations on the globe. George Washington, whom the Second Continental Congress summoned to mold a force capable of sustaining the Revolution, opted to create an army on the British model. He hoped to train a force that could defeat British professionals in European-style combat. While Washington never wavered in his objective and ultimately succeeded in fielding a first-rate professional army, his early defeats, recurrent recruitment and logistical problems, and the dominance of the British navy forced his commanders to rely on the militia at key points during the conflict. One of the legacies of the American Revolution is the debate over the efficacy of the professional versus the citizen-soldier. The authors highlight the fact that while it may be argued that Washington's professionally trained Continental Army was the key to victory over Britain, many Americans were convinced that the militia, the immortal Minuteman, was mainly responsible for independence.

After the Revolution, Americans were wary of strong central authority, which they equated with the tyrannical policies of Parliament and the king. They also remained fearful of a professional standing army and were confident that Minutemen or citizen-soldiers could be summoned to meet any threat. The Articles of Confederation, the nation's first constitution, did not allow Congress directly to raise a national military force. Under the Articles, states provided troops for the central government on a quota system. The Newburgh Conspiracy of 1783 reinforced public anxiety about a professional standing force. After a decade of turmoil under the new government, the Articles of Confederation were replaced by the U.S. Constitution in 1788. Under the Constitution, the powers of the central government were expanded and Congress was given the authority to raise and support an army and a navy. During the 1790s, Congress maintained a small professional army, but the militia, mainly under state control, continued to provide the preponderance of the nation's military strength. The

Uniform Militia Act of 1792, which remained the basic law until the twentieth century, embodied the concepts of universal military service and the citizen-soldier.

The beginning of the French Revolution in 1789 would drastically alter political affairs in Europe and bring about dramatic changes on the battlefield. Owen Connelly examines the impact of the Wars of the French Revolution and the subsequent Napoleonic Wars on the military art. In Europe, the limited wars of the eighteenth century gave way to intense nationalistic struggles. Nations conscripted mass armies in order to decide the fate of the Continent. The United States was fortunate to be separated from Europe by a vast ocean and largely to escape the devastation of the Napoleonic Wars. An undeclared naval conflict with France (the Quasi-War) in the late 1790s briefly brought the nation to arms and helped establish a naval tradition, but the prudent leadership of President John Adams prevented a full-scale clash with a European power, at least for the moment. Americans were slow to understand the full meaning of the military changes in Europe, which Connelly describes, but over time they would begin to apply the lessons of that great European struggle to their own circumstances.

Before the conflict in Europe ended, the United States became engaged in a second war with Britain. Provoked mainly by violations of its neutral trading rights, America declared war in 1812. J. David Valaik analyzes the War of 1812 as the first of two distinctly limited wars fought by the United States in the first half of the nineteenth century. Given its long-standing fear of a large standing army and over a decade of rule by frugal Democratic-Republican presidents, it is not surprising that America was not prepared for the 1812 conflict. Despite some solid performances by the militia, most notably under Andrew Jackson at New Orleans, Valaik argues that it was the successes of professional officers that allowed the Americans to stalemate the British by 1814. Afterward, the United States took steps to incorporate some of the lessons learned from the earlier Napoleonic Wars. The revamping of West Point into a formal military academy, for example, would pay dividends during the second conflict, the Mexican War. Essentially, however, the nation reverted to its traditional reliance on a small professional army supported by the militia system. The Mexican War showed that the professionally trained officers were more than capable of defeating an ineptly led enemy in a limited conflict. Still, the myth persisted that volunteers, many with militia training, were largely responsible for the victory over Mexico.

The Mexican War, and especially the new western territory acquired as a result of it, helped to propel the nation toward the Civil War. William Piston explains why the Civil War can be considered the first modern war. Professionally trained generals sought to duplicate Napoleon's decisive victories of fifty years before, but too much had changed in the interim for them to succeed. The use of rifled muskets and other improved weaponry made the war the deadliest in U.S. history. More than 600,000 soldiers were killed and large sections of the South were devastated. As in the case of America's previous wars, the nation quickly returned to peacetime conditions despite the turbulent period of Reconstruction. By 1876 the army's strength was slashed to about 27,000 men, and the navy fared little better. Most of the land force was stationed on the western frontier. Jerome Greene examines the complex problems faced by the U.S. Army in its attempts to pacify Indian tribes. While the country rapidly industrialized and some leaders entertained visions of great-power status, the army continued to be engaged in short, violent campaigns against the powerful Indian tribes.

By the end of the nineteenth century the United States had embarked upon a course of imperial conquest. The navy had been reconstructed into a modern force, but the army remained undermanned and provincial, at least for a nation seeking great-power status. A short "splendid little war" against Spain (1898) marked America's emergence as a world power and provided the nation with a modest but sprawling empire. The Spanish-American War also exposed many organizational deficiencies in the U.S. Army. During Theodore Roosevelt's administration, the army was reorganized under the general staff concept, but on the eve of the Great War (1914–1918) it remained smaller and far below the standards of the major European powers. David Woodward traces the course of American mobilization and its military contribution to the Allied victory in World War I. By the end of the conflict the United States had sent about two million soldiers to Europe and had built a navy second to none. But, as in the case of previous wars, America quickly demobilized its large army and relied on sea power as the bulwark of defense in the interwar years.

As international conditions deteriorated during the 1930s, President Franklin Roosevelt took halting steps toward rearmament, including, in 1940, the first peacetime draft. Japan's surprise attack on Pearl Harbor in the following year catapulted the nation into the greatest war in its history. Colin Baxter examines America's contribution to the Allied war effort in Europe, to which Roosevelt and his military advisers gave the highest priority. Concurrent with the Allied drive against Adolf Hitler in Europe, the United States mounted a nearly separate war against Japan in the Pacific. H. P. Willmott explains the complex origins of the Pacific war in the 1930s and analyzes how and why U.S. forces eventually defeated the Empire of Japan and devastated its home islands by August 1945.

The dawn of the nuclear age with the explosion of two atomic bombs over Japan in 1945 portended a new and more dangerous era of warfare. When the Grand Alliance of World War II broke down shortly after the end of the conflict, two superpowers, the United States and the Soviet Union, confronted one another in a tense struggle of stratagems called the Cold War. The Soviet development of an atomic bomb in 1949 caused many observers to fear that the next war, World War III, would result in a nuclear holocaust. But America's next two wars, both undeclared, were limited conflicts undertaken to contain Communist expansion in Asia. Pierce Mullen examines U.S. problems and frustrations in fighting a limited war in Korea in the early 1950s. The stalemate in Korea, however, did not dampen America's enthusiasm enough to thwart what it perceived to be another Soviet-inspired move in Southeast Asia. John Carroll traces the origin and development of the U.S. involvement in the Vietnam War within the context of the Cold War. America's longest conflict overextended the nation's resources in the face of worldwide responsibilities and resulted in a tempering of its willingness to engage in further limited wars. One of the prime reasons for America's involvement in these two wars, of course, was one of the alternatives, nuclear war. Walter Hixson examines the nuclear arms race between the United States and the Soviet Union from its origins in the 1940s and speculates on the prospects of nuclear disarmament in the post–Cold War era.

During the last two decades, many changes have taken place that have affected—and will continue to affect—the future military posture of the United States. The collapse of Communist regimes in Eastern Europe and the Soviet Union have ended the so-called Cold War after a half century, but also have led to some instability in these regions. During the mid-1990s, political leaders in Washington made significant cuts in military appropriations but continued to face crises resulting largely from political instability and/or aggression in various parts of the globe, including among others southeastern Europe (Bosnia/Kosovo), Latin America (Panama), and the Middle East (Iraq/Palestine).

The whole direction and focus of America's military strategy changed dramatically after the stunning terrorist attacks of September 11, 2001. A nation that had been enjoying a period of relative tranquility abroad and prosperity at home in the aftermath of the Cold War was suddenly traumatized and called to arms by President George W. Bush. Christopher Harmon provides some background on international terrorism, an analysis of events that have taken place since 9/11, and a look at how the United States' military focus has changed since that tragic day.

The Colonial Wars and the American Revolution

DAVID H. OVERY AND KEVIN M. GANNON

IN THEIR CHAPTER, David Overy and Kevin Gannon trace the development of the military art from early colonial times through the American Revolution. They suggest that the primitive environment in North America helped shape the kind of warfare that British colonials employed against Indian tribes, the French, and other colonial powers. Isolated in beachhead settlements along the Atlantic Coast and hemmed in by dense inland forests, the colonials were keenly aware that their survival depended upon the Royal Navy as well as upon a vigilant system of defense. Drawing on English tradition, they relied upon the militia as their first line of defense against enemies. These soldiers, who were drawn from every stratum of colonial society, established an American legacy of relying on ordinary citizens to provide the nucleus of an armed force in times of conflict.

Although colonial leaders made every effort to train militiamen in European tactics, the hardworking colonials had little time to master Old World military doctrine and found that the European open-field style of combat was of little use when it was employed in the dense forests of North America. Although they never mastered the Indian style of brush warfare, militiamen and provincial troops, who were recruited to fight in the long series of wars against France in North America (the Imperial Wars), adopted some native methods of warfare that emphasized irregular and individualized combat. During the Imperial Wars, the American volunteers, who augmented British regular forces, employed a combination of Indian and European tactics when they were engaged in battle. British regulars made some slight modifications in adjusting to the rugged terrain, but they never fully adapted to the primitive conditions in America.

It was mainly the superiority of British forces, financed by England's Secretary of State William Pitt, that proved decisive in defeating the French and their Indian allies in the final Imperial War, the French and Indian War (1755–1763). American volunteers came home from that conflict convinced that they had been instrumental in driving the hated French from North America. Many believed that they were better soldiers than the British professionals who had fought with them. Colonial veterans of the Imperial Wars boasted of their own military prowess and belittled that of the British. English professional recruits and officers, including Gen. Jeffrey Amherst, were equally convinced that the colonials were "the worst in the world" and all but worthless without British leadership. The exaggerated confidence of both the British and Americans in their military superiority was, in itself, one of the causes of the Revolution.

After more than a decade of political turbulence that followed the defeat of the French, colonial leaders were determined to resist what they considered to be Parliament's tyranny over the thirteen colonies. After American and British forces clashed near Boston in April 1775, a hastily summoned Second Continental Congress assembled in Philadelphia and authorized the creation of a Continental Army to resist British oppression. George Washington, a Virginia planter and veteran of the French and Indian War, was appointed to lead it. From the beginning, he was determined to train a professional army and fight in the tradition of open-style European combat. A series of stunning and nearly catastrophic defeats in and around New York City (1776) forced General Washington to assume a more defensive posture after he retreated southward through New Jersey and across the Delaware River into Pennsylvania. For the next several years he cautiously kept his Continental Army intact by largely avoiding battle with the main body of the British force opposing him. In the meantime, he made every effort to upgrade the quality of his professional force. As the authors point out, this was one of the keys to winning the Revolutionary War.

In northern New York and in the South, however, combat was more irregular and sometimes resembled what twentieth-century commentators might call guerrilla warfare. Under these conditions the rawboned American militia made a significant contribution: it played a role in defeating Gen. John Burgoyne's army in northern New York (1777) and during the British southern campaign toward the end of the war. Nevertheless, Overy and Gannon argue that it was American professional forces fighting European-type battles as well as the significant aid from France that led to the victory over Britain. When the war ended, however, Americans continued to be wary of professional standing armies and relied on a militia-based system of defense. Some leaders questioned whether or not this would be adequate for the future security needs of the young republic.

In the seventeenth and eighteenth centuries, a system of limited warfare evolved in Europe that bore less heavily upon its long-suffering people. English colonists in North America, however, rarely enjoyed a similar reprieve. From their first battles with aboriginal Americans, who also became enemies during many conflicts with other European colonials, war was more pervasive and perilous than for their transatlantic cousins. The English colonies were a crucible that blended Old World military practices with the environment and circumstances of the New World, fusing them into a society that uniquely challenged Britain during the American Revolution.

The North American wilderness had been the scene of battles long before European contact. Among native peoples, warfare was fairly common, though waged on a small scale and highly individualistic. Leaders exercised little control over warriors who moved independently, rapidly, and almost invisibly to spring unexpectedly upon their enemies. After what were typically short battles, losers withdrew, often to places where unwary pursuers could themselves be ambushed. Victors paused to kill or capture survivors, loot, and collect trophies before moving on. Stealth, a sudden raid or ambush, and then rapid withdrawal characterized the Indians' way of war, which later generations would call partisan, irregular, or guerrilla.

This style of warfare, the colonists discovered, was also deadly. As the pace and scope of English settlement increased through the seventeenth century, natives realized the threat that these colonists posed to their traditional lands and activities. Even in areas where Indian-colonist relations were initially cordial (such as Plymouth, Rhode Island, and Pennsylvania), tensions would eventually rise; by the end of the century, the English colonies displayed a uniform pattern of deteriorating relations and episodic violence. Perceiving their very survival to be at stake, colonists organized militias based on the English model. Most males became citizen-soldiers, required to bear arms, drill periodically, and fight if their communities were threatened—though in older areas of settlement where the threat was less acute, militia activities often served more of a social than a military function. Though the militia was organized on the English model, their way of fighting became distinctively something else fairly rapidly. European tactics, which prescribed mass formations and intricate maneuvers, were hard to master and ineffective against enemies in deep forests. So colonial militiamen learned from their enemies. Using quietly moving scouts to detect concealed foes, they ambushed, fought from cover, and raided Indian villages, sparing no one as they destroyed food stores, crops, and dwellings. Victory over hostile tribes often resulted from indiscriminate violence and devastation that appalled contemporary Europeans. Acts of massacre, torture, and treachery on both sides made warfare in the colonies singularly ferocious.

Both European and American styles persisted in the colonies after England and France went to war in 1689 (King William's War). For the next seventy-five years, Anglo-French antagonism, though focused primarily at sea and on European battlefields, increasingly spilled over into the nations' North American dominions.[1] Along the colonial frontiers English and French settlers, both with Native American allies, raided and massacred, while English colonists—at times with British regulars—waged more conventional campaigns against enemy towns and fortifications. The first three Anglo-French conflicts were indecisive, and England's military commitment in North America was limited until the ministry and Parliament decided finally to make the continent a major arena—and prize—in a showdown fight.

The English took full charge of the French and Indian War. They dictated strategy, employed large ground and naval forces, and brought European-style warfare to the continent in its most complete form to date. British regulars did most of the fighting, and sieges followed traditional European practice, but these methods were not initially successful. Early campaigns in America were a debacle; in 1755, Gen. Edward Braddock, attempting to take Fort Duquesne from the French, ignored colonial warnings about the nature of French and Indian warfare and attempted to march a conventional force through heavily forested terrain. Because the large

Colonial North America (U.S. Army Center of Military History)

British force moved as a unit, it was necessary to carve an actual road through the wilderness. Taking advantage of the Britons' excruciatingly slow pace and complete lack of stealth, the French and their native allies were able to ambush Braddock's forces near Duquesne, routing the British and mortally wounding Braddock. Succeeding British campaigns did not fare much better. Commanding officers, such as John Campbell, Earl of Loudoun, were more effective in antagonizing the colonial assemblies than in their engagements with the French. The British command's explicit disdain for the colonial militia ensured a steady degree of resentment, not only from high-ranking colonial officers who found themselves under the youngest British lieutenant in the chain of command, but from colonial officials who saw little incentive to work with the British commanders. Colonial militiamen were often appalled at the lowly character of the British enlisted ranks, whose camp habits of drinking, gambling, and whoring were a decided contrast to the lofty reputation the British army had enjoyed in the colonies before it was actually present in them. The harshness of camp discipline (where lashings were meted out regularly and in staggering numbers) also shocked colonial militia—both enlisted men and officers—used to a more democratic, less punitive system of unit command.

The early phase of the war in America was essentially a series of skirmishes along the New York–Canada frontier, while the British concentrated their efforts against France and its allies on the European continent and the high seas. That changed, though, in 1757. The new minister of war, William Pitt (one of the most respected British political figures in the colonies), made the strategic decision to focus the war effort in North America, thus transforming the character of the conflict from another chapter of Anglo-French conflict into a climactic war for empire. Reinforcements, including more able commanders, were sent to North America, and the strategy paid significant dividends. In 1759, Gen. James Wolfe decisively defeated Montcalm's French forces at Quebec, a victory predicated upon disciplined battle tactics and deadly massed volleys. Despite this major victory's European-style characteristics, there were concessions to the American terrain in this new phase of the British war effort as well. Regulars operating as light infantry, organized in small units using loose formations, provided flexibility and mobility in forested areas. Rangers were even better adapted to the environment. Lightly equipped, wearing garments that blended with the undergrowth, they moved Indian-like ahead of their slow-footed, crimson-uniformed comrades to detect ambushes, gather intelligence, and fight as skirmishers. The most famous of such units was Rogers' Rangers, whose skilled woodsmen, raiding hostile villages deep in French-claimed territory, were essentially eighteenth-century commandos.

When French power was eliminated from the North American continent via the 1763 Treaty of Paris, Britons and colonists alike exulted in the outcome of this great "War for Empire," but the years of struggle had planted the seeds of estrangement as well. Ignoring—or resenting—the mother country's dominant role in the war, colonists blamed generations of British official neglect for exposing them to the "savagery" of the French and Indians. They resented the fact that the redcoats viewed their contributions with contempt and so recalled monumental British blunders. The ill-fated Braddock expedition of 1755 became emblematic of these, as did James Abercrombie's 1758 assault on French-held Fort Ticonderoga, where he drove hundreds of his soldiers to their death in suicidal charges against the fort's nearly impregnable defenses. American colonists concluded that British troops were mindless hirelings led by arrogant martinets who were unwilling to acknowledge their own mistakes or stupidity.

The British, in turn, ignored their own mistakes and significant colonial efforts in this and earlier wars to condemn what they saw as the unreliability, indiscipline, and general incompetence of American forces. But their disgust with provincial troops, however justified, rested upon a fundamental misunderstanding of the colonists and their military "system." Many of the American soldiers whom they had seen were not members of the militia at all but rather were propertyless conscripts and volunteers with little incentive to fight. Militiamen might have been unprofessional, halfhearted, or unwilling in campaigns far from home, but they usually had a stake in society and could fiercely defend what they held dear.

British and American military institutions had come to rest upon very different bases. The former depended upon disciplined professionals fighting European-style, while the latter depended upon casually trained militia who used tactics learned on the frontier. Ideology had a good bit to do with this difference; colonial fears regarding professional "standing armies" as an instrument of tyranny (here the example of the 1688–1689 "Glorious Revolution" was important) mitigated against the evolution of anything resembling the British professionalization of the military developing in North America. As one contemporary observer noted, both traditions were valid, at least for their particular circumstances: "American irregulars would easily be confounded by regular troops in the open fields of Europe and regular troops would be as easily reduced to the like confusion by American irregulars in the woods here." Neither side saw it that way in 1763, however, and it would be over a decade before the issue would be disputed once again, this time on the battlefield during the American Revolution.

Victory over the French ultimately brought no peace, but instead a dozen years of growing animosity between the British political establishment and the American colonists. The colonists expected London's usual inattention to their internal affairs (a "salutary," or benign, neglect) to continue. The home government, on the other hand, was determined to bind its empire more tightly together and make the colonists help pay for their own administration and defense. Adding to the urgency and determination associated with this new direction in policy was the fiscal crisis faced by the British government; as a result of the global and extended nature of the Seven Years' War, the national debt had increased to a staggering twenty times the amount of Britain's annual budget. Parliament and the ministry thus imposed new taxes (designed explicitly to produce revenue, as opposed to measures earlier in the century which had been primarily regulatory in nature). British troops were kept in the colonies, due mostly to an uprising of Native Americans in the Ohio Valley—Pontiac's Rebellion—that was not suppressed until 1765. The British also sought to bring colonial governments and economies under stricter control, ending such informal traditions as lax enforcement of customs statutes and the de facto autonomy of the colonial assemblies. Colonial legislatures responded with official protests and nonimportation agreements; citizens boycotted British goods and often joined mobs in sometimes-violent protests against imperial policies. The British troop presence in the colonies—especially in Boston, the center of much of this resistance—increased significantly in response, and the troops themselves were a constant irritant to the colonists. In 1770, they killed several civilians while confronting a Boston mob. This so-called Boston Massacre (a title bestowed by the leadership of Boston's Sons of Liberty) became another cause célèbre for opponents of British policy.

The conflict between colonial autonomy and imperial control escalated rapidly after 1773, when Bostonians dumped into the harbor immense cargoes of tea that bore a hated English tax; the tea had become the symbol for the larger ideological and constitutional dispute between colonies and metropolis. After Parliament responded to the Boston Tea Party by imposing harsh sanctions against Massachusetts (dubbed the "Intolerable Acts" in America), the colonies sent delegates to a Continental Congress in Philadelphia in the fall of 1774. The Continental Congress discussed common grievances against Britain and how best to resist, adjourning in October with the agreement to reconvene the following May to once again assess the situation. In the intervening months, tensions were high— especially in Massachusetts, where Boston had essentially become a safe haven for troops and loyalists penned into the city by an overwhelmingly hostile countryside. Throughout the winter and early spring, the environs outside of Boston resembled nothing so much as an armed camp, as potential rebels stockpiled arms and powder in anticipation of push coming to shove. Prodded by his superiors in London, Royal Governor Thomas Gage (also commanding general of British troops in Boston) finally decided to take the fight to the countryside. Learning through informants that militia in nearby Concord were stockpiling munitions, Gage ordered an expedition to sally forth and destroy the weapons caches, as well as capture patriot leaders Samuel Adams and John Hancock, who were supposedly hiding near Concord as well. In the early morning hours of April 19, 1775, British troops marching toward Concord encountered some eighty militiamen assembled on the green at Lexington, approximately halfway between Boston and Concord.

The battle was brief, and its outcome seemed to confirm British disdain for the colonial militia. Several Minutemen were killed, and the rest scattered before the redcoats, who continued toward Concord. But the numerous towns around Boston had been alerted to the movements of the British; General Gage was not the only party who possessed intelligence about his counterpart's activities (Paul Revere was only one of some sixty riders who fanned out from Boston to alert the countryside as the British column began its march). As the British troops marched on to Concord, Minutemen from throughout the region converged in the hills and forests around the village as well. Finding neither munitions nor Adams and Hancock, the regulars retreated after receiving fire from some forward elements of the various Minutemen groups surrounding the village's environs. On their way back to Boston, the British regulars ran a sixteen-mile gauntlet of withering fire from enraged colonial citizen-soldiers shooting from behind trees and fences and from upper stories of buildings along the Concord road. The exhausted British reached Boston early in the evening, having suffered several hundred killed, wounded, and missing.

For the next two months, rebels massed around Boston while British forces and loyalists remained within the refuge of the city. Commanding (more by default than anything else) the hastily assembled yet committed force was Gen. Artemas Ward, an aged Massachusetts veteran. By June, some 13,000 colonial militia were massed around Boston. The Americans put the city under siege, culminating in the daring overnight fortification of Breed's Hill on the Charlestown peninsula, which commanded Boston and its harbor; a continued colonial presence there would have rendered the British position in Boston, as well as their troop and supply ships' positions in the harbor, untenable. Still contemptuous of Americans, British forces launched simple frontal assaults on the colonial breastworks, per the orders of Gen. William Howe. Twice repulsed, they finally took the hill on a third attempt, but lost in dead and wounded some 40 percent of their soldiers. The Battle of Breed's Hill (immortalized as Bunker's Hill, due to poor local maps) gave rebellious colonists even more confidence in their military process. The British command was shaken. The rebels had been driven from the heights overlooking Boston Harbor, but it was a pyrrhic victory. Sir Henry Clinton, one of the British generals sent to Boston (along with Howe and John Burgoyne) to oversee the suppression of the rebellion, understood the cost of taking Breed's Hill. "It was a dear bought victory," he admitted. "Another such would have ruined us."

In the meantime, the Second Continental Congress had reconvened in Philadelphia in May. While radicals in favor of independence were present, they were outnumbered by moderate and conservative delegates who favored continued attempts at reconciliation with Britain. Yet the escalated military situation, and the presence of some 13,000 troops around Boston, made it necessary in the eyes of the delegates for them to do something lest events continue to develop without political or military oversight. Thus, while the moderates were able to adopt a general agenda that tended toward efforts at negotiation with the British government, the immediate measures taken by Congress reflected the military necessity thrust upon it and favored the long-term goals of the radicals. Congress "adopted" the force around Boston and appointed Virginian George Washington as commanding general. Washington clearly wanted the job, arriving for the daily sessions of Congress dressed in his Virginia militia officer's dress uniform. After arriving at Cambridge (immediately outside of Boston) in July to take command of his forces, Washington was not convinced that recent British setbacks forecast future American victories. Having commanded militia and fought with the British army during the French and Indian War, he believed that defeating the king's regulars required an army built on their model. Accordingly, Washington began immediately to forge a new Continental Army out of the mob of unruly Americans he encountered. Congress passed resolutions authorizing enlargement and equipping of the forces, as well as the printing of paper currency to facilitate such activities as recruitment and requisitions. Thus, in the uncertain months between the summers of 1775 and 1776, while American independence was just one of several options under consideration, the Continental Congress assumed a janus-faced character—professing a willingness to reconcile with King George III while undertaking measures explicitly aimed at bringing harm to his forces in America.

For the next year there was neither peace nor war. Small-scale fighting erupted in other colonies, and King George III declared the Americans to be rebels. In December 1775, Parliament passed the Prohibitory Act, which imposed a Royal Navy blockade on the colonial coast. In March 1776, as Congress continued to debate war aims, Washington was able to force a British evacuation of Boston. In the early winter months of 1776, Henry Knox, a Boston bookseller who became Washington's trusted artillery chief, pulled off a spectacular logistical feat when he and a small force brought heavy guns through some three hundred miles of icy and snowy terrain from Fort Ticonderoga to Boston. On the night of March 4, Washington placed many of the cannon on Dorchester Heights, which overlooked Boston proper. When the British awoke to find themselves under colonial guns, William Howe negotiated an arrangement with Washington whereby he would hold off bombarding the city and the British regulars and local loyalists would evacuate. Washington, his specific mission still not clearly defined, moved his army to New York, where he believed British forces would reappear. In July, the Continental Congress officially declared the colonies independent from Great Britain, a culmination of events spurred on significantly by the previous months' military developments, as well as the publication in January of Thomas Paine's enormously influential tract *Common Sense*, which stated forcefully and clearly the case for independence. By August, then, Washington's army was not only the line of defense against British aggression, but the very vehicle of revolution and independence. That month, Howe moved his army to New York, where the British threatened the city with powerful land and naval forces. Washington's task was now evident: defend New York and win his country's independence.

His immediate situation was perilous. Washington's army of 19,000 ill-trained and poorly equipped men faced over 30,000 British regulars whose naval support provided an enormous tactical advantage. New York City, located as it was on Manhattan Island, was vulnerable to amphibious attack, and American avenues of retreat went northward along the Hudson River, which enemy ships could easily navigate. On August 27, Howe attacked American forward positions on Long Island and outflanked their defenders, who fled first to Brooklyn, then into New York City proper. Within two months, British landings behind American lines routed the inexperienced Continental troops and drove Washington from Manhattan to White Plains, north of the city along the Hudson. During November and December, a detachment of Howe's forces commanded by Lord Charles Cornwallis chased Washington and his depleted army out of New

York, through New Jersey, and across the Delaware River into Pennsylvania. As Christmas approached and winter intensified, Cornwallis stopped his deliberate pursuit. The Continental Army was in desperate straits, as was their commander. Washington had been outmaneuvered and outfought and now led an army that casualties, short enlistments, and defections had reduced to some 2,000 ragged Continentals. "I think," he worriedly wrote, "the game is pretty much up."

Washington's despair arose not only from the bleak military situation, but also from its larger importance in the course of the revolution. Keenly discerning the principle, later famously articulated by Clausewitz, that "war is politics by other means," Washington knew that with collapse of his army would come the collapse of the revolutionary efforts and thus American independence itself (and he would surely be one of those the British government would find guilty of treason—a capital offense). Additionally, Washington understood that without some sort of victory upon which patriot supporters could hang their hats, efforts to recruit and supply his forces would be made infinitely more difficult by declining civilian morale. Acting on these considerations, and aware that European armies rarely fought in winter, he found reinforcements, recrossed the Delaware River on Christmas night, and near sunrise attacked a Hessian garrison at Trenton, New Jersey. Washington's force killed forty and took over nine hundred prisoners before quickly retreating back into Pennsylvania. Surprise was no longer an ally, however, when he returned to Trenton several days later. General Cornwallis appeared with 6,000 British regulars, and Washington withdrew rather than fight a battle he could not win. But when Cornwallis did not attack, Washington seized the initiative once again; that night under the cover of darkness, with their campfires still ablaze, his troops quietly marched away. At Princeton, they defeated a British detachment bound for Trenton and, before Cornwallis could catch them, returned to Morristown, New Jersey, for the winter. In less than two weeks, Washington's bold initiatives had won small but significant victories—they saved his command (a significant bloc of congressmen had grown weary of retreats and were calling for Washington's replacement) and restored a semblance of Continental, political, and public morale.

Trenton and Princeton notwithstanding, the British army was yet to be defeated—a task as vital as it was improbable. Washington and most of his officers were inexperienced, though dedicated, amateurs. The small Continental Army was inadequately trained and even more inadequately supplied. Militia were comparatively plentiful, but Washington believed that "to place any dependence upon [them] is assuredly resting upon a broken staff." They could not—or would not—fight British regulars in the open, and even when protected by entrenchments often broke and ran. At one point, Washington was said to have raged, "Are these the men with whom I am to defend America? Good God, have I got such men as those?"

Forced to fight from a position of great weakness, Washington developed a sort of Fabian strategy designed to sap Britain's resolve. Its key was to preserve his army—put simply, retreat and survive. While the army lived, so did the revolution; it was really the only true "national" institution (save Congress) for the fledgling United States at this point. He could not, therefore, risk pitched battles with larger forces, defend any position to the last man, or fight without a "moral certainty" of winning. As at Trenton and Princeton, he had to avoid the enemy's main body, but smash enemy outposts and detachments and then withdraw. Washington envisioned a lengthy war with the hope, though not the guarantee, that his men could outlast the British.

Despite much larger, more experienced forces, King George's government had enormous problems. The Atlantic Ocean was a 3,000-mile, several-weeks-long impediment to communicating with and supplying and reinforcing its armies. The Royal Navy could attack America's vast coastline at will, but the country was huge, much of it heavily forested, with few of its significant towns possessing decisive strategic importance. And the people—some loyal to the British, some hostile, some neutral, and many of them armed—could make military operations extremely difficult, because friends were not easily distinguishable from enemies. Americans themselves would learn this some two hundred years later in Southeast Asia; indeed, some historians—pointing toward the difficulties of distance and coping with nationalist forces who blended easily into the general populace—have described the American Revolution as Great Britain's Vietnam. Continuing the metaphor, the British had to reckon with the fact that a strategy of total war that would destroy civilian lives and property and fight enemy armies to extinction might crush the rebellion, but logistical, moral, and political factors argued against it. Such an effort would consume military resources that were difficult to replace and violated the accepted principles, in terms of politics and public opinion, regarding limited war. England's desire for eventual reconciliation (from some quarters of the government, at least) with the colonies was another consideration.

Because America's vast territory precluded effective military occupation, and the cost alone made a permanent one unthinkable, colonials must one day accept British sovereignty, even if they practiced de facto home rule. Total war was thus unlikely to win hearts and minds, especially those of the neutral colonists—perhaps as many as one-third of the entire colonial population. English generals always hoped that by occupying places they would rally loyal Americans as the nucleus for a successful counterrevolution. British strategy during the entire war would revolve around this fundamental assumption and hope—including Gen. John Burgoyne's strategy for the campaign of 1777.

Burgoyne successfully sold the London ministry on his plan to isolate New England (the seedbed of the American rebellion in the eyes of the British government) by seizing the Hudson River Valley; the logic was simple: cut off the head, and the body would die. Burgoyne landed in Canada and moved southward during the summer of 1777. According to Burgoyne's plan, as he and the ministry understood it, Howe was to move northward from New York City to meet Burgoyne's forces, "liberating" a good many Americans along the way. Then Howe would move on Philadelphia to force Washington into action, defeat the Continentals, and free the city from rebel control. But Howe changed the plan without notifying Burgoyne, and moved on Philadelphia while the latter was moving south from Canada. Howe would direct a successful campaign against General Washington in 1777 as he had the year before. By moving his army by way of the Chesapeake Bay to positions outside of Philadelphia, he forced the elusive Washington to follow him, take a stand, and engage the British forces. In September, Howe attacked the American forces along Brandywine Creek, drove away the patriot army, and entered the rebels' largest city and capital. Washington's riposte—a surprise assault on a British garrison at outlying Germantown—was futile, though daring. Two of the four attacking American columns failed to arrive. The others fought well before they collided in a dense fog, fired upon each other, then retreated. British counterattacks drove the Americans off and ended the debacle. Washington lost Philadelphia, as he had New York; his army was still overmatched; and this time there would be no Trenton or Princeton to assuage the harshness of a winter encampment at Valley Forge (while the British enjoyed the comparative luxury of Philadelphia).

But there was Saratoga. As successful as Howe had been in driving the rebels away from their capital, this was no European-style war in which capturing the enemy's capital brought surrender. Howe's thrust to Philadelphia meant abandoning Burgoyne's forces as they marched south through the Hudson River Valley; ultimately, taking Philadelphia would weigh much less in the balance than the eventual disastrous defeat of Burgoyne's army in upstate New York. Early in 1777, Burgoyne had divided his invasion force of nearly 10,000 men into two components. Barry St. Leger, with 1,900 men, over half of them Iroquois warriors, moved eastward from Lake Ontario through the Mohawk River Valley. Burgoyne led his contingent down Lake Champlain, planning to continue along the Hudson to Albany, where he would meet with St. Leger and Howe's forces, who he assumed were moving northward from New York City. The only American obstacles were a small garrison at Fort Stanwix on the Mohawk and a larger one at Fort Ticonderoga on Lake Champlain.

St. Leger easily put Stanwix under siege, but his Iroquois, duped by an American general, doomed the campaign. In early August 1777, frustrated by weeks of inactivity, they ambushed a relief column of American militia at Oriskany. After several hours of intense fighting, both sides were badly mauled, but the Iroquois—unaccustomed to close, pitched battles with heavy losses—were traumatized. When they returned to Stanwix and learned that a large American force was approaching, they fled, leaving St. Leger with little choice but to retreat. The architect of this British misfortune was American general Benedict Arnold. He had forced a mentally deranged Tory (loyalist) to warn St. Leger that American soldiers "numerous as leaves on the trees" were coming. The British were skeptical, but the Iroquois—whose cultural traditions attached a degree of awe to those whom Europeans might deride as lunatics—were not. When Arnold arrived at the fort with only 1,000 men and found the enemy departed, it was apparent his ruse had worked.

Meanwhile, Burgoyne's waterborne army quickly captured Ticonderoga, but then he defied both history and geography. Rather than continue on to Lake George, a faster and safer route to the Hudson, Burgoyne decided to march overland. Barely two decades earlier in Pennsylvania, Gen. Edward Braddock had learned too late the danger of moving an army European-style though heavy forests, and British invasions of French Canada during the French and Indian War had proven the utility of Lake Champlain to move quickly through the region. Overland, however, Burgoyne's objective lay to the south, through land occupied by hostile forces, and for three weeks his men consumed valuable supplies as they labored in rough terrain along narrow wagon trails that rebel forces obstructed with trees, boulders, and diverted streams. By the time the British reached open country and stopped to rest, the presence of Burgoyne's army and rumors of atrocities committed by its attached Indian contingents were bringing New Englanders out in force. In August, aroused Yankees annihilated a British detachment at Bennington, Vermont, and during the next few weeks, hundreds more joined the main rebel army near Saratoga, New York.

By September, there stood between Burgoyne and Albany an American army, commanded by Gen. Horatio Gates, that totaled nearly 7,000 men—mostly regulars—and uncounted numbers of militia. Burgoyne had lost one-tenth of his army at Bennington and was not being reinforced; his supplies continued to dwindle, and roving bands of patriots made foraging increasingly dangerous. On the ninth, Burgoyne took heavy casualties while driving Gates from positions at Freeman's Farm, and then paused to await help from New York City. Of course, William Howe had moved south to Philadelphia rather than north to reinforce Burgoyne. Thus, the only force that arrived was more Americans, and they sealed Burgoyne off from the countryside. On October 7, desperately short of food, Burgoyne was routed by rebel forces along Bemis Heights and retreated to Saratoga. Ten days later, after more pitched fighting that went the way of the Americans, Burgoyne surrendered his entire force to Gates.

Burgoyne's defeat was not entirely his own fault. Because the ministry in London had not more explicitly coordinated strategy, Howe could move toward Philadelphia and leave Burgoyne without reinforcements that he was counting upon. Gates's regulars, for their part, had fought well; especially conspicuous for feats of bravery and leadership was Benedict Arnold, who led charges on British positions even after being seriously wounded in the leg. Burgoyne had erred, though, in moving overland from Lake Champlain, and he persisted in this error too long in trying to reach Albany. As his army tarried, it did not attract eager loyalists as planned, but rather throngs of armed rebels who attacked outposts, patrols, and foragers. The Americans, recalled a British sergeant, "swarmed around the little adverse army like birds of prey." In the end they made even retreat impossible.

The American victory at Saratoga had fundamentally important results. Most significantly, it won for the United States an alliance with France (Franco-American Treaty, 1778). Still smarting from its defeat in the Seven Years' War, France was sympathetic to the American cause but unsure of its chances of success against the British army—until Saratoga offered the French government reason for confidence in the Americans. As for the British, Saratoga dashed their hopes of defeating the northern rebels and forced a change in strategy. Henceforth, British armies remained on the defensive in the north and launched major offensives only in the south. Accordingly, early in 1778, Gen. Sir Henry Clinton, who had replaced Howe, began moving his army from Philadelphia to New York, a more defensible base from which to launch operations against southern ports.

Saratoga and the French alliance also stimulated patriot morale and army enlistments—perhaps their most immediately crucial effects. Thus, General Washington's army emerged from Valley Forge early in 1778 stronger in numbers and, thanks to Prussian drillmaster Friedrich von Steuben, more proficient in the skills required on eighteenth-century battlefields. In late June, Washington's forces attacked Clinton's rear guard at Monmouth, New Jersey. The battle was tactically indecisive, and Clinton's troops continued their march, but Continental soldiers had finally engaged enemy regulars on equal terms and fought them to a standstill.

After Monmouth, military operations in the north were essentially a sideshow to the more significant activities southward, though sometimes a bloody one. Except for sporadic British raids and an occasional attack against each other's outposts, Clinton remained in New York while Washington kept vigil around the city. However, along the Pennsylvania and New York frontiers and in Kentucky, Britain's Native American allies terrorized white settlements. In return, George Rogers Clark led a punitive expedition into the Illinois country, John Sullivan ravaged Iroquois villages, and American militia matched atrocity with atrocity. Neither side gained a decisive advantage or gave quarter as unconventional warfare in its grislier forms continued remorselessly in the backcountry.

England's new post-Saratoga strategy envisioned a systematic, purposeful effort to restore the king's authority in the southern colonies. Assumptions that military success, or even the mere presence of British regulars, would evoke a groundswell of loyalism had been unrealistic for the northern colonies—as both Howe and Burgoyne could attest. In Georgia and the Carolinas, however, where conflict between Tories and patriots had been bitter and continuous—virtually civil war in some areas—the presence of antirevolutionary sentiment seemed ideally suited for a deliberate attempt at pacification. "The basic concept," explains historian John Shy, "was to regain military control of some one major colony, restore full civil government, and then expand both control and government in a step-by-step operation conducted behind a slowly advancing screen of British regulars."

Initially, British power in the South was overwhelming, and the southern strategy appeared poised for imminent success. In late 1778 an amphibious force took Savannah, Georgia. Using it as a base, the British began to plan for an assault on Charleston, South Carolina—the most important settlement in the southern colonies. In May 1780, General Cornwallis's army took the city with only light resistance, capturing the entire American force of some 5,000 troops commanded by Gen. Benjamin Lincoln. In a stinging and humiliating surrender, Cornwallis denied Lincoln's Continentals the "honors of war" in the surrender ceremony, evidence of the firm attitude of the British toward southern rebels. The fall of Charleston was the worst military catastrophe for the patriot forces during the entire Revolution, and it sent shock waves throughout America. Congress sent Horatio Gates— the "Hero of Saratoga"—to South Carolina to assume command of the Continental forces in the region and try to undo the pattern of British success. However, Gates proved a remarkably incompetent commander in the southern theater. After an ill-conceived march on the British outpost at Camden, South Carolina, Gates's army instead encountered the bulk of Cornwallis's regulars, who had been sent out from Charleston once word of the Americans' maneuvering had reached the British command. On August 16, the two armies collided in the hours before sunrise; the day's battle saw the Americans thoroughly routed, suffering twice as many casualties as the larger British force. Gates himself fled the field of battle, outracing his own troops and not stopping his ride until he had crossed into North Carolina. The magnitude of the defeat at Camden, coupled with Gates's stunning act of cowardice, drove American morale as low as it had been at any point thus far in the war. Another Continental force in the South had been lost to the British, and there was no reason to believe that the British southern strategy would not prove successful.

The defeats suffered by patriot forces in the South were not the only reason for the general air of despondence on the American side by the end of the summer of 1780. At sea, the Americans had proven no match for the British either. In 1775, Congress had created the Continental Navy, which eventually comprised about fifty ships, including thirteen new frigates, and had joined state governments in granting letters of marque and reprisal, which licensed civilian shipowners to seize enemy commercial vessels. Most states also formed navies of shallow-draught ships for coastal defense. Given England's enormous advantage in fighting ships, American sailors operated most successfully as privateers, and their taking of some eight hundred commercial prizes during the war seriously affected British trade. John Paul Jones, the Continental Navy's most celebrated hero, oversaw the sinking of two Royal Navy warships and raids on the enemy coast. But his exploits, especially his thrilling victory over HMS *Serapis* in September 1779 ("I have not yet begun to fight"), were only morale-raising anomalies. By 1780 only the privateers were still a threat to the British. With most of its fleet—including all of its frigates—captured or sunk, the Continental Navy, reduced to less than half a dozen vessels, had basically ceased to exist.

The Continental Army was always too small. Recruiting, easiest after Trenton and Princeton, had brought the army to its greatest strength—nearly 19,000 men—in 1777. Thereafter, all efforts to increase or even meet those numbers failed. Congress offered cash bounties and land to men enlisting for one year or more and bonuses to recruiting officers. Then it assigned quotas to the states, which also paid bounties; when these quotas were unmet (and that was usually the case), it began to conscript men from their militia. Draftees, though, were allowed to hire others ("substitutes") to take their place. This process usually provided recruits from lower socioeconomic classes: former convicts and indentured servants, British deserters, poor farmers, landless whites, recent immigrants, and the unemployed. Thus, the Continental Army was a double source of irony: the republican ideology of the revolutionary generation cautioned against professional "standing armies," which is exactly what Washington and other commanders were trying to make the army into, arguing that this was crucial to the war effort. Additionally, this republican ideology envisioned an army of citizen-soldiers—propertied men with a tangible stake in the society they were fighting to create; what was occurring instead, though, was the creation of an army whose ranks were filled with the poor and propertyless. The disinclination to serve in the Continental Army shown by many propertied citizens was dismayingly tangible. In short, the Continental Army's enlisted ranks looked more like those of traditional European forces than the idealized republican army originally conceived by the revolutionary leadership.

The total number of men serving in the armies (perhaps 100,000 to 200,000 or more) has puzzled scholars; indeed, their numbers and composition perplexed commanders as well. Armies included regulars committed to one year, three years, or the duration of the conflict; militia whose participation often depended upon the agricultural calendar and the proximity of campaigns to their homes or state boundaries; and "partisans"—irregular or guerrilla fighters—obedient primarily to their own leaders (these groups were particularly common in the southern colonies, especially South Carolina).

Women and African Americans also contributed to the diverse social and cultural composition of America's Revolutionary forces. The female camp followers who regularly accompanied European armies as cooks, laundresses, and prostitutes had their counterparts during the Revolution, but American women served the military in many other ways. There were perhaps 20,000 "Women of the Army" who worked as nurses or ammunition- and water-carriers, helped bury the dead, and recovered usable material from the battlefields. They were carried on army rosters, drew pay and rations, and could be dismissed and court-martialed. Some women wore men's clothing and joined the Continental Army, and others were members of the militia, but most became combatants because their homes and communities were attacked either by regular forces or, especially on the violent frontier, by Indians and partisans. Although their numbers are unknown and their deeds largely unrecorded, these women, according to historian Linda DePauw, participated in the war by the "tens of thousands."

Because most African Americans were held as slaves, they had little choice of whether or how to provide military service. In the North, there was great opposition to accepting them as soldiers, until a decline in white enlistments forced states to meet manpower quotas by conscription. Thereafter, many slaveholders drafted for military duty offered their chattels as substitutes. Free African Americans in the North also served; Rhode Island sent two battalions of black men into war, and more than 10 percent of Massachusetts' free blacks fought in the Continental ranks. Between 5,000 and 8,000 African American men—mostly northerners—served in the regular army, usually in integrated units.

In the South, slaveowners remained unalterably opposed to arming slaves, despite the chronic shortage of fighting men. The British also hesitated to use them as soldiers, even though hundreds fled to their lines. Many slaves crossed over to the British as a result of the 1775 proclamation by royal governor of Virginia, Lord Dunmore, that slaves who aided the British in suppressing their rebellious masters would be granted their freedom. For many slaves, then, it was the British side in the Revolution that promised liberty. Both Britons and patriots employed slaves as laborers, teamsters, personal servants, guides, and spies, and neither side objected to using them as sailors. African Americans commonly worked in both navies as seamen or highly valued pilots who navigated in dangerous coastal waters and guided ships into southern ports. Tragically, many slaves who expected their wartime service—on either side—to bring emancipation were cruelly disappointed.

Disillusionment among Revolutionary soldiers partly explains declining enlistments as the war continued. Camp duty was irksome, tedious, dirty, and often exhausting. When victory or (more often) survival depended upon long marches and swift movement, there were days or weeks of withering heat and choking dust, numbing cold, or ankle-deep mud that relentlessly impeded each weary step. Battles fought at close range with musket, bayonet, and cannon were mouth-parching, bowel-loosening horrors that left behind sickening human debris: severed heads and limbs, faces mangled beyond recognition, torsos "split like fish to be broiled." Treatment of the sick and wounded was entrusted, in the best-case scenario, to physicians lacking anesthetics and effective medicine (to say nothing of proper sanitary conditions). If captured, one might be exchanged for Britons in American custody or, at worst, confined belowdecks in filthy, vermin-infested, and disease-ridden prison hulks anchored offshore in American ports. Disobedience or insubordination brought harsh punishment. Flogging was commonly prescribed for minor offenses (though not usually on the scale of British disciplinary standards); deserters were shot or hanged. Despite this attempt at deterrence, however, an estimated 20 percent of American soldiers deserted, and mutinies proliferated after 1778. Military executions during the Revolution numbered in the hundreds.

Basic to the discontent that drove soldiers to desertion or mutiny, and indeed a basic fact of military life, was the absence of bare necessities: enough food, adequate shelter and clothing, and regular pay. The starvation and nakedness identified with Valley Forge were common in Washington's armies, but the men continued to fight, and the cost to those who did was high. Of an estimated 25,000 American soldiers killed during the Revolution, about 6,500 were killed in battle, perhaps 10,000 succumbed to hunger, disease, exposure, or wounds, and over 8,000 did not survive imprisonment by the enemy.

The army's poverty was not General Washington's fault, nor was it solely the fault of the Continental Congress. The latter was fearful of levying direct taxes for revenue, and the Articles of Confederation (ratified in 1781 and formalizing most of the government's extant practices) granted it no authority to do so. The central government, in fact, depended mainly upon the individual states for money, supplies, and manpower. Military oversight was entrusted to various congressional committees whose members, even if knowledgeable and conscientious, had other responsibilities. These were far from optimal conditions to coordinate political and military needs and strategy, and they would bedevil relations between Congress and Washington's command. Congress also created independent departments to supervise payrolls and provisions, but officers were often incompetent and sometimes dishonest (notable exceptions in this regard were Nathanael Greene and Timothy Pickering). Formal training in this realm simply did not exist, as it would be many years before logistics would become a formal military specialty. Attempts to meet expenses by printing paper money failed when, due to rampant inflation, Continental dollars plummeted in value until they became worthless to soldiers and civilians alike. The Royal Navy's blockade of the American coast forced whatever supplies that were available to travel along what was essentially a nonexistent road system—and that was only if enough wagons could be procured to carry them. In 1780, Congress threw up its hands in despair and turned over to the states all responsibility for sustaining their troops, but they were no more successful in doing so than Congress had been. Generals warned that men were about to mutiny, a prediction that Connecticut, Pennsylvania, and New Jersey troops soon confirmed.

Benedict Arnold's notorious defection to the British in September 1780, after his plot to surrender West Point had failed, was only the most dramatic of Washington's problems with his officer corps.[2] Whether commissioned by the states (as they were through the rank of colonel) or appointed by Congress as generals, few officers had the training that might have improved the army's performance. The only exceptions in this regard were the few Americans who had received training in the British army, and foreign officers who attached themselves to Washington's service, such as Baron von Steuben and, later on, French officers such as Rochambeau. American officers continued to learn mostly from experience, for the army provided no systematic military education. Ironically, two British-trained generals were conspicuous disappointments. Charles Lee withdrew his men during the Battle of Monmouth and was relieved of his command. Horatio Gates—dubiously the hero of Saratoga and then humbled at Camden—

worked tirelessly to undermine Washington's authority (particularly with Congress). The lust for rank and recognition underlying Gates's maneuvering and Arnold's treason obsessed many officers whose interminable rivalries exasperated their commander in chief. Even Nathanael Greene and Daniel Morgan, whose military talents were indisputable, had spells of jealousy and oversensitive pride.

The rebellion seemed to be collapsing by the end of the summer in 1780, as British officials in the South had begun their pacification strategy. They placed troops in a series of outposts throughout the Carolina piedmont and backcountry to ensure order, and also recruited loyalists into military units. Many citizens swore their allegiance to the king. But the policy, for a number of reasons, began to come apart during its implementation. British troops abused civilians whom vindictive loyalists further alienated by acts of wanton vengefulness. Officials often treated neutrals as harshly as rebels, and their Anglican-inspired hostility toward Presbyterians angered the numerous Scots-Irish of the region. Disaffected citizens swelled the ranks of partisans who, led by such figures as Thomas Sumter, Andrew Pickens, and Francis Marion, fought savagely against the Tories and harassed Cornwallis's army—especially its communication and supply lines. The most significant blow to the British efforts in the backcountry came at King's Mountain, just over the North Carolina border, where in October 1780, patriot militia and Continental soldiers decimated a force of British troops and loyalist militia. The violence of the defeat put a quick brake on British recruitment efforts among Carolina loyalists, significantly hampering Cornwallis's continuing efforts to implement the British southern strategy.

Violence was pervasive but random when Gen. Nathanael Greene arrived in the Carolinas as Gates's replacement in late 1780. A protégé of Washington, and perhaps the war's finest strategist, he gave the Revolution in the South new hope. Greene had only 1,500 men, but the Carolinas by this point teemed with partisans and militia whose efforts, properly directed, could have a decisive impact. The genius of Greene's command is that he understood and acted upon this. After consulting with guerrilla leaders, Greene made his move. In December he defied conventional military wisdom by splitting his already small army, dispatching Gen. Daniel Morgan into northwestern South Carolina. Greene's strategy was not as reckless as first appearances indicated, however; Cornwallis took the bait and divided his own forces, sending Banastre Tarleton's forces after Morgan.

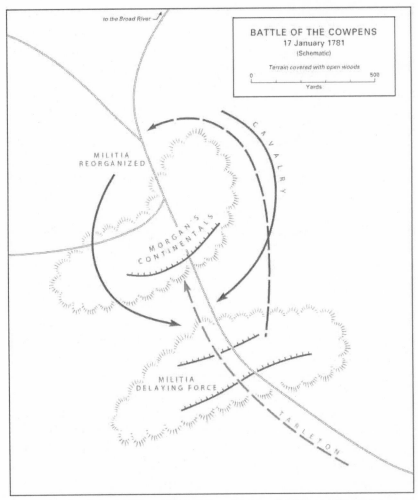

to the Broad River

BATTLE OF THE COWPENS
17 January 1781
(Schematic)

Terrain covered with open woods

0   500

Yards

MILITIA
REORGANIZED

CAVALRY

MORGAN'S
CONTINENTALS

MILITIA
DELAYING FORCE

TARLETON

Battle of the Cowpens (U.S. Army Center of Military History)

As Greene's strategy unfolded, Morgan achieved military immortality at the Cowpens, South Carolina (near present-day Spartanburg), in January 1781. Another of Washington's amateur officers, he deftly used a mixed force of militia and Continentals to win the rebellion's most stunning victory over a British army. Facing Tarleton's 1,100 men with his own 1,000-man force, Morgan placed the militia in front of his regulars (see map). Understanding the militia's liabilities and limitations, Morgan assured them that they needed to fire only two volleys before retreating, but instructed them to then reassemble at the rear of his right flank. He then stationed the cavalry to his left. When Tarleton attacked, the militia resisted briefly, as the British expected. But the Continentals stood firm, holding their attackers in place while the militia and cavalry swept in from both sides to effect an annihilating double envelopment. Tarleton, who barely escaped, lost over nine hundred men; Morgan, fewer than eighty.

However, Greene's strategy had indeed separated his army from Morgan's. If Cornwallis had acted with alacrity, he might have defeated the two in detail. But he did not; Morgan reunited with Greene and their combined forces turned north toward the Dan River at the Virginia/North Carolina border before Cornwallis's forces could begin pursuit. Trying to catch Greene in North Carolina, Cornwallis rashly sacrificed sustenance for speed, ordering his men to burn anything they could not carry, and then plunged into pursuit of the Americans. For weeks, the chase continued. As Greene had planned, hovering patriot bands denied the enemy food and reinforcements. Greene's advance guard commandeered every usable boat on the way as well. The result was a maddening finish to the race for Cornwallis's harried and exhausted troops—they arrived at the Dan in time to look to the other shore and see the last of Greene's men disembark from the last boat in the area that could have been used to ford the river.

Before Cornwallis's army could recover from the "race to the Dan," during which fatigue and hunger had reduced its fighting strength by nearly 20 percent, Greene turned back into North Carolina to fight at Guilford Courthouse in March. Cornwallis won the battle (only by dangerously ordering his artillery to fire over the heads of their own forces to hit the American ranks), but he lost 500 men while rebel forces remained intact. With his situation desperate and unlikely to improve, Cornwallis retreated to Wilmington and abandoned his remaining forces in South Carolina. Greene returned to engage the larger garrisons only to lose again at Hobkirk's Hill and Eutaw Springs. But the British, also sorely battered, returned to their coastal bases. Meanwhile, rebel partisans overwhelmed small outposts and detachments. In just a few months, English power— which once seemed so dominant in the lower South—had been confined to a few seaboard towns, and the victory was uniquely Greene's. His genius, writes historian Russell Weigley, lay in "weaving the maraudings of partisan raiders into a coherent pattern, coordinating them with the maneuverings of a field army otherwise too weak to accomplish much and making the combination a deadly one."

Having lost the Carolinas, Cornwallis decided that their recovery—and any hope of success for the British southern strategy—depended upon extinguishing the rebellion in Virginia. Thus, in May he moved his force there and spent weeks chasing rebels led by the Marquis de Lafayette. General Clinton, however, reacting to reports of a French fleet in American waters, ordered Cornwallis to occupy a position along the coast from which he could be either evacuated or reinforced. When Cornwallis chose Yorktown, Washington's long wait for a conclusive victory was almost over.

The American commander had known many disappointments since Monmouth. Until Morgan's and Greene's victories, the arrival of 4,000 French regulars in fulfillment of the Franco-American alliance had been the only good news. But by August 1781, Washington no longer had to act from a position of weakness. Early cautious urgings for a siege of Clinton's forces in New York were overruled by the opportunity waiting to be seized southward. With an army of 10,000 (nearly half of it French), a sizable French fleet that could be quickly en route to southern waters, the active support of the commanding officers of both the French army and navy, and Cornwallis isolated on the Virginia coast, Washington executed a plan that (for once in the conflict) worked perfectly. Leaving behind a few thousand men to deceive Clinton, he marched the army to the Chesapeake Bay, where French ships carried it to join the rebel forces already near Yorktown (see map). Meanwhile the French naval squadron had gained control of the lower Chesapeake, effectively blocking any potential effort to resupply or reinforce Cornwallis's forces barricaded inside Yorktown. By late September, 18,000 French and American troops and the French navy had trapped Cornwallis behind his fortifications. French experience in siege-craft allowed Washington's artillery to scourge the British with murderous fire. By October 17, the British forces had had enough; Cornwallis asked for a cease-fire and, on October 19, unconditionally surrendered his army to Washington.

For all practical purposes, the war ended at Yorktown. The defeat of Cornwallis brought to a climax growing British domestic opposition to a costly, futile, and seemingly endless conflict that had escalated beyond North America into war not only with France, but also with Spain and the Netherlands. In 1782 the British government began peace negotiations that resulted the next year in the Treaty of Paris and the recognition of the independent United States of America.

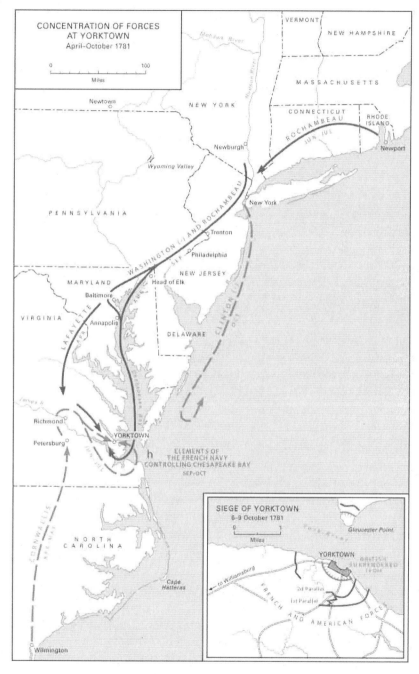

Concentration of Forces at Yorktown (U.S. Army Center of Military History)

Scholars who have studied the United States' improbable victory over a powerful European nation have come to different conclusions about the war and its principals. George Washington has been compared to Julius Caesar, dubbed a lucky amateur, and extolled for his character, wisdom, adaptability, and endurance. Some indict British generals for lacking a comprehensive strategy or for being overly timid or too aggressive. Others suggest that Britain's effort to subdue an armed people from a great distance was doomed from the beginning; or, conversely, that Parliament suffered a critical failure of will in choosing to negotiate, and that with further efforts it could have crushed the rebellion.

Perhaps so, but Britain did seek peace rather than spend more blood and treasure on a venture with such dubious prospects. From this perspective, whatever sustained America's war effort beyond the limits of British endurance led to ultimate victory: Washington's Fabian strategy of prudence and attrition, Burgoyne's surrender, Britain's conflict with other nations that ultimately diluted its commitment in North America, French francs that barely kept the Revolution afloat, or the French military assistance that made victory at Yorktown possible—or some combination of these elements. The most significant single factor, though, seems to have been the failure of the British to pacify the Carolinas. Due especially to the successes of Nathanael Greene in coordinating the activities of the numerous partisans with the Continental army, and the success of his efforts to overextend and exhaust Cornwallis's forces as he drew them out of South Carolina, the endgame scenario of Cornwallis's forces being barricaded inside Yorktown surrounded by over 16,000 American and French troops played out as it did. Not all historians have recognized the fundamental importance of the southern theater, but it is very doubtful that without events unfolding the way they did in South Carolina there would have been a decisive confrontation on such favorable terms for the Americans as that which occurred at Yorktown.

Even had Britain won, the question of reconciliation would have remained. British generals had won battles and occupied territory, but pacification would have been difficult in any case—this was a people's war, much more complex than dynastic squabbles among European royalty. Moreover, the popular masses of Americans were not docile, unarmed, or remote from the conflict. Hostilities between rebel and Tory, tantamount to civil war within a revolution, together with the presence of many neutrals, immensely complicated British attempts to simultaneously wage war and win peace. This was especially true in the southern colonies, as Cornwallis and Tarleton discovered to their dismay in 1780 and 1781. Soldiers are rarely politicians (good politicians, anyway), and the situation in America was such as to confound the wisest and most patient of diplomats. Future harmony between the colonies and the mother country would have required keeping loyalist support while bringing neutrals and at least some of the rebels back into the fold, yet nothing the British did augured this result. Lenient treatment of rebels infuriated Tories, while harsher methods further embittered rebels and, if indiscriminately applied, angered fence-sitters as well (again, this was especially true in the southern theater). British soldiers usually antagonized civilians, and the inability of commanders to restrain Tory vengeance caused even more resentment.

The militia, often justly maligned but accurately reflecting the Revolution's character as a people's war, baffled the British, because it was—in one way or another—always there to augment the small regular army, harass enemy forces, neutralize or overpower Tory militia, and nullify pacification efforts once British troops were gone. Yet militia alone could not have sustained the Revolution, and what may have followed the Continental Army's collapse raises intriguing questions. Would Congress also have capitulated, depriving the war effort of even its uncertain leadership? Could Parliament then have resolved the issues that had led to revolution and healed the bitterness that the war had caused? Would Americans have accepted reunion with Britain, or would their animosity toward England and the hatred between patriots and loyalists have plunged the country into widespread and intense partisan warfare? Had the latter occurred, what could Britain have done, and for how long? What seems certain is that reconciliation was, at best, highly unlikely by the end of the first few years of war: the ideological, cultural, and political chasm between the colonies and the mother country had grown impassable, and a few years of war served only to cement this gulf more firmly in the consciousness of each side's adherents.

Counterfactual speculation aside, independence had indeed been won, and Congress now had to decide the Continental Army's future. Its decision not to retain the sizable regular army, as General Washington desired, was based not only on the country's poverty but also on the traditional dread of standing armies in peacetime. That fear had come to American shores with early English colonists, lain dormant when many years of

British official neglect had fostered colonial self-rule, and resurfaced after 1763 as English troops remained in the colonies only, it seemed, to enforce the will of a tyrannical Parliament. It had grown during the war when American soldiers had looted civilian property and their leaders had often condemned (though with good reason in most cases) selfish civilians and an incompetent Congress, and it climaxed in 1783 at the Continental Army's encampment at Newburgh, New York. With the war essentially over, officers had openly challenged the Confederation government and hinted at reprisals if they did not receive the pensions that it had promised them. Washington personally defused the crisis, and Congress made concessions. But in 1784, it reduced the army to eighty officers and men.

Even as the Continental Army disintegrated, hostile Indian tribes threatened backcountry settlements and British troops remained in forts throughout the Northwest Territory. In 1784 and 1785, Congress, lacking a substantial army, asked the states to provide 700 militiamen for extended service, but this force was too weak to intimidate natives or expel Britons. Then, in 1786, during the sharp postwar economic depression, Congress stood by helplessly while state forces in Massachusetts put down a protesting "army," led by Revolutionary veteran Daniel Shays, which had risen against heavy debts and burdensome taxation. Many Americans, including former Continental Army officers such as Washington, became convinced that the government's impotence was a chronic disease that had to be cured at its source: the dependence upon the states to defend American territory and preserve domestic order. Thus, the Revolution was barely over before internal unrest, opposition to the existing government, and dangers along U.S. borders indicated to some that the road ahead would be hazardous.

The American Revolution did not significantly alter European military thought and practice. It would, however, inspire others who wished to end monarchical rule and the subordination of colonial peoples, and this is where much of its significance for later eras' politico-military activity lies. In the war's immediate aftermath, though, massed infantry fighting in conventional style and the use of conventional weapons continued to decide European conflicts; the importance of colonial irregulars went largely unnoticed across the Atlantic. The minuscule American navy contributed nothing to naval doctrine and, except for the distress it and the privateers caused British commerce, might as well never have existed. The most important naval engagement of the war, which drove British ships from the Virginia coast near Yorktown, was a French victory.

However, there were distinctive aspects to American warfare. From the outset, observes historian John Ferling, conflict between Native Americans and Europeans "descended to a level of almost indescribable terrorism and malevolence" and assumed "a tone of barbarism perhaps not witnessed in the Western world since antiquity." That pattern persisted during the Revolution. Tories and patriots fought each other without mercy; English officer Banastre "Butcher" Tarleton deserved his gruesome nickname, and few of his fellow British commanders controlled the ferocity of their Indian allies, whose own villages in turn suffered brutal American reprisals. Unconventional warfare, also more common in the New World than the Old, had become so familiar to Americans as to be almost instinctive. Even Washington, whose career represented in many ways an attempt to emulate European military custom, occasionally urged his men to fight in what they called "Indian fashion," and his frequent use of evasion, surprise, and deception had deep roots in the colonial American military environment and tradition.

Although Americans faced an uncertain future, their military experience, encompassing more than eight generations, had established enduring guideposts: faith in the militia and fear of professional armies. After the Revolution, the reputation of the Minutemen would attain mythological proportions, much to the detriment of the regular army's prospects. Yet, these archetypical citizen-soldiers were rare in an age of limited wars fought by professionals interested primarily in pay and personal survival. The Revolution had been, in may ways, an exception to this trend. A Washington explained, Americans were fighting "neither [for] Glory nor extent of territory, but [in] defense of all that is dear and valuable in life." When a like principle emerged in Revolutionary France, it continued to challenge the eighteenth-century status quo, producing huge civilian armies and profoundly altering the nature of warfare.

Notes

1. In America, the War of the League of Augsburg (1688–1697) was known as King William's War (1689–1697); the War of the Spanish Succession (1701–1714), as Queen Anne's War (1702–1713); the War of the Austrian Succession (1740–1748), as King George's War (1743–1748); and the Seven Years' War (1756–1763), as the French and Indian War (1755–1763).

2. In some ways, Arnold's "turning coat" was an outgrowth of the general problems the army faced. Arnold had earlier employed significant amounts of his

own funds to equip troops under his command and was never reimbursed by Congress, fueling his resentment toward what he saw as a lack of proper recognition of his sacrifices and accomplishments. Listening to Congress dub Horatio Gates the "Hero of Saratoga" rankled him as well, as the two had quarreled over command and strategy during that campaign. One could make the argument that Arnold's conduct on the field at Saratoga was more distinguished than that of Gates; Arnold certainly did.

Sources and Suggested Readings

Alden, John R. *A History of the American Revolution*. New York, 1969.

———. *The South in the Revolution, 1763–1789*. Baton Rouge, La., 1981.

Anderson, Fred. *A People's Army: Massachusetts Soldiers and Society in the Seven Years' War*. Chapel Hill, N.C., 1984.

———. *The Crucible of War: The Seven Years' War and the Fate of Empire in British North America, 1754–1766*. New York, 2001.

Babits, Lawrence E. *A Devil of a Whipping: The Battle of Cowpens*. Chapel Hill, N.C., 2001.

Buchanan, John. *The Road to Guilford Courthouse: The American Revolution in the Carolinas*. New York, 1997.

DePauw, Linda. "Women in Combat: The Revolutionary War Experience." *Armed Forces and Society* (Winter 1981).

Dull, Jonathan R. *A Diplomatic History of the American Revolution*. New Haven, Conn., 1985.

Ferling, John E. *A Wilderness of Miseries: War and Warriors in Early America*. Westport, Conn., 1980.

Fischer, David Hackett. *Washington's Crossing*. New York, 2004.

Flexner, James T. *George Washington in the American Revolution, 1775–1783*. Boston, 1967.

Foner, Jack D. *Blacks and the Military in American History*. New York, 1974.

Fowler, W. M., and Wallace Coyle, eds. *The American Revolution: Changing Perspectives*. Boston, 1979.

Gruber, Ira D. *The Howe Brothers and the American Revolution*. Chapel Hill, N.C., 1972.

Higginbotham, Don. *George Washington and the American Military Tradition*. Athens, Ga., 1985.

———, ed. *Reconsiderations on the Revolutionary War: Selected Essays*. Westport, Conn., 1978.

———. *The War of American Independence: Military Attitudes, Policies, and Practices, 1763–1789*. New York, 1971.

Leach, Douglas E. *Americans for Empire: A Military History of the British Colonies in North America, 1607–1763*. New York, 1973.

Martin, James Kirby, and Mark Edward Lender. *A Respectable Army: The Military Origins of the Republic, 1763–1789*. Arlington Heights, Ill., 1982.

Matloff, Maurice, ed. *American Military History*. Washington, D.C., 1969.

Millett, Allan R., and Peter Maslowski. *For the Common Defense: The Military History of the United States, 1607–1983*. New York, 1984.

Millis, Walter. *Arms and Men: A Study in American Military History*. New Brunswick, N.J., 1956.

Peckham, Howard H. *The Colonial Wars, 1688–1763*. Chicago, 1964.

Quarles, Benjamin. *The Negro in the American Revolution*. Chapel Hill, N.C., 1961.

Royster, Charles A. *A Revolutionary People at War: The Continental Army and the American Character, 1775–1783*. Chapel Hill, N.C., 1979.

Shy, John A. *A People Numerous and Armed: Reflections on the Military Struggle for American Independence*. New York, 1976.

———. *Toward Lexington: The Role of the British Army in the Coming of the American Revolution*. Princeton, N.J., 1965.

Weigley, Russell F. *The American Way of War: A History of United States Military Strategy and Policy*. New York, 1973.

———. *A History of the United States Army*. New York, 1967.

TWO

Napoleonic Warfare

OWEN CONNELLY

D URING THE 1780s the United States operated under its first constitution, the Articles of Confederation. The document gave few powers
to the national government that sat in Philadelphia, and reserved
most of the authority for the states. In the realm of military affairs, Congress
was virtually powerless. The tiny Continental Navy of the Revolution became
extinct, and the professional army consisted of only one regiment, inadequate
even to deal with western Indian tribes. Fortunately, international conditions
mainly were placid in the 1780s, and the young republic struggled through
the decade without major foreign policy problems. At home a serious depression sparked agrarian unrest and caused some leaders to doubt whether the
Philadelphia government could even suppress domestic turmoil. After the
abortive Shays's Rebellion (1786) in Massachusetts, a concerted effort was
made to revise the Articles of Confederation with an eye toward strength-
ening the central government. The resulting U.S. Constitution of 1787
assigned more power to the national government and allowed for the creation of an adequate defense force, but citizens' continuing suspicion of
standing armies and the government's inadequate financial resources pro-
hibited a more aggressive strategy of national defense.

Under President George Washington's administration, Congress dealt a
blow to nationalists who desired a strong professional army when it passed
the Calling Forth Act and the Uniform Militia Act in 1792. The former allowed

the president to mobilize the militia in times of national emergency, but the latter called for universal military service, which continued into the twentieth century, and essentially placed control of the militia—the main element of national defense—in the hands of state governments. In the early 1790s, Washington utilized his power to call out the militia to help pacify Indians on the northwestern frontier and to quell a protest over excise taxes in western Pennsylvania, the Whiskey Rebellion (1794). But, when international conflict followed the outbreak of the French Revolution (1789), the United States lacked a sizable, professionally trained army and navy to meet the crisis.

Owen Connelly examines the wars of the French Revolution (1792–1799) and the subsequent Napoleonic Wars (1800–1815) and their impact on the development of the military art. These conflicts, which can be viewed as the prototypes of the modern world wars, helped transform warfare from the relatively limited disputes between monarchs of the eighteenth century to struggles of intense nationalism. Over the course of a generation, the size of European armies doubled and tripled, and a number of refinements were made in weaponry, tactics, and strategy. By the end of the long series of wars, France's Napoleon Bonaparte, even in defeat, was regarded as the supreme master of modern warfare. European generals studied his maxims and sought to emulate his methods both on the battlefield and behind the lines. At the time, few leaders clearly understood the full implications of mobilizing a country's citizenry and waging war in the name of nationalism.

Although it wished to remain separate from the European struggle, the United States could not avoid some involvement. As the world's leading neutral trading nation, it was caught in a squeeze by two of the world's premier naval powers, Britain and France. After avoiding war with Britain by ratifying the domestically unpopular Jay's Treaty (1795), America became engaged in an undeclared naval war with France. The Quasi-War (1798–1800), in combination with a small naval building program in previous years to counter the menace of pirates in the Mediterranean, led to the establishment of the Navy Department under Benjamin Stoddert and the beginning of a naval tradition for the new nation.

After the conclusion of the Quasi-War, President Thomas Jefferson drastically reduced naval expenditures and preparedness, but in 1802 he did establish a military school at West Point for the training of engineers. In 1817, following the War of 1812 (which will be covered in the next chapter), President James Monroe appointed Captain Sylvanus Thayer to be the superintendent. Thayer, who studied in France, transformed West Point into a military school based on the French model. (The Navy Department did not follow the army's lead until 1845 with the establishment of the U.S. Naval Academy at Annapolis.) Although stressing engineering and field tactics, West Point instituted a few classes in military strategy initially under the direction of Dennis Hart Mahan. These classes emphasized the teachings of the Swiss strategist Antoine Henri de Jomini, who viewed the Napoleonic conflict from a flawed perspective, but future American officers at least got a sense of the European style of combat. By the time of the Mexican War (also covered in the next chapter), American officers demonstrated some of the lessons learned from Napoleonic warfare. But still few, if any, fully understood the volatile forces of nationalism unleashed by the French Revolution and harnessed by Napoleon in his quest to conquer Europe.

The West Point *Military History and Atlas of the Napoleonic Wars* has a flyleaf quotation from Hendrik Willem van Loon, which reads in part:

> Should I hear the sound of heavy drums and see the little man on his white horse, in his old and much-worn green uniform, then . . . I am afraid I would leave my books . . . and my home . . . and follow him wherever he cared to lead. My own grandfather did this, and Heaven knows he was not born to be a hero.

At the United States Military Academy, where Napoleon's campaigns have long been studied, the man himself is revered for his charisma and leadership ability, and held in some awe. The American public also seems to be fascinated with the little man who beat heavy military and political odds to dominate Europe, as frequent television shows and movies attest.

The United States has drawn heavily on military developments in Europe from 1776 through the twentieth century and beyond. (For a trivial example, the helmets worn by U.S. soldiers in the Gulf Wars beginning in 1991 and 2003 were modeled after German helmets of World War II.) Before the American Revolution, colonial officers had taken the British military as a model. During and after the Revolution, Americans looked to France and the German states as well. Further, Europeans were in the American Revolutionary War—many French volunteers, such as the Marquis de Lafayette—and some 7,800 regulars under the Count de Rochambeau, who fought at Yorktown (1781) under General Washington. Other foreigners were the Baron Friedrich von Steuben, drillmaster at Valley Forge, the Baron de Kalb (killed at Camden, South Carolina), and the Polish noble Thaddeus Kosciusko. After the Revolution, the American army sent officers to Europe to study and observe maneuvers and wars.

Warfare changed radically during the wars of the French Revolution (1792–1799) and Napoleonic Wars (1800–1815), which was predicted by eighteenth-century developments. There was a population explosion in the eighteenth century that saw an increase of almost 100 percent Europe-wide (44 percent in France, first in contraceptives). Thus men were available for mass armies. The Industrial Revolution, which began in the eighteenth century, produced (among other things) reliable weapons in larger quantities than ever before.

The weapons used by the French armies of the Revolution and Napoleon were inherited from the monarchy. General Count Jean-Baptiste Vaquette de Gribeauval designed new field cannon for Louis XV and improved them as Louis XVI's inspector of artillery. His light, smoothbore, 12-, 8-, 6-, and 4-pound guns were the best in Europe until 1825. They were of standard caliber, as were the carriages and limbers, and had packaged shot and powder.[1] Gribeauval's followers standardized small arms, producing the 1777 Charleville musket, five feet long, muzzle-loading, .69 caliber (17.5 mm) for infantry; the .69 musketoon or carbine, ten inches shorter, for the cavalry; and others. They designed the standard sidearm, the .69 muzzle-loading flintlock pistol. There were cartridges for these weapons also. The rifle was known, but was used only by French snipers and skirmishers.[2]

Prussia equipped one regiment of Jäger (light infantry) with rifles, however, before the death of Frederick the Great (1786), but no more. In the 1780s also, the British armed a company of infantry with rifles; and after 1793, to fight the French, the Ninety-fifth Rifle regiment and part of the Sixtieth Infantry and the King's German Legion (KGL). Napoleon met the Ninety-fifth and the KGL at Waterloo.

According to General Charles de Gaulle, French military theorists made an eighteenth-century "military enlightenment."[3] Chevalier Jean de Beaumont du Teil advocated concentrated artillery fire on the enemy at the point of attack—and his book was one of Napoleon's texts. General Pierre de Bourcet, a French staff officer in the Seven Years' War, devised what is now called an "estimate of the situation." After the war, he directed a staff college at Grenoble (beginning in 1764) and promoted planning in his *Principes de la guerre de Montagnes*. In 1766 he organized a general staff, the *Service d'état major des logis des armées*, which was abolished, but was restored in 1788.

Jacques-Antoine-Hippolyte de Guibert (1743–1790) was a junior officer in the Seven Years' War. Afterward, he rose to the rank of general and became France's foremost military reformer. His *Essai général de tactique* (1772) proposed a national militia, patriotically indoctrinated, that would live off the enemy's land and overwhelm him with flexible tactics. In *Defense du système de guerre moderne* (1779) he concentrated on tactics, having decided that a citizen army was politically impossible. However, in his last book, *De la force publique* (1790), he proposed a militia comprising all healthy male adults, and discussed conscription.[4] Guibert advocated the battalion column for maneuver, but deployment into line in combat for maximum firepower; this much was formalized in the *Drill Regulations of 1791*, the drill manual of the Republican army. It is a myth that the revolutionary armies always attacked in column. Generals decided whether column, line, or a combination was best for their troops, or left it to battalion commanders.

The Marshal de Broglie introduced the division to the French army in 1759. In 1780, it became the largest unit of maneuver. (Napoleon made the division—8,000 to 10,000 men—a part of the *corps*, which he made standard.)

Earlier (1751), Louis XV, influenced by Madame de Pompadour, founded the *École Militaire* in Paris. (The British Royal Military College, Sandhurst, dates from 1802, as does the United States Military Academy at West Point.) The Count de Saint-Germain (minister of war 1775–1777) persuaded Louis XVI to create twelve *écoles royales militaires* so that more impecunious country nobles (the backbone of the officer corps) could be educated. He reserved the *École Militaire* in Paris for high nobility and exceptional students from the "feeder" schools. One of the latter was Brienne, where Napoleon got his initial training, but he spent his final year at the *École Militaire*. Four quarterings of nobility were required to enter the king's schools, but most country nobles qualified. If poor, many had the oldest titles in France.

Advanced schools for artillery and engineer officers had been founded before the cadet schools. These arms admitted graduates of the *écoles* who excelled in mathematics and science, but also commissioned commoners who were qualified (Lazare Carnot was one of these). The French army should have had the most professional officer corps in Europe, but, says Lee Kennett: "French society was . . . far from being militaristic. It was a . . . breach of court etiquette to appear at Versailles in uniform."[5] Then too, aristocratic tradition held that nobles were *born* to lead. The highest-ranking officers often had attended none of the king's schools. For example, in 1777, arriving in America, the Marquis de Lafayette (age twenty) demanded a commission as major-general, and the Continental Congress gave it to him.[6] In France he had been a mere captain, assigned to a regiment he seldom visited.

The government of Terror (1793–1794) in the French Revolution most radically changed the conduct of war. The king was deposed (August 1792)—after a three-year attempt at constitutional monarchy—and executed (January 1793). The republic was established, but proved weak. The government of Terror (so called at the time) under Maximillien Robespierre's Committee of Public Safety, was voted in to protect France from foreign and internal enemies. Lazare Carnot, later dubbed the "Organizer of Victory," was the military member of the Committee. In 1793–1794, he created the largest army ever seen in Europe—800,000 men under arms (1,000,000 on paper)—using the *levée-en-masse*, which made all male Frenchmen between eighteen and twenty-five liable for military service. Under loyal generals of the royal army[7] and commoner-generals, many former NCOs, the peoples' armies—whipped up to patriotic frenzy by *représentants* from Paris—gradually won out over professional armies of European monarchs, using barbaric tactics. Henry Lachouque, historian of the Imperial Guard, wrote:

> The battle of this period was a fearsome spectacle. No longer a contest of honor, as in the 17th and 18th centuries, with its rules of elegance and somber beauty, this was a struggle to the death, often without quarter, a veritable hell.

In the first battles won by republican armies, the keys to victory were the democratic arms of the French army. It was the royal artillery, in blue uniforms (rather than royal white), that won the Battle of Valmy against the Prussians (September 1792). At that time, 42 percent of career artillery officers were with the army, but only 18 percent of cavalry and infantry officers.[8] In exile, Napoleon said: "If France . . . promptly set on foot such a good army, it was because it had a good foundation, that emigration [of noble officers] made better, not worse."[9]

Napoleon began his career as an officer in the royal army. He was born Napoleone Buonaparte (August 15, 1769) on the Italian-speaking Mediterranean island of Corsica to Carlo and Letizia Buonaparte. He was legally French, however, since Louis XV had bought the island in 1768 from Genoa, which had been unable to suppress an independence movement. Napoleon's father, Carlo Buonaparte, had been a rebel, but he was an opportunist and a lawyer who spoke French. He made himself useful to his new lords. As a result, he became a French count (converting an Italian title), secretary of the Corsican Estates, royal prosecutor, and generally "a big fish in a small pond." He was able to get free tuition at French schools for his elder children, but died in 1785 at age thirty-nine.[10] Louis XVI gave Napoleone a "scholarship" at Brienne. He entered at age nine, and a friar registered him as "Napoleon," but he did not change his surname to Bonaparte until 1796, when he had army command. He did well, especially in mathematics, and was sent to the *École Militaire* in Paris for his last year. He graduated in 1785 (forty-second in a class of fifty-eight) and was commissioned in the artillery.

In 1791, Napoleon took advantage of the Revolution, which had created the National Guard, to become elected lieutenant colonel of a Corsican battalion. But in 1793 Corsica declared independence and expelled the Buonapartes as Francophiles; they fled to France, then under the government of Terror. Napoleon had already sworn loyalty to the republic and become a Jacobin (the party of the Terror), and he rejoined the army as a captain. His politically correct status was a factor in getting him a post that brought him to national attention.

A French army was besieging Toulon, a major seaport, which was in revolt against the government of Terror, assisted by Richard Lord Howe's British fleet. The French artillery general was wounded; Captain Buonaparte applied for his post, presenting himself to the *représentants* as a trained artilleryman and a Jacobin. He was given command of the artillery, and got approval from his general and Carnot (in Paris) for a plan that used the army to get him a high promontory overlooking the harbor. From there, his guns drove the British fleet from the harbor, and Toulon fell. A captain in September, Bonaparte was brigadier general at year's end, courtesy of Carnot, always looking for talent.

He faded into obscurity when the Terror ended, but in October 1795, he was called on by Paul Barras, who knew him from Toulon, to defend the Convention from the Paris mob, so that it could put in power the Directory—a moderate government. Napoleon delivered a "whiff of grapeshot" against the marching people and was shortly given command of the Army of Italy.

With the Army of Italy (38,000 effectives), Napoleon in one year defeated five armies—one Piedmontese and four Austrian, all larger than his own—and captured 160,000 prisoners. At the same time, two French armies in Germany, totaling 160,000 men, had gotten nowhere. He became *stupor mundi* (the wonder of the world)—or at least the world press—and a national hero. Bonaparte blundered many times, but he was a "scrambler"—an improviser—who overcame his mistakes and won repeatedly. He also knew his men, and that their zeal for "spreading liberty" had worn thin. Thus in his famous speech that began, "Soldiers! You are naked and hungry," he promised them cities and rich provinces to loot (by implication).[11]

Napoleon's next venture, an attempt to capture Egypt and ruin British trade in the Middle East and India, was a disaster. He defeated the mameluke rulers of Egypt at Shubra Kitt and Embabeh (Battle of the Pyramids; although he was nowhere near them, his address to the troops, "Forty centuries look down upon you . . ." became famous). However, on August 1, 1798, Admiral Horatio Nelson's British fleet destroyed Napoleon's fleet, and he was marooned with his army. He marched into Turkish Syria anyway, but had to retreat because of disease among his men and attacks by strong Turkish and British forces. Back in Egypt, however, he destroyed a Turkish invasion force of 20,000 at Aboukir with 7,700 men and seventeen cannon.

He returned to France and was welcomed as a savior, since France was at war with a new coalition and the public perception was that France was losing. In Paris, a coup d'état to overthrow the Directory had been planned by a group under the veteran politician, the (once) Abbé Emmanuel Sieyès, and including Talleyrand, the foreign minister; Fouché, minister of police; and Napoleon's brothers Joseph and Lucien. Sieyès wanted a "sword" to control the army, but had not found one, and took a chance on Napoleon. He should not have. On 18–19 Brumaire (November 9–10, 1799), the coup reduced Sieyès to equal footing with Bonaparte, who then won the support of the outgoing legislators. The new constitution made Bonaparte First Consul of France, with kingly powers.[12]

In 1800, riding a donkey, Napoleon took an army over the Alps—Hannibal style—and defeated the Austrians (the last land power fighting) at Marengo. In 1801–1802, he made peace with all the major powers. However, he violated the provisions of the treaty with Britain, which resumed war at sea in 1803. In May 1804, the French Senate proclaimed

Napoleon Emperor of the French; the people, in plebiscite, approved. On December 2, 1804, in Notre Dame, Napoleon crowned himself "in the name of the French people and the *Army*."

Since 1803, Napoleon had been reorganizing the French army, which totaled about 600,000. He trained his field army of 200,000 from headquarters at Boulogne. This was the *Grande Armée* of which he created an *Armée d'Angleterre* (Army of England), threatening invasion. He gave it all the glamour of the old royal army, and more. Regiments, notably the cavalry, got uniforms in blazing colors. Regimental flags had eagles atop the staffs ("The Eagle" of the Regiment). Every regiment had a band. He restored the identity of foreign regiments—Poles, Swiss, and others—for healthy competition. However, he introduced no new weapons or tactics. And contrary to what many have assumed, he did not expand the artillery. Throughout his wars, he maintained an average of three cannon per 1,000 men, often fewer than his enemies. Napoleon's emphasis was on organization, discipline, morale, training, hardening, and better use of weapons (but not marksmanship for the infantry, who continued to use area fire). Napoleon restored the grade of marshal (1804) to the army and promoted to it generals he considered outstanding (and for political reasons, a few heroes of the republic)—sixteen in 1804, ultimately twenty-six.[13] He made the *corps* the standard unit-of-all-arms, capable of fighting alone. It had 20,000 to 30,000 men and was normally commanded by a marshal. It comprised two or more infantry divisions (8,000 to 10,000 men each), a brigade of light cavalry (2,000 to 3,000 men), six to eight companies of artillery, and engineers, medics, trains, and headquarters.

In August 1805, Austrian and Russian armies were moving against France on the continent; Austrian general Karl Mack von Leiberich was at Ulm, waiting for Russian reinforcements. Napoleon sent the *Grande Armée* racing into Germany. His corps, describing great arcs, crossed the Rhine and then the Danube. (See map.) Early historians, tracing these movements, thought it obvious that Napoleon had planned to encircle Mack. *Not so.* He thought Mack would retreat to a position behind one of the tributaries of the Danube to the south. The path of his army was toward the Isar River or Munich. At midnight on October 13, he discovered that Mack was behind him and might cut his supply lines. He ordered the corps nearest Ulm, and the reserve cavalry (Murat), back across the Danube, rerouted other corps to back them, and followed, bringing up the Guard and much

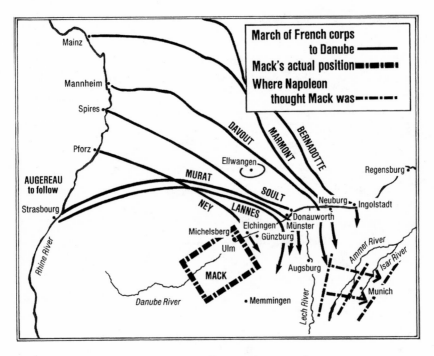

Ulm (Owen Connelly, *Blundering to Glory:*
Napoleon's Military Campaigns, SR Books, 1999)

artillery. The army drove the Austrians into Ulm and bombarded them into
surrender, capturing Mack and 26,000 men (October 20). Ulm was a triumph of improvisation, however, not strategy.

On October 21, Lord Nelson sank the better part of the French and
Spanish fleets off Cape Trafalgar (Spain), but Bonaparte captured the press,
except in Britain. Napoleon marched on through Vienna and found the
Russians and a few Austrians in Moravia. Czar Alexander I had taken command. He had 86,000 men to Napoleon's 67,000, and on December 2, 1805,
ignoring Mikhail Kutuzov's advice to wait for reinforcements, the czar
attacked Napoleon's supposedly weak south wing, determined to envelop
the French army. His troops, mired in swampy ground, were stopped by
fire from Nicholas Davout's corps, which had arrived during the night.
Alexander kept sending in troops, however, until he weakened his north
wing. Napoleon sent Jean Soult's corps south to drive the Russians facing

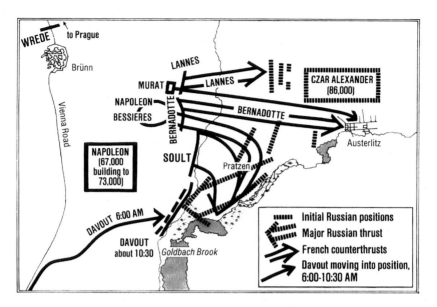

Austerlitz (Owen Connelly, *Blundering to Glory:*
Napoleon's Military Campaigns, SR Books, 1999)

Davout into swamps and lakes. He then unleashed the rest of his army eastward on Austerlitz. Alexander escaped, but his army was destroyed.

Austerlitz was a classic Napoleonic tactical triumph. Napoleon held back a large reserve (two corps, the Guard, and Joaquim Murat's reserve cavalry), waited until his enemy made mistakes, took advantage of the mistakes, and crushed him. None of Napoleon's battles were alike, but, unless conditions dictated something different (as at Waterloo), there was always the big reserve, the wait, the enemy mistake, and the attack. At both Ulm and Austerlitz, however, he accomplished what was always his purpose—to destroy the enemy army.

In 1806, Napoleon overwhelmed the Prussian Army, which he surprised and outnumbered at Jena, while Davout won the twin battle of Auerstädt. In 1807, at Friedland, he demolished the Russian army of 60,000 under General Theophil von Bennigsen, caught with his back to the Alle River. Napoleon called in corps until he had 80,000 men, and attacked the Russians, half of whom were killed or drowned. On Bennigsen's advice, the czar surrendered, and became Napoleon's ally—until 1812.

By this time, with ever-increasing numbers of French and foreign troops at his disposal, Napoleon seems to have decided to depend on mass rather than maneuver for victory. He had won by greater numbers in the 1806–1807 campaign. In every subsequent campaign through 1812, he began with superior numbers. But he never mastered the art of commanding great masses. His forte was maneuver, as he would demonstrate in 1814, in France, fighting his most amazing campaign, against odds of two or three to one. In late 1807 and 1808, Bonaparte seized Spain and Portugal and deposed their monarchs. General Andoche Junot took Portugal; Joseph Bonaparte became king of Spain. Joseph was chased from Madrid (July 1808) by a grassroots uprising; Sir Arthur Wellesley (later Duke of Wellington) ousted Junot. Napoleon went to Spain with most of the *Grande Armée*, amassed 300,000 troops, and crushed the Spanish (100,000 at best). He restored Joseph to the throne, but left Wellington to his marshals, who could not displace him. Spanish enthusiasm at the grassroots level died quickly; Spanish armies always lacked trained troops and repeatedly lost to the French, but guerrilla bands persisted, robbing and killing the French and taking subsidies from the British.

Napoleon never returned to Iberia, which was a cardinal error. His armies sustained 300,000 casualties, and the war (1807–1813) cost billions of francs, which weakened the Empire before the disaster in Russia (1812). Meanwhile, in 1809, with Napoleon in Spain, Austria attacked the French in Germany, expecting aid from the Germans, but got none. Pan-German nationalism infected only intellectuals until the mid-nineteenth century. Napoleon quickly challenged the archduke Charles, commanding Austrian forces. Charles (helped by the Danube in flood), defeated Napoleon at Aspern-Essling (May 1809), but Napoleon beat him at Wagram (July 1809), where he commanded 190,000 troops (the most ever in one battle) against Charles's 140,000. The victory enabled Napoleon to marry a Habsburg archduchess, Marie-Louise, by whom he had a son (1811), whom he expected to be recognized by European monarchs.[14]

Russia challenged on December 31, 1810. After spending 1811 in preparation, Napoleon attacked in 1812. His army, two-thirds non-French, numbered 720,000, of whom 611,000 marched into Russia (490,000 in the first wave). Czar Alexander arrayed only 180,000 against him. Napoleon had hoped that the czar, assessing the odds, would make terms. But Alexander was determined to fight, made desperate by fear that his court, hurt in the pocketbook by the French alliance, would revert to the Russian "national sport" of assassinating czars.

Napoleon had not planned to march on Moscow, but the Russians retreated along that road, and he followed, hoping to destroy the enemy army. The Russians refused serious battle until the czar put Mikhail Kutuzov in command. He stood at Borodino, 550 miles into Russia, 70 from Moscow. The battle of Borodino (September 7, 1812) cost the Russians 45,000 casualties and the French more than 31,000. The Russian army remained intact, but left the field the next morning. Napoleon went on to Moscow, which had been evacuated and was soon burned. The French emperor remained there, attempting to negotiate with the czar. He thought any rational ruler would make peace, and he feared that his allies would desert him and/or his government would face a coup in Paris. In mid-October, he finally marched—too late in an unusually early and cold winter. The retreat in the ice and snow, which killed most of the *Grande Armée*, is too well known to merit description here. Estimates of Napoleon's losses range from 400,000 to 570,000, complicated by many factors, such as Russia's claim to have captured 200,000.

Nonetheless, Napoleon raised another army (of green troops and jaded generals) and returned to Germany in 1813 to face the Allies. He won battles, but agreed to a truce in June, during which Wellington defeated King Joseph in Spain. Afterward the troops of all the major powers stood against him. In earlier campaigns, usually because of lack of coordination between allies, he had fought one power at a time. With a maximum of 400,000 troops, he could not contend with the 600,000 of the Allies, who, in a climactic battle at Leipzig (November 1813), drove him from Germany.

In 1814, he fought an amazing campaign in France, primarily against the Austrian prince von Schwarzenberg and Marshal Blücher of Prussia, both of whom had him outnumbered. For four months, he struck first at one, then at the other, making incredibly fast marches between the two. But his two enemies finally joined forces, and more armies entered France, and again he was overwhelmed by enemy numbers. On April 6 he abdicated and was exiled on the island of Elba, off the west coast of Italy.

In March 1815, with the French unhappy with King Louis XVIII, returned "in the baggage of the Allies," and the Allies squabbling at the Congress of Vienna, Napoleon returned to France (the flight of the Eagle).

During the "Hundred Days," he ruled France again. But the Allies made him an outlaw before he landed, and refused to believe his promise to keep the peace. He raised an army of 125,000 troops and struck at the nearest Allied armies in Belgium, under Wellington (110,000) and Blücher (125,000), hoping to beat each separately. However, on June 18, 1815, they combined to defeat him in the battle of Waterloo. Urged by crowds in Paris to fight on, Napoleon instead abdicated again and was sent into exile on St. Helena, in the south Atlantic, 1,300 miles from Africa and 2,400 from Brazil. There he died in May 1821.

Napoleon was a military genius, which he believed was a gift of God. That aside, his triumphs can be attributed to his awesome energy (in his prime, not in Russia or later), his ability to "scramble," his refusal to accept defeat, and his leadership. In peace, he counted on his charm and could persuade men to do almost anything. In war he drove his marshals like a drill sergeant (he was *un homme terrible*, he said) and rewarded them afterward if they had done well. With the men he was familiar, and he was among them at danger points often enough that they counted him as one of themselves, "the little corporal."[15]

No doubt he also owed his success in part to the ineptitude of his enemies, and he was lucky, although he denied it. War, he said, was "nothing but accidents," and luck, the ability to exploit them. He also had superior subordinates, among whom marshals André Masséna and Louis Davout stand out. In Italy (1796–1797) Masséna literally won battles for him. In the later campaigns, Davout very often insured victory by incredible marches and personal initiative, for example at Austerlitz (1805), where his corps arrived and deployed in the dark to stop the czar's planned envelopment; at Auerstädt (1806), where his corps won unaided; and at Wagram (1809), where he turned the Austrian flank.

Napoleon began almost every campaign with a strategic blunder, as in 1805, when he overshot Mack at Ulm and had to double back to defeat him. Often he began campaigns or battles with mistakes, but he never quit; instead, he rewrote his plans as he went. In midcareer he acquired superior numbers that covered his mistakes and ensured his victories—until the last years.

Exiled on St. Helena, Napoleon said many things about the "art of war," some of which are contradictory, but many of which ring true, he told Bertrand: "The art of war is a simple art . . . it is all common sense; nothing about it is theoretical."[16] His most consistent pronouncements concerned great commanders. Among these are many that describe the secrets of his success. For example, *"S'engage et alors on voit"* [Engage and then wait and see] appears repeatedly, if in different words. For example:

> The outcome of a battle . . . is the result of one instant, one thought: one approaches with various combinations, you mix it up [*on s'mêle*], you fight for a time, the decisive moment arrives, a mental spark [*une étincelle morale*] tells you so; the smallest of reserves [wins the battle].[17]

Such was Napoleon's tactical doctrine. As to strategy, he said repeatedly to keep corps close enough together for quick concentration; do not divide forces in the presence of the enemy; maneuver to outnumber the enemy on the battlefield.

Napoleon was probably the greatest commander of all time, but his genius lay in scrambling, not carrying out plans. Napoleon's charisma and bold strategy and tactics captivated American officers, surely at the United States Military Academy (USMA). Dennis Hart Mahan (USMA, 1824), who joined the West Point faculty in 1832, founded the "Napoleon Club," where officers talked about Bonaparte. As principal instructor in warfare, one of his texts was Captain J. M. O'Connor's translation of S. F. Gay de Vernon's treatise *The Science of War and Fortification*, which included a précis of the strategic precepts of Antoine Henri, Baron de Jomini.

The baron's milquetoast version of Napoleonic warfare dominated teaching at West Point until Clausewitz was translated into English in 1873. This was unfortunate, since Jomini omitted the "chaotic and the demoniacal" in Napoleon's methods of war.[18] He presented the principles of war in a neat system, which Napoleon himself, on St. Helena, found laughable.[19] Napoleon was an improviser.[20] Jomini emphasized control of places— territory, capitals. Napoleon's purpose was always to destroy the enemy army. Jomini was Napoleonic only in his emphasis on the offensive. In 1846, Mahan's student Henry Wager Halleck published *Elements of Military Art and Science*, and in 1847, Mahan published his own book, known by its short title, *Outposts*. Both were influenced by Jomini.

West Point had no course in Napoleonic warfare before the Civil War, but Jomini's version of Napoleonic warfare was included in the general course. Of generals in the Civil War, Jomini's interpretation influenced

Halleck, of course, who lost battles but became President Lincoln's general-in-chief. Somehow, the principal commanders—of the United States and the Confederate States—took different lessons from Napoleon. Grant adopted a strategy of annihilation; Lee searched for the climactic battle and destroyed his own army.

It is Grant's strategy that has become the American "way of war."[21]

Notes

1. Interchangeable parts were engineered by Honoré Blanc but were rejected as too expensive. More accurate casting made lighter gun barrels that delivered the same fire. Ken Adler, *Engineering the Revolution: Arms and Enlightenment in France, 1763–1815* (Princeton, N.J., 1997), 40–43. Geoffrey Parker, *Military Revolution: Military Innovation and the Rise of the West* (Cambridge, 1988), 148.

2. Though more accurate, rifles were still muzzle loading (except for expensive hunting models); cartridges were more difficult to ram home, and the few seconds of delay could spell death for soldiers, who did not like them.

3. Pierre Messmer and Alain Larcan, *Les Écrits militaires de Charles de Gaulle: Essai d'Analyse thématique* (Paris, 1985), 228–229.

4. Peter Paret, *Understanding War* (Princeton, N.J., 1992), 58.

5. Lee Kennett, *The French Armies in the Seven Years' War*, 81.

6. Marie Joseph Paul Yves Roch Gilbert du Motier, Marquis de Lafayette (1757–1834).

7. For whom defeat meant a trip to the guillotine.

8. Adler, *Engineering the Revolution*, 56–57, 76, 83.

9. "Si la France . . . a mis si promptement sur pied de bonnes armées, c'est qu'elle avait un bon fond, que l'émigration l'améliora plutôt qu'elle ne le détériora." *Correspondance de Napoléon Ier. Publiée par ordre de l'Empereur Napoléon III*, 32 vols. (Paris, 1858–1870), XXIX, 342. Hereinafter *Correspondance*.

10. Joseph, Napoleon, Lucien, and Elisa. There were eight in all; Napoleon was the second. Carlo died of stomach cancer, which killed Napoleon in 1821. That he was poisoned (arsenic) can be easily disproved.

11. Actually the speech was composed on St. Helena (1816), but no doubt he made a similar one.

12. Americans warmed to Bonaparte when he approved a treaty ending an undeclared "Corsair War" with France, which had ruined U.S. shipping. But, in fact, war did not end.

13. The top grade in revolutionary armies was major general, called commander-in-chief if commanding an army. Under Napoleon, grades were brigadier general, major general, lieutenant general (temp), and marshal.

14. He divorced Josephine de Beauharnais in November 1809.

15. *Correspondance*, XXXII, 286.

16. Napoleon, *Correspondance*, XXX, 171, 263.

17. E. Las Cases, *Mémorial de Sainte Hélène*, I, 256.

18. Russell F. Weigley, *The American Way of War* (Bloomington, Ind., 1973), 82.

19. "Jomini établit surtout des principes. Le génie agit par inspiration. . . . Générals sont battus en disant qu'ils ont suivi les principes qu'on leur inculqués. Il y a tant d'éléments divers dans la guerre!" Ernest Picard, *Préceptes et jugements de Napoléon* (Paris, 1913), 210.

20. "[A prime quality of a great general] is the courage of the *improviste*. . . . War is composed altogether of accidents. . . . A [great] commander never loses sight of what he can do to profit by them." E. Las Cases, *Mémorial de Sainte Hélène*, I, 256.

21. To borrow from Russell Weigley's title, cited above.

Sources and Suggested Readings

Bertaud, Jean Paul. *La Révolution Armée: Les soldats citoyens et la Révolution française.* Paris, 1979. Trans. by R. R. Palmer as *The Army of the French Revolution: From Citizen Soldiers to Instrument of Power.* Princeton, N.J., 1988.

Blanning, T. C. W. *The French Revolutionary Wars, 1787–1802.* London and New York, 1996.

Blaufarb, Rafe. *The French Army, 1750–1820: Careers, Talent, Merit.* New York, 2002.

Chandler, David O. *The Campaigns of Napoleon.* New York, 1966.

Clausewitz, Karl von. *On War.* Princeton, N.J., 1976.

Connelly, Owen. *Blundering to Glory: The Military Campaigns of Napoleon.* Wilmington, Del., 1987, 1990, 1999.

Dwyer, Philip G. *Napoleon and Europe.* New York, 2002.

Esdaile, Charles. *The Peninsular War: A New History.* Houndmills, UK, and New York, 2003.

Esposito, Vincent J., and John R. Elting. *A Military History and Atlas of the Napoleonic Wars.* New York, 1964.

Eysturlid, Lee W. *The Formative Influences, Theories, and Campaigns of the Archduke Carl of Austria.* Westport, Conn., 2000.

Forrest, Alan. *Conscripts and Deserters: The Army and Society during the French Revolution and Empire.* London and New York, 1989.

———. *Napoleon's Men: Soldiers of the Revolution and Empire.* London and New York, 2002.

———. *Soldiers of the French Revolution.* Durham, N.C., 1990.

Hamilton Williams, David. *Waterloo: New Perspectives: The Great Battle Reappraised.* New York, 1994.

Haythornthwaite, Philip J., et al. *Napoleon: The Final Verdict.* Foreword by David G. Chandler. London and New York, 1996.

Hofschröer, Peter. *1815: The Waterloo Campaign—Wellington, His German Allies and the Battles of Ligny and Quatre Bras.* London, 1998.

———. *The Waterloo Campaign: A German Victory.* London, 1999.

———. *Wellington's Smallest Victory: The Duke, the Modelmaker, and the Secret of Waterloo.* London, 2004.

Hopkin, David. *Soldier and Peasant in French Popular Culture, 1766–1870.* Woodbridge, Suffolk, and Rochester, New York, 2003.

Howarth, David A. *Lord Nelson: The Immortal Memory.* New York, 1989.

———. *Trafalgar: The Nelson Touch,* 2nd ed. New York, 1975.

Jomini, Antoine Henri de. *The Art of War.* Harrisburg, Pa., 1952. [First French ed. 1838.]

Lynn, John A. *The Bayonets of the Republic: Motivation and Tactics of the Army of Revolutionary France, 1791–94.* Urbana, Ill., 1984; Boulder, Colo., 1996.

Markham, Felix. *Napoleon.* New York, 1963.

Quimby, Robert S. *The Background of Napoleonic Warfare.* New York, 1957.

Ross, Steven T. *Quest for Victory: French Military Strategy, 1792–1799.* New York, 1973, 2002.

Rothenberg, Gunther E. *The Art of Warfare in the Age of Napoleon.* Bloomington, Ind., 1978.

Rowe, Michael, ed. *Collaboration and Resistance in Napoleonic Europe: State Formation in an Age of Upheaval, c. 1800–1815.* Basingstoke, UK, 2003.

Schenk, Hans G. *The Aftermath of the Napoleonic Wars: The Concert of Europe Experiment.* New York, 1967.

Scott, Samuel F. *From Yorktown to Valmy: The Transformation of the French Army in an Age of Revolution.* Niwat, Colo., 1998.

———. *Response of the Royal Army to the French Revolution.* Oxford, UK, 1978.

Shanahan, William O. *Prussian Military Reforms, 1786–1813.* New York, 1966.

Trinkle, Dennis A., and Scott A. Merriman. *The History Highway: A Guide to Internet Resources,* 3rd. ed. 2002.

Urban, Mark. *The Man Who Broke Napoleon's Codes.* New York and London, 2002.

Woloch, Isser. *The French Veteran from the Revolution to the Restoration.* Chapel Hill, N.C., 1979.

The Wars of 1812 and 1846: The Leadership Factor

J. DAVID VALAIK

D ESPITE THE long series of wars that erupted in the wake of the French Revolution and the momentous changes in the military art that they would entail, Americans felt relatively secure and complacent behind the ocean barrier that separated them from Europe. With the conclusion of the Quasi-War (1800), Thomas Jefferson, the first opposition leader elected to the presidency, took office and stressed simple republican values. Representing the agrarian majority, Jefferson immediately embarked on a program of economy in government. He drastically cut back the high-seas navy, which his constituents considered too costly, and assigned the nation's coastal defense to a gunboat fleet that eventually grew to 176 fifty-foot, one-gun crafts. Suspicious of standing armies, Jefferson also reduced the size of the regular army. The president was convinced that the nation's security could be preserved by assuming a defensive posture.

By the beginning of Jefferson's second term in 1805, however, the escalation of the Napoleonic Wars drew the United States into the vortex of the European conflict. Constant violations of America's commercial rights as a neutral on the high seas by both Britain and France forced Jefferson and his successor, James Madison, to take steps to protect the nation's rights and honor. Britain, with the larger fleet, became the main focus of American anger, especially after an English naval vessel fired on the USS *Chesapeake* in 1807. Western Americans avidly supported war against Britain in part because of accumulating evidence that the English were arming northwestern Indian tribes. For some the issue was whether the United States was truly an independent nation or merely a vassal of the major European powers. In 1812, Madison felt compelled to preserve the nation's honor by asking Congress for a declaration of war against Britain.

J. David Valaik examines how a nation that was prepared for only a defensive conflict was forced to launch an offensive war against Britain through Canada to redeem its honor. Fortunately for America, the British already were fully engaged with Napoleon's massive forces in Europe and thus could afford to fight only a limited war against the United States. Valaik stresses the leadership factor in accounting for America's dismal military performance in the early stages of the conflict. It is not altogether surprising that a nation that had failed adequately to nurture a professional military tradition and was unprepared for an offensive war might suffer from a crisis of leadership when it began. Fortunately, some able officers were found who, at critical times in the war, led American forces to victory. All in all, they fought one of the world's leading powers to a draw, which was formalized in the Treaty of Ghent (1814). In an outpouring of nationalism, the country celebrated the conclusion of the War of 1812 as a victory, highlighted by Andrew Jackson's magnificent stand before New Orleans (1815) and a number of spectacular naval triumphs.

For a few years after the War of 1812, the United States basked in the glow of nationalism and launched a military program designed to protect the nation in a future war against a European power. The regular army was maintained at a relatively high level, and Congress authorized the construction of a number of ships of the line. As previously mentioned, West Point was converted into a military academy based on the European model. By the 1820s, however, it became apparent that the Concert of Europe established at Vienna in 1815 had ushered in an era of relative peace and tranquility in the Old World. Responding to the easing of international tensions, Congress embraced traditional republican values and ordered deep cuts in both land and sea forces. At this point, Secretary of War John C. Calhoun proposed that the regular army, even at its reduced level, form the basis of national defense in a plan he called the "expansible" army concept. Calhoun's model called for a small, officer-intense regular force with many skeleton companies and regiments that could be expanded to a formidable army in wartime. Congress rejected Calhoun's proposal in 1821 and, in effect, placed the burden of national defense in the hands of the state-controlled militia.

From the 1820s through the mid-1840s the regular army was maintained at an anemic level barely able to perform its frontier duties. On the administrative side, however, the army was reformed to better carry out technical and logistical functions that had been deficient in the War of 1812. Although America's small navy was minuscule by European standards, the Navy Department made some effort to keep abreast of the new technological developments including steam-powered vessels, the screw propeller, exploding artillery shells, and armor plating.

By the time of the Mexican War, many officers in the army and navy had benefited from training at both academies. General in Chief of the Army Winfield Scott, although not a West Point graduate, instituted some Napoleonic tactics and training procedures in the regular army. His masterful campaign against Mexico City (1847) was reminiscent of limited wars of the eighteenth century, but his tactics reflected a decidedly Napoleonic flavor. Scott's use of divisions to outflank Mexican forces and skillful deployment of mobile artillery contrasted to Gen. Zachary Taylor's frontal assaults in northern Mexico, which, although successful, were a reminder of a long-standing amateur tradition in the American military. But even European observers were impressed by Scott's direction and the navy's support of the amphibious invasion at Vera Cruz in 1847. All in all, as Valaik points out, U.S. armed forces were better trained and better led in the Mexican conflict than they had been in 1812. The fact that Americans faced a less able foe in 1846 than in 1812 did little to tarnish their overwhelming victory in the limited war against Mexico.

We have always been fascinated by the place that war has played in our history. Much of the colonial era was shaped by a lengthy conflict with the French and their Indian allies, and of course it was only after years of warfare on land and sea that our founding fathers were able to create an independent nation.

In 1812 and again in 1846 the fate of the young republic would once again hang in the balance. If American forces had been vanquished in the earlier conflict, there is little reason to believe that the victorious British would have been magnanimous in their peace terms. They might well have detached much of New England and Louisiana from the union and retained control of the Great Lakes and adjacent western lands. Only a "rump republic" perhaps would have remained in the South, a weakened state whose political system would have been badly strained and whose recuperative powers would have been suspect.

A nation such as this would not have been well positioned or able to respond effectively to the difficult matter of Texas annexation, which arose in 1845. This also involved the much larger question of acquiring California and other territory and thereby creating a vast transcontinental republic. Such a dream was almost as old as the republic itself, and so the eventual war with Mexico was hardly a minor question in American history. Control of an entire continent was at issue, and a victory was hardly guaranteed. In fact, some Americans actually predicted defeat, while others even hoped for failure in what to them was a shameful struggle to extend the "slave power." Many self-proclaimed military experts of that day viewed U.S. forces as weak and heavily outnumbered. Earlier military actions against a few thousand Seminole warriors gave little reason for optimism. Had Zachary Taylor, "Old Rough and Ready," lost a few early rounds against his Mexican antagonists, would Winfield Scott have been unleashed against Mexico City? What questions might then be raised concerning America's tenuous situation in California, which had long been the prize for President James K. Polk? Had there been no victory over Mexico, would the American nation have ever realized its "manifest destiny"?

From today's perspective, these limited conflicts of the nineteenth century were small in comparison to the world wars of the twentieth. Then, there were no great drafts of manpower, dragging millions of young men into military service. The daily lives of the vast majority of Americans were not affected by distant encounters at sea or battles on the nation's periphery. Marauding Indians or Mexican guerrilleros posed no threat to Bostonians or Philadelphians. Nonetheless, American survival and expansion were at stake in these small wars of the nineteenth century.

What is clear, however, is that some of our national leaders did not understand this as clearly as might have been the case, and that their conduct before and during the wars was not always of the highest order. The neglect of the military by the public and politicians before the wars was typically American (especially Jeffersonian), but their manipulations during these conflicts also manifested prejudice and ignorance. To be sure, the military itself was not blameless. There were numerous incidents of cowardice and many more of incompetence at all levels. Many displayed acts of bravery and dedication, but one man stands out in both wars for his leadership qualities. That man, as will be seen, was Winfield Scott, "Old Fuss and Feathers."

In 1812 the U.S. Army had an authorized strength of 36,000 troops; this was to be augmented by 50,000 volunteers and 100,000 militiamen. The navy had virtually ceased to exist as a blue-water force, thanks in part to Thomas Jefferson, a man who, like many Americans, spoke of liberty but begrudged the funds necessary to defend it. Since Britain's forces were then fully engaged against the legions of Napoleon, the American numbers appear more potent, especially when one considers that there were no more than 8,000 British troops in Canada, and about 2,000 of these were raw militia. Numbers, however, can be misleading, and this was the case in 1812. As for the British, locked in a battle to the death with Napoleon, they certainly did not want a war with the United States. But with their recruitment of sailors by impressment, the British pushed the Americans too far.

When President James Madison asked his followers in Congress for a declaration of war in June 1812, there were no more than 8,000 regulars in his army, and these men were scattered in small frontier outposts. Their commander was the aging and notorious Gen. James Wilkinson of Maryland, a man who might well have been executed years before for his part in Aaron Burr's conspiratorial adventures or for having been secretly in the pay of the Spanish government. In addition, the condition of the American forces left much to be desired. Madison should have realized this, because he knowingly had retained William Eustis as secretary of war. Eustis, a medical doctor during the Revolution, had only one qualification for office: staunch loyalty to the Jeffersonian Republicans. The U.S. Army, in short, was not prepared for war in 1812. Furthermore, its leadership, both in and out of uniform, was woefully deficient. In the navy the situation was as bad, if not worse.

At the top, Paul Hamilton, the secretary of the navy, was a party regular from South Carolina. As a plantation owner he may have known something about cotton and slaves, but his knowledge of naval affairs was minuscule at best. In addition, he was a habitual drunkard. With the British brazenly blockading the port of New York and having already impressed at least 6,000 seamen working under the American flag, Congress in January 1812 refused to appropriate additional monies to construct a new frigate. Hamilton, therefore, commanded a fleet that numbered only seven frigates, while the Royal Navy could count as many as six hundred warships flying the white ensign of battle. When the war began there were

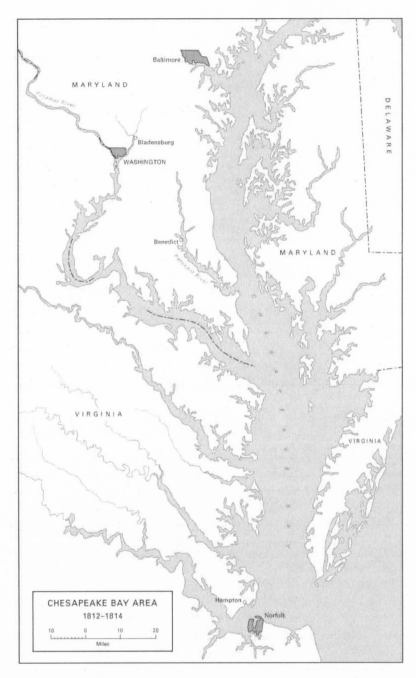

Chesapeake Bay Area, 1812–1814 (U.S. Army Center of Military History)

only twenty-five British warships in American waters, but this number included one sixty-four-gun ship of the line and as many as six frigates. The U.S. fleet was soon driven into the protection of different ports to avoid certain destruction, thus leaving the coasts virtually defenseless. Only sixty-three of Jefferson's inadequate gunboats were still in active service, and as these tiny craft mounted only one cannon each, they were hardly a match for the British fleet that sailed boldly up the Chesapeake Bay. With little opposition the fleet disembarked an invasion force of infantry, which swept aside hopelessly untrained and poorly led militiamen at Bladensburg, Maryland, and proceeded to set the American capital at Washington ablaze (1814).[1]

Thus, the United States began the war badly unprepared but boldly entertaining not one, but two, ambitious objectives: first, to put an end to Britain's humiliating violations of U.S. sovereignty, especially at sea; and second, to seize British Canada while the English were engaged in Europe in the massive struggle against Napoleon, therefore fulfilling an ambitious dream that dated back to the Revolution. It is no surprise that America did not succeed in this momentous undertaking, although it was fortunate—perhaps miraculous—that the nation did not lose its independence or impair its future development. For those persons who do not believe in miracles, there is one very sound explanation for America's ultimate good fortune: leadership.

The U.S. Military Academy at West Point has defined leadership as an "art"—of influencing and directing people to an assigned goal by commanding their obedience, their confidence, and their respect. Those who would be leaders must insist upon high standards of training and discipline that will enable them to know their subordinates' strengths and weaknesses, thereby capitalizing on the former while minimizing the latter. There were many men in leadership positions in the War of 1812, and far too many of them failed in their appointed tasks. The country was fortunate that a few did not.

The senior major general, Henry Dearborn, was not one of these successful leaders. Along with President Madison and Secretary Eustis, he was charged with the important task of determining grand strategy, and he failed in this fundamental but crucial role. Dearborn, a medical doctor and formerly Jefferson's secretary of war, along with others sent one American force up Lake Champlain to attack Montreal, a second force

250 miles west in the Niagara region, and a third army another 200 miles west to Detroit.

In doing so, he violated two fundamental principles of war, objective and concentration of force; and, in failing to coordinate his three-pronged offensive effectively, he totally vitiated the concept of unity of command. In the end his effort was a failure, as evidenced by the surrender of Gen. William Hull outside Detroit in 1812. Abandoned by his Ohio militiamen and frightened by the specter of wild savages in the nearby forest, Hull surrendered to British Gen. Sir Issac Brock, who advanced resolutely from the east. Despite occupying a strong defensive position fortified with ample artillery and outnumbering Brock's forces, Hull capitulated without firing a shot. For this he was court-martialed and ordered to be shot, although President Madison remitted the sentence. Certainly neither Dearborn nor Hull was an effective military leader.

It would be equally inappropriate to describe General Wilkinson as a leader in anything other than name. He was to advance upon Montreal, an essential objective in the war's earliest stages since it constituted a chokehold on all British forces farther west, but he too failed shamefully. The terrain was difficult and there was some opposition, but Wilkinson's failure was the result of a lack of talent, drive, and, most importantly, will.

In the center—that is, along the Niagara frontier of western New York—British forces seemed vulnerable. Once again, however, the clumsy and timorous efforts of the Americans were sadly wanting. This was not for lack of manpower. In September 1812, Brig. Gen. Alexander Smyth brought 1,650 regulars to Buffalo; this force augmented the 900 regulars and 2,500 militiamen at Lewiston commanded by Maj. Gen. Stephen Van Rensselaer. In all, there were nearly 5,000 American troops along the Niagara frontier. They were opposed by only 1,500 British under the command of General Brock. Victory seemed certain, but once again unity of command was lacking and ineffective leadership was to prove disastrous. Because Van Rensselaer was a New York militia officer, General Smyth had no intention of serving under his command and even refused to meet with him. Van Rensselaer, therefore, struck out on his own and failed to achieve a victory. It might be more accurate and fair to say that his men failed him.

On the night of October 10–11, 1812, Van Rensselaer's forces prepared to make their way across the mighty Niagara River in the hope of seizing Queenston Heights, Canada, across from Lewiston. Heavy rain and the lack of sufficient boats, however, caused the Americans to call off the attack.

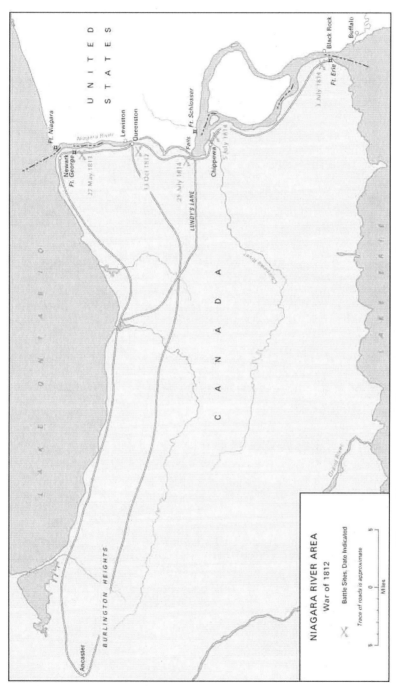

Niagara River Area, War of 1812 (U.S. Army Center of Military History)

The militiamen were disappointed and urged Van Rensselaer to plan another action. Early on October 13, with some covering artillery fire, they renewed the assault with a first wave of 300 regulars and an equal number of militia in thirteen boats. Only ten of the boats managed to cross the river and land at the agreed-upon point of attack. The militiamen were immediately pinned down, but the regulars made it to the top of the heights and drove off the British and Canadian defenders. Under the command of Lt. Col. Winfield Scott, a twenty-six-year-old Virginian, the Americans continued to battle new British units, which were rushing to the site. Soon, only 300 Americans remained, clinging stubbornly to the heights but continuing to take casualties and running low on ammunition. Although General Brock had been killed earlier in the battle, the British fought on, and the Americans were near collapse.

Just across the river, however, more than 1,000 militiamen constituted an overwhelming mass of reinforcements. These men, bragging loudly before the battle of their prowess and determination, now refused to leave the state of New York, which was their legal right, to fight beside their beleaguered comrades only a few hundred yards away in Canada. They could hear the firing and see the wounded returning by boat, but no one could move them.

By late afternoon, facing more than 1,000 British and Canadian troops and their Indian allies, with little or no ammunition, Scott's men were forced to surrender.[2] More than 500 Americans had been wounded, and more than 900 eventually became prisoners of war. The British counted fewer than 100 casualties. It was a sad day for American arms in general but an even worse one in the annals of the militia. Van Rensselaer resigned in shame; General Smyth went on extended leave, never to return to the war. It would be some time before the Americans again would launch an invasion of Canada. Despite the failure of the invasion, Scott stood out as a leader. It was fortunate for the American cause that he was spared Brock's fate and returned to fight another day.

Scott had been a serious student of the military arts since his first days as a soldier, and as a captive of the British for some months after the Battle of Queenston Heights, he had ample opportunity to reflect upon its lessons before being paroled. When he returned to Buffalo in 1813, he set about preparing his troops for battle in a way that few soldiers of that day had experienced. A full colonel now, Scott was adjutant general to Dearborn, but in reality he exercised practical daily command, which in a matter of months transformed his raw recruits into disciplined, fighting regulars. From basic camp hygiene to linear battlefield movements, from uniform discipline for the ranks to basic leadership lessons for junior officers, Scott drilled his men with a firm hand and effective discipline. The results were dramatic: healthy, tough troops ready for battle; and battle they did.

On May 27, Scott led his men in an assault against Fort George, across the Niagara River from Fort Niagara. Scott was in the forefront, and he personally seized the British ensign as his men routed the enemy troops. When the smoke of battle cleared, fifty-two British regulars lay dead and 300 were wounded. Total American casualties were only fifty-nine. Had Scott been permitted to pursue the broken enemy force, he might have been able to destroy them, but the cautious and timid Dearborn forbade this.

For reasons of health Dearborn was soon gone, and for some months thereafter nothing would happen in this area—nothing good, that is. Humiliating minor clashes resulted in the capture of two American generals, and in December 1813 Wilkinson's ill-conceived and poorly executed assault against Montreal came to naught. Meanwhile, the British took Fort Niagara in a daring surprise attack. Wilkinson lost his command and was ordered to appear before a court-martial. Finally, an angry delegation of western New Yorkers called in person upon President Madison to demand that a competent officer be named to command in this area, and they recommended Scott.

The twenty-seven-year-old Scott returned to Buffalo as the youngest brigadier general in the army. Now, in 1814, as before, he renewed his regimen of disciplined training in anticipation of launching a new offensive. Under the overall command of Maj. Gen. Jacob Brown, 3,500 men were soon ready for action. On July 3, with Scott in the lead boat, an American force seized Fort Erie, across the Niagara River from Buffalo, and turned east in the direction of Lake Ontario where the British had established a major base in Burlington. In response to the bold American initiative, British and Canadian troops, with Indian allies, rushed to block the invaders. Commanded by the aggressive general Phineas Riall, they were to encounter the Americans on July 5 on the banks of the little Chippewa River.

There is no need to recount in detail the battle that occurred there, or the engagement a few weeks later on July 25 at Lundy's Lane. Both sides employed simple linear tactics of the day; there was no finesse. In fact, the question of who won what at Lundy's Lane is still debated on both sides of the Niagara. What cannot be disputed, however, are two important facts. First, well-trained and spirited American regulars (clad in gray New York militia uniforms for lack of proper dress), with General Scott in the first rank, met British regulars toe to toe and bested them.[3] Nearly 150 British troops died at Chippewa to forty-four Americans. Elements of the vaunted British army that had sent Napoleon into exile were staunchly repulsed, and the tradition of excellence on the battlefield begun in the days of George Washington's Continentals was mightily enhanced. Second, the spirit of the American people was buoyed by the gallant leadership of Brown and Scott, both of whom were wounded at Lundy's Lane and forced to retire from the field.[4] It was reported after the fact that, just before the armies clashed at Chippewa, Scott exhorted his men: "They say that the Americans are good at long range shot but cannot stand cold iron!! I call on you instantly to give lie to that slander! Charge!"

We will never know if Scott uttered those words, or, if he did, that they were heard all along the American front, but we do know that he was in the forefront of those troops, that he had trained them for that day, and that neither he nor they shrank from battle. Furthermore, even though the lesson was not learned in Washington, our political leaders should have expended more energy and money to support the regular army than they did to raise and arm a blundering militia. More victories, not defeats, would have been their reward.

Of course, every great general need not be a scholarly student of the military arts, able to quote Clausewitz and recount Napoleon's maneuvers in detail. It is safe to assume that Andrew Jackson would have failed even the most simple exam on such matters, but he was a most effective battlefield commander. Perhaps his lifelong combativeness sprang from his Scots-Irish heritage, or his youthful clashes with the British during the Revolution had bred soldierly instincts in him, but, whatever it was, Jackson emerged from the War of 1812 as our foremost hero. While the Battle of New Orleans was fought after the peace had been agreed upon at Ghent, in Belgium, his leadership then and before remains highly noteworthy.

Jackson crushed the Creek Indians at Horseshoe Bend (1814), killing as many as 900 warriors, and razed the British base at Pensacola. In the latter action, he realized the importance of denying the British a base of operations in the South. It was, however, his conduct of the New Orleans campaign that earned him recognition as one of America's great generals. This is not to ignore the arrogance and plodding of Lt. Gen. Sir Edward

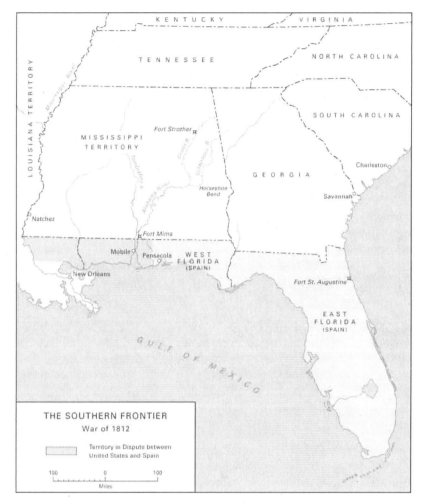

The Southern Frontier, War of 1812 (U.S. Army Center of Military History)

Pakenham, the British commander. A more skillful foe might have caused Jackson greater problems, but it was Jackson who won the day and Pakenham whose remains were returned to his grieving widow in England. Jackson's task, however, was not an easy one. When he arrived in New Orleans in December 1814, Jackson had only 800 regulars in his command, not a large number to face the British veterans—not even a large-enough number to bring order to the frenzied city whose vain Creoles had been under the American flag for only eleven years. Yet the hard and high-handed

Indian fighter won the hearts of the Creoles, and by the day of battle he commanded at least 5,000 militiamen, the vast majority of whom had never experienced combat. Such a force could not engage the battle-hardened British in offensive operations, but thanks to a slow enemy advance Jackson had time to choose a near-perfect defensive site, with well-anchored flanks, and to construct a system of stout breastworks. On January 8, 1815, behind these defensive works, against which British artillery was completely ineffective, the militia, carefully intermixed with regulars, stood steady and poured volleys of deadly fire into the closed British ranks.

In less than one hour, more than 2,100 British soldiers, including General Pakenham, lay dead or wounded. Seven Americans died in the battle. The finest British arms had been defeated, this time by rank amateurs, and General Jackson's heroic stature grew beyond measure. Some critics faulted him for not immediately pursuing the retreating enemy force; such a charge is often leveled by critics after successful battles. Jackson's caution on that day of heady victory, however, was wise indeed. Had he unleashed his raw recruits against the bloodied survivors of the British force, they probably would have suffered a similar fate.

New Orleans was a great American victory. It was one of the few land victories of the war. There were two additional clear-cut victories that should be noted, however. These were naval victories; and while the bodies of water upon which they were fought were small, had the American flag fallen into the waters of Lake Erie or Lake Champlain, the outcome of the War of 1812 would have been much different.

On September 9, 1813, Lt. Robert H. Barclay, commanding a British squadron of six small ships, sailed forth on the recently constructed HMS *Detroit* to engage an American force under the command of Master Commandant Oliver Hazard Perry. His flagship, the USS *Lawrence*, carried a battle flag emblazoned with the immortal words, "Don't Give Up the Ship."[5] Both captains enjoyed advantages as well as disadvantages: each lacked an adequate number of trained seamen and was therefore obliged to fill out his crew with soldiers, both regulars and militiamen; British guns outranged the American batteries, but these were in greater number, and that would tell if Perry could bring his ships to close quarters.

At about noon on September 10, as the British opened fire at long range, the wind on Lake Erie shifted, to Perry's advantage, and he closed with the enemy without hesitation, a daring decision that the great Nelson would have applauded. Devastating broadsides were exchanged. Barclay and his second in command were wounded and taken below deck, and even though Perry's ship was sinking beneath him, he transferred his flag to another and won the battle. In destroying or capturing the entire British force in the area, Perry conquered Lake Erie for the American cause, and in doing so he effectively isolated the western outposts of the British. As a direct consequence, Gen. William Henry Harrison in early October was able to defeat the British on the Thames River, a battle in which their foremost Indian ally, Tecumseh, was killed. This was a significant victory and one that could not have been won by a timid commander.

The same was true with regard to the Battle of Lake Champlain. On September 1, 1814, over 10,000 British troops crossed over from Canada in the direction of the lake. Under the command of Lt. Gen. Sir George Prevost, most of these men were blooded regulars who had served under the Duke of Wellington. By September 6 this force had reached Plattsburgh, New York. Scattered elements of New York militia had failed to impede their advance, but at Lake Champlain, together with advancing British ships, they encountered a small American naval force whose presence they could not ignore. Commanded by Master Commandant Thomas Macdonough, one frigate, three smaller vessels, and ten gunboats awaited them; only this little flotilla could stop the British from moving on to the Hudson River and thus cutting off eastern New York and New England from the rest of the nation, which would have shaken the American cause.

While nearly equal in firepower, the two fleets began to exchange punishing broadsides on September 11, but careful planning and preparation before the battle resulted in a decisive American victory.[6] Macdonough, commanding the USS *Saratoga*, a twenty-six-gun sloop of war, had positioned his ships close to the west shore, thereby blocking the passage of General Prevost's infantry by land and also making it impossible for the British ships to outflank his command. Then, by anchoring his vessels stem to stern, Macdonough guaranteed his stationary ships a degree of maneuverability that the oncoming British did not enjoy. He had given his ships, in effect, underwater springs by laying out extra cables to their anchors, thus allowing them to be turned completely around and thereby presenting both broadsides to the enemy. The British, who attempted to anchor, were quickly engaged and could not spring around in time. Suffering terrible punishment, they were forced to withdraw, and Macdonough won a great victory only one year after Perry's triumph at Lake Erie. General Prevost retreated to Canada, and New England was saved. This was the most decisive battle of the war, and news of it was not lost on the British diplomats meeting in Ghent.

It would be foolish to imagine that the War of 1812 had been America's "finest hour." Most often the militia did not fight well; because of poor leadership and inadequate training, they fought badly if at all. The commander in chief, President Madison, and senior generals failed to give effective direction to the war effort; there was no well-defined objective. Finally, Congress, or at least the war hawk element therein, blundered into a war against a dangerous enemy with an inadequate and ill-prepared army and navy that had been woefully neglected for decades.

That the United States did not lose the War of 1812 was a victory in itself, one that must be attributed to professional officers such as Brown, Scott, Perry, and Macdonough and to the well-trained and disciplined men whom they commanded. Moreover, while the expansionist objectives of many Americans were not realized, some important gains were achieved. As a war of conquest it was not successful, but Great Britain, in agreeing to settle for less than total victory, gave undeniable testimony that American independence finally had been secured.

By 1835, there were only 4,000 men in the United States Army. The ongoing struggle against the Indians and the difficult Seminole wars had toughened these regulars, and the introduction of the percussion cap greatly enhanced their firepower. Earlier, under President James Monroe, Secretary of War John C. Calhoun had breathed new life into the military, sharpened its internal organizations, and strengthened professional education at West Point. Now, under the tutelage of Sylvanus Thayer and Dennis Hart Mahan, a new and better-prepared generation of young officers was entering the army. The role they would play would be most important. Finally, in 1841 a new general assumed command of the U.S. Army: Winfield Scott, the first officer to wear three stars since George Washington.

While most Americans persist in the certainty that we "won" the War of 1812, and take pride in its outcome, similar feelings concerning the conflict with Mexico in the 1840s do not abound. Texans may still remember the exploits of their wild Rangers, which were bold, indeed, if not always honorable, and Mississippians may still recall their dashing Mounted Rifles, commanded by a West Point graduate named Jefferson Davis, but this is not a war well remembered.

Some Americans view this conflict as a war of aggression—nothing like the struggle for independence in 1776 or the fight against the Axis powers in World War II. President Polk's assertion in 1846 that Mexico had "shed American blood on American soil" failed to convince many of his contemporaries that this was a just war, and the question of the disputed territory between the Nueces and Rio Grande rivers still is not beyond argument. However, it is indisputable that the bellicose government in Mexico City had ordered an attack before the first clash of arms, which Polk then used to his own advantage. Quite foolishly the Mexican government wanted war because Texas had joined the American republic, and Polk gave it to them. Furthermore, the army he commanded, while quite small, was not to be taken lightly: it was, in fact, Scott's army. These regulars drilled in classical European style, which would stand them in good stead when they fought the Mexicans, but before that moment these professional soldiers had gained much experience in fighting innumerable battles with the Indians.

Having mentioned Polk, one might consider his conduct as commander in chief. There is much to admire. He was a tireless worker, and his energy and attention to the complexities of the conflict generally resulted in the troops' being well supplied with weapons and ammunition. However, his preoccupation with politics did not constitute a positive contribution to the war effort. To deny immediate command to the nation's most competent and experienced soldier, General Scott, and to ignore his strategic vision, was simply wrong and motivated almost solely by narrow Democratic partisanship.[7] Then later to strip Gen. Zachary Taylor of nearly all of his regulars was an act of the same political partisanship. This may well have ended the favorable press coverage enjoyed by the Whig general, but, in shifting troops to Scott's command, Polk was admitting his original error in ignoring the general in chief's strategic vision.

Finally, Polk's covert intrusion into diplomatic minefields, whereby he made possible the return to Mexico of Gen. Antonio López de Santa Anna, did not hasten the war's end but prolonged it. No other Mexican general was as able as Santa Anna to oppose Scott's assault on Montezuma's capital. On paper, the Mexican army was formidable. Generally, it was well armed, and its considerable cavalry force, with its long, flag-festooned lances, was widely acclaimed. In battle after battle the Mexicans outnumbered the Americans by as much as three or four to one, but with the exception of a few minor clashes the Mexican forces were shattered and defeated in every confrontation. In May 1846 at Palo Alto the Mexicans suffered over 200 casualties, compared to approximately 50 for the Americans;

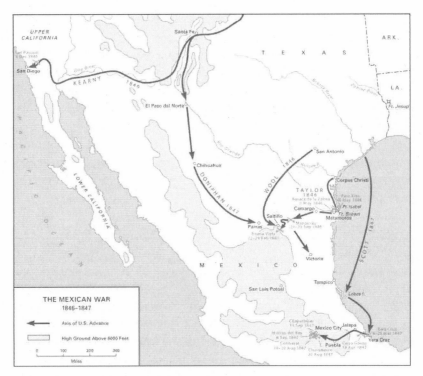

The Mexican War, 1846–1847 (U.S. Army Center of Military History)

and at Resaca de la Palma there were almost 400 Mexican casualties to 100 for the Americans. And at bloody Buena Vista (February 1847) the figures were 1,800 Mexicans to 673 Americans, and so it went: victory after victory for the United States.

While each of these battles can be studied in detail, and all should be credited to General Taylor, there were marked similarities. Although the Mexican cavalry was numerous, neither it nor its American counterparts played an important role in the war. Artillery, on the other hand, was often decisive: usually outnumbered, the U.S. infantry was rescued time after time by the omnipresent artillery. Lt. Col. James Duncan and Capt. Samuel Ringgold led their batteries of flying artillery to the crucial sectors of the front and invariably broke the thick ranks of Mexican infantrymen, who did not lack courage. In battle after battle, these artillery elements were swift and deadly accurate; officers and men stood to their pieces and brutally punished the onrushing Mexicans. In the end the battlefields were held and the Mexicans swept away by American infantry.

Since the earliest recorded battles to the Iraq War, the foot soldier has proved irreplaceable, and his campaigns in Mexico were no exception. It is important to remember as well that these were extremely tough foot soldiers. Under the professional leadership of General Scott for over twenty years, this little army of professionals had made great strides.[8] Using his training manuals, written and rewritten over the years, junior officers drilled and maneuvered their men, engaged in summer exercises, and instilled a deep pride of professionalism in the ranks. "Old Fuss and Feathers" was certainly cantankerous, vain, and hotheaded, but when the call to arms came, his army of nearly 8,000 men was more than equal to the challenge.

General Scott effectively integrated the large number of volunteers who enlisted into this army. The proud regulars and a significant number of West Point–trained junior officers drilled these amateurs so that in battle they were able to resist the Mexican masses with a toughness that belied their recent civilian status. At Buena Vista, for instance, 4,500 volunteers, side by side with only 500 regulars, withstood the onslaught of 20,000 Mexicans commanded by Santa Anna. The battle went badly at first, and one of Taylor's aides rode up to inform him that the men were whipped. "I know it," Taylor replied, "but the volunteers don't know it. Let them alone; we'll see what they do." We know what they did that day; and while the volunteer units did fail upon occasion, these men were a far cry from the militia of 1812.

As we know, many of the junior officers who led these men were graduates of West Point, and the roles they played in every battle were often crucial. The difficult Mexican terrain caused almost every potential grand battle to degenerate into a series of frenzied small-unit clashes, and there was a premium on quality leadership on the platoon and company levels. The West Pointers earned their pay: they sited the guns, they discovered the paths that made it possible to outflank strongly positioned enemy forces, and they led the men in hand-to-hand combat. To glance at a list of Civil War senior officers is to encounter the lieutenants and captains who served so bravely in Mexico: Lee, Beauregard, Grant, and others. It was General Scott himself, some years after the war, who praised them for their many contributions, suggesting that without these men victory would have been more difficult to attain, and of the men, it was Grant himself who wrote that "a better army, man for man, probably never faced an enemy." As generous and correct as that assessment may have been, to mention Scott again is to raise the most important reason for the many victories in the war. As often as it was lacking in the War of 1812, the indispensable factor—leadership—was most apparent in Mexico in 1846 and 1847.

The exploits of numerous other individuals are also worthy of note and acclaim. The march of Gen. Alexander Doniphan and his volunteers across a seemingly endless and hostile wasteland was an epic achievement. This was also true of the campaign of Col. Stephen W. Kearny, who commanded the little Army of the West, which marched over 850 miles in less than two months. But when one considers the war in general, one invariably thinks first of Scott and Taylor.

Indeed, Taylor managed to parlay his military acclaim into a ticket to the White House. Scott, on the other hand, ended his Mexican command under a cloud. The leaders of the Mexican government were so pleased with his firm, but fair, postwar administration that they offered him a handsome purse and their nation's presidency. President Polk recalled him to Washington to answer general criticisms of his command. Not surprisingly, Scott overwhelmed his critics, but in the eyes of the American public Taylor was the greater hero of the war. He was compared to Caesar and Napoleon.

Zachary Taylor was a typical rough-and-ready frontiersman. Mounted on Old Whitey, wearing a sombrero and a baggy frock coat with no insignia of rank, he would be difficult to spot on the battlefield—that is, unless one were looking for real action. There, he could always be found, exposed to danger while calmly directing subordinates. His cool presence amid the heat of battle was an important source of strength for all who came under his command.

There was no silver service at mess, no host of sentinels to guard the general's august person, but that was not all that was missing for those in his command. Careful study of his battles has led some critics to argue that his concept of warfare was rather unsophisticated. There is, in short, more to soldiering than marching, shooting, and charging. In battle, Taylor's men suffered from ambiguous orders, piecemeal commitment of infantry units (often without the benefit of available artillery support), and little, if any, planned coordination. Finally, it should be noted that Taylor's regimen of discipline left much to be desired. As a consequence of comparatively loose discipline, his units experienced serious problems of desertion, excessive incidence of violence directed against Mexican civilians, and serious health problems, which often rendered 20 percent or more of his troops incapable of effective service.

While Scott was not faultless in any one of these areas, he was clearly superior in most. The student of this war must bear in mind that since it had begun in May 1846, Scott, as general in chief, had been compelled to remain inactive as a consequence of President Polk's politically motivated decision to appoint Taylor to battlefield command. Furthermore, Scott's correct counsel to direct the major offensive operations against Mexico City was ignored in favor of a campaign in northern Mexico, which, while it was marked by victory after victory, became frustrating and embarrassing for want of strategic success. That Scott did not resign from the service is mute but mighty testimony to his professionalism and patriotism. When Polk finally turned to the Vera Cruz strategy, it was fortunate that Scott was still at hand to command in the field.

With a force of 12,000 men, Scott sailed for Mexico, and it was soon apparent that he was the man to lead the expedition. In a single day, 10,000 men, with animals, supplies, and equipment, were ferried to the shores of Vera Cruz without mishap. Twenty days later the Mexican garrison surrendered; only nineteen Americans had died. This signal victory was not a matter of luck or accident; rather, it was the end result of Scott's meticulous planning. Under his careful direction specially designed landing craft were constructed; the troops were drilled in amphibious landing techniques, and the transport vessels were loaded with the skill and foresight of World War II marines. Under the protective guns of a hundred-ship fleet, America's first major amphibious landing was conducted flawlessly.[9] Nevertheless, Scott came under immediate criticism. His men had not wildly stormed the Mexican defenses, flags aflutter, bugles blaring. Rather, they carefully besieged the city with its 5,000 defenders and three hundred cannons effectively trapped therein. Then for a week naval guns and field artillery bombarded the enemy into submission. Some armchair critics thought this cowardly, but Scott reasoned wisely that he needed no casualties here, that he would need all of his men for the decisive struggle that lay ahead. Scott clearly understood his objective: to seize Mexico City and compel the enemy to sue for an American-dictated peace as soon as possible. To fight the wily Santa Anna in one battle after another would result only in bloody attrition of the small U.S. force against an enemy that had already displayed amazing recuperative powers. Winfield Scott, in the footsteps of the Spaniard Hernán Cortés centuries before, abandoned a secure base of operations, and set off for Mexico City over two hundred difficult miles to the west.

On learning of Scott's bold decision, the Duke of Wellington opined that Scott's force was doomed. Santa Anna was of a similar opinion. He intended to stop Scott at Cerro Gordo and force him back to the coast where the dreaded yellow fever, *el vomito*, would decimate what remained of Scott's little army. The Mexican general had underestimated his antagonist's talents. With 12,000 men in his command, Santa Anna had taken up an extremely strong position to block the 8,500 Americans under Scott, and when one U.S. brigade engaged his main force, Santa Anna not surprisingly entertained visions of glory. The self-styled Napoleon of the West was, however, wrong. American engineers and Scott himself had reconnoitered the Mexican position; shortly after the battle was joined, 1,000 Mexicans were dead, 3,000 were captured, and Santa Anna and the remnants of his army were fleeing pell-mell from the scene. The initial attack on April 18 had been only a feint. Using a hidden and treacherous mountain trail discovered by the young Robert E. Lee, Scott had moved his main force to the Mexican rear in a nearly perfect envelopment. The Mexicans were routed, and the road to Mexico City beckoned. After seizing Pueblo, however, Scott was forced to halt his army when, thanks to the wisdom of Congress, he was ordered to release 4,000 short-term volunteers from service. It was not until August that Scott again commanded a force of 10,000 effectives for the march on Mexico City, now defended by a force of around 35,000.

Final victory was at hand, but it did not come easily. The Mexican soldiers, fighting for the capital of their nation, were pitted against a force of equally brave men, regulars and volunteers, for whom winning had become a morale-boosting habit. In clash after clash, costly frontal assaults were largely avoided thanks to the young West Point engineers, and one Mexican position after another fell to the maneuvering Americans. Padierna, Contreras, Churubusco, and finally Chapultepec itself fell. The Americans entered Mexico City on September 14, 1847. When the Treaty of Guadalupe Hidalgo was finally signed in February 1848, President Polk's western expansionist dreams were partially fulfilled.

General Scott had demonstrated beyond doubt the qualities of a great captain. This had been America's greatest war to date, with more than 100,000 soldiers, sailors, and marines having taken up arms. It was also the bloodiest conflict ever experienced by the nation: more than 1,500 Americans died in combat and over 10,000 died of disease. However, in

Scott, the country found a leader of great military intellect whose compassion for his men's lives and their well-being also demonstrated great humanity. His record as a general between 1814 and 1861 was unmatched, and his Mexican campaign was nearly faultless. Scholars of his last, decisive campaign have used adjectives such as bold, brilliant, masterful, and audacious to describe both his strategic vision and his tactical conduct of the battles themselves. They did not exaggerate.

Following the victories of Taylor and Scott, much time and energy were expended by citizens and politicians to make transcontinental America a reality, but the fruits of victory soon proved to be as divisive as they were abundant. The gulf between North and South grew wider and more bitter as the question of slavery's future in the United States dangerously exacerbated tensions. It is not surprising, therefore, that many of the lessons that might have been learned from this conflict, not unlike the lessons of 1812, were once again neglected.

Military appropriations, both for the army and navy, were permitted to shrink until these forces again were reduced in size and efficiency to a woeful degree. Small military units were sent to distant western outposts where they were both out of sight and out of mind. Cadets at West Point still studied and memorized the old lessons of Napoleon's campaigns and strategy, but many promising young officers left the military service for advancement in the civilian world. Little attention was given to technical advancements in weapons systems. The myth of volunteer prowess on the battlefield was not studied seriously; and if another great war were to come about, the evidence suggested that many costly errors would be repeated. The enemy of the future would not be as weak as Mexico; in fact, the enemy would be fellow Americans. The coming "people's" war between the North and the South would not be a game of chess to be won by brilliant maneuvers.

Notes

1. Earlier, American troops had burned York—that is, Toronto, Canada.

2. Among the Canadian militia was a unit made up of African Americans who had fled from slavery in the United States.

3. Shortly thereafter, cadets at the new military academy at West Point adopted gray uniforms in recognition of these New Yorkers.

4. Scott nearly died of his wounds and did not return to action for the remainder of the war.

5. This phrase was uttered by Capt. James Lawrence of the Chesapeake in June 1813, as he was mortally wounded, before his frigate was captured by the British in action at Boston.

6. The U.S. force had sloops and ten gunboats; the British, under Capt. George Downie, had three sloops, twelve gunboats, and the large frigate HMS *Confiance*.

7. This is not to suggest that Taylor and Scott were without political ambitions.

8. The regular period of enlistment at the time was five years. A private earned five dollars per week.

9. The victory once again demonstrated the great importance of sea power in warfare.

Sources and Suggested Readings

Bauer, K. Jack. *The Mexican War, 1846–1848*. New York, 1974.

Berton, Pierre. *Flames across the Board: The Canadian-American Tragedy, 1813–1814*. Boston, 1981.

Connor, Seymour V., and Odie B. Faulk. *North America Divided: The Mexican War, 1846–1848*. New York, 1971.

Dupuy, R. Ernest, and Trevor N. Dupuy. *Brave Men and Great Captains*. New York, 1959.

———. *Military Heritage of America*. New York, 1956.

Elliott, Charles Winslow. *Winfield Scott, the Soldier and the Man*. New York, 1937.

Grant, U. S. *Personal Memoirs*, vol. 1. New York, 1885.

Heller, Charles E., and William A. Stofft, eds. *America's First Battles, 1776–1965*. Lawrence, Kans., 1986.

Hitsman, J. Mackay. *The Incredible War of 1812: A Military History*. Toronto, 1965.

Johannsen, Robert W. *To the Halls of Montezuma: The Mexican War in the American Imagination*. New York, 1985.

Lavender, David. *Climax at Buena Vista: The American Campaigns in Northeastern Mexico, 1846–1847*. New York, 1956.

Mahon, John K. *The War of 1812*. Gainesville, Fla., 1972.

Malcomson, Robert. *A Very Brilliant Affair: The Battle of Queenston Heights, 1812*. Toronto, 2003.

Maltoff, Maurice, ed. *American Military History*. Washington, D.C., 1969.

Roosevelt, Theodore. *The Naval War of 1812*, vol. 2. New York, 1882.

Weigley, Russell F. *The American Way of War: A History of United States Military Strategy and Policy*. New York, 1973.

———. *A History of the United States Army*. New York, 1967.

FOUR

The American Civil War, 1861–1865

WILLIAM GARRETT PISTON

B Y THE TIME of the Mexican War, the United States was already on the verge of entering into an era of rapid modernization. Although the nation was still an overwhelmingly agricultural republic with a preindustrial economy, the war with Mexico clearly highlighted some important progress in technological development. Advancements in transportation and communication allowed President James K. Polk actively to assume his constitutional authority as commander in chief of the armed forces. The army and navy utilized railroads, steamships, and Samuel F. B. Morse's new telegraph to shrink the distance between the home front and the battlefield. For the first time, newspaper reporters were attached to U.S. forces and relayed accounts of battles to the nation in a matter of days. America was no longer a fragile republic but an energetic nation of over twenty million citizens. Its growing manufacturing sector made it one of the leading countries in the world in terms of gross national product.

The rapid growth all but guaranteed that in the future the nation could launch and sustain longer and more deadly wars. As a result of the Mexican War, the junior officer corps, largely graduates of West Point, had gained important experience that might be useful in future conflicts. Officers trained at West Point had been taught military strategy based on the writings of the

Swiss interpreter of Napoleon's campaigns, Antoine Henri de Jomini. While Jomini emphasized the offensive thrust of Napoleon's design, he tended to highlight the French general's more rational maxims pertaining to communication and movement rather than to the sustained violence used by him to subdue aroused foes. In Mexico, the lessons gleaned from Jomini seemed applicable but proved to be a poor guide for officers soon to be engaged in a war of intense nationalism.

By the 1850s many of the battlefield tactics and grand strategies perfected and practiced during the Napoleonic Wars and taught at military schools around the world became obsolete. The development of the rifled musket, adopted by the U.S. Army in the mid-1850s, made offensive operations much more difficult. In Napoleon's time, forces using smoothbore muskets with an effective range of only fifty yards could close rapidly with the enemy in offensive engagements. The invention of the conical-shaped rifled bullet that expanded when fired to "grip" the rifling of a musket drastically altered the advantage on the battlefield in favor of the defender. Perfected by a French Army captain, Claude Étienne Minié, the so-called minié ball could be rapidly loaded, unlike with previous rifled weapons, and gave the rifled musket an effective range of four hundred to six hundred yards. By the time of the Civil War, the standard infantry weapon for both sides was a .58 caliber, muzzle-loading rifled musket that was made more reliable by the use of a percussion cap. The net result was that offensive forces came under effective enemy fire at a distance about ten times greater than in earlier wars. Because the rifled weapons continued to be muzzle-loaded, soldiers were exposed even when reloading. Despite what now clearly seems like a revolutionary change on the battlefield, officers were slow to adjust their tactics and strategy to the new reality. The result was inordinately high casualties in the Civil War, especially for attacking forces.

William Garrett Piston describes the Civil War as an escalating conflict of extreme nationalism and the most important event in the nation's history. It was an event that marked a transition from the rather leisurely, limited wars of the eighteenth century to the violent, total wars of the next century. Both North and South, imbued with the fever of nationalism, raised huge volunteer armies and supported their respective causes with a spirit and energy unseen in any previous American conflict. Pressed by a need for more and more forces, first the South and then the North resorted to the first drafts in the nation's history. Although commanding officers on both sides began the war hoping to conclude the conflict in one or two "climactic battles" that would spare the civilian population from the agony of a protracted struggle, it became apparent after two years of inconclusive engagements that this was not only a war between armies but also a clash between two peoples and societies. Toward the end of the struggle, Union commander General Ulysses S. Grant formulated a strategy of total war to subdue the Confederacy. His relentless attacks on Southern armies as well as on Confederate economic resources shocked those who were wedded to a concept of the more polite warfare of another era. The Civil War was America's bloodiest and a harbinger of what would come in the next century.

No event has impacted American history more than the Civil War. Ten thousand five hundred battles, from Gettysburg, Pennsylvania, to Bull's Gap, Tennessee, led to the deaths of approximately 630,000 Americans, far more Americans than died in World Wars I and II combined. One in four Confederate soldiers died, compared to one in ten Federal soldiers. During the first year after the war, Mississippi devoted one-fifth of its budget to artificial limbs. Among the few who foresaw the terrible nature of the coming war, William T. Sherman warned, "you people of the *South* don't know *what you* are *doing!* You think you can tear to pieces this great Union without war! But I tell you there will be *blood-shed*—and plenty of it! And *God only knows how it will end!*" Sherman was right. The death toll, human grief and suffering, children without fathers, women who never married, families that never united—all left an indelible scar. At the same time, the Civil War preserved the United States, abolished the system of slavery that had mocked the very idea of freedom, ensured that democratic government would not perish, and consecrated the nation in what Lincoln called in his Gettysburg Address "a new birth of freedom."

The Civil War has seared the American memory, and controversy over that epic struggle will echo through time. Even the war's name has been the subject of long-lasting disagreement: The Civil War, or The War of the Rebellion, or The War between the States, or, most extreme, The War of Northern Aggression? How traditional, modern, or total was the Civil War? Why did the South lose, and why did the North win the war? Some have argued that the Confederacy fell from within when Southern women withdrew their support for the war, or because whites concluded that God was punishing them for slavery. What was the influence of Napoleonic thinking on the conduct of the war? But in terms of what actually happened, rather than the eternal "might-have-beens," the picture is clearer. The Confederacy lost the war on the battlefield—or more properly, the Union won it there—and the reasons have never been a mystery. The Union won primarily because it possessed greater manpower and resources and managed its war effort more effectively.

The path to Northern victory was not easy or a forgone conclusion. At first, Lincoln and his generals hoped to fight a short and relatively bloodless war that would not cause so much bitterness that reconciliation would be impossible and possibly lead Southerners to adopt permanent guerrilla warfare. Instead, the war between the North and the South became a people's war with both sides committed to victory.

A comparison of the two sides reveals Northern superiority in most significant categories. The Union (excluding distant Oregon and California) had a population of 18.5 million compared to the Confederacy's 9 million, of whom 3.5 million were slaves. The North possessed almost 22,000 miles of railways, compared to the South's 9,300. Only a very few facilities in the Confederacy could produce locomotives, and none could produce rails. The Union had almost five times as many factories and nearly ten times as many industrial workers as the Confederacy. Banks in the North had deposits totaling $189,000,000, while Southern banks possessed only $47,000,000. The Confederacy led in the production of rice, mules, cattle, and swine but was second to the Union by a considerable margin in corn, wheat, oats, horses, milk cows, and sheep.

Of course, the odds were never as simple as a comparison of data suggests, and different perspectives suggest different possibilities. Although developing less rapidly than the North, the South enjoyed prosperity before the war, and it was no agricultural backwater. Had the Confederacy sustained its independence it would have been the world's fifth most heavily industrialized nation, with the world's second-largest railway network, dwarfing all European rail competitors. Against this one must remember that the Confederacy was burdened by large pockets of Unionism in northwestern Virginia, western North Carolina, East Tennessee, and northwestern Arkansas. Before the war ended, tens of thousands of men from these regions enlisted in the Union army. Moreover, the slave labor that initially helped to sustain the Southern economy evaporated steadily as slaves, scenting freedom in the air, ran away and slavery collapsed.

The decisions Lincoln made and the actions his administration took in 1861 had long-term ramifications. Perhaps the most important decision came on April 21, when the newly elected president met with his cabinet. They agreed that they were defending a nation rather than the Constitution. For political reasons Lincoln could not avoid calling Congress into special session, but by selecting July 4 as the date for it to convene he freed himself from any immediate interference from the elected representatives of the people. It was a bold move for a man who had won only 40 percent of the popular vote. Lincoln rejected all appeals for compromise. He saw the crisis as a war to be won on the field of battle rather than a political or constitutional dilemma to be resolved by negotiation or court action. He took his role as commander in chief quite literally; the result was an unprecedented and arguably unconstitutional expansion of executive power. In the first six weeks after Fort Sumter's fall, Lincoln spent thousands of dollars without authorization, and suspended the writ of habeas corpus in the area between Philadelphia and Washington, where mobs had attacked Union troops passing through Baltimore. Suspension of the writ of habeas corpus enabled the government to arrest Confederate sympathizers and hold them without trial. Later, Lincoln extended this authority to all parts of the Union where "disloyal" elements were active. For critics of his possibly unconstitutional acts against civil liberties, Lincoln had a question: "Are all the laws, *but one*, to go unexecuted, and the government itself to go to pieces, lest that one be violated?"

Both sides spent the first months of the war recruiting troops. Options were limited by an American military tradition that distrusted standing armies, celebrated the citizen militia, ignored sea power, and underfunded everything. The navy possessed some ninety vessels with a dozen of them truly modern and powerful, but it had no battle fleet. Service at sea was unpopular, and the navy was so chronically short of crewmen that Congress had long ago authorized the enlistment of African Americans. The United States Army—the Regulars—consisted of just under 17,000 men, all of whom were white. Although they were generally well-trained and equipped with modern small arms and artillery, most were scattered among small forts and outposts in the West, far from the current points of danger. State militia existed, but their numbers and training barely began to furnish the necessary manpower. Perhaps because Lincoln knew the shortcomings of the militia from his own brief service in the Black Hawk War, he revived the United States Volunteers. It was one of his most crucial decisions, for it gave the Union an effective, efficient way of harnessing its numerical advantage.

The volunteer system, which the Confederacy also adopted, produced the vast majority of the soldiers who fought in the Civil War. Unlike eighteenth-century soldiers, Civil War volunteers had well-developed ideas of what the war was about. Whether the cause was preservation of the Union or the cause of Southern independence, about half of the armies consisted of ideologically motivated troops. The explosion of popular support for war in 1861 was as powerful as that which mobilized the armies of the French Revolution. Of the more than three million Civil War soldiers, two-thirds were younger than twenty-three years of age and came from rural communities.

In times of crisis Congress had always authorized an expansion of the U.S. Army, but strict discipline and long terms of service made the blue coat unpopular with even the most ardent patriots. Recruitment never reached authorized levels. Consequently, in both war and peace a majority of the Regulars were foreign-born, mostly impoverished bachelor Germans or Irishmen for whom the military provided a means of acculturation. The U.S. Volunteers were raised by the states and bore state designations, but they were paid and supplied by the federal government (if states supplied arms or uniforms, they were compensated). On being sworn into federal service, volunteers accepted longer terms of duty, usually at least a year, and acknowledged that they could be sent anywhere, even outside the country.

In early May Lincoln called for 42,000 volunteers to serve for three years. Several thousand were inadvertently enlisted for shorter terms, which proved annoying, but this initial call allowed the federal government to harness the *rage militaire* prevalent in the early months of the war. Each state was assigned a quota. Iowa provides an example of the system's operation. Across the Hawkeye state, newspapers carried Governor Samuel J. Kirkwood's announcement that citizens should enroll themselves into companies of eighty-seven men, elect captains and lesser ranks, and notify him by telegraph when they were ready for service. Within forty-eight hours men and women had gathered in local town halls, churches, or schools to hear patriotic speeches and enroll the willing—and perhaps even the unwilling. Like other Americans, most Iowans lived in small communities where they knew their neighbors well. The social pressure to enlist was enormous, the negative consequences of shirking immediate and highly public. Personal reputations mattered highly in a nineteenth-century world in which kinship networks, employment, political loyalties, and church affiliations carefully delineated daily lives and governed future prospects. Individual honor was at stake, but so, too, was the honor of communities, which competed overtly against one another to produce the first and best companies. Communities raised large sums of money to support the families of the volunteers during their absence, and in public ceremonies such as flag and sword presentations the soldiers pledged to die rather than compromise the honor of their hometowns. Since the federal government had few stocks of uniforms, local women frequently took the initiative, organizing themselves to produce wonders of sartorial splendor in every color imaginable. Companies adopted names that reflected their community ties, and in some cases their ethnic makeup. Units like the Burlington Zouaves, the Davenport Rifles, the Mount Pleasant Grays, and German Rifles might possess a leavening of Mexican War veterans, but the doctors, lawyers, and county clerks who were elected captains, lieutenants, and sergeants were able to discipline their men because they were the natural community leaders. Because they were commanding their friends and neighbors, and would have to answer to their home communities at conflict's end, that level of discipline was never great. But the tradeoff in terms of rapid assembly, self-motivation, dedication, and pride made the volunteer system worth it.

The volunteer system worked because it delegated recruitment to the community level and maintained rather than disrupted existing relationships. Prewar militia units, volunteer fire companies, political clubs, college freshman classes—all joined *en masse* and served together. State governors supported it because they could use the appointment of colonels as a form of patronage. For the soldiers, pride in their state and a determination to sustain the honor of their hometowns served as a glue that compensated for the absence of strict discipline. As the war progressed, regiments developed an *esprit* based on shared hardships and a determination not to let comrades down, but hometown pride and prewar social connections were vital for the first full year of service.

Although the federal government later utilized conscription, the volunteer system fed a steady stream of regiments into the Union armed forces throughout the course of the war. It also provided flexibility in relation to command. The United States Army had 1,105 officers on active duty in 1861, of which 824 had been educated at West Point. Promotion was by seniority rather than merit, there was no system of retirement, and rank was jealously guarded. Military culture dictated that the lowest-ranking

Regular outranked the highest grade of militia officer. Officers in the volunteers, however, were on par with the Regulars. A brigadier general in the U.S. Volunteers was senior to a colonel in the U.S. Army even if the general was a former lawyer and ward boss and the colonel a veteran of twenty years' service. The conspicuous failure of politicians Lincoln appointed to high rank, such as Benjamin Butler and David Hunter, has obscured the system's vital contribution to the war effort. It immediately brought back into uniform from civilian life 114 former West Pointers and gave them ranks higher than seniority would have dictated in the Regulars. William T. Sherman and Ulysses S. Grant are the foremost examples. It also allowed civilians who demonstrated significant military talent—men like John A. Logan and Francis P. Blair Jr.—to achieve responsible positions. Political officers were inevitable. Even if 184 West Pointers had not resigned to join the Confederacy, the wartime expansion of the Union armed services to number almost one million men necessitated giving critical commands to complete amateurs.

At the same time that the Lincoln government mobilized Union land forces, it began the process of blockading the South. Success soon followed when combined Army-Navy operations seized control of Hatteras Inlet, North Carolina (August 1861); Port Royal, South Carolina (November 1861); Ship Island, Georgia (November 1861); and Fernandina, Florida (March 1862).

The border states demanded immediate attention as well, and only Lincoln's heavy-handed measures prevented a possible Maryland secession, which would have placed Washington, D.C., inside the Confederacy. Both Kentucky and Missouri had governors who favored secession but legislatures with clear Unionist majorities. In the Bluegrass state, Lincoln responded for pleas to neutrality, accepting a situation in which both Union and Confederate agents recruited troops openly, but neither side sent outside forces into the state. He also dispatched agents to recruit men among the Unionists in East Tennessee. This failed when the Confederates rushed troops into the region, but before the summer ended enough "loyal mountaineers" had crossed into Kentucky to form an entire East Tennessee brigade. Yet officially Kentucky "neutrality" remained un-violated. The situation could never last, but it allowed the Union to focus resources elsewhere for the time being.

Thus in the first few months of its tenure, Lincoln's administration took steps that in retrospect placed the Union solidly on the road to vic-

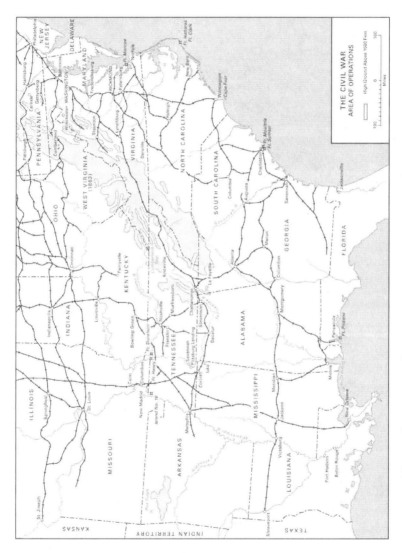

The Civil War Area of Operations (U.S. Army Center of Military History)

tory. It adopted the volunteer system, an efficient means of mobilizing manpower and maximizing military talent. It began a blockade and started securing offshore bases. It firmly controlled Maryland and crucial parts of Missouri, and made sure the Confederacy did not have the upper hand in Kentucky. These accomplishments have often gone overlooked because many other things did not go well for the Union in 1861.

Much of the Confederacy's initial success stemmed from the fact that it so closely resembled the Union. Except for its explicit protection of slavery, the Confederate constitution was almost identical to that of the United States. Like Lincoln, President Jefferson Davis took his responsibilities as commander in chief quite literally. He, too, saw the crisis primarily as a military one, and as a West Point graduate and former Secretary of War he approached the contest with decided advantages. His government did not try to reinvent the wheel. The Confederate Congress created both a navy and a regular army, although the latter was never very large. Each Confederate state had its militia, but the majority of soldiers enlisted in volunteer regiments, which formed the Provisional Army of the Confederate States. The names were different, but the Confederate system functioned just like the U.S. Volunteers and provided the same advantages in terms of recruiting and officer advancement.

In June the Confederate government moved its capital to Richmond, Virginia, the largest city in the South's most populous state and an important center of iron manufacturing. It had better rail connections than Montgomery, and its physical facilities were superior. Confederate strategy could never have sacrificed Richmond's important resources without a maximum defense, but placing the Confederate capital less than one hundred miles from Washington had an unforeseen effect, quite like the proverbial waving of a red flag in front of a bull. The fate of Richmond eventually took on for both sides a political and psychological significance that far exceeded its military value. From his office in the building that became known as the White House of the Confederacy, Davis could contemplate the South's relative strengths and weaknesses. Southern white males were rushing to arms. Thanks to stockpiles in state arsenals, and the capture of important federal sites, such as the arsenal at Baton Rouge, there were enough arms for immediate defense. Robert E. Lee, Albert Sidney Johnston, Joseph E. Johnston, and other soldiers of the highest reputation had resigned their commissions to join the Confederate army. Interior railway and telegraph lines gave the promise of rapid troop movements and quick long-distance communication. But some factors were hard to evaluate. The Confederacy could never build enough forts or ships to defend the entire length of its coastline or challenge the U.S. Navy for control of the seas. On the other hand, the vast extent of the coast made the Union blockade a challenge. Confederates might convert existing ships into ironclads to protect ports and break the blockade, while privateers and commissioned vessels preyed on Union commerce.

Resting its claim to legitimacy on the majority vote of adult white males, the Confederacy's military policy was defensive. Davis therefore created a series of military departments that in effect spread the Confederacy's forces in a cordon across the boundary with the North. Throughout 1861 this approach seemed to work rather well.

The Confederates failed to stop Federal forces under General George B. McClellan from occupying key points in the mountains of northwestern Virginia, where Unionism was rampant. But the war's first major battle was a disaster for northern arms. Responding to the popular demand, "On to Richmond," Lincoln's government ordered General Irvin McDowell and his 35,000 men to advance on the Confederate capital. McDowell objected that his men were poorly trained and unready for combat. Lincoln replied: "You are green, it is true. . . . But they [the Confederates] are green also. You are all green alike." Twenty-five miles southwest of Washington, on July 21, 1861, the Federals attacked 25,000 Confederates led by General P. G. T. Beauregard, the victor of Fort Sumter. Beauregard had deployed his brigades along a stretch of the stream called Bull Run. From this position the Confederates held the railroad town of Manassas Junction and blocked the direct overland approach to Richmond. McDowell might well have defeated the outnumbered Beauregard but for the Confederates' use of the railroad to rush additional troops under General Joseph E. Johnston to the Bull Run battlefield. These reinforcements, together with the defensive stand by General Thomas J. Jackson, who earned the nickname "Stonewall" for holding the line against Federal attacks, turned the tide of battle. Just as McDowell had feared, the Federal retreat turned into a rout as Northern soldiers and civilians stampeded back to Washington. In the South there was jubilation over this confirmation of what they already knew—one Southerner could lick ten Yankees.

The humiliating defeat at Bull Run led to a shakeup of the Union high command, and Lincoln replaced McDowell with General George B. McClellan, who had won a series of minor victories in western Virginia

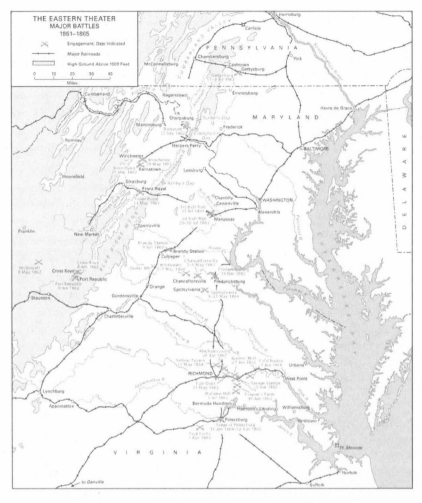

The Eastern Theater, 1861–1865 (U.S. Army Center of Military History)

that led an admiring public to call him the "Young Napoleon." Although McClellan promised action, and he is to be credited with building the Army of the Potomac, he proved to be a timid commander. Future operations were not helped by the fact that McClellan detested Lincoln, whom he called "the original Gorilla."

Before McClellan advanced on Richmond, Union forces in the West won some important victories. In February 1862, a joint military-naval operation, commanded by General Ulysses S. Grant, captured Fort Henry on the Tennessee River and Fort Donelson on the Cumberland. Grant's demand for "unconditional and immediate surrender" made him an instantaneous celebrity in the North. Fourteen thousand Confederate prisoners were taken in what was the first major Union victory of the war.

The Confederate army was forced to withdraw from Kentucky and middle Tennessee. Nashville, Tennessee's capital and an important supply center, was abandoned without a fight. The Army of Tennessee, commanded by General Albert Sidney Johnston, a close friend of President Jefferson Davis and widely considered the South's finest commander, was now in full retreat.

Engagements such as Bull Run (Manassas), Ball's Bluff, Wilson's Creek, and Lexington loomed large in the popular mind at the end of 1861, for they seemed to confirm Southerners' prewar claims of superior military prowess. In actuality, by beginning the process of marshaling the North's enormous strength, by doing so without wasting a moment or quibbling over legal niceties, and by preventing the border states from falling to the Confederacy, Lincoln in the first months of his tenure as war president took what proved to be the single most crucial steps toward ultimate victory.

A comparison of the campaigns that followed in the eastern and western theaters of the war in 1862 illustrates two important, related points. The first is that superior amounts of men and material did not guarantee Union victory. In the East, Lee seemed to be able to set numbers to naught, winning battle after battle against formidable odds. But the second point is that superior Federal resources really were important, even decisive at key points, particularly in the West. Successful campaigns by Grant, Sherman, and others set the Union on the road to victory, but it was superior resources as much as good generalship that allowed them to keep the territory they had conquered in the face of Southern countermoves. The payoff was cumulative, as Union advances in the West denied the Confederacy resources so critical to waging war that it is very difficult to imagine a purely military Southern victory after November 1863.

As Jefferson Davis's principal military advisor, Robert E. Lee was acutely aware of the Confederacy's inferior numbers. From the start of the war, however, Southern civilians, newspaper editors, and political leaders demanded decisive action on the battlefield. In the spring of 1862, McClellan landed a Federal army on the Virginia coast southeast of Richmond and began advancing up the peninsula formed by the York and James rivers. McClellan's 105,000-man army eventually faced Joe Johnston, who had only 60,000, at the very gates of Richmond. When Johnston was wounded, Lee assumed command of the Army of Northern Virginia.

Over the next six and a half months Lee used a combination of maneuver, surprise, and concentration of force so audaciously that he began to develop a psychological dominance over his enemies. This did not come easy, however. In the Seven Days battles, Lee's men drove the Federal forces back several miles from the Confederate capital at Richmond, but at great cost, incurring some 20,000 casualties to McClellan's 16,000. Lee predicted a long and bloody war that would demand tremendous sacrifices in the Confederacy. To Lee, winning the war was the highest priority, and even states' rights and individual rights should be subordinate to achieving Confederate victory.

Lee had spent the first twelve weeks of his field command staving off the disaster facing Richmond. Now free to maneuver, he applied for the first time the strategy that guided him throughout the war. He adopted an offensive-defensive policy. His overall goal was defensive, as the Confederacy sought no territorial conquests. Whenever practicable, however, Lee would seize the initiative, disrupting the enemy's plans and forcing battle on his terms rather than theirs. Thus despite being outnumbered overall he might be able to amass a temporary superiority of numbers at the decisive point, which he did at the second battle of Bull Run (Manassas), where he defeated General John Pope.

Rather than let his enemy rest for even a moment, Lee crossed the Potomac on September 4, an offensive move welcomed by Southerners eager to see "those barbarians" suffer who had been "so long robbing and murdering our quiet and unoffending citizens." He wanted to retain the initiative and draw the Federal forces north out of Virginia during the harvest season. If he could reach Pennsylvania and cut railroad lines there, he might undermine Northern morale and, most importantly, win foreign recognition of the Confederacy. Lee's reasoning was sound, but he failed to take into account the poor condition of his army, which was worn down and exhausted. He also slowed his operations by detaching Jackson to capture the Federal garrison at Harpers Ferry, which surrendered on September 15. In the meantime, McClellan, in sole command of the pursuing Union field forces, learned of Lee's plans and positions through a captured document. Warned of the security breach, Lee hastily assembled his army behind Antietam Creek near Sharpsburg, Maryland. He had no more than 39,000 men, his ranks having been depleted by a third due to straggling and desertion. McClellan brought some 70,000 to the fight, and had he not attacked ineptly he might have destroyed the Confederate army. The Battle of Antietam, fought on September 17, remains the single bloodiest day in American military history (13,700 Confederate and 12,350 Union casualties) and was quite possibly *the* turning point of the war. A victory by Lee in Maryland would most likely have resulted in British recognition of Confederate independence. Instead, Lee retreated back to Virginia. Desertions increased and soldiers threw away their shoes to avoid service. Finally, on September 22, 1862, Lincoln issued his preliminary Emancipation Proclamation to end slavery. Receiving no favorable response from the South, Lincoln went ahead on January 1, 1863, and declared that all slaves in those areas under enemy control "shall be . . . thenceforward, and forever free." Almost 200,000 African Americans, most of them newly freed slaves, would eventually serve in the Union army and navy, where they made a vital contribution to the North's victory. One such heroic contribution is graphically depicted in the award-winning film *Glory* (1989), in which the Fifty-fourth Massachusetts Colored Regiment, the first African American regular army unit recruited in the Civil War, attacked Confederate Fort Wagner, South Carolina, in July 1863.

Convinced after the Battle of Antietam that General McClellan had a fatal case of "the slows," Lincoln removed him from command of the Army of the Potomac for the last time, replacing the admittedly popular but timid McClellan with the aggressive, bewhiskered General Ambrose Burnside, whose facial hair inspired the term "sideburns." Burnside planned a rapid move to cross the Rappahannock at Fredericksburg, the largest river barrier before Richmond. What followed, during December 13–15, 1862, was a series of horrendous direct attacks to try to cross the Rappahannock River and take entrenched Confederate positions. Fifteen charges by courageous Federal troops against the stone wall along the Sunken Road were mowed down by Confederate rifle fire. At Fredericksburg, Northern forces suffered more than twice as many casualties as their enemy (12,600 Union losses against 5,300 Confederate casualties). "It is well that war is so terrible . . . ," remarked Lee of the slaughter, "[lest] we should grow too fond of it."

On the eastern front, Lee's offensive-defensive strategy had prevented the Union from capturing Richmond in 1862 (at a cost of 48,000 Confederate casualties), but in the West, Union forces won some important victories. On April 6, 1862, Southern general Albert Sidney Johnston launched a surprise

attack on Grant's army at Pittsburg Landing just north of the Mississippi
state line. On the battlefield was a small wooden church known as Shiloh
Meeting House. Although his army of 40,000 was only slightly superior in
numbers to that of Grant's (Johnston reportedly said, "I would fight them
if they were a million"), his surprise attack came close to driving Grant's
army back into the Tennessee River. Neither Grant nor his senior general
William T. Sherman had expected an attack or given orders for their troops
to entrench. Only the timely arrival of Union reinforcements and Grant's
stubbornness ("Lick 'em in the morning, though") forced a Confederate
withdrawal. Shiloh horrified both North and South. In two days' fighting,
the South suffered 10,700 casualties; Northern losses totaled 13,700. It continued to be a cruel month for the Confederates. On April 26, Flag Officer
David G. Farragut captured the port of New Orleans after boldly running his wooden steamships past the forts below the city. The North had
captured the South's most populous and wealthiest city. On top of this success, the Union had captured coastal bases from which to enforce its blockade of the southern coast. The last serious challenge to the Union blockade
ended on March 9, 1862, when the Confederate ironclad *Virginia* (originally the USS *Merrimac*) was battled to a draw by the Union ironclad
Monitor. The Southern coast was equivalent to a third front; lacking the
resources to defend nearly 3,000 miles of coastline, the seceded states lost
that front to the North.

Popular films and literature often portray 1863 as the crisis of the war,
beginning with Lee's tactical masterpiece, the Battle of Chancellorsville,
Virginia, in May 1863. With an army less than half the size of its Northern
counterpart, Lee once again demonstrated dazzling generalship. With leg-
endary audacity, he divided his forces, sending Stonewall Jackson on one
of the best-executed surprise flank attacks of the war. Lee had won again,
but nothing like an Austerlitz-type Napoleonic decisive victory. Not only
had Lee's Army of Northern Virginia absorbed 22 percent casualties, it
had suffered a major loss in the death of Lee's "right arm," the irreplaceable Stonewall Jackson, who died as a result of wounds received from
friendly fire.

In the West, however, Ulysses S. Grant conducted one of the boldest
campaigns of the war in a yearlong effort to capture the almost inaccessi-
ble Confederate bastion of Vicksburg, Mississippi. Vicksburg civilians hud-
dled in shelters to withstand a forty-seven-day bombardment and siege, some
of them reduced to eating rats. The Confederate government in Richmond,

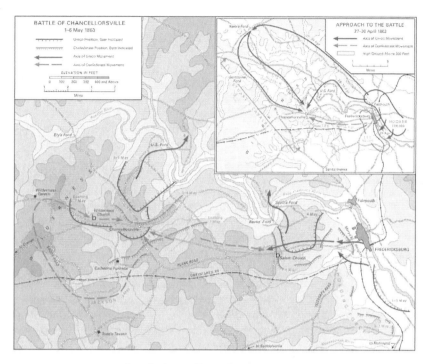

Battle of Chancellorsville, May 1–6, 1863
(U.S. Army Center of Military History)

meanwhile, weighed the alternatives of either sending reinforcements to the western theater to break the siege of Vicksburg or adopting General Robert E. Lee's proposed strategy, which called for an invasion of Pennsylvania. A dramatic victory in the North might change the course of the war. President Jefferson Davis approved Lee's plan for an all-out invasion of the North, and by the end of June Southern troops were in southern Pennsylvania. Leading elements of the two great armies crashed into each other near the small Pennsylvania town of Gettysburg, where on July 1–3, 1863, there took place the largest battle ever fought on American soil.

The Confederates won a major victory on the first day of Gettysburg, but the bulk of the Union army now occupied the high ground in strong defensive positions on Cemetery Ridge and Culp's Hill. On July 2, Confederate attacks failed to dislodge General George Gordon Meade's troops from the high ground they occupied. On the third day, Lee launched a direct attack on the enemy's center, Cemetery Ridge. Northern soldiers chanted, "Fredericksburg, Fredericksburg," as they fired into the ranks of

Battle of Gettysburg, July 1–3, 1863 (U.S. Army Center of Military History) the oncoming 13,000 Confederates. Only a few made it to the top of the ridge, and they were killed or captured. Defensive rifle fire and artillery canister (acting like a giant shotgun) had defeated what became popularly known as Pickett's Charge. After the failure of the charge, Lee blamed only himself. During the three days of combat, Blue and Grey casualties totaled over 50,000. As Lee withdrew his battered army back to Virginia (he lost nearly 20,000 men at Gettysburg), news was received of the fall of Vicksburg on July 4. Northerners rejoiced at the simultaneous Independence Day victories in the East and in the West.

However, as historian Albert Castel notes in retrospect, the impact of the fall of Vicksburg is easily misunderstood and exaggerated. One is tempted to wonder whether or not the 80,000 Union soldiers and large naval forces involved in the Vicksburg campaign were a diversion from a more critical objective such as Chattanooga, the "Gateway to the Deep South." *If* Chattanooga had fallen in the summer of 1863, Atlanta *might* have fallen a year earlier.

Unlike the Mississippi River towns, Chattanooga was vital to the Confederacy. From there rail lines that ran across northern Mississippi and Alabama branched north through East Tennessee into Virginia and south through Georgia into the Carolinas. In September 1863, Federal troops under General William S. Rosecrans maneuvered the Confederates out of the city, only to be driven back at Chickamauga. The Union army retreated into Chattanooga, where it was encircled by Confederate forces. After Grant arrived from Vicksburg to take command, the siege was broken by the charge up the rugged slopes of Missionary Ridge and Lookout Mountain. With Chattanooga in Federal hands, the road into the Deep South lay open.

Grant's victories in the West earned him promotion to general in chief of all the Union armies. Grant's plan called for the western armies under Sherman to invade Georgia, while in the east he engaged Lee's army. In May 1864, the Army of the Potomac crossed into northern Virginia and fought an unprecedented campaign of bloodletting in the Wilderness area of northern Virginia. It resembled nothing that had come before: no maneuver, combat, and withdrawal, but a six-week slugfest in the densely wooded Wilderness in which the armies seldom broke contact for more than a few hours. The North lost almost sixty thousand men— more than twice the number of Confederate casualties. At Cold Harbor, a frontal Union attack cost 7,000 casualties in less than an hour. Despite the unpopularity of "Butcher" Grant among many Northerners, Lincoln was

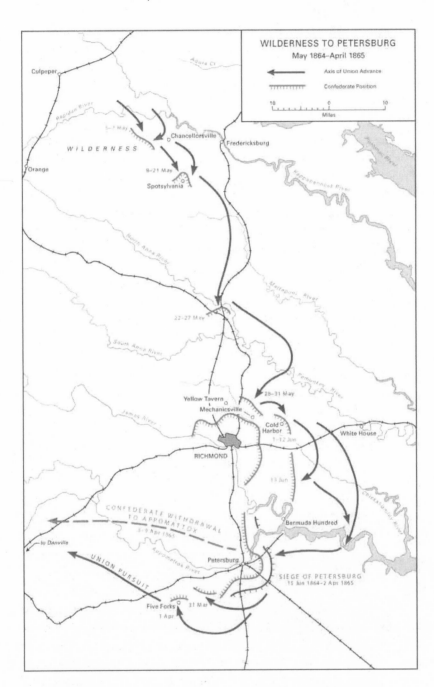

Wilderness to Petersburg (U.S. Army Center of Military History)

pleased with Grant's determination to keep fighting. Grant was determined to defeat the Confederate army "by mere attrition, if in no other way." A delighted Lincoln urged Grant to "hold on with a bull-dog grip, and chew & choke, as much as possible." Confederate soldiers could see that this kind of fighting would wear them out eventually.

Recognizing that he could not directly break through to Richmond, Grant moved the Army of the Potomac to the south of the Confederate capital and settled down to a long, drawn-out siege of Petersburg, a rail center twenty miles south of Richmond. For ten months, Lee and Grant faced one another across a trench-scarred landscape—a foretaste of World War I.

Politically, the military deadlock in Virginia caused northern morale to plummet during the summer of 1864. War weariness had set in, and even Lincoln confessed privately that he would probably be defeated in the November election. What saved Lincoln was the fall of Atlanta to Sherman on September 2, 1864. A Confederate manufacturing center and one of the most heavily fortified cities in the Confederacy, its capture by Sherman electrified the North and helped ensure Lincoln's reelection two months later. Lincoln won 212 of a possible 233 electoral votes and 55 percent of the popular vote.

By late September, the North had additional good news. Grant had wanted the rich agricultural resources of the Shenandoah Valley of Virginia—"the breadbasket of the Confederacy"—utterly destroyed so that "crows flying over it" would have to carry their own food. By October, General Philip H. Sheridan reported to Grant that the Shenandoah Valley was a "smoking, barren waste" and that "the people here are getting sick of the war." During the first two years of the war, hoping to avoid excessive bloodshed and bitterness, Lincoln and his generals had fought a limited, almost eighteenth-century type of war. Hoping to avoid a "remorseless revolutionary struggle" that might see the South shift into guerrilla warfare, Lincoln had urged his generals to fight a limited war. But it was now clear that this was a people's war, and that the Southern people as well as the South's armies must be conquered before the war could end.

In November, William T. Sherman and his army of 62,000 left Atlanta and began his famous "March to the Sea" that would, as he said, "make Georgia howl!" Sherman's army cut a path sometimes fifty miles wide through the heart of the Confederacy demonstrating that anyone "directly or indirectly" waging war against the Union was subject to the effects of its harsh realities. The story of Sherman's march through Georgia, then the Carolinas, became the stuff of legend: from "Sherman neckties," rails heated and twisted into "neckties," to "Sherman sentinels," buildings burned to the ground with only a chimney left standing. Private homes were generally spared, but food and valuables were fair game. Most black people welcomed the arrival of Sherman's army with jubilation—the inevitable working out of God's will. Thousands set out to follow the Union columns. Sherman captured Savannah on December 22 and presented the city to Lincoln as a Christmas present. Sherman's marches through the South vividly demonstrated the inability of the Confederate government to protect its own people and deepened an already growing pessimism and defeatism. In the West, in the Battle of Franklin, a town about thirty miles south of Nashville, Confederate general John Bell Hood launched a larger and even more disastrous frontal attack than Pickett's Charge at Gettysburg. Across two miles of open ground, 18,000 Confederates charged against well-prepared Federal defenses. More than half became casualties. Among the dead were five Confederate generals.

As the new year 1865 dawned, Grant laid plans for the Confederacy's final destruction. Lee remained pinned down in Virginia, while Sherman started north into South Carolina. Federal cavalry pushed through the rugged mountains of East Tennessee, passing through western North Carolina and into western South Carolina. All across the South bridges, rail yards, salt works, grist mills, tanneries, smoke houses, and iron furnaces went up in flames.

At Petersburg, the siege heated up in March, as the Federals continued to extend their lines to the west, threatening the rail lines that supplied both that city and Richmond. Unable to hold, Lee began evacuating Richmond on April 2. At last, determined to avoid useless sacrifice, Lee surrendered the Army of Northern Virginia at Appomattox Court House on April 9. Over the next few months the remaining Confederate armies followed Lee's example. Unlike Jefferson Davis and others, Lee rejected the idea of fighting a guerrilla war, and advised his soldiers to go home and be loyal citizens. This was Lee's finest hour and greatest service to the South.

Could the Confederacy have won? Prior to the 1960s most popular literature and academic analysis concluded that it could not. Historians writing after the Vietnam War, however, reminded readers that God does not always side with the largest battalions, and that a nation's will to victory, its civilian morale, can be as important as the number of soldiers it fields and how well they are fed and clothed.

While laudably shattering a great many moonlight and magnolia myths, and presenting a fuller and more accurate understanding of internal conditions within the South during the war, the trend of post-Vietnam interpretation has obscured battlefield realities. Granted, the Confederacy had real problems with internal dissent, particularly in relation to conscription—"a rich man's war but a poor man's fight"—but in retrospect, Southern defeats there were fatal. The South lost geography without which an independent Confederacy was an improbability. It lost resources that undercut its ability to continue the war or recover what it had lost. Blocked access to international markets and the unavailability of wagons, horses, and mules had a far greater impact on the war than Stonewall Jackson's death. Confederates themselves made much of the possibility of a political victory, of breaking the North's will to victory, either directly or by helping to engineer Lincoln's defeat in 1864. But this was a fantasy in the most important sense. Southerners always envisioned a peace in which the North would not only recognize the Confederacy, but also restore what it had conquered. The North had no reason to do so. To win back what it lost on the battlefield in 1862, the South needed more men. These it might have gotten had areas like East Tennessee and western North Carolina supported the cause. But the Confederacy also needed a large fleet of river ironclads and factories to turn out locomotives, boxcars, and—most of all—rails. Without these, even a master of maneuver warfare such as Lee stood no chance of reversing the tide.

Sources and Suggested Readings

Beringer, Richard E., et al. *Why the South Lost the Civil War.* Athens, Ga.: University of Georgia Press, 1986.

Castel, Albert. "Vicksburg: Myths and Realities." *North & South* 6 (November 2003): 62–75.

Catton, Bruce. *This Hallowed Ground: The Story of the Union Side of the Civil War.* New York: Doubleday, 1956.

Connelly, Thomas L., and Archer Jones. *The Politics of Command: Factions and Ideas in Confederate Strategy.* Baton Rouge: Louisiana State University Press, 1973.

Esposito, Vincent J., ed. *The West Point Atlas of American Wars.* 2 vols. New York: Praeger, 1959.

Foote, Shelby. *The Civil War: A Narrative.* 3 vols. New York: Random House, 1958–1974.

Freeman, Douglas Southall. *Lee's Lieutenants: A Study in Command.* 3 vols. New York: C. Scribner's Sons, 1942–1944.

Gallagher, Gary. *The Confederate War: How Popular Will, Nationalism, and Military Strategy Could Not Stave Off Defeat.* Cambridge, Mass.: Harvard University Press, 1997.

Grimsely, Mark. *The Hard Hand of War: Union Military Policy toward Confederate Civilians, 1861–1865.* Cambridge: Cambridge University Press, 1995.

Jenkins, Wilbert L. *Climbing up to Glory: A Short History of African Americans during the Civil War and Reconstruction.* New York: Scholarly Resources, 2002.

Leonard, Elizabeth D. *All the Daring of the Soldier: Women of the Civil War Armies.* New York: W. W. Norton, 1999.

McPherson, James. *Battle Cry of Freedom: The Civil War Era.* New York: Oxford University Press, 1988.

———. *For Cause and Comrades: Why Men Fought in the Civil War.* New York: Oxford University Press, 1997.

Nevins, Allan. *The War for the Union.* 4 vols. New York: Scribner, 1959–1971.

Thomas, Emory. *The Confederate Nation, 1861–1865.* New York: Harper & Row, 1979.

Trudeau, Noah Andre. *Like Men of War: Black Troops in the Civil War, 1862–1865.* Boston: Little, Brown, 1998.

Weigley, Russell F. *A Great Civil War: A Military and Political History, 1861–1865.* Bloomington: Indiana University Press, 2000.

Websites

The American Civil War Homepage. sunsite.utk.edu/civil-war/.

Civil War Women. scriptorium.lib.duke.edu/women/cwdocs.html.

History of African Americans in the Civil War. www.itd.nps.gov/cwss/history/aa_cw_history.htm.

National Civil War Association. www.ncwa.org/.

Selected Civil War Photographs. memory.loc.gov/ammem/cwphtml/cwphome.html.

U. S. Civil War Center. www.cwc.lsu.edu/.

Films

The Civil War. A documentary film series by Ken Burns. 1990.

Cold Mountain. Miramax, 2003. Contains a vivid recreation of the Battle of the Crater, July 1864.

Glory. Columbia TriStar Pictures, 1989. Story of the Fifty-fourth Massachusetts Colored Regiment.

Gods and Generals. Ted Turner Pictures, 2003.

FIVE

Indian Wars of the Trans-Mississippi West, 1850s–1890s

JEROME A. GREENE

AS STATED in a previous chapter, Native Americans—or Indians, as Christopher Columbus called them—represented one of the first dangers for European settlers in the British colonies. But due to their alliance mainly with the French during the Imperial Wars of the colonial period, the military power of most Indian tribes east of the Mississippi River was on the wane by the time of the founding of the American nation. By the 1790s even the tiny army of the feeble republic under President George Washington was able to subdue hostile Indians in the Old Northwest (that is, the region northeast of the Ohio River) at the Battle of Fallen Timbers (1794). The conclusion of the War of 1812 terminated British subsidies to American Indians and, for the most part, led to the end of Indian power east of the Mississippi. The year 1832 saw the defeat of the Sauk and Fox warrior Black Hawk in Illinois, which effectively cleared the area of hostile tribes, and also marked the establishment of the Office of Indian Affairs under the War Department. By that time, the Indian bureau, as well as most Americans, considered the area west of the ninety-fifth meridian as a "Great American Desert" and thus suitable as "Indian country." During this period, a number of eastern tribes were "removed" beyond the Mississippi River. The few Indian wars of the 1830s and 1840s (the Seminole conflict being the most notable) were the exception rather than the rule.

In 1849 the Office of Indian Affairs was transferred to the Department of the Interior, which was dominated by westerners who were not sympathetic to the Indians. By this time, land-hungry frontiersmen had discovered that farming was practicable on the grassy sod of the Great Plains. The rapid white migration into the region previously set aside as Indian country led to conflict. Indian Affairs officials made policy and the War Department enforced it. The undermanned pre–Civil War army was strung out in a chain of scattered forts attempting, with only modest success, to maintain an uneasy peace between the settlers and Indian tribes. During the Civil War, western state and territorial militia as well as volunteers manned the frontier garrisons, and Indian-white conflict escalated.

Jerome Greene chronicles how the U.S. Army as well as state and territorial forces enforced federal Indian policy from the 1850s through the 1890s, when most Indians were confined to reservations. By the end of the Civil War, the idea of territory set aside for Indians became obsolete. An 1851 congressional act initially called for the restriction of tribes to territorial boundaries or reservations. The wartime passage of the Homestead Act (1862) and a postwar boom in trans-Mississippi railroad construction, moreover, helped stimulate white migration and development in the western states and territories and reinforced the settlers' demand that Indians be confined to reservations. Many of the nomadic tribes who depended upon the buffalo to support their way of life resisted the government policy. The regular army, gradually reduced to a modest force in the years after the Civil War, was assigned to police the frontier and mediate between whites and the western tribes as federal policy sometimes fluctuated during the fifty-year period.

During the reservation era, the army was given the thankless task of enforcing government policy. Denied their nomadic lifestyle and ancestral lands, a number of tribes rebelled against being "civilized" and turned into sedentary agriculturalists. Although many army officers had mixed feelings about such a policy, they carried out orders, prohibiting Indians from leaving reservations and fighting them when they did. Undermanned and facing extremes in topography and weather as well as the vastness of the area that it had to patrol, the army was hard-pressed to fulfill the mission. Soldiers sometimes faced Indian warriors armed with repeating weapons. But no matter what their armament, repeater or bow, Indians were extremely mobile and elusive because they traveled on swift ponies in a wide area. To compensate, army officers often launched winter campaigns against fixed Indian encampments, which frequently resulted in a terrible toll on the inhabitants.

By the 1890s the army had completed the task of annihilating or pacifying the western Indians. While the military's role in subduing the Indians was substantial, it should be noted, as Greene points out, that the economic development of the West and the accompanying decimation of the buffalo herds contributed significantly to the demise of the Plains Indians. An era in U.S. Army history was complete. During the final decade of the nineteenth century, the last hostile Indians were either dead or pacified, and the army drastically reduced the number of its western garrisons. By the end of the century, its officers pondered what their next mission would be.

As white Americans advanced beyond the Mississippi River during the decades immediately preceding and following the Civil War, they again encountered Native American peoples who ranged over broad geographic expanses. Many of these Indian tribes refused to move, and the result was the same kind of guerrilla-type warfare that had dominated frontier expansion "back East" since the seventeenth century. Between the time of the war with Mexico and the 1890s, conflicts occurred with assorted Indian tribes inhabiting the territory from the Mississippi west to the Pacific coast and from Canada south to Mexico. In operations spanning four decades, in an area stretching from Canada to Mexico, and ultimately embracing more than 1,200 encounters large and small, United States troops acting as the agents of federal policy gradually completed the inevitable process of territorial conquest begun in 1492.

The Treaty of Guadalupe Hidalgo, ending the war with Mexico, helped define the broad extent of land over which ensued major army efforts against the tribes. That 1848 convention, legitimizing large territorial concessions to the United States, accelerated overland migrations to Oregon and California and practically ensured conflict between emigrants and natives whose lands lay in their course. The new territory augmented that of the Louisiana Purchase of 1803 and embraced parts of geographic provinces today recognized as the Great Plains, Great Basin and Inter-Mountain region, Pacific Coast and Northwest, and Desert Southwest. In the late 1840s, these vast tracts harbored numerous native peoples who practiced agriculture and/or competed among themselves for wild game for sustenance. Their encounters with emigrants in the years following the war with Mexico generally reacted to the interlopers' appropriation of land and game resources on which the Indians depended.

The principal travel routes by which the emigrants accessed Indian lands were the Oregon Trail, the Mormon Trail, the California Trail, and the Santa Fe Trail and their secondary arteries. In addition to the ever-constricting land base that these routes imposed on the tribes, the Indians witnessed repeated incidents of land exploitation by settlers and entrepreneurs, all of which in turn exacerbated long-standing intertribal feuds over land and increasingly limited resources. Although most emigrant traffic ceased during the Civil War years, its resumption after 1865 brought renewed opposition from the tribes. The period between 1865 and 1886 witnessed some of the most wide-ranging army-Indian conflicts in the nation's history as the peoples resisted the further encroachment of whites into the plains, deserts, and mountains.

A large number of tribes speaking different languages occupied diverse parts of the lands beyond the Mississippi before, during, and following the Civil War. Some of those with whom the federal government alternately made peace and warred included the Dakotas (Santee Sioux), Lakotas (Teton Sioux), Northern Arapahos, Northern Cheyennes, Blackfeet, Crows, Southern Arapahos, Southern Cheyennes, Kiowas, Kiowa-Apaches, and Comanches, all denizens of the prairies and plains; the Bannocks, Paiutes, Nez Perces, and Shoshonis, who occupied the intermountain plateau; and the Navahos, Chiricahua Apaches, Mescalero Apaches, and other Apache groups of the southwestern deserts. Several of these tribes were more frequently engaged in army-Indian warfare over several decades, especially the Lakotas, Northern Cheyennes, Southern Cheyennes, Comanches, and Kiowas—all peoples of relatively large numbers more or less situated along the principal lines of emigration and capable of offering substantial resistance to government forces. It is important to note that singly or otherwise these tribes had previously sought to extend their dominance in the area through warfare with neighboring Indian groups. The presence of horses among most tribes by the mid-to-late eighteenth century had facilitated their migration onto the plains, precipitating their transformation from agricultural to buffalo-hunting cultures and promoting rivalries among them. Intertribal warfare was common, and mounting pressures influenced by white expansion, notably the fur trade, promoted competition over hunting grounds. By the mid-nineteenth century, economic motivations

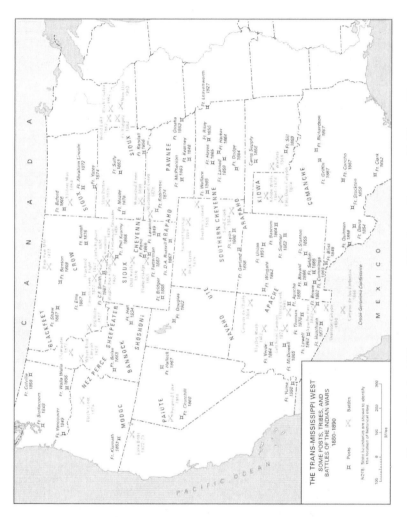

Trans-Mississippi West, 1860–1890 (U.S. Army Center of Military History)

grounded initially in the buffalo herds had become compounded with the peoples' established dependence on horses and firearms. Similar conditions affected the various Apache groups in the Southwest. In California and Oregon, smaller tribes like the Modocs and Nez Perces, located in more secluded regions, fought enthusiastically against inroads by whites but often lacked tribal cohesion and unanimity.

The Regular Army, which waged most of the campaigns against these people, reflected diversity of composition and leadership, especially following the Civil War. At that time the massive volunteer force was disbanded and the regular establishment reorganized into ten cavalry, twenty-five infantry, and five artillery regiments. Two regiments of cavalry (Ninth and Tenth) were segregated black units, as were two of infantry (Twenty-fourth and Twenty-fifth). Between 1866 and 1891, army strength averaged almost 31,000 officers and men, but ranged from a high of 57,194 in 1867 to a low of 24,140 in 1877. Many of these troops rotated among the well over two hundred garrisons scattered throughout the West. Assorted regional army divisions, departments, and districts administered the post–Civil War army. During the 1870s, the primary management sphere affecting Great Plains army commands was the Military Division of the Missouri, which was headquartered in Chicago, Illinois, and embraced all of the country from the Great Lakes to the Rocky Mountains. The division was divided into multiple departments, among them the Department of Dakota, administered from St. Paul, Minnesota; the Department of the Platte, administered from Omaha, Nebraska; and the Department of the Missouri, administered from St. Louis, Missouri. Departments, in turn, were often further subdivided, with the Department of Dakota, for example, incorporating the District of Western Montana, governed from Fort Shaw, Montana Territory, and the District of the Yellowstone, headquartered at Fort Keogh, Montana. Typically, a major general (rarely a lieutenant general) commanded a geographical division, a brigadier general a department, and a colonel a district.

Among the officers who commanded divisions during the western Indian campaigns were Lieutenant General Philip H. Sheridan (Division of the Missouri) and Major General Irvin McDowell (Division of the Pacific, headquartered at San Francisco). Commanders of departments included Brigadier General Alfred H. Terry (Department of Dakota), Brigadier General George Crook (Department of the Platte), and Brigadier General John Pope (Department of the Missouri)—all part of Sheridan's

Division of the Missouri—and Brigadier General Oliver O. Howard (Department of the Columbia, part of the Division of the Pacific). Among the districts, Colonel John Gibbon commanded the District of Western Montana with headquarters at Fort Shaw, Montana, within the Department of Dakota. Other officers administered similar organizational sectors elsewhere in the country; those identified above, along with their predecessors and successors in comparable stations, were responsible for overseeing the movements against the principal western tribes during the last half of the nineteenth century. Within these commands, at one time or another, operated elements of all ten cavalry regiments and all twenty-five infantry regiments (along with occasional artillery support) then comprising most of the army.

Campaigns were the army's method of prosecuting Indians for their perceived wrongs and for eliminating them as obstructions to white expansion. A definition from the 1880s cited war as a contest "carried on by force, either for defense or for revenging insults and redressing wrongs, for the extension of commerce or acquisition of territory, or for obtaining and establishing the superiority and dominion of one [nation] over the other." Campaigns, within such a context, consisted of "a connected series of military operations, forming a distinct stage or step in a war." Occasionally, "campaign" is interchanged with "expedition," which precisely refers to the sudden, rapid movement of land forces for the purpose of surprise assault of an enemy. Field-grade commanders (majors, lieutenant colonels, and colonels) usually managed campaigns, although department commanders infrequently directed large, multiforce enterprises against one or more large bodies of Indians. Sometimes company-level officers (lieutenants and captains) led scouts or sorties directed toward smaller numbers of tribesmen. In the field the troops were armed with single-shot small arms, .45-caliber breech-loading Springfield carbines for the cavalry and rifles for the infantry. Cavalrymen additionally carried .45-caliber Colt or Schofield revolvers. Artillery that accompanied the larger campaigns often consisted of 12-pounder Mountain Howitzers, 12-pounder Napoleon cannon, M1851 Ordnance Rifles, and Gatling Guns, and later included 1.5-inch-caliber breech-loading Hotchkiss cannon. This superiority in firepower, together with renewable manpower and resources, virtually assured victory against the tribes in the West.

Most army campaigns, once organized, set out from permanent posts situated on the edge of a broad area occupied by the targeted Indians, or from temporary stations termed "camps" and "cantonments" within that sector. Matters of logistics, including supply, and with troop organizational preparations normally occurred at the regular forts before opening the campaign, and the involved forces consisted of regiments or companies of infantry, cavalry, and artillery soldiers (the latter most frequently employed as infantrymen) and officers; bodies of Indian scouts (often enlisted from among tribes who were enemies to those deemed "hostile" by the government); and a contingent of civilian scouts and trailers, guides, teamsters, and drovers. The army usually contracted for the large number of ox- or mule-drawn wagons that transported tons of forage and equipage into the field, as well as for the herds of beef cattle that accompanied and fed the large commands. These self-sufficient yet lumbering columns of troops and impedimenta, sometimes several strong, progressed slowly in their courses, their very size and composition often hampering results. Consequently, smaller commands of cavalry often ranged far ahead of the converging columns, providing speedy mobility to help offset their measured advance; thus, the comparatively free-moving cavalry commands normally composed the essential attack mechanism when the army actually caught up with the Indians. Some officers were innovative. General Crook, for example, employed large numbers of scouts, ideally recruited from within the tribe being prosecuted, to aid in seeking and fighting enemy warriors. He also championed the use of sure-footed, rapidly moving pack mule trains over customary supply wagons.

Because of this manner of campaigning, the opportunities for striking the Indians were limited. As for actual combat, it is important to note that army-Indian warfare lacked formal precepts. No provision for its unconventional qualities existed beyond experience gained on campaign; because Indian warfare was viewed as but temporary duty in the realm of possible conflicts with standard international foes, West Point texts and classes taught budding officers only the time-tested processes of conventional warfare based upon European precedent. As a result, the army's evolving modus operandi against Indians included the application of conventional methods to existing conditions and prosecuting the people by means later known as "total warfare," which embraced the killing of their warriors, the destruction of their property, especially ponies, and the psychological terrorizing of their people through ambush-style attacks. (The term is often associated with its use during the Civil War, particularly in the campaign in the Shenandoah Valley of Virginia in 1864 and that for Atlanta in

1865, although it was used against Indians on the trans-Mississippi frontier before 1861.) Within the scope of "total warfare," the army employed what was known as an "offensive battle," in which, traditionally, troops sought out and attacked an armed adversary wherever located. On the frontier, "offensive battle" became transposed to comprise not surprise assaults on well-armed opponents, but daybreak strikes against Indian villages usually harboring large numbers of noncombatants, occasionally resulting in the deaths of women, children, and the elderly. However altered the tactic became, its transposition on the frontier apparently did not, for officers and the army, change the existing definition of "offensive battle."

In typical encounters, cavalrymen raced their horses through a camp, shooting into the tepees while driving the warriors' ponies away and squeezing off escape routes, leaving the villagers dismounted and disoriented as they tried to flee or were captured. Food, shelter, livestock, arms and ammunition, and all material supplies were burned and otherwise ruined following these assaults, with the purpose to end all means for future resistance. By the nature of the assaults, entire Indian families often suffered, and the deaths of noncombatants, inevitable although usually incidental, held scant consequence for many officers as they pursued victory. Military authorities deemed winter the ideal season for such attacks because freezing weather immobilized the people and their ponies in the villages. Almost universally, defeated tribesmen were quickly relocated and virtually imprisoned in venues far removed from their homelands to punish them as well as to exemplify their fate to other potentially disruptive tribes. Today the tactic of rushing Indian villages and occasioning the deaths of women and children is often viewed as immoral. But the nineteenth-century army validated it as expedient because of the Indians' customary elusiveness and the signal need to protect American citizens on the frontier; arguably, the tactic of assaulting Indian villages shortened the span of the violence and protected life by forcing the people onto reservations.

Because of economic incentive among the plains tribes, the practice of warfare that had evolved among many of them by the 1850s—perhaps the height of intertribal conflict—incorporated characteristics that were highly individualized and intratribally competitive and that carried over into the warriors' encounters with U.S. soldiers. Almost universally paramount was the act of "counting coup," by which means a man achieved war honors and subsequent enhanced status by striking or touching an enemy and getting away unhurt, rather than by killing him (although coups were also counted on the bodies of slain antagonists). Other means of distinction in combat consisted of wresting a weapon from an adversary's hands, stealing a picketed horse from within an enemy camp, rescuing a downed comrade from the clutches of the enemy, and leading a successful war party. Scalping and killing were considered less credible. Intertribal warfare was composed of raids and forays conducted by small parties of mounted warriors encouraged by the prospect of acquiring horses. Because of the relatively small number of individuals in a war party, along with the primary objective of distinguishing one's self by counting coup, deaths during intertribal combat, except where outright reprisal was the main inspiration, were relatively few.

One product of intertribal warfare during the last half of the nineteenth century—during the period of the army's major Indian campaigns—was the gradual realignment of tribes in relation to one another that occurred for reasons of conquest or of security. For example, longtime cultural associations to include intergroup marriage overcame occasional enmity between Cheyennes and Lakota Sioux for the sake of gaining territorial dominance, and were further militarily solidified when both groups first confronted pressure from the U.S. Army in the 1850s; the same was true of the Arapaho-Cheyenne-Lakota alliance. On the other hand, as these groups—and especially the Lakotas—achieved regional dominance in the 1850s, 1860s, and early 1870s, smaller groups like the Crows, while equally combat proficient, saw the wisdom of affiliating themselves with the federal government for protection. Tribes like the Crows, Arikaras, and Shoshonis furnished scouts to the army during the campaigns of the 1870s, thus advancing the tradition of intertribal warfare under new conditions. Most elements of warfare practiced by the Indians continued much as in the days when their principal antagonists were opposing tribesmen. The overriding aspect remained one's individuality in combat, and it was within this cultural context that the attributes of warfare against soldiers continued.

During the course of army-Indian warfare, the tribal groups hunted by the troops usually steered clear of large conflicts with them whenever possible. The Indians inhabited camps loosely segregated from one another to ensure access to available game, but which could pull together for security on knowledge of troops operating in the vicinity. When taking the offense against the army, it was usually via surprise techniques, that is, striking and running, and usually only when the warriors were assured superiority in numbers. Native arms, initially technologically inferior to those of the soldiers, consisted of bows and arrows, clubs and axes, trade knives, and lances—all of which had been used in the course of intertribal fighting and continued to be used during the pre– and post–Civil War periods in combat with troops. But by then many of the people had also acquired muzzle-loading guns from traders, and they later received improved pistols, rifles, and carbines. Yet their inability to access ammunition components proved costly and retarded their ability to make war of substantial duration against the army. Furthermore, in their peregrinations, the people followed traditional practices in keeping to established trails and camping in specific areas, generally along creeks and rivers where grass, water, and game afforded sustenance and shelter. On the plains, these villages with their skin tepees (or rancherias with brush-covered lodges in Apache country), often became targets of attack by the army. Rarely, large numbers of emboldened warriors would surprise troops in open terrain to preempt attacks on their own camps.

As indicated, the first major confrontations with tribes in the trans-Mississippi West occurred with the influx of whites onto the plains following the war with Mexico. The Mexican Cession introduced United States military authority to new areas, and together with increased emigration via the Oregon Trail and its ancillary routes, contact with Indians for trade was assured. But contact too often engendered misunderstanding, mutual mistrust, and, ultimately, hostility. At first, the government attempted to negotiate with Indian tribes to remove them from the routes of emigration. The conventions promised trade, annuities, training, and even money, although many provisions went unfulfilled. In time, the agreements sparked disorder among the tribesmen, many of whom comprehended little of their meaning just as white negotiators could not fathom the Indians' concept of oneness with the land.

Treaties concluded on the Northern Plains involved the Teton Sioux, Northern Arapahos, Northern Cheyennes, Crows, Shoshonis, and other tribes, with the principal object being to isolate them from the overland arteries. Similar accords were formulated on the Southern Plains with the Southern Cheyennes, Kiowas, Comanches, and Southern Arapahos, and with smaller groups, while still other treaties sought to ensure white interests in the far Southwest and Northwest. A principal defect in the treaty-making process, however, remained the inability of the negotiators to predict which tribesmen and leaders might subscribe and adhere to the documents' provisions. The process encouraged confusion and nonad-herence, and often led to violence when the army was sent to force compliance or to deal with nonsubscribing bands. Of all the provisions in all the treaties, it was the government's establishment of reservations that brought the most resistance and promoted the long period of army campaigning. By the 1870s—the height of the Indian wars—the paradoxical "Peace Policy" cultivated during the administration of President Ulysses S. Grant embraced a concept of Indian administration guided by representatives of selected religious denominations. Obviously, this course collided clumsily with the army's forceful subjugation of the tribes on the frontier, thereby confusing and compounding issues of war and peace.

On the Northern Plains, a dispute with long-term repercussions arose in 1854, scarcely six years after the close of the war with Mexico. It involved the rights of emigrants passing near Fort Laramie, in present-day Wyoming but then part of Nebraska Territory. When Sioux Indians trading near the post killed a Mormon pioneer's cow, a small body of soldiers responded from the fort. The lieutenant in charge of the men overreacted, firing on the tribesmen, who outnumbered him and who in turn killed the entire detachment. Within a year, the government responded, sending Brevet Brigadier General William S. Harney and an army of 600 dragoons, infantry, and artillery to find the Sioux and punish them. Harney met them at Blue Water Creek, Nebraska Territory, not far from a rendezvous point on the Oregon Trail, and attacked their camps on September 3, 1855. The army assault on the people of Little Thunder and Spotted Tail destroyed their villages, killing and wounding some ninety tribesmen. For the Lakotas, and by extension for their Cheyenne colleagues, Blue Water brought devastation, yielding seeds of dissension for future relations with the whites.

Federal dealings with the Indians intensified following Harney's expedition and carried south onto the Central Plains, where troops protecting emigrants attacked a camp of Cheyennes near the Platte River. Following up, in July 1857 a body of Fourth Cavalry under Colonel Edwin V. Sumner confronted 300 warriors along Solomon's Fork of the Republican River in Kansas, dispersing them under a charge that only assured retaliatory attacks. The consequences of the Harney and Sumner expeditions resonated among many tribes throughout the plains and influenced the years of conflict that followed. And the passions kindled did not end as regular troops were pulled east to fight in the Civil War. When volunteer units from the states and territories replaced them in the western garrisons, relations with the tribes continued much as before.

During the Civil War years, two events of paramount importance occurred that presaged a volatile future for Indian-white relations west of the Mississippi. The first took place in Minnesota following repeated incursions into the lands of the Santees, or Eastern Sioux (Dakota), and the recurring swindling by agents of their annuities. In August 1862, the Indians rose against the settlers, killing more than 800 whites during a month-long rampage led by the principal Dakota leader, Little Crow. State forces under Colonel Henry H. Sibley finally curbed the Indians, although Santees fleeing west instigated further campaigns to protect citizens from their retribution. In the summer of 1863, Sibley led a force to defeat the Santees and related Yanktonai tribesmen; another campaign, composed of state volunteers and headed by Brigadier General Alfred Sully, struck a large body of Santees near Whitestone Hill, Dakota Territory, destroying their camps and killing as many as 300 people while capturing a large number of noncombatants. Sully's victory pressed the warfare farther west in 1864—all the way to the Yellowstone River, to eventually provoke Lakota kinsmen of the Santees, some of whom had met and fought Harney earlier at the Blue Water. Further, the fears inspired among settlers by the Minnesota outbreak affected other burgeoning white communities in the West.

In the Colorado Territory, those fears culminated in the Sand Creek Massacre, an event rooted in attempts by territorial officials to check raiding by Indians along the emigrant trails in the country around Denver. Intent on protecting citizens, Governor John Evans won authority to raise a regiment of U.S. Volunteers to supplement existing territorial forces. On November 29, 1864, the Coloradoans, led by Colonel John M. Chivington, a former Methodist minister, stormed into a village of Cheyennes and Arapahos headed by noted peace chiefs Black Kettle and White Antelope. The action degenerated into mob violence as soldiers of the First and Third Colorado Cavalry regiments slaughtered the surprised people without discrimination, in many instances aggravating the brutality by defiling the remains of the dead. Chivington's losses were minimal. Although most of the Indians managed to flee the melee, at least 160 and probably many more lay dead. The government quickly denounced Sand Creek as a national disgrace, but the event galvanized the Cheyennes, Arapahos, Lakotas, and other plains tribes to heartily resist further white aggression in what they considered their country. Moreover, among Indians Sand

Creek came to symbolize the injustice and brutality of white Americans, compounding tenuous Indian-white relations for the balance of the nineteenth century.

In retaliation, Cheyenne, Arapaho, and Lakota warriors ranged the emigrant paths in Colorado, Wyoming, Kansas, and Nebraska attacking wagon trains, stealing livestock, and destroying property. Military escalation followed. In 1865, Brigadier General Patrick E. Connor inaugurated a three-pronged campaign into Montana and Wyoming using state volunteer forces. While his own column routed a village of Arapahos under Black Bear near the foot of the Big Horn Mountains in northern Wyoming, the cooperating commands endured weather and logistical troubles that instead rallied the tribes. Again the government negotiated treaties to keep the Indians away from emigrant lines, but again they had little effect. Complicating all, a new route to the Montana gold fields called the Bozeman Trail, blazed across north-central Wyoming in 1864, brought new emigrant traffic that cut through prime Lakota-Cheyenne hunting lands. The army raised three posts—Forts Reno, Phil Kearny, and C. F. Smith—to monitor the route, but warriors continued to harass passing convoys, inciting responses from troops of the Eighteenth Infantry and Second Cavalry. Several encounters took place, but that of December 21, 1866, wherein Chief Red Cloud's Sioux and their Cheyenne and Arapaho allies ambushed and annihilated Captain William J. Fetterman and eighty soldiers near Fort Phil Kearny, stunned the nation. After more fighting the next summer near Forts Phil Kearny and C. F. Smith, the government negotiated the Fort Laramie Treaty of 1868, temporarily conceding the region to the Indians by closing the Bozeman Trail and abandoning the posts. Coincidentally, completion of the Union Pacific Railroad assured alternative routes to western Montana.

The Fort Laramie Treaty granted the affected tribes unrestricted hunting rights in eastern Wyoming and southeastern Montana. It also established the Great Sioux Reservation embracing the Black Hills in what is now the western half of South Dakota. It was only a matter of time before rekindled economic interest in the Black Hills reopened the issue of Indian occupation of potentially valuable lands. In the meantime, the army prosecuted other tribes for perceived grievances against settlers. Perhaps no people endured more calamity during this period than the Piegans, a division of the Blackfeet alliance in northwestern Montana. The Piegans drew the attention of Major Eugene M. Baker, seeking marauders who had killed area settlers and destroyed their property. At dawn on January 23,

1870, Baker and his Second Cavalry troops attacked the village of Heavy Runner along the Marias River, and in partial repetition of Sand Creek, regular soldiers killed more than 170 people, nearly a third of them noncombatant women and children. The "Massacre on the Marias" flew in the face of the Peace Policy, and, as with Sand Creek, evoked harsh media criticism wherein eastern humanitarians called for a reevaluation of military tactics in striking camps containing noncombatants. Most immediately, public and political backlash from the incident stymied then-current plans for transferring the administration of Indian affairs from the Department of the Interior to the War Department.

The foremost warfare on the Northern Plains again involved the Lakotas and Northern Cheyennes. In 1873, engineering survey parties for the projected Northern Pacific Railroad edged into Montana hunting lands specified for the tribesmen in the 1868 treaty, producing clashes between Seventh cavalrymen and Indians along the Yellowstone River. Then a cavalry expedition to the Black Hills in 1874 found gold, setting off a rush of miners onto Sioux land. When government negotiators failed to purchase the Black Hills from the Lakotas, they set a course leading to the Great Sioux War, the nation's largest Indian conflict. Instigated by the refusal of Sioux who had spurned the 1868 accord to go onto the reservation, the Bureau of Indian Affairs turned to the War Department to force the issue.

Over the course of twenty months between February 1876 and September 1877, the Great Sioux War ranged over a boundless tract in present-day Wyoming, Montana, South Dakota, and Nebraska. Army strategy called for prosecuting the nonagency Sioux during the winter, but an early campaign under Brigadier General George Crook compounded matters by striking a village of Northern Cheyennes along Powder River in Montana, thereby aligning those people more solidly with the Sioux. Next, three columns closed on the Yellowstone–Powder River country where the Indians, now designated "hostiles," were presumed to be located. One under Crook pushed north from Wyoming, while another under Colonel John Gibbon headed east along the Yellowstone from stations in western Montana. A third, commanded by Brigadier General Alfred Terry, included infantry but also the Seventh Cavalry under Lieutenant Colonel George A. Custer.

Crook's column of Second and Third cavalry and Fourth and Ninth infantry first met the Indians, who attacked his troops on the upper reaches of Rosebud Creek, Montana, on June 17, 1876. After an all-day encounter with the soldiers and their Crow and Shoshoni auxiliaries, the warriors bested Crook, who turned south to replenish his supplies and ammunition. Unaware of the setback, Terry and Gibbon united and sent Custer and the Seventh Cavalry to find the Indians in the direction of the Little Big Horn River. On June 25, that officer attacked a village containing as many as 5,000 people, including some 1,500 warriors led by war chief Crazy Horse. In less than two hours, Custer and his immediate command lay dead on the heights above the river—"Custer's Last Stand"—while the remnants of the regiment occupied a defensive position a few miles away. The battle remains a hotly debated topic. Terry and Gibbon reached the battlefield two days later to learn of Custer's catastrophe. More than 265 soldiers had been killed at the Little Big Horn, while Indian losses likely did not exceed 100.

In the midst of the nation's centennial celebrations, outraged Americans read in their newspapers of a massacre of brave soldiers by bloodthirsty "savages." During the following weeks and months, reinforcements arrived and the Great Sioux War settled into a seek-and-destroy mode. With refurbished troops, Crook trailed one body of Indians east into the Dakota Territory, the men living on butchered cavalry mounts as they pursued the tribesmen. Crook's cavalrymen presently forced encounters with the Sioux in Dakota and with the Northern Cheyennes in Wyoming, events that wore significantly on the tribes. With men of the Fifth and Twenty-second infantry regiments, Colonel Nelson A. Miles scored victories over Sitting Bull and Crazy Horse in Montana during the winter of 1876–1877, and by midsummer of the latter year most tribesmen had yielded or fled into Canada. In 1881, Sitting Bull accompanied his people back from Canada, signifying the end of conflict with the Lakotas. The Indians' defeat of Custer during the nation's centennial observance captured the public imagination and has since come to symbolize the entire span of the Indian wars in American history.

Other army actions quelled smaller eruptions on the Northern Plains. In 1887 a Crow shaman who tried to lead a resurgent movement against mounting white influence in the Yellowstone country died in a clash with First Cavalry troops from Fort Custer, Montana. The so-called "Sword-Bearer Outbreak" presaged a broader movement involving tribes throughout much of the Great Plains in the late 1880s but predominately affecting the reservation Lakotas in South Dakota. Government agents perceived Sioux reaction to their declining condition as a manifestation of hostility, and the army responded with a massive buildup that ultimately composed parts of eighteen cavalry, infantry, and artillery regiments. The Ghost

Dance movement promised to restore the old days. Tensions heightened when Indian police killed the venerated Sitting Bull; they exploded altogether at Wounded Knee Creek, South Dakota, on December 29, 1890, when soldiers of the Seventh Cavalry killed more than 250 Lakota men, women, and children in an unpremeditated encounter that escalated into a massacre of grievous proportion. Wounded Knee was the last major armed clash between troops and Indians in American history.

Post–Civil War Indian campaigns on the Central and Southern Plains mostly paralleled operations in the north. There, tribes like the Southern Cheyennes, Southern Arapahos, Kiowas, and Comanches went through the same cultural convulsions. For years, those people witnessed penetration of their ancestral hunting grounds by caravans of whites moving along the Santa Fe and collateral trails, and since the 1830s and 1840s they had endured forced juxtapositioning caused by the arrival of tribes removed from the East by the government. Following the annexation of Texas in 1845 and the subsequent Mexican Cession, more whites entered the region. In Texas, where warfare between settlers and Comanches spanned several decades, U.S. troops joined Texas rangers and militia in quelling Indian raids. As at Fort Laramie, a treaty formalized at Fort Atkinson in 1853 attempted to halt marauding by Kiowas, Comanches, and Kiowa-Apaches. Fueled by the Sand Creek Massacre, after 1864 incendiary conditions flared among tribes from Texas to Kansas and Colorado, their anger focused on white gold-seekers en route to Colorado Territory and workmen building railroads through their country. While Sand Creek proved a horrific blow to the Cheyennes and Arapahos, its impact similarly carried over to other tribes outraged by the event. Treaties concluded at the Little Arkansas (1865), and Medicine Lodge (1867), Kansas, tended only to aggravate matters by further reducing the tribal lands.

Hostilities heightened in 1867. Following repeated Indian raids, the army sent Major General Winfield S. Hancock with 1400 cavalry and infantry, together with a complement of artillery, to impress the tribes and force their acquiescence. Yet army movements in Kansas, Nebraska, and eastern Colorado failed to cow the warriors. In one instance in September 1868, at what became known as Beecher Island of the Arickaree Fork of the Republican River in eastern Colorado, Cheyennes under Roman Nose assailed a force of fifty civilian scouts with Major George A. Forsyth, inflicting severe casualties. Continued attacks by Cheyennes and Arapahos prompted government inauguration of a winter expedition to punish the tribesmen responsible. Under Sheridan's direction, the campaign of November 1868 departed Camp Supply, Indian Territory (present-day Oklahoma), and resulted in Custer and his Seventh Cavalry striking and destroying the Washita River Cheyenne village of Black Kettle, killing the peace chief who had survived Sand Creek four years earlier, along with approximately thirty people. Over succeeding months, Custer, now supported by Kansas volunteers, pursued the Cheyennes and forced peace with them early in 1869. Elsewhere, army strikes against Cheyenne Dog Soldiers at Summit Springs, Colorado, followed by intimidation of the Comanches and the arrest of Kiowa chiefs Satanta and Big Tree, brought temporary peace, with the Indians relegated to reservations. After several years of starvation, however, caused by the government's failure to provide sufficient food, the Kiowas, Comanches, and Southern Cheyennes retaliated yet again. The Red River War of 1874–1875 saw infantry and cavalry columns under Colonels Miles and Ranald S. Mackenzie maneuver to destroy key villages at McClellan Creek and Palo Duro Canyon in Texas before the tribes finally submitted to reservation life.

With the conclusion of the Great Sioux War in 1877, the Northern Cheyennes had been sent to join their southern kinsmen near Fort Reno in the Indian Territory. In September 1878, with a year of disease and starvation behind them, leaders Morning Star and Little Wolf started with about 340 of their people for Montana, precipitating yet another campaign to stop them and return them south. Seeking food and livestock, the Indians attacked and killed white settlers during their flight through Kansas and Nebraska as horse and foot soldiers converged on them from different army jurisdictions. Over seven autumn weeks the troops repeatedly engaged the elusive tribesmen. Finally, they halted Morning Star and his people and imprisoned them in an abandoned barracks at Fort Robinson, Nebraska. In January 1879, the people broke out. More than sixty died within weeks at the hands of pursuing Third cavalrymen, while others turned themselves in at the post. Public opinion favoring the plight of the tribesmen resulted in their eventually being permitted to return to Montana, where Little Wolf and his followers had surrendered in the spring of 1879. The army campaign against the Northern Cheyennes in 1878–1879 signified the failure of the government's policy of forced removal, while it exhibited the martial skills of the people in evading the troops for so long.

Concurrent with army maneuvers against the tribes of the Southern Plains were those directed toward controlling the myriad tribes of the

Pacific Northwest. Many of those peoples had befriended traders and white explorers, including Lewis and Clark, yet the inroads of settlers and entrepreneurs exploiting regional resources in the years preceding and following the Civil War threatened their existence. Prolonged missionary activity in the region had introduced European concepts of education and religion, causing cultural schisms in some Indian societies, and the 1847 Cayuse uprising against Marcus Whitman's mission on the Walla Walla River in Washington Territory told of underlying grievances. Federal and territorial troops countered the Indians in lengthy campaigns, but attempts to treat with the tribes in 1855 proved unsuccessful. Large numbers of warriors from among the Yakimas, Walla Wallas, Cayuses, and other tribes struck out at whites in their country, and both regular and territorial forces took the field to prosecute the Indians in 1856. Following the Battle of Big Meadows, in which regulars suppressed the so-called Rogue River tribes who had resisted the plundering of lands in southern Oregon, many of the tribesmen succumbed to the reservation. Regional militia meantime subdued the Yakimas and Walla Wallas, and although Colonel George Wright's column of Third Infantry and Third Artillery soldiers took up the chase, the fighting ended inconclusively with two forts erected to monitor future Indian activities. Wright renewed his offensive in the spring of 1858, and on May 17, a command under Lieutenant Colonel Edward J. Steptoe was repulsed by a coalition of Palouses, Coeur d'Alenes, and Spokans in an encounter in which the soldiers barely escaped annihilation. Wright's army retaliated in September, registering victories over the warriors at Spokane Plain and Four Lakes in present-day Washington State; in the end, the tribesmen submitted and several of their chiefs and headmen were hanged. Despite its harshness, Wright's campaign fostered increased white settlement and brought semipermanent peace to the country with the Indians consigned to reservations.

Elsewhere in the Northwest, increasing government conflicts with the Southern Shoshonis of northern Utah and southern Idaho Territory resulted in the massacre of one of their villages along Bear River in January 1863 by state troops under Colonel Patrick E. Connor. Continued settlement of the Salmon River region of Idaho and eastern Oregon, coupled with gold discoveries in the 1860s and 1870s, provoked dissension among the Nez Perces, most of whom had previously befriended the whites. Between June and October 1877, Nez Perce bands that had refused to subscribe to treaties with the government fought a wide-ranging war of survival. Spearheaded by chiefs Looking Glass, Joseph, and White Bird, the people led a pursuing column of infantry, cavalry, and artillery under Brigadier General Oliver O. Howard on a 1,200-mile odyssey through parts of present-day Idaho, Montana, and Wyoming that was punctuated by frequent clashes, notably those at White Bird Canyon, Clearwater, and the Big Hole River. As the tribesmen attempted to reach sanctuary in Canada, they were besieged near the Bear's Paw Mountains in northern Montana by Seventh cavalrymen and Fifth and Twenty-second infantrymen under Colonel Miles, until Joseph surrendered. Although some Nez Perces escaped into Canada, those taken prisoner were sent to Kansas and the Indian Territory; it was not until 1885 that they were permitted to return to the Northwest. In 1878, like cultural pressures faced groups of Bannocks, who led cavalry, infantry, and artillery in similar fashion through parts of Idaho, Washington, Oregon, and Wyoming, killing some settlers until defeated by the soldiers. Another local war in 1879 involved displaced Paiutes. During that year, too, bands of Ute Indians upset over annuity issues and ineptly introduced reforms killed their agent, forcing confrontations with soldiers. In particular, the weeklong siege of a command of Fifth Cavalry and Fourth Infantry at Milk Creek, Colorado, which cost the lives of one officer and nine men, ended only after timely arrival of military reinforcements from Colorado and Wyoming.

Meantime, in California the situation during the last half of the nineteenth century was largely different and involved the army but peripherally, with certain exceptions. There, a concentrated Indian population, estimated at upwards of 260,000 people as of 1800, had dwindled dramatically under successive Spanish administrations. By 1850 there were perhaps 140,000 tribal members belonging to a multitude of small, linguistically related tribes. Many of the people roamed the landscape in loosely ordered bands living on roots, small game, and seeds. Following the Mexican War, gold-hungry whites rushed into the region, killing with impunity large numbers of the mostly defenseless tribesmen. They further introduced diseases that killed off thousands in what seemed an orchestrated campaign of extermination by those intent on seizing Indian lands and resources. In the thirty years from 1850 to 1880, California's Indian population declined to 16,000 people.

Few California groups were sufficiently populous to offer significant resistance. In 1867–1868, then–Lieutenant Colonel George Crook headed operations against Paiutes defiant over the inroads of whites in southern

Oregon and northern California. Disagreements over treaties and reservation conditions also persisted among the small but resilient Modoc tribe. In 1872–1873, a full-blown military contest erupted with them, with warfare in the lava fields of northern California requiring cavalry, infantry, and artillery troops to access some of the toughest landscape extant. During wide-ranging action, the warriors killed many settlers. Several pitched battles took place before the army command succeeded in bringing the Modoc spokesmen to council, an effort that saw the murder under truce conditions of Major General Edward R. S. Canby, commanding the Military Division of the Pacific. The Indians thereafter inflicted repeated casualties among the troops, and then withdrew to their lava-bed stronghold. Eventually, rising factionalism within the Modoc community, together with the arrival of military reinforcements, forced some of the tribesmen to acquiesce. They presently united with troops under the command of Brigadier General Jefferson C. Davis in pursuing and capturing the warriors and their leader, Captain Jack. He and several other headmen were hanged following sentence by a military commission, and the remaining Modocs were relocated to the Indian Territory.

The army experienced perhaps the most difficult Indian-fighting conditions in the desert Southwest, where searing temperatures, lack of water, and inhospitable terrain converged to enhance native resistance, frustrate the troops, and prolong the warfare. Between the decades of the 1850s and 1880s, native inhabitants of the region included the large Navaho tribe and assorted groups of Apaches. In the 1850s, army columns under Lieutenant Colonel Philip St. George Cooke marched against the Jicarilla Apaches, forcibly removing them as an impediment to white progress. Within a decade, as the Civil War raged in the East, armies of state volunteers headed variously by Colonel James H. Carleton and Christopher ("Kit") Carson pursued Mescalero Apaches and Navahos, implementing a "scorched earth" policy in seizing their stock, burning their gardens, and imprisoning them at the barren Bosque Redondo in eastern New Mexico. Farther west, episodes like the 1861 "Bascom Affair," during which army Second Lieutenant George N. Bascom, Sixteenth Infantry, hanged relatives of the Chiricahua Apache leader, Cochise, accelerated the deterioration of army-Apache relations. Compounding that, the Camp Grant Massacre of 1871, during which Aravaipa and Pinal Apaches were attacked and indiscriminately murdered by a mob composed largely of citizens, further corrupted relations between whites and Apaches.

Later campaigns in Texas, New Mexico, and Arizona through the 1870s and 1880s involved army prosecution of disparate Apache groups who continued to raid settlements throughout the border country. Incursions into both the United States and Mexico were led by Cochise, Victorio, Chato, and Mangas Coloradas. Major efforts against the Apaches included Crook's Tonto Basin expedition of 1872–1873, in which he supplemented his cavalry with Apache scouts to help stabilize the region, and the Sierra Madre campaign, in which a Sixth Cavalry command pursued Geronimo's Chiricahuas deep into the mountains of Mexico (in accordance with existing reciprocity agreements) following their outbreak from the San Carlos reservation in 1883. Again, Crook employed Apaches to help locate and fight their kin, and in the end the Indians surrendered. In 1885–1886, with the scouts and elements of the Fourth Cavalry and Eighth Infantry, Crook again took the field against Geronimo and his followers, who once more broke away from San Carlos. Following policy disagreements between Crook and Sheridan, Brigadier General Nelson A. Miles, using methods similar to Crook's, forced Geronimo's surrender in September 1886. To preclude further outbreaks, the government removed the Apaches to Florida as prisoners of war. Army movements against the Apaches in 1885–1886 represented the last of the true campaigns against Indians; episodes thereafter, including the aforementioned 1887 Crow rebellion and the events surrounding Wounded Knee in 1890, besides an 1898 incident involving the Pillager Chippewas in Minnesota, are more accurately categorized as civil disturbances warranting army constabulary action within reservation boundaries.

Between 1850 and 1891, more than 1,300 officers and men were killed or wounded during confrontations with Indians; conversely, at least 2,000 tribesmen—and doubtless many more—died as a consequence of army operations in the West. During campaigning on the Northern Plains in the mid-1870s—the peak of the warfare—the ratio of army casualties in proportion to numbers of troops engaged in fact surpassed that of either side during the Civil War. In the end, the Indians lost because the tribes were unable to unite militarily for common purposes, because of the diminishing warrior base versus the ease of troop replacement, because of the peoples' inability to absorb repeated destruction of their homes and material goods by the troops, and because of the tribes' inability to ensure sustainable resources, principally arms and ammunition. As well, toward the end of the period of major army-Indian confrontation, the proliferation of railroads and their facility for quickly deploying troops proved valuable to the government's capability to anticipate and stem disruption among tribal populations. Coincidently, by the 1890s the elimination of the buffalo herds largely at the hands of white hunters ended the primary source of sustenance for many tribes, and they were forced to the reservations to survive.

The direct result of the army's prosecution of the Indians throughout the trans-Mississippi region was the opening of former tribal lands to settlement, farming, mining, railroads, and other forms of commercial enterprise that benefited the government and its people. The four-plus decades of sporadic warfare ensured that the expansionist designs of white Americans surmounted the interests of the Indians in accordance with "manifest destiny." Relegated to reservations where troops initially guarded them, the people faced starvation and disease epidemics while striving to survive as cultural entities over the next century. With passage of the Dawes Severalty Act in 1887, many tribes lost treaty-guaranteed lands through the breakup of reservations for sale to white homesteaders. Through it all, the army had served as promoter of settlement and protector of white populations in accordance with national interests. While troops participated in the campaigns, they also took part in the establishment and operation of agencies and reservations. They further promoted military domination of the tribes on many reservations by controlling their activities and assuring their continued compliance with government wishes.

For the army, the Indian wars brought change. Tactically, even as the conflicts proceeded, officers gave more attention to their unconventional features than previously, several at the department level even disseminating edicts (for their immediate commands) specifically governing campaigns against Indians. In future years, many tactical and logistical judgments grounded in Indian-war experience found application in other arenas, as when officers with frontier service encountered guerrilla-style warfare in the Philippines and elsewhere after 1898. Similarly, technological advances in armament and equipment conceived during four decades in the West, especially regarding such weapons as the breech-loading Hotchkiss gun, first used in combat during the Nez Perce campaign and subsequently employed at Wounded Knee, found practical use elsewhere as the nation—and the army—shifted its attention to the Pacific and beyond. In these respects, the Indian-fighting experience provided an important crucible of learning for an army soon challenged in more worldly ways to defend and advance the nation's interests.

Sources and Suggested Readings

Athearn, Robert G. *William Tecumseh Sherman and the Settlement of the West.* Norman: University of Oklahoma Press, 1956.

Cozzens, Peter, ed. *Eyewitnesses to the Indian Wars, 1865–1890.* Vol. 1, *The Struggle for Apacheria*; Vol. 2, *The Wars for the Pacific Northwest*; Vol. 3, *Conquering the Southern Plains*; Vol. 4, *The Northern Plains*; Vol. 5, *Army Life and Leaders.* Mechanicsburg, Pa.: Stackpole, 2001–2004.

Frazer, Robert W. *Forts of the West.* Norman: University of Oklahoma Press, 1965.

Gray, John S. *Centennial Campaign: The Sioux War of 1876.* Fort Collins, Colo.: Old Army Press, 1976.

Greene, Jerome A. *Nez Perce Summer, 1877: The U.S. Army and the Nee-Mee-Poo Crisis.* Helena: Montana Historical Society Press, 2000.

———. *Washita: The U.S. Army and the Southern Cheyennes, 1867–1869.* Norman: University of Oklahoma Press, 2004.

———. *Yellowstone Command: Colonel Nelson A. Miles and the Great Sioux War, 1876–1877.* Lincoln: University of Nebraska Press, 1991.

Hedren, Paul L. *Fort Laramie in 1876: Chronicle of a Frontier Post at War.* Lincoln: University of Nebraska Press, 1988.

———. *We Trailed the Sioux: Enlisted Men Speak on Custer, Crook, and the Great Sioux War.* Mechanicsburg, Pa.: Stackpole, 2003.

Hutton, Paul A. *Phil Sheridan and His Army.* Lincoln: University of Nebraska Press, 1985.

Leckie, William H. *The Military Conquest of the Southern Plains.* Norman: University of Oklahoma Press, 1963.

Madsen, Brigham D. *The Shoshoni Frontier and the Bear River Massacre.* Salt Lake City: University of Utah Press, 1985.

McDermott, John D. *Circle of Fire: The Indian War of 1865.* Mechanicsburg, Pa.: Stackpole, 2003.

———. *A Guide to the Indian Wars of the West.* Lincoln: University of Nebraska Press, 1998.

Monnett, John H. *The Battle of Beecher Island and the Indian War of 1867–1869.* Niwot: University Press of Colorado, 1992.

Paul, R. Eli. *Blue Water Creek and the First Sioux War.* Norman: University of Oklahoma Press, 2004.

Rankin, Charles E., ed. *Legacy: New Perspectives on the Battle of the Little Bighorn.* Helena: Montana Historical Society Press, 1996.

Rickey, Don G. *Forty Miles a Day on Beans and Hay: The Enlisted Soldier Fighting the Indian Wars.* Norman: University of Oklahoma Press, 1963.

Robinson, Charles M., III. *General Crook and the Western Frontier.* Norman: University of Oklahoma Press, 2001.

Schlicke, Carl P. *General George Wright: Guardian of the Pacific Coast*. Norman: University of Oklahoma Press, 1988.

Thompson, Erwin N. *Modoc War: Its Military History and Topography*. Sacramento, Calif.: Argus, 1971.

Thrapp, Dan L. *The Conquest of Apacheria*. Norman: University of Oklahoma Press, 1967.

Utley, Robert M. *Frontier Regulars: The United States Army and the Indian, 1866–1890*. New York: Macmillan, 1973.

———. *Frontiersmen in Blue: The United States Army and the Indian, 1848–1866*. New York: Macmillan, 1967.

———. *The Last Days of the Sioux Nation*. New Haven, Conn.: Yale University Press, 1963.

Weigley, Russell E. *History of the United States Army*. New York: Macmillan, 1967.

Wooster, Robert. *The Military and United States Indian Policy, 1865–1903*. New Haven, Conn.: Yale University Press, 1988.

Videos

Geronimo and the Apache Resistance. Pacific Arts Video for PBS, *The American Experience*, 1990.

How the West was Lost. 7 vols. The Discovery Channel and 9 KUSA (Denver), 1993, 1995.

Websites

Frontier Heritage Alliance. www.frontierheritage.org/.

Little Big Horn Associates. www.lbha.org/.

The National Indian Wars Association. www.indianwars.org/.

SIX

The Military Role of the United States in World War I

DAVID R. WOODWARD

F OR A BRIEF period at the end of the Civil War the United States had the most formidable army and navy in the world. The development of iron-clad ships during the conflict ushered in a new era in naval warfare and made the U.S. Navy a leader in the new technology. But in the decades after the war, Congress mandated drastic cutbacks in both services. During the era of the Indian wars, the army was reduced to a mere domestic constabulary sufficient to patrol frontier areas. It was not until the Indian campaigns were over in the 1890s that army troopers were issued a modern repeating rifle, the smokeless-powder Krag-Jorgensen.

As the first line of national defense, the navy fared better. A building program in the 1880s made America's White Squadron a formidable maritime force. In 1884 the Naval War College was established in Newport, Rhode Island, in order to develop naval strategy for the modern age. Captain Alfred Thayer Mahan, an instructor at the college, emerged as the prophet of naval expansion. His 1890 book, *The Influence of Seapower upon History*, as well as his other works linked national greatness to naval strength. During the last decade of the century, an elite class of Americans championed Mahan's ideas as a powerful rationale for overseas expansion.

A crisis with Spain over its Cuban colony in the Caribbean near the U.S. mainland provided the spark that propelled the nation into an era of imperial conquest. In the Spanish-American War (1898), the U.S. Navy performed well against its vastly inferior Spanish counterpart. Public support for naval expenditures, moreover, was enhanced by Admiral George Dewey's triumph at Manila Bay and other naval successes and the need to protect America's far-flung colonies—Puerto Rico, Guam, and the Philippines—acquired as a result of the conflict. During the first decade of the new century, one of the heroes of the Spanish-American War, Theodore Roosevelt, demonstrated as president the nation's naval prowess and its emerging status as a world power by sending the Great White Fleet around the world (1908). By that time, however, the British development of superbattleships of the HMS *Dreadnought* class had made most of the world's top-of-the-line naval vessels obsolete. Roosevelt prevailed upon Congress to begin construction of a number of *Dreadnought*-type vessels. On the eve of the Great War in 1914, the United States had kept pace with most of the world's leading naval powers with a fleet that included fourteen post-*Dreadnought* battleships.

The U.S. Army entered the Spanish-American War in an undermanned and ill-prepared state. As in previous wars, volunteers were called up to meet the national emergency. A small invasion force of less than 20,000 men, composed mainly of regulars, launched an attack on Cuba from a base in South Florida. With the aid of Cuban rebels, the Americans were able to overcome weak Spanish resistance on the island in a little more than a month. The apparent ease with which U.S. forces triumphed in Cuba belied the fact that the army had been plagued by serious supply, logistical, and command problems during the war. The army performed better in its brutal suppression of a Filipino insurrection that degenerated into guerrilla war in the western Pacific (1899–1902), but some army officers and administration officials, including President Roosevelt, demanded reform of the U.S. Army structure. Secretary of War Elihu Root spearheaded the reform movement, which included the implementation of a chief-of-staff system based on the Prussian model and an overhaul of the National Guard. In other areas, the army engaged in a modernization program that included the adoption of the Springfield M1903 rifle, the M1902 3-inch artillery piece, and a light, substandard automatic machine gun. The War Department also created motorized and aerial branches of the service that received some field testing during incursions into Mexico just prior America's entry into the European conflict.

Despite the reforms and efforts at modernization, the army was still ill prepared to mobilize for and fight in the Great War in Europe. In unleashing a new wave of unrestricted submarine warfare in 1917, Germany gambled that the United States could not sufficiently mobilize within two years to play a significant role on the Western Front. By that time, the German High Command reasoned, the Central Powers would be victorious. However, the U.S. Army and Navy beat the German estimate, although the margin was slim indeed. David Woodward examines the nature of the world's first total war and the American contribution to the Allied victory. He concludes that U.S. naval and army forces played an important role in bringing the war to a decisive conclusion in late 1918. "American forces alone did not actually win the war," he writes, "but they almost certainly kept the Allies from losing or accepting a stalemated peace."

Few events in world history compare to the slaughter and consequences of what contemporaries called the Great War. Over twenty million lives would be lost in the maelstrom of violence that followed the assassination of the archduke Franz Ferdinand, heir to the Austro-Hungarian Empire, by an adolescent fanatic, Gavrilo Princip, on the streets of Sarajevo on June 28, 1914. The possibilities for a general European war had existed since German unification in 1871. Extreme nationalism, hostile alliance systems, and Social Darwinian ideas ("survival of the fittest"), as well as other ingredients, made up the witch's brew that led far too many to welcome war as a force for "renewal" and a test of idealism. Why a general European war in 1914? Millions of words have been written in the attempt to answer the question about the origins of World War I: the answer of contemporaries was quite simple—"the enemy"; later, in the 1920s and '30s, "revisionists" blamed the Allies; today, the historical wheel has turned: while none of the major powers were without some responsibility for the unwanted catastrophe, there remain the haunting words of the German chancellor Bethmann-Hollweg, who thought war "the best and most radical solution" to the Balkan problem.

The nineteenth century had brought forth a vast new Pandora's box of new rapid-fire and high-explosive weapons that dramatically raised the lethality of the battlefield. Industrialization and technology forced soldiers to adapt to a new and unexpected style of warfare. More than twice as many people were killed in this war as in all of the major wars combined from 1790 to 1913. Europe's position in the world diminished while the United States emerged as a global power. The United States, whose industry was on the verge of outproducing all of the European countries combined, further increased its influence in international affairs by sending a great army to Europe to fight as a member of the anti-German coalition.

When it began in August 1914, the war took shape exactly as the European general staffs expected. Great masses of troops and equipment, transported to the enemy's border by rail, were on the move. Generals expected to engage their adversaries in one or two monster battles of annihilation. The French plunged headlong into Alsace and Lorraine, provinces they had lost to Germany forty years earlier; the Germans conducted a gigantic flanking movement, the infamous Schlieffen Plan, through Belgium into northern France with the object of enveloping the French Army. The Russian Army meanwhile launched a two-pronged assault against East Prussia. To the surprise of civilian and soldier alike, the war was not fought to a quick conclusion. All of the carefully laid prewar plans came to grief. The Germans enjoyed the greatest success, overrunning Belgium and threatening Paris, but their advance was stopped at the First Battle of the Marne in September 1914. In the east, Russia was thwarted in its efforts to overrun East Prussia, was engaged against Germany and Austria-Hungary, and would soon be at war with Turkey.

By the end of 1914 the general staffs on the Western Front faced an entirely unexpected development: firepower proved to be supreme, and siege warfare replaced offensive warfare with an elaborate trench system being constructed with ever-increasing sophistication from the North Sea to Switzerland. Rather than two parallel trenches, there existed a series of usually continuous defensive positions with connecting trenches. From the air it looked like a gigantic spider web. Before the war, the British Army's annual requirement for spades and shovels was 2,500. During the war, 10,638,000 were manufactured. Digging never ceased as new trenches were made and old ones repaired or expanded. Along the some-475-mile front there were thousands of miles of fortifications.

The military stalemate was largely a result of the industrialization of warfare and the development of mass-conscript armies and large reserves in the major continental powers. Millions of soldiers were thus available to man the defenses. Rapid-fire weapons, especially the machine gun, helped the defense more than the offense. The machine gun fired six hundred rounds to a skilled rifleman's fifteen rounds per minute. Six of these

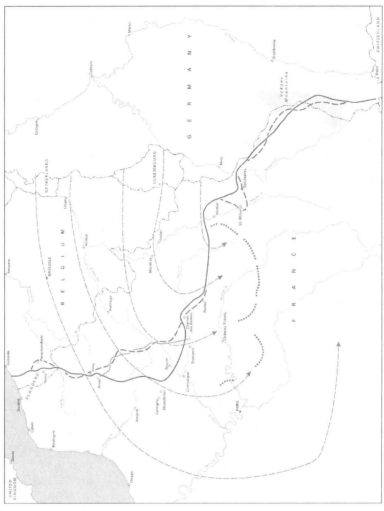

Western Front, September 1914–March 1918 (U.S. Army Center of Military History)

guns could defend a front against a brigade. The deadly effect of the potent weapon, however, cannot be explained solely by its increased rate of fire. The uncertain human element became less a factor in battle. As precise as a machine tool, the machine gun mounted on a tripod could be adjusted to sweep a section of the battlefield, making it almost impossible for soldiers to advance upright without being hit in this prearranged field of fire. Machine gunners might be filled with terror, their teeth chattering and their pants fouled, but the nerveless weapon in their sweaty hands continued to do its deadly work, even in fog or darkness.

Despite the increased strength of the defense, few general staff officers at first viewed trench or static warfare as anything more than a temporary interruption of a war of movement. The labs and factories of the industrialized countries produced weapons designed to help them break the deadlock. The British were the first to manufacture an armored vehicle, powered by a combustion engine, that crunched across the barbed-wire-strewn battlefield on caterpillar tracks. The tank was a match for the machine gun and served to demoralize an adversary, but the 1916–1918 versions were neither fast enough nor sufficiently battleworthy to be a war winner.

Artillery (especially heavy artillery and the high-explosive shell) along with chemical warfare proved to be the most effective and lethal weapons against entrenched forces. It is claimed that artillery caused up to 70 percent of battlefield deaths. The industry of the belligerents, when mobilized for total war, turned out vast quantities of big guns and shells. Poison gas, eventually fired in mortar canisters and shells, was used to terrify defenders while massed artillery attempted to smash and neutralize the opponent's machine guns and artillery. The destructive and terrifying impact of artillery has been vividly described by the Frenchman Henri Barbusse in his book *Under Fire*:

A diabolical uproar surrounds us. We are conscious of a sustained crescendo, an incessant multiplication of the universal frenzy; a hurricane of hoarse and hollow banging, of raging clamour, of piercing and beast-like screams, fastens furiously with tatters of smoke upon the earth where we are buried up to our necks, the wind of the shells seems to set it heaving and pitching.

Toward the end of the war, the airplane, which was first used for military reconnaissance, was employed as a supplement to the artillery bombardment to weaken an enemy's defenses and hamper his movements. The infantry's role in theory was to occupy territory that had already been conquered by shell, gas, and bomb.

The employment of these weapons enabled a determined attacker to break into his adversary's fortifications, but the freedom from trench warfare that he sought remained an illusion. The cratered and pulverized earth in his path made the forward movement of his artillery, without which no successful advance against trenches could take place, slow and difficult. The infantry, even when supported in the case of the Allies by both tanks and airplanes, could not advance rapidly enough to prevent enemy reserves from being brought forward by rail and digging in. It was thus possible to break into but not out of the enemy's fortifications. Some generals saw galloping horse soldiers as the answer to maintaining the momentum of the assault, but it did not take the frontline soldier long to realize that cavalry did not belong on the same battlefield with barbed wire and machine guns.

The war initially centered on Europe, but fighting soon spread to other corners of the globe—from East Africa to Baghdad to the Turkish Straits to the Shantung province of China. Since most of the major powers had imperial possessions, they felt compelled to defend and in some cases to add to their colonies. In a few cases, the need for natural resources or the necessity of denying them to the enemy helped expand the conflict. Japan took advantage of the war to seize German colonial holdings in the Far East. All of these factors combined to make this a truly global conflict.

Most Americans watched the bloodletting in Europe and its spread to other parts of the world with mixed feelings of horror over the slaughter and relief that their country was neutral. President Woodrow Wilson, who from the beginning had urged his countrymen to be "impartial in thought as well as in action," was reelected in 1916 with the slogan: "He Kept Us Out of War."

It has been argued that the American tradition of civilian supremacy over the military, in combination with Wilson's concept of the military's proper role in a country at peace, handcuffed the professional army and naval officers in preparing their country for possible participation in the conflict. When the influence of the European general staffs in the chain of events leading to World War I is remembered, Wilson's concern that diplomacy might be shaped in unfortunate ways by military expediency was not without some validity. But the president went too far when he insisted that the military had no role to play in the formulation of national policy.

Peacetime officers were not expected to advise civil authorities unless asked; and Wilson believed that a neutral response to the war in Europe was exclusively the responsibility of civilians. When he read a newspaper report in 1915 that members of the army general staff were war-gaming with Germany in mind, he ordered an investigation and the relief of any officers found guilty of contingency planning.

One effect of this artificial and unrealistic separation of civil and military responsibilities was that the country's "preparedness" campaign had little connection with the real war that the United States was most likely to fight. Even the most security-minded Republicans in Congress demanded a regular army of only 250,000, a force hardly calculated to make the Kaiser and his generals tremble in their boots. The U.S. Navy actually fell from third in the world to fourth during the first two years of the war. When Wilson, attempting to have a fleet that could support the national interest, announced in early 1916 that the United States would construct a navy second to none, plans were made for a battleship-dominated fleet that would have little impact against submarine warfare, which constituted the real German threat on the high seas.

When America entered the war in April 1917, nine out of ten warships were inadequately manned, two out of three were not materially fit, and the required antisubmarine ships, minelayers, and auxiliaries had not been built. The Naval Air Service and the U.S. Army Signal Corps had only a handful of pilots and a few obsolescent planes. For the army there were 127,588 regulars and 80,446 National Guard officers and men, a total of 208,034. These soldiers had no tanks or gas masks, little ammunition, and few artillery pieces and machine guns. Staff work at all levels was inadequate for any conflict involving masses of men and supplies. The new army general staff, created in 1903, whose chief of staff was expected in theory to the be principal military adviser to the president, was undermanned and had neither the inclination nor the vision to give doctrinal or strategic leadership to involvement in a great war raging some three thousand miles on the other side of the Atlantic. The U.S. Army, according to Robert H. Ferrell, "was a home for old soldiers, a quiet, sleepy place where they killed time until they began drawing their pensions."

Given the magnitude of the military task before it, the U.S. Army, essentially a nineteenth-century force, was less prepared to fight than during the War of 1812 or even the Revolutionary War. The hollow and misdirected "preparedness" campaign and Wilson's separation of political from military policy made it impossible for the United States to play an immediate part in the war. It is tempting to play the game of "what if" with John J. Pershing, who was chosen to command the American Expeditionary Force (AEF). Pershing writes in his memoirs: "Let us suppose that, instead of adhering to the erroneous theory that neutrality forbade any move toward preparation, we had taken the precaution in the Spring of 1916 to organize and equip an army of half a million combatant troops, together with the requisite number of supply troops for such a force." Pershing's point is that if such a force had existed, the United States could have ended the war a year earlier. Perhaps, but given the prevailing antiwar and isolationist sentiment of the time, the creation of an expeditionary force of some twenty combat divisions was simply not possible.

Once the United States was forced into the war in April 1917 by Germany's return to unrestricted submarine warfare, President Wilson demonstrated leadership through his vigorous support for the draft (or selective service, as it was called). Before the war ended, no fewer than 24,234,021 Americans had registered for the draft. As for women, they also served with the AEF as telephone operators and nurses. The U.S. Navy enlisted 11,000 women during the war, and other women served overseas in such volunteer organizations as the YMCA.

With the United States so unprepared, it is not surprising that there was no initial consensus for participation in the land war in Europe. "Good Lord! You're not going to send soldiers over there, are you?" one startled senator exclaimed to a general staff officer at a senate hearing. President Wilson, however, quickly concluded that American forces could most effectively support national goals by fighting in France.

The enormity of the task ahead for American arms was not underestimated by knowledgeable U.S. and European military leaders. The British Army in 1914 had been both modern and antique: a small, all-volunteer force, or a "contemptible little army," as the Kaiser is said to have referred to it. After two years, the British had raised and trained a mass citizen army capable of engaging the Imperial German Army on equal terms. Equipping and supplying such a mass force created another set of problems. Despite the colossal arms race during the prewar years, none of the combatant nations in 1914 had the big guns and ammunition to fight a long war. Every country soon had serious munitions shortages. It took time, trial, and error before peacetime economies could be mobilized. The practical chief of the British imperial general staff, General Sir William Robertson,

who along with Lord Kitchener, the secretary of state for war, was responsible for creating and supplying the largest British force ever employed, recognized how unprepared the Americans were. Shortly before the United
States entered the war, he wrote to a fellow officer: "I do not think that it
will make much difference whether America comes in or not. What we
want to do is to beat the German Armies; until we do that we shall not win
the war. America will not help us much in that respect." The U.S. Army
general staff did not really disagree with Robertson's pessimistic assessment. Although it planned to have a force of some 500,000 men in France
by 1918, it argued that America could not play a decisive role in Germany's
defeat until 1919.

With the United States apparently months, even years, away from
engaging Germany on the Western Front, the French and British initially
asked the Wilson administration to send over raw draftees to be trained,
equipped, and utilized by the French and British armies. An added benefit
to the Allies would be that their essential transatlantic flow of war supplies
from America would not be interrupted by the inevitable demands from
Washington for building a large army from scratch. This Allied request for
manpower to serve as cannon fodder was the first of many that threatened
to delay or prevent the creation of an independent American army.

Pershing became his country's strongest and most effective advocate
of an independent American army. He was every inch a soldier. Although
he stood only five feet nine inches tall, he had such a formidable presence
that many thought he was above six feet. He had been nicknamed Black
Jack, a reference to his once having led black troops, by his students at West
Point, who resented his aloof and strict nature. His previous combat experience included skirmishes with Indians, the attack on San Juan Hill in
Cuba in the Spanish-American War (where he won a commendation for
gallantry), pacification of the Moros in the Philippines, and command of
the so-called Punitive Expedition that pursued the bandit Pancho Villa into
Mexico. He also had seen the ability of entrenched defenders to inflict horrendous casualties on assaulting forces with rapid-fire weapons in 1905
when he served as an American military observer attached to the Japanese
Army in Manchuria during the Russo-Japanese War.

President Wilson and Secretary of War Newton D. Baker conferred
upon Pershing more authority and responsibility than any American general had previously been given. Pershing decided when and how America's
land forces in Europe were to be used, and he had the authority of the

president behind him when he discussed questions with Allied prime min-
isters that had political as well as military ramifications. He also was independent of the army general staff in the War Department, which worked
with Baker to mobilize the country. Before America entered the war,
Wilson had ignored the soldiers. Now, he gave one of them virtual control
over the national contribution to the war effort in Europe. Wilson's sharp
distinction between civil and military responsibilities meant that he was
rejecting what many Allied politicians now believed: war was too serious
a business to be left to the generals.

In late June 1917, advance elements of the First Division, the Big Red
One, arrived in France. The U.S. Navy was already present on the maritime
front. One week after entering the war, the Wilson administration decided
to send a flotilla of six destroyers to the war zone. During the next months
America's naval commitment grew in a cooperative effort with Britain's
Royal Navy. Before the war ended, sixty-eight destroyers were serving in
European waters, and five battleships, commanded by Rear Admiral Hugh
Rodman, formed the Sixth Battle Squadron. The United States also played
the dominant role in erecting a vast mine barrier from Scotland across the
North Sea to Norwegian waters, the North Sea Mine Barrage, to limit the
effectiveness of German submarines.

Pershing and the nucleus of his staff preceded American units to
Europe. The AEF planners had much to accomplish before their troops
engaged the enemy. Anglo-French strategical priorities (the French were
determined to defend Paris, and the British, the Channel ports) and logistical considerations helped determine the placement of any future
American army on the Western Front. The first U.S. troops were billeted
in the French zone in the rear of the Lorraine sector on the southeastern
end of the Western Front, which eventually terminated at the Swiss frontier. The prospect of important strategic objectives also made the Lorraine
sector attractive to Pershing and his staff.

Although an independent army seemed in the distant future, the AEF
leaders from the beginning assigned American arms a decisive role in the
conflict. They developed an ambitious plan for capturing the fortress city of
Metz in 1919. If the German railway lines running laterally to the south
of the Ardennes Forest and north of the Vosges Mountains were cut, then
the AEF planners expected the Germans to be forced back beyond the
Rhine. The American plan also envisaged the crippling of German industry through the seizure of the coal and iron mines of the Saar. A prelude

to the Metz offensive would be the reduction in 1918 of the pronounced St. Mihiel salient, situated southwest of Metz, which posed a threat to any American advance on that city.

As opposed to previous Allied offensives that expended men and metal for little more than the wearing down of the enemy and the occupation of a few miles of bloodstained territory, Pershing and his staff were confident that their 1919 offensive would defeat Germany. Initially they thought in terms of a force of five American corps of thirty divisions, commanded by a major general, consisting of four regiments of infantry, three regiments of artillery, fourteen machine-gun companies, an engineer regiment, a signal battalion, a troop of cavalry, and other auxiliary units. These oversized divisions of some 28,000 men were twice the size of their European counterparts. Before the war ended, Pershing increased dramatically his manpower needs to one hundred divisions, an unrealistic request that would have made the AEF larger than the combined Allied forces on the Western Front.

Russell Weigley, in *The American Way of War*, argues that Pershing's strategy of annihilation was consistent with the prevailing view of the American military, who sought total victory as opposed to the more limited and indirect strategy of attrition that usually does not seek the destruction of the enemy. "The Civil War," Weigley writes, "tended to fix the American image of war from the 1860s into America's rise to world power at the turn of the century, and it also suggested that the complete overthrow of the enemy, the destruction of his military power, is the object of war."

In truth Pershing's offensive plan was probably as illusionary as the previous plans of French and British generals to end the war. German defenses around Metz were some of the strongest on the Western Front. Moreover, the lateral railway ran well beyond rather than through Metz as the American planners believed, and German industry got only about 10 percent of its coal and iron from the Saar.

Pershing planned a prolonged offensive with distant objectives at precisely the time when many Allied political and military leaders had lost faith in the cult of the offensive and believed in limited assaults with limited objectives to reduce their casualties and inflict heavy losses on the defender—in short, a strategy of attrition. The primary reason for American optimism was the widely held assumption at Pershing's general headquarters of U.S. superiority in fighting men and tactics. "The fact is,"

Pershing informed Secretary of War Baker, "that our officers and men are far and away superior to the tired Europeans." Following the American triumph at St. Mihiel, a confident Pershing told his intelligence officer, Brigadier General Dennis Nolan: "The reason for the American triumph lay in the superior nature of the American character. Americans were the product of immigrants who had possessed the initiative and courage to leave the Old World . . . to make a mighty nation out of a wilderness. Americans had the willpower and spirit that Europeans lacked." When asked by a reporter at a press conference in the fall of 1917 if he thought a breakthrough possible after three years of stalemate, Pershing confidently asserted: "Of course, the western front can be broken. What are we here for?" To be blunt, Pershing believed that the Americans had almost nothing to learn from French and British officers who, during the previous three years, had paid dearly in blood for their knowledge of siege warfare and the lethality of the new military technology.

An important consideration for Pershing was that he fervently wanted his country to play the leading role in Germany's defeat. American subordination to either Allied strategy or tactics might diminish the AEF's military role. With some justification Pershing also thought that the Anglo-French forces were nearing exhaustion and had lost their offensive spirit.

Pershing's answer to breaking the stalemate was the aggressive American rifleman, whose tradition of marksmanship and frontier warfare he believed made him a natural for "open" warfare or a war of movement as opposed to trench warfare. Doctrinally, however, Pershing's methods had little chance of success on a battlefield dominated by automatic weapons and artillery. He expected scouts to lead the advance and pinpoint the enemy's position. Massed and accurate infantry rifle fire would then be organized to suppress the enemy defenders until other infantrymen got close enough to attack with the bayonet.

There is probably another, more complex reason for Pershing's controversial tactics. As was the case with many of his military contemporaries, he had difficulty reconciling his deep-rooted traditional values with the industrialization of warfare. He recognized that the new military technology, especially the rapid-fire weapons, had changed the nature of warfare. But in important ways, his prewar image of battle was not altered by these new conditions. To him the valiant soldier and his trusty rifle, not the adaptation of the new weaponry to siege warfare, were paramount to success. As he once explained: "Close adherence is urged to the central idea that essential principles of war have not changed, that the rifle and the bayonet remain the supreme weapons of the infantry soldier and that the ultimate success of the army depends upon their proper use in open warfare."

Many of Pershing's subordinates were more flexible and innovative. Nonetheless, the AEF's official doctrine never deviated in its reliance upon the rifleman in open warfare. General Sir Henry Rawlinson, the commander of the British Fourth Army in 1918, admired greatly the physical and fighting qualities of the Americans attached to his forces, but he could not say the same for their staff work and tactical doctrine. "Staff work is shocking," he reported to the War Office in May 1918. "They can't move or feed themselves and they know nothing even of the rudiments of tactics. Pershing's 'Schedule of Training' is shocking. Nothing in it."

Rawlinson's critical comments unfortunately were not far off the mark. Frequently the U.S. infantry followed a rigid plan of attack, made poor use of fire and maneuver, and, except for self-timed barrages by the artillery and machine guns, did not get adequate help from the supporting arms. In Pershing's defense, it should be noted that the AEF's tactical mistakes had been made many times over by European commanders. The tragedy is that some of these mistakes might have been avoided if there had been a readiness on the part of AEF planners to learn from the experiences of the French and the British. As French Premier Georges Clemenceau remarked, "If the Americans do not permit the French to teach them, the Germans will do so." On the other hand, intense rivalry between national armies is commonplace, especially at the command level, and it is perhaps asking too much to expect the Americans to be any less nationalistic or parochial than their European comrades in arms.

Whatever the merits of Pershing's strategy and tactics, his grandiose plan to capture Metz and win the war profoundly shaped the AEF's participation in the anti-German coalition. Its granite-willed commander was determined that nothing would stand in the way of the creation of an independent American army and the husbanding of the necessary resources for the reduction of the St. Mihiel salient in 1918 and the capture of Metz in 1919. It is little exaggeration to say that he was prepared to accept the British being driven into the sea and a Germany victory parade in Paris under the Arc de Triomphe before he allowed the Allies to thwart his plans.

The course of the war during 1917 put Pershing's ambitious plans in considerable jeopardy. The failure of the French offensive in April resulted in a widespread mutiny in the French Army. Subsequently, the massive British operations in Flanders during the summer and fall, Passchendaele, or the third battle of Ypres, floundered in rain and mud. A surprise Austro-German offensive against Italy in October almost drove the Italians from the war. Only reinforcements from the depleted Anglo-French forces from the Western Front saved the day. On the high seas, unrestricted German submarine warfare took a terrible toll on Allied shipping. On the Eastern Front, revolution in Russia eventually took that country out of the war. As 1917 came to an end, the Allies had reason to fear that Germany might win in 1918. The first of some one million German troops from the moribund Eastern Front began arriving on the Western Front. These reinforcements eventually gave Berlin a numerical advantage on that front for the first time since 1914.

Faced with a critical manpower shortage, Allied requests for soldiers took on a desperate note at the beginning of 1918. Although the United States had been in the war for nine months, only one of its divisions, the First Division, defended a sector of its own. Three other divisions were in various stages of training, and altogether only 175,000 American troops had reached France. The first American battle deaths had occurred on November 3, 1917, when three doughboys in training had been killed during a German trench raid. When an American driver accidentally struck a Parisian, some Frenchmen complained that the Americans were a greater menace than the Germans. An even more unfair comment was that the AEF stood for "After Everything's Finished."

The Allies insisted that the brigading of U.S. combat battalions with French and British divisions, or amalgamation, was the most practical way for Pershing to assist his allies. Anglo-French divisions, corps, and field armies had logistical support and experienced staffs but not the infantry to keep them up to strength. The Allies argued that the fresh American troops would develop faster in veteran divisions under experienced officers. Another advantage was that the serious shipping crisis might be alleviated if the Wilson administration sent combat troops without artillery and without the large number of service troops that would be required if Pershing moved immediately to create an independent army.

This was asking a lot from the political and military leadership of a great nation. Only the clear threat of the imminent collapse of the anti-German coalition could possibly justify such a self-effacing military role by a country that was already the dominant economic power in the world and seemed destined to assume a leading political role in international affairs under the guidance of President Wilson. Wilson's ability to implement his "new diplomacy," in fact, might depend upon his county's military contribution to Germany's defeat.

On March 21, 1918, Germany launched the first of five offensives on the Western Front to win the war before American participation might turn the tide in favor of the Allies. The first onslaught (which would not be surpassed in scale until May 10, 1940, when German armies invaded France, Belgium and the Netherlands) pitted seventy-one of its divisions against twenty-six British divisions. A forty-mile-wide and forty-mile-deep chunk was bitten out of the British front before the German drive lost its momentum in early April. The British, losing almost 70,000 men per week, were faced with a desperate manpower situation. "For God's sake, get your men over!" officials in the War Office told the U.S. military attaché in London.

Under intense pressure Pershing negotiated with the Allies. The resulting compromise was very much in his favor. He continued to resist amalgamation, which would destroy his plan to create an independent army in 1918. Backed by his president, he would agree only to attach U.S. divisions to the British and French armies while they underwent further training. In return he got two important concessions. First, the British diverted scarce shipping tonnage to transport American troops, which dramatically increased the flow of U.S. divisions across the Atlantic. The 306,000 Americans who came across in July almost equaled the number of troops that Pershing had commanded at the end of March. A German prisoner of war, observing the steady stream of soldiers arriving by ship at Le Havre, exclaimed, "Mein Gott im Himmel!" and tears filled his eyes. Second, the Allies accepted in principle Pershing's goal of an independent American army with its own sector. As soon as this army became a reality, Pershing planned to reclaim most of his divisions then training in quiet Allied sectors.

Before the Germans were put on the defensive in July 1918 at the Second Battle of the Marne, there were going to be many anxious moments for the Allies. Pershing believed that the French and British would bend but not break under the weight of the five German offensives that occurred at the rate of one per month. And he was right—but it was a close call. His conserving of his undertrained but rapidly expanding forces, slightly more than half of which were brought over in British-owned or British-controlled ships, put the anti-German coalition in peril.

Western Front, March 20–November 11, 1918 (U.S. Army Center of Military History)

The AEF finally went on the offensive on May 28 when the dough-boys captured the village of Cantigny. Prior to this attack, the United States had been at war for a little over a year and had suffered only 163 combat deaths. At Cantigny, Pershing utilized the Twenty-eighth Infantry Regiment, First Division. As H-hour approached on May 28, members of the Twenty-eighth listened to a massive bombardment of German defenses. Each soldier was equipped with 220 rounds, two hand grenades, and one rifle grenade. He also carried two water canteens, chewing gum, and emergency rations. His only American-made weapons were his rifle and bayonet. During the advance into Cantingy the Twenty-eighth encountered only light resistance and had only fifty casualties. In repulsing vigorous German counterattacks, however, the Americans suffered 1,000 casualties.

During the next two months, American forces, predominantly under French command, gradually increased their role. At Belleau Wood and Chateau-Thierry in June, the Americans fought with reckless abandon. At Belleau Wood on June 6, Sergeant Dan Daly of the Marine Brigade of the Second Division issued these much quoted words: "Come on, you sons of bitches," he shouted. "Do you want to live forever?" (The resulting 1,087 casualties made this the most costly day in U.S. Marine Corps history until Tarawa some twenty-five years later.)

After the final German offensive ground to a halt in July, the Americans supported the French counteroffensive. During the Battle of Soissons, July 18–22, the soldiers and marines who participated were as eager for battle as they were unprepared. Douglas V. Johnson II and Rolfe L. Hillman Jr. have described their lack of readiness as follows: "partly trained, dubiously led, questionably administered and managed, reasonably well equipped thanks to the Allies, and operating under a mixture of doctrines understood by only a few." Losses were heavy: more than 12,000 casualties. As July came to an end, no American army yet existed, but nine U.S. divisions had been engaged with the French and two with the British.

This limited and subordinate role dramatically changed from August onward. Created by Pershing's orders of July 24, the First Army, AEF, became operational on August 10. Pershing now had his independent field army, but coalition warfare began to interfere with his determination to launch an offensive in the direction of Metz. Generalissimo Ferdinand Foch, the Allied supreme commander, insisted that Pershing shift his attention north toward Mézières and Sedan to assist a series of converging

Allied attacks along the length of the front from the Meuse River to the sea. Pershing, anxious to reduce the St. Mihiel salient in 1918 as a prelude to his win-the-war offensive against Metz in 1919, strenuously objected. He made a counterproposal, accepted by Foch, that unhappily stretched the capabilities of the inexperienced American army to the breaking point. Pershing proposed to eliminate the St. Mihiel salient to the east and then launch an even greater offensive within weeks to the north between the Meuse and the Argonne Forest. This plan constituted a logistical nightmare for even the most experienced command and staff.

During this period American forces remained almost totally dependent upon the British and the French for their tanks, planes, machine guns, heavy artillery, trench mortars, and flamethrowers. This was partly due to the decision to ship men rather than equipment across the Atlantic, but it was also a result of breakdowns in mobilizing the home industry for war. American factories, for example, produced only 26 tanks before the war's end, although 23,000 had been ordered. Aircraft production has been called "the outstanding industrial fiasco of America's part in the World War." None of the 3,010 guns, 267 tanks, and 1,500 aircraft available to Pershing for his St. Mihiel offensive was of American manufacture.

On September 12, Pershing positioned 216,000 Americans and 48,000 Frenchmen on the St. Mihiel salient, which was approximately twenty-five miles across and sixteen miles deep. At precisely 0100 hours the ground shook and the sky lit up as the preliminary bombardment began. One doughboy compared the sound "to what one hears beneath a wooden bridge when a heavy vehicle passes overhead." At 0500 hours the artillerymen, nearly half of whom were French, shifted to a creeping barrage intended to blast a path through German barbed wire and trenches for the advancing tanks and infantry. The timing of the American offensive could not have been more fortuitous. The AEF attacked just as the Germans began a planned withdrawal. Except for local operations that continued until the sixteenth, the Battle of St. Mihiel was over in approximately thirty hours. Two hundred square miles of French territory were liberated, with 450 guns and 16,000 prisoners captured. The AEF suffered 7,000 casualties, an extremely modest figure by the standards of the Western Front.

Some have characterized this American success as "the stroll at St. Mihiel" or the "sector where the Americans relieved the Germans." This is hardly fair. Pershing's forces had come a long way from their regiment-sized attack against Cantigny in May. A successful major offensive had been launched, and the weak German resistance could not detract from its success.

The next phase of American operations, the Meuse-Argonne campaign, proved far more difficult. The U.S. military was about to fight its largest battle in its history with many green troops and divisional staffs, and with corps and army staffs that had fought independently of the Allies only in the abbreviated Battle of St. Mihiel. The rugged terrain of woods, steep hills, and ravines over which the Americans had to advance gave every natural defensive advantage to the Germans, who had constructed a sophisticated network of fortifications that included pillboxes and miles of barbed wire.

On September 26, only two weeks after St. Mihiel, the AEF launched a new and more powerful offensive. Pershing hoped to advance ten miles on the first day. During forty-seven days of continuous fighting at Meuse-Argonne, however, the AEF advanced only thirty-four miles, the most rapid advance coming in the last eleven days of the war when Germany had exhausted its reserves. During the battle, twenty-two of the AEF's twenty-nine combat divisions were sent into action. Opposing them was perhaps one-fourth of the German division strength on the Western Front. Casualties were high. Over 25,000 Americans died in combat, and nearly 100,000 were wounded. Because of this heavy fighting at Meuse-Argonne, most of America's battle deaths came during the last six weeks of the war.

Among those who died for their country were black soldiers who found themselves waging war against both Germans and Jim Crow. In all, about 200,000 African Americans served in the armed forces; two black divisions, the Ninety-second and the Ninety-third, fought on the Western Front. Most blacks in France were commanded by white officers and given shovels rather than rifles. (None was awarded the Congressional Medal of Honor. An attempt to correct this injustice was made in 1991 when President George H. W. Bush awarded the medal posthumously to Corporal Freddie Stowers, a farm worker from South Carolina, who was mortally wounded while assaulting a German machine-gun position on September 28, 1919.)

Almost as soon as the guns were silenced by the Armistice of November 11, 1918, a war of words began that continues to the present day over the conduct of the war and America's contributions to victory. Pershing's tactical doctrine and his dominant influence on the U.S. role in the land war have been subjected to especially critical analysis by modern scholarship.

Pershing's emphasis on rifle training and open warfare is an especially controversial subject. The commander of the AEF remained unrepentant. "Ultimately, we had the satisfaction of hearing the French admit that we were right, both in emphasizing training for open warfare and insisting upon proficiency in the use of the rifle," Pershing wrote in his memoirs. One of his research assistants, however, could find no such admission by any of the French war leaders. Pershing's tactical solution to trench warfare that emphasized the rifle was dated by dramatic advances in weaponry, especially in automatic weapons and improved artillery. It is also debatable that the AEF ever truly engaged in open warfare. At Meuse-Argonne, the American advance was slow and costly against the rugged German defenses until the breakthrough came on November 1. During the next ten days the AEF advanced further than it had during all of October. German reserves had been exhausted through attrition; there were no reserve divisions to bring up to stop the American advance.

Pershing consistently pursued his government's objectives, even to the point of placing the anti-German coalition at risk from March to July 1918. Throughout American participation, his strategy was shaped by a determination to launch a war-winning offensive on the Lorraine front in the direction of Metz. He took a hard-line position on reinforcing the depleted Anglo-French forces through amalgamation because it threatened the rapid creation of an independent American field army. The constraints of coalition warfare did force him to fight the Meuse-Argonne campaign to assist the broad-front Allied counteroffensive after the Germans had been stopped on the Marne in July. But an independent American campaign that gave the United States the decisive role in defeating Germany was never far from his mind. If Germany had fought on into 1919, he planned to return to his original plan of rupturing German railway communications and capturing Metz and the Saar. By 1919 he was certain that his forces would have the strength, experience, and efficiency to force Berlin to accept unconditional surrender. And he was right. Whatever the flaws in Pershing's strategy—and there were many—Germany, with its allies out of the war and its armies demoralized and depleted, almost certainly would have been forced to accept unconditional surrender in 1919. Germany's defeat by largely American arms and the resulting preeminent position of the AEF might well have given President Wilson the dominant position he desired at the Paris Peace Conference.

The termination of hostilities in November, when a few months earlier most Allied leaders had expected the conflict to continue until 1919 or even 1920, meant that the American contribution did not overshadow Allied accomplishments. Perhaps America's most amazing achievement had been building a great army from scratch. In April 1917, the size of the regular U.S. Army placed it in seventeenth place in the world, tied with Chile, Denmark, and the Netherlands. Nineteen months later Washington had raised an army of some 4,000,000, with one-half of this number operating in the European theater. The AEF represented 31 percent of the forces opposing Germany on the Western Front when the war ended. On the battlefield, however, America's role was arguably no more and probably less than that of the French and the British for all of 1918. AEF casualties during the last year of the war, for example, were roughly one-third of those suffered by the British. (U.S. losses represented about 1 percent of the total casualties suffered by all of the belligerents during the war.) Out of every one hundred artillery shells fired during the last year of the war, the Americans fired six, the British forty-three, and the French fifty-one. During the last five months of the war, with the Germans retreating along the entire Western Front, the British and French recaptured considerably more ground than the AEF. The British for their part took almost four times as many prisoners and twice as many guns. On the other hand, there can be no doubt that America's rapidly growing military presence in Europe raised Allied morale as much as it lowered German hopes of victory. Also, the costly Meuse-Argonne offensive drew off German reserves, making it possible for the British and French to advance against weakened German defenses in the north.

Perhaps the most balanced assessment one can make is that U.S. naval and army forces, as part of the victorious coalition, played an essential role in bringing the Great War to a successful conclusion in 1918. American forces alone did not actually win the war, but they almost certainly kept the Allies from losing or accepting a stalemated peace.

Sources and Suggested Readings

Coffman, Edward M. "The American Military and Strategic Policy in World War I." In *War Aims and Strategic Policy in the Great War, 1914–1918.* Edited by Barry Hunat and Adrian Preston. London, 1977.

———. *The War to End All Wars: The American Military Experience in World War I.* New York, 1968.

DeWeerd, Harvey A. *President Wilson Fights His War: World War I and American Intervention.* New York, 1968.

Eisenhower, John S. D. *Yanks: The Epic Story of the American Army in World War I.* New York, 2001.

Ellis, John. *Eye-Deep in Hell: Trench Warfare in World War I.* New York, 1976.

Ferrell, Robert H. *Woodrow Wilson and World War I, 1917–1921.* New York, 1985.

Finnegan, John Patrick. *Against the Specter of a Dragon: The Campaign for American Military Preparedness, 1914–1918.* Westport, Conn., 1975.

Gilmore, Russell. "'The New Courage': Rifles and Soldier Individualism," *Military Affairs* (October 1976).

Harries, Meirion, and Susie Harries. *The Last Days of Innocence: America at War, 1917–1918.* New York, 1997.

Johnson II, Douglas V., and Rolfe L. Hillman, Jr. *Soissons 1918.* College Station, Tex., 1999.

Kennedy, David M. *Over Here: The First World War and American Society.* New York, 1980.

Mead, Gary. *The Doughboys: America and the First World War.* Woodstock, N.Y., 2000.

Millett, Allan R. "Cantigny, 28–31 May 1918." In *America's First Battles, 1776–1965.* Edited by Charles E. Heller and William A. Stofft. Lawrence, Kans., 1986.

———. "Over Where? The AEF and the American Strategy for Victory, 1917–1918." In *Against All Enemies: Interpretations of the American Military from Colonial Times to the Present.* Edited by Allan Millett and Williamson Murray. Westport, Conn., 1988.

Nenninger, Timothy K. "American Military Effectiveness in the First World War." In *Military Effectiveness*, vol. 1, *The First World War.* Edited by Allan Millett and Williamson Murray. Boston, 1988.

———. "Tactical Dysfunction in the AEF, 1917–1918." *Military Affairs* (October 1987).

Pershing, John J. *My Experiences in the World War.* 2 vols. New York, 1931.

Smythe, Donald. *Pershing: General of the Armies.* Bloomington, Ind., 1986.

Stallings, Laurence. *The Doughboys: The Story of the A.E.F., 1917–1918.* New York, 1963.

Trask, David F. *The United States in the Supreme War Council: American War Aims and Inter-Allies Strategy, 1917–1918.* Middleton, Conn., 1961.

U.S. Department of the Army. Office of Military History. *United States Army in the World War, 1917–1918.* 17 vols. Washington, D.C., 1948.

Weigley, Russell F. *The American Way of War: A History of United States Military Strategy and Policy.* New York, 1973.

Woodward, David R. "The American Military Experience in World War I." In *Encyclopedia of the American Military*, vol. 2. Edited by J. E. Jessup. New York, 1994.

────. "'Black Jack' Pershing: American Proconsul in Europe." In *First World War: Personalities in Conflict*. Edited by Matthew Hughes and Matthew Seligmann. London, 2000.

────. "Military and Diplomatic Course of World War I." In *The Oxford Companion to American Military History*. Edited by John Whiteclay Chambers. New York, 1999.

────. *Trial by Friendship: Anglo-American Relations 1917–1918*. Lexington, Ky., 1993.

Woodward, David R., and Robert Franklin Maddox, eds. *America and World War I: A Selected Annotated Bibliography of English-Language Sources*. New York, 1985.

Website

World War I: Trenches on the Web. www. worldwar1.com/.

Films

All Quiet on the Western Front (Louis Milestone), U.S., 1930.
The Big Parade (King Vidor), U.S., 1925.
The Dawn Patrol (Howard Hawks), U.S., 1925.
Sergeant York (Howard Hawks), U.S., 1941.
What Price Glory (Raoul Walsh), U.S., 1926.

The United States, World War II, and the Grand Alliance

COLIN F. BAXTER

I N THE AFTERMATH of World War I, much of the world's population, including many military leaders and strategists, were appalled by the terrible carnage of 1914–1918. As the exuberance of victory and the ignominy of defeat faded into memory, many citizens were determined that another conflict of this magnitude and destruction must be avoided at all costs. In several nations, peace organizations sprang up in response to the public revulsion against the recent slaughter in Europe. The weight of public opinion ensured that in the United States, as in other countries, military spending would be kept under tight rein by government leaders. Some military experts believed that the stagnation and stalemate of trench warfare and the strategy of attrition that led to the end of the war were unacceptable models for future conflicts. Strategists such as B. H. Liddell Hart and J. F. C. Fuller in Britain, Giulio Douhet in Italy, Heinz Guderian in Germany, Charles de Gaulle in France, and William "Billy" Mitchell in the United States theorized that small, elite mobile forces might return decisiveness to large-scale warfare at a fraction of the casualties of the Great War. The development of air power and motorized weapons, especially tanks, seemed to offer hope for avoiding another costly stalemate in the trenches.

In the United States, most of the American Expeditionary Force of more than 1.2 million was quickly demobilized. The War Department hoped to maintain the regular army at a peacetime strength of 500,000 under a system of universal training, but Congress rejected that proposal as too costly and unnecessary. In addition to pressures from disarmament advocates, many congressmen were impressed by the view that, with Europe relatively weakened by the war, there was little reason to maintain a sizable land force. Under the National Defense Act of 1920, maximum regular army strength was set at 280,000 men, with heavy reliance to be placed on the National Guard in time of war. The act focused on the need for rapid industrial mobilization should a new conflict threaten and also called for the institutionalization of the Reserve Officers' Training Corps (ROTC).

Under the conservative and austerity-oriented Republican administrations of the 1920s, the regular army was maintained at less than one half of the authorized maximum, or at about 130,000 men, with very little funding left over for modernization. With the meager defense budgets, the army spent only small sums on the development of new weapons, mechanization, and air power. Of the funding devoted to these areas, the development of air power was given priority, while the nation fell behind in the areas of motorized capability and tracked vehicles. During the 1920s, General Billy Mitchell, influenced by contemporary European ideas on air power, began a campaign for a separate air service, which he envisioned as the nation's first line of defense in time of war. Mitchell failed to gain approval for his idea, but his campaign was important in focusing public attention on the U.S. Army Air Corps (1926) and in channeling more funds to the air service. By the onset of the Great Depression (1929), however, all elements of America's land forces were in a shabby state of preparedness.

In 1930 the War Department produced its first official Industrial Mobilization Plan (IMP). But because of political controversies associated with the Depression, little was done to implement the IMP until 1938. Despite some efforts by Army Chief of Staff Douglas MacArthur to emphasize modernization during the Depression years, dwindling congressional appropriations proved inadequate to make much progress. After the Second World War broke out in Europe with the German invasion of Poland (1939), President Franklin D. Roosevelt and army leaders began to prepare the nation for possible intervention in the European conflict. In 1940, Congress, with Roosevelt's support, instituted the first peacetime draft in American history. In the following year U.S. military planners adopted a British-backed proposal that held that if the United States entered the war, the defeat of Germany would be Washington's number-one priority.

As the United States drifted toward war in 1941, Colin Baxter emphasizes, many American military experts, impressed by Adolf Hitler's stunning triumphs with the blitzkrieg in Europe, expected that air power and highly mobile mechanized divisions would be crucial in turning the tide of battle in that theater. Despite these projections, Baxter points out that American army commanders, as well as their Soviet counterparts, would find that massive ground forces supported by heavy firepower from conventional artillery and by enormous logistical support behind the lines would be necessary to defeat Germany. Air power and armor were important in the European campaign, but it was large infantry forces with considerable artillery support, similar in many respects to the armies of World War I (except for their increased mobility and use of air power by the 1940s), that ultimately vanquished the Third Reich.

A t dawn on September 1, 1939, the European phase of the greatest war in human history began with Nazi Germany's invasion of Poland. Two days later, Britain and France declared war on Germany. On June 22, 1941, Hitler attacked the Soviet Union and began what Russians simply refer to as The Great Patriotic War. Six months later, on Sunday, December 7, 1941, the Japanese navy attacked the American Pacific Fleet based at Pearl Harbor, Hawaii. Hitler and Mussolini quickly declared war on the United States. After Pearl Harbor and Hitler's declaration of war, the isolationist effort to keep the United States out of the war ended and the American people united as one to defeat the new barbarism.

Although the defeat of Germany, Japan, and Italy would require the combined efforts of the *then* British Empire, the *then* Soviet Union, and the United States, together with China, the debate continues over who won the war. To historian Gerhard L. Weinberg it is clear that "the majority of the fighting of the whole war took place on the Eastern Front: more people fought and died there than on all the other fronts of the war around the globe put together."[1] Few would deny that Russia bore the brunt of the ground combat after 1941, suffering 11 to 13 million soldiers killed and even more civilian deaths.

American and British casualties were far less, but Russian survival in no small degree depended on the contributions of the Western powers in the common cause against Hitler's Third Reich. The U.S. mobilized only

12 percent of its population for the military, but it provided two-thirds of the Allied munitions. More than 200,000 Americans died in the European theater, and another 200,000 died in the Pacific war. Britain lost over 300,000, and 60,000 civilians through bombing; Canada lost 35,000, India 32,000, Australia 19,000, New Zealand 11,000, South Africa 8,000, and other British colonies 20,000. French combat deaths were 250,000. Italian losses were about 200,000. Approximately 4 million Germans were killed, including 500,000 civilians. World War II claimed an average of 27,600 lives every day.

What had begun as an almost old-fashioned war of unprovoked German aggression against Poland was transformed to a total war, a war that would be characterized to an unprecedented degree by racial and ideological brutality and fanaticism. Adolf Hitler, the leader of Germany since 1933, had two objectives: "solve the Jewish problem (safeguard the racial purity of Germans)" and expansion in eastern Europe to secure "living space" for German peoples. The twisted and perverted idea of a struggle for survival among races and nations found its ultimate practitioner in Adolf Hitler, who eventually carried out the genocidal murder (the Holocaust) of six million Jews.

Blitzkrieg, or "lightning war," was a word unknown before the German defeat of Poland in one month. Western reporters described the speed and destructiveness of the one-month Polish campaign as a new type of warfare, a blitzkrieg, involving tanks and "Stuka" dive-bombers. In practice, the German army had not yet fully evolved or embraced the concept of blitzkrieg: only *six* of the fifty-five German divisions that defeated Poland were armored or panzer divisions. The bulk of the German army, in 1939, as in 1914, marched on foot, with supply and artillery pulled by horses. At the same time, the Poles did not have even one armored division. More importantly, the Germans had more men, far superior equipment, and 2,000 aircraft against Poland's 350 planes. Warsaw, Poland's capital, was encircled by September 17 and terror-bombed into unconditional surrender. "Take a good look around Warsaw, "Hitler told journalists, "That is how I can deal with any European city."[2] That same day Soviet troops advanced into Poland. Under the terms of the Nazi-Soviet pact of August 23, 1939, Poland was about to be partitioned between Hitler and Stalin (the Baltic countries of Estonia, Latvia, and Lithuania were annexed by Marshal Joseph Stalin to the Soviet Union in 1940). Poland would now be at the mercy of new systems of terror—the Nazis motivated by race and the Soviets by class ideology.

Within four weeks of September 1, over 100,000 Polish soldiers, and 25,000 civilians, had been killed. Thousands of Poles did escape and fought on every front until 1945. Thanks also to the Poles and French, British code-breakers at Bletchley Park, northwest of London, were ultimately able to decipher radio messages sent on the Enigma machine used by the German military. Amazingly, the *Ultra* secret, the intelligence derived from Enigma, and whose possession by the Allies shortened the war, was not revealed until thirty years after the end of World War II.

From the first day of the Polish campaign, Hitler had made it clear to his military leaders that crushing the Polish people, not simply defeating the Polish army, was Nazi Germany's aim. Hitler demanded the liquidation of the ruling and intellectual leaders of Poland. The ordinary Poles would remain as cheap slaves. It was during the invasion of Poland that the *Einsatzgruppen* (special action groups) gained experience in the practice of mass murder.

During the winter of 1939–1940, the French and British military staffs decided to stay put on the defensive. France placed its faith in the Maginot Line, their answer to the futility of World War I infantry attacks. As far as the Maginot fortifications existed—87 miles—they provided protection, but that left 250 miles of completely unfortified frontier. The French troops in the Maginot Line, which included Indo-Chinese and Madagascan machine gunners, became prisoners of their positions and unavailable to act as a mobile reserve.

As an uneasy calm settled over western Europe, American correspondents labeled it the "Phoney War." The British expected to wear down the German economy by naval blockade and bombing before delivering the final coup de grâce on a weakened and demoralized enemy. Conventional military wisdom assumed that heavy artillery and the machine gun still dominated the battlefield as they had done in the last war. These notions would soon be proven to be outdated in the coming storm.

Would blitzkrieg warfare win in the west? The answer came with stunning suddenness in April 1940. Hitler launched surprise attacks on the two neutral Scandinavian countries of Denmark and Norway. Threatened with the bombing of Copenhagen, Denmark surrendered in a day. After recovering from the surprise German attack, the Norwegians, with the assistance of British, French, and Polish troops, bitterly resisted the invasion. Though the Germans won on land and in the air, they suffered a severe reverse at sea, losing ten destroyers—half of that type—to the British navy.

Early in the morning of May 10, 1940, the German blitzkrieg in the west began with the invasion of the Netherlands and Belgium. To hasten a Dutch surrender, the Luftwaffe wiped out the center of Rotterdam, killing almost a thousand civilians. In Belgium, eighty glider-borne German paratroopers landed directly on top of the supposedly impregnable fortress of Eban Emael, the key to Belgium, and captured the fort in twenty-eight hours, just in time to greet German troops marching west.

The German plan for victory depended upon making the Allies think it was the Schlieffen Plan of 1914 all over again. The Allies in fact did take for granted that a German attack in the west would again come through neutral territory and so bypass French fortifications, including the famed Maginot Line. Although the original German war plan *did* call for just such a repeat of 1914, the plan had pleased no one, including Hitler. The final plan of attack was risky but brilliant: it called for the main German thrust to be struck to the south rather than the north, through the heavily wooded terrain of the Ardennes. Fortunately for the Germans, they achieved complete tactical surprise—both the date of the attack and the point of their main blow were unexpected—and the Allies played completely into their hands.

On May 10, while the best of the French army and the highly mobile British army (containing *not one* armored division, however) rushed into Belgium to assume their defensive positions, the German hammer blow fell precisely on the weakest spot along the Allied front, the heavily wooded terrain of the Ardennes, an area defended by the lowest category of reservists. It was no accident that the Germans attacked this weak spot, the linchpin of the Allied line. The Germans had successfully decoded French signals and knew of Allied intentions, strength, and troop dispositions. A spearhead of ten panzer divisions—only 7 percent of the attacking German force—drove rapidly to the Meuse River, and after a successful two-day struggle, which panzer leader General Heinz Guderian called "almost a miracle," German tanks crossed the Meuse on May 13. The margin of German success had been slim, but the speed of the penetration and breakthrough were decisive as the panzer divisions drove rapidly to the Channel coast, threatening to cut the supply lines of the Allied armies in Belgium. Covering 135 miles in a week, German tanks reached the Channel on May 20. The slower-moving marching infantry, dependent on horse-drawn transport, followed. The unimaginable had happened and the German blitzkrieg had defeated France in a mere *six weeks*! Miraculously,

338,000 British and French troops were evacuated off the beaches of Dunkirk back to Britain. Many writers have claimed that the German panzer divisions were halted short of Dunkirk because Hitler wanted peace with Britain. This was most definitely *not* the case. The panzers were halted because Hermann Goering's Luftwaffe was expected to wipe out the British army on the Dunkirk beaches. The decision was a military mistake, and the Germans were now faced with the annoying fact that the English Channel served as a huge antitank ditch.

Another myth concerning 1940 is the view that France was defeated by overwhelming German superiority, both numerically and qualitatively. It was neither: the two sides were roughly equal in strength—about ninety divisions each—and in tanks, the French outnumbered the Germans, 3,000 to 2,400. The key difference was in tactical doctrine: German blitzkrieg consisted of panzer (armored) divisions and combined-arms warfare. The often superior French tanks were scattered piecemeal among their slow-moving infantry divisions. Combined with good, tactical ground support from the German air force, and an effective system of radio communication, the Wehrmacht had caught the best-equipped French troops in the wrong place at the wrong time. With at least 2,000 modern aircraft, including the Messerschmitt 109 fighter, the Junker 87 ground-attack "Stuka" dive-bomber, and Heinkel and Dornier medium bombers, Germany did have air superiority over the battlefield.

Would France remain in the war? Marshal Henri Pétain, the famed defender of Verdun in the first war and the new leader of France, quickly accepted defeat, signed an armistice with the victorious Germans, and declared that the French government would not go overseas to continue the fight from its empire. Having achieved one of the great military victories in history, the Germans imagined that they had won the war. Would Britain fight on alone or follow the example of Vichy France?

The answer came from Prime Minister Winston Churchill, whose speeches and radio broadcasts breathed a spirit of defiance: "I have nothing to offer but blood, toil, tears, and sweat. . . . We shall fight on the beaches, we shall fight on the landing grounds, we shall fight in the fields and in the streets, we shall fight in the hills; we shall never surrender. . . ." After the Nazis' stunning victory in France, Hitler imagined that he had won the war and that an isolated Britain would make peace. Hitler wasted weeks waiting for British peace feelers that never arrived. Churchill's advice to his people should they be invaded was "you can always take one with you." In the back of Churchill's mind lay the twin hopes of a break between Hitler and Stalin, and intervention from the New World.

By July, Hitler ordered plans for the invasion of Britain, and in the summer of 1940 occurred the Battle of Britain in which Spitfires and Hurricanes fought life-and-death battles thousands of feet high against the Luftwaffe. By mid-September, the Battle of Britain was over. The Royal Air Force had lost 792 aircraft (and 507 pilots); the German air force, 1,389 aircraft and 6,000 aircrew. Churchill, in Britain's and his own finest hour, paid a well-deserved tribute to the RAF: "Never in the field of human conflict was so much owed by so many to so few."

The fall of France and the Battle of Britain did not bring about American intervention into the war, but President Franklin D. Roosevelt did abandon any semblance of strict neutrality, and against isolationist opposition Congress passed the Lend-Lease Act in March 1941, which made the United States the "Arsenal of Democracy." Those who fought against Nazi Germany would have free access to American production. Secret American-British strategic talks took place in Washington in March 1941, producing document ABC-1, which declared that in case of war with Japan and Germany, they would pursue a "Germany first" strategy. By late 1941, although most Americans favored "all aid short of war" to the Allies, the desire to avoid war remained uppermost in the public mind.

Leaving the defeat of Britain to U-boats and bombers, Hitler turned to what he considered to be his life's mission, more living space for the German people in the east and a solution to the "Jewish question." The attack on the Soviet Union, Operation *Barbarossa*, was to be not only a war against the "subhuman Slavic peoples," but a crusade against the "Jewish-Bolshevik" menace, a fantasy that existed only in Hitler's demented mind. In Hitler's *rassenkampf*, or race war, in the east, international law ceased to exist as the Wehrmacht violated all the laws of war. Hitler and many of his generals shared the conviction that the Soviet Union was a "rotten structure" that would come "crashing down" like a house of cards under the impact of a German blitzkrieg attack, an expectation that nearly succeeded thanks in part to Stalin's blind refusal to give any credence to reliable warnings from the west and his own sources that a German invasion was imminent. He dismissed the warnings as a mere western ploy to involve him in the war. Stalin continued to ship massive amounts of raw materials *to* Germany until a few hours before the German invasion of Russia on June 22, 1941.

Hitler and his generals expected another quick and easy victory, six months at the most. After that, they could prepare to deal with Britain and the United States. What would have been the most spectacular victory in history seemed to be tantalizingly close in the first weeks of Operation *Barbarossa*. Three million German troops, supported by 3,300 tanks and 2,000 aircraft, destroyed 3,500 tanks and over 6,000 aircraft and killed or captured some two million men. German mobile panzer divisions cut through and encircled entire Russian armies, trapping them in a *kessel* or cauldron. Ominously, however, the German blitzkrieg continued to depend heavily on 600,000 horses to tow artillery, ambulances, and supply wagons.

Panzer leader General Heinz Guderian wanted to continue the spectacular advance east and capture Moscow, assuming there would a single decisive battle for its defense. Since 1945, Hitler has been blamed for reversing Guderian's advance so as to seize the food supplies of the Ukraine and the Caucasian oilfields. If the Russian war could not be won in 1941, Hitler's decision was probably correct, but his actions violated blitzkrieg doctrine, which called first for defeat of the enemy's armed forces. As it was, the German armies scored one of the greatest victories of the war when they trapped five Russian armies, 665,000 men, in the Kiev pocket. Too late, the advance on Moscow resumed in October when "General Winter" arrived with a vengeance as temperatures fell to minus twenty-five degrees centigrade. German tank engines froze solid. Frostbite cases topped 100,000 by Christmas. German hopes that the weather would make a Red Army attack impossible were shattered on December 5, when salvos of *Katyusha* rockets, fired from multiple launchers, opened the Soviet counteroffensive. Eight Soviet divisions from Siberia, wearing padded jackets and white camouflage suits, supported by 1,700 highly mobile, wide-tracked T-34 tanks (which coped with the snow and ice far better than German tanks) and 1,000 aircraft, pushed the invaders back.

In the German rear, Soviet cavalry divisions, mounted on Cossack ponies, and with sabers drawn, made surprise attacks on enemy artillery batteries and supply depots. With troops in the open exposed to temperatures of minus forty degrees centigrade, German soldiers took clothes and boots from civilians for themselves. Officers complained that their men looked liked Russian peasants. The civilians died of cold and starvation. Earlier, Stalin had ordered that all houses and farms for up to forty miles behind German lines were to be destroyed so as to deny the enemy shelter. He did not consider the fate of Russian civilians for an instant.

In hindsight, it might be argued that the Germans should have gone on the defensive until 1942 instead of renewing the attempt to take Moscow in October. On the other hand, to that point, German successes had been astonishing, having killed or captured at least four million Soviet soldiers since June. With the stakes so high, defeat, even by the narrowest of margins, is unforgiving. The failure of blitzkrieg in Russia, together with America's entry into the war, were pivotal turning points in World War II.

Isolationism and neutrality in the United States had come to an abrupt end on Sunday, December 7, 1941, when the Empire of Japan launched a surprise attack on the U.S. Pacific Fleet moored at Pearl Harbor, Hawaii. Japanese nationalist zealots had decided that the war in Europe presented Japan with a golden opportunity to dominate Asia. Three days after the "day that will live in infamy," Hitler declared war on the United States. The isolationist debate was over as an enraged American public geared up for total war.

Ranking seventeenth in size among the world's armies in 1939, with not one armored division, by the summer of 1941 the United States Army numbered 1,500,000 or thirty-six divisions. Nevertheless, Congress passed the Selective Service Extension Act by only a one-vote margin—less than four months before the attack on Pearl Harbor. There was a continuing public belief that there was no immediate danger. Many recruits carried wooden models of mortars and machine guns and brooms rather than the new M1 Garand semiautomatic rifle. A peacetime frame of mind continued as Detroit auto assembly lines prepared to manufacture the 1942 models. The attack on Pearl Harbor changed everything.

During 1942, another thirty-seven divisions were formed, and by the end of the year the American army numbered over 5,000,000. The Army Air Forces grew from 270,000 to 1,270,000. Manpower had to be shared with a large navy, eventually some 4 million strong. The number of divisions stabilized at eighty-nine in 1944. Not all were on the sharp edge: when 50,000 American troops went ashore at Normandy on D-Day, 1944, they were backed up by ten times that number of support troops, who provided everything from clothing to dental care, ammunition, and gasoline.

In hindsight, Nazi Germany appears doomed to inevitable defeat by its overwhelming enemies. Superior numbers alone, however, have not and do not decide the outcome of wars. A key reason for Allied victory was the special friendship that developed between Roosevelt and Churchill. The resulting "special relationship" led to the creation in 1942 of a Combined

Chiefs of Staff to direct the conduct of the war. Given their past wars and differences, however, would the Americans and the British be able to work together as a team? Their future wartime operations were often marked by disagreements, and tempers became frayed; according to one eyewitness, at a session of the Cairo Conference in November 1943, the American naval chief "almost climbed over the table" to hit the British military chief: "God, he was mad! I wish he had socked him."[3] Later, Allied Supreme Commander Dwight D. Eisenhower would place things in their proper perspective, writing that "these [disagreements] paled into insignificance alongside the miracle of achievement, represented in the shoulder-to-shoulder march of the Allies to complete victory in the West."[4]

A persistent strategic difference between the Americans and the British involved what is commonly called the "Second Front" controversy. The American army chief of staff, General George C. Marshall, advocated an early invasion of France for three basic reasons: a cross-Channel invasion was the quickest way to defeat the German army; it would have offered an immediate diversion to the hard-pressed Russians, who were also demanding a second front; and, lastly, Marshall wanted to end the European war as quickly as possible so that America's full strength could be focused on Japan. The late military historian Russell F. Weigley argued that Marshall's approach—a sheer power, head-on attack—was in the American tradition of Civil War general Ulysses S. Grant. The British opposed a 1942 invasion of France for a number of reasons: first, such a landing would depend very largely on British troops; second, with fifty German divisions in western Europe and operating on interior lines of communication, the Wehrmacht could concentrate its forces quickly to overwhelm any Allied beachhead; third, the Allies lacked the specialized amphibious landing craft to carry out what would be history's greatest amphibious operation. The raid on the French port of Dieppe in August 1942 offered convincing evidence of what lay in store for a premature landing: over 1,000 Canadian and British troops were killed in the attack. As author Rick Atkinson noted in his brilliant book *An Army at Dawn*, the American proposal for a cross-Channel landing in 1942 "had been audacious to the point of folly."[5]

The delay of the second front in 1942 raised the question of where the United States and Britain could fight and win in the short run. With Russia engaged in a life-and-death struggle with the Nazis in the east, doing nothing was out of the question. But where? Churchill suggested they invade French North Africa, an idea also favored by Roosevelt, who wanted American public opinion involved in the European war at a time when Pearl Harbor had riveted its attention on the Pacific. Marshall and his military advisers, anxious to avoid dispersion of effort, opposed the venture as a mere sideshow that would delay the main invasion of the Continent, the second front. A direct order from President Roosevelt, as commander in chief, overruled his military advisers and committed American troops to landings in French North Africa in Operation Torch. The Allied landings began on November 8, overcoming—not without suffering casualties—those Vichy French troops who fired on the Allied landings. With Morocco and Algeria in Allied hands, they began to move east toward Tunisia. Hitler decided at once not to give up Tunisia without a fight, and poured in men and supplies. Coming from the west, overconfident Americans expected the Germans to retreat eastward on their approach. Field Marshal Erwin Rommel had other ideas, and on February 14, he launched a surprise attack against the inexperienced American forces at Kasserine Pass. At Sidi bou Zid, the first Stukas attacked. Sherman tanks burst into flames. Stung by the defeat at Kasserine Pass, Eisenhower replaced the incompetent American commander with the aggressive George S. Patton with orders to clear out the deadwood in his command.

Before his arrival in Tunisia, Rommel and his panzer army had survived a headlong flight from Egypt, where he had been defeated at the Battle of El Alamein (October 23–November 4, 1942) by the recently appointed British general Bernard L. Montgomery (known as "Monty"). Years of fighting back and forth across the desert had finally resulted in Rommel's Italian-German forces on the verge of seizing the Middle East. The new British commander told his men before El Alamein, "If we can't stay here alive, then let us stay here dead." In November, in El Alamein, Rommel wrote that he wished he were "just a newspaper vendor in Berlin."

The Allied campaign in North Africa, in terms of sheer numbers of troops engaged, was dwarfed by the colossal battles that raged in Russia, but the strategic consequences of the North African campaign cannot be overestimated. Downplayed by critics as a mere sideshow (only a handful of German divisions fought in North Africa), Hitler was prevented from seizing the Middle East, the campaign knocked Italy out of the war, and in terms of combat experience, American general Omar Bradley wrote, "In Africa we learned to crawl, to walk—then run." When Tunis fell in May 1943, 250,000 Axis troops surrendered to the Allies.

Southern Approaches to Europe (U.S. Army Center of Military History)

At the Casablanca Conference in Morocco in January 1943, the Americans and British again debated the Second Front question. General Marshall struggled once again to get a full-scale cross-Channel invasion in 1943, only to be bitterly disappointed when Roosevelt and Churchill settled on Sicily as the next objective (and, by implication, Italy after that). Hitler's decision to defend Tunisia resulted in that campaign's taking longer than expected; the Germans held on until May 1943, thus making a cross-Channel invasion impossible before 1944. Beyond the problem of moving troops from the Mediterranean back to Britain in preparation for the invasion, there was the larger question of the shortage of shipping due to the U-boat crisis. With shipping losses exceeding new construction, at the Casablanca Conference the highest priority was assigned to the battle against German U-boats. Among the other decisions made at Casablanca was that preliminary planning for the cross-Channel invasion would begin (Operation Overlord) as soon as the North African campaign was terminated. In addition, the Allies demanded the "unconditional surrender" of the Axis powers, in part to reassure Stalin that there would be no separate peace made with Hitler.

On the Eastern Front, the Great Patriotic War continued in full fury. The Soviet Union had survived the Nazi blitzkrieg of 1941, but at the cost of losing control of some 40 percent of its population and even more of its industrial base. In 1942, the Germans renewed their rapid advances, and the German soldier or *landser* remained convinced that after so many successes, they must be close to final victory. Ahead stretched the great Volga River, and along its banks for twenty miles, the city of Stalingrad. From August 1942 until January 1943, the epic battle of Stalingrad captured the imagination of the world. Stalin had ordered, "Not one step back," and thousands upon thousands of Russian soldiers or "Ivans" did just that. The Soviets executed over 13,000 of their own soldiers at Stalingrad. Any sign of wavering was brutally stamped out.

On February 1, 1943, newly promoted Field Marshal Friedrich Paulus surrendered his Sixth Army to the Russians. Over 200,000 German troops had been trapped in Stalingrad, and of these 91,000 now marched east into a captivity few survived. Soviet losses were as many as half a million. Stalingrad was a catastrophic defeat for the Germans, whereas Russian morale soared upward. The victory also boosted Soviet and communist prestige worldwide.

Between July 5 and 12, 1943, the Germans launched their third and last summer offensive on Russian soil in an effort to regain the initiative in the east. In the battle of Kursk occurred the largest tank battle until the Gulf War. In losses, it was a draw, with the Soviets losing 400 tanks and Germans somewhat fewer. But the Red Army received three new tanks for each loss, while the Germans received only one. As the Red Army moved west, it would exact a terrible revenge. Pillage, murder, and mass rape awaited many who were in the path of the Soviet advance.

With the battle of Kursk already decided, Hitler broke off the attack and sent some of his crack SS divisions to defend his southern front in the Mediterranean: at dawn on July 10, 1943, the Americans and British landed in Sicily. The Allies would go on to conquer Sicily, but only after thirty-eight days of some of the hardest battles of the war. Soon after the fighting on Sicily, there occurred *"l'affaire* Patton," involving two slapping and cursing incidents that nearly ended the career of America's brilliant battlefield commander. Enraged at a soldier who said he "couldn't take it [combat]" anymore, Patton lost his temper and slapped the soldier's face with a glove and kicked him out of the hospital tent. Patton weathered the crisis thanks in no small part because of the support of Eisenhower, who realized that Patton was needed.

The Allied campaign in Italy that followed on the heels of success in Sicily became one of the controversial subjects of World War II. Benito Mussolini's fascist regime had fallen, the Allies responded slowly, and Hitler poured reinforcements into Italy. The Germans quickly disarmed Italian soldiers and shipped most of them off to work in slave-labor camps. In September 1943, General Mark Clark's Fifth Army of four divisions landed at Salerno, thirty miles south of Naples. Disaster quickly threatened as the Germans counterattacked the beachhead with five divisions. With his army facing possible annihilation, Clark considered withdrawal at one point. Allied naval gunfire support proved decisive, however: a Brooklyn-class cruiser fired 1,500 five-inch shells in ten minutes at German concentrations. Allied warships fired a total of over 11,000 tons of shells in direct support of the ground forces at Salerno.

With Rome barely eighty miles away, it seemed inconceivable that Allied forces would not capture the city until just two days before D-Day. The famous American reporter Ernie Pyle captured the toughness of the war in Italy when he wrote, "The land and the weather were both against us. It rained and it rained. Vehicles bogged down and temporary bridges washed out. The country was shockingly beautiful, and just as shockingly hard to capture from the enemy."[6] The Italian hilltops were always occupied by well-dug-in German troops looking down on the Allies below. "Willie and Joe," the bearded, sunken-eyed, unsmiling GI characters made famous by combat cartoonist Bill Mauldin, captured on their faces the grimness and exhaustion of combat, as well as their humor.

In January 1944, the Allies attempted an amphibious end run around the German defensive lines at Anzio, some thirty-five miles south of Rome. The two-division landing force was too small for its task, and the result was another close call with disaster. Although the landing achieved complete surprise, the Allies were quickly besieged by six German divisions and were in grave danger of being driven back into the sea. American and British troops dug in and fought a magnificent defensive battle on a beachhead only eight miles in depth. Instead of a threat to the enemy rear, the Anzio landing became a besieged outpost that had to be rescued by the Fifth Army. Prime Minister Churchill remarked that he had expected to land a "wildcat" ashore, but instead it was "a beached whale." Other hard battles were to follow, such as that of Monte Cassino, a mountain guarding the highway to Rome. The Eternal City fell on June 4; two days later, all eyes turned to Normandy. Critics at the time and since labeled the battle for Italy as a sideshow that wasted lives; the other side notes that it tied down twenty-seven German divisions that might have been used elsewhere to much greater effect.

While the fighting in Italy ground on, the "Big Three" met together for the first time at the Teheran Conference in November 1943. There should be no more delays of a cross-Channel invasion, insisted Stalin. Churchill could no longer resist the demand, and the target date of May 1944 was set. Two key prerequisites for a successful invasion had been met: the Allies had won both the Battle of the Atlantic against the German submarine and the war in the air. For American power to be applied in Europe, the Atlantic sea lanes had to be kept open. German surface ships, such as the battleship *Bismarck*, had to be neutralized—it was sunk in May 1941—but the enduring enemy was the U-boat. Until the end of 1941 the average number of naval escort ships per convoy was only *two*. In 1942, Allied merchant ship losses rose to nearly 800,000 tons a month, or nearly 8 million tons for the year (1,664 ships sunk). After Pearl Harbor, Nazi U-boat commanders scored a "second Pearl Harbor" off the American east and Gulf coasts, sinking scores of merchant ships often within sight of land. Military historian John Keegan writes that "Hitler's investment in his U-boat fleet thus more than justified the cost."[7] Their operations delayed

Allied offensives and delayed the buildup of American forces in Britain for the eventual liberation of Europe. Slowly, the seesaw battle against the U-boat was won as more escort vessels, more powerful depth charges, escort carriers, *Ultra* intelligence, and long-range aircraft gained the upper hand. The B-24 Liberator bomber became "flying death to a surfaced U-boat." By 1944 the Atlantic became a highway crowded with men and munitions making for either Britain or the Allied armies in liberated Europe.

At the 1943 Casablanca Conference, Roosevelt and Churchill had agreed to the combined bomber offensive against Germany, or, as they informed a skeptical Stalin, a "second front in the air." Before the war, the prophets of air power had promised far more than technology could deliver. A glimpse of the future became very real for the people of Guernica in 1937, when, during the Spanish Civil War, the German air force destroyed Guernica, an attack memorialized by the artist Pablo Picasso. Rotterdam, London, Coventry, and other cities would follow, but bombing was in its infancy.

Few World War II subjects are as controversial as that involving the Allied bombing of Germany (and Japan). A few critics at the time, and many more since World War II, argue that the Allied bombing campaign was immoral, a war crime, unproductive, or even counterproductive. Some recent accounts view the German civilians as innocent victims of the Allied bombing, which they equate with the Jews who died in the Holocaust.

In any discussion of Allied strategic bombing, it is necessary to keep in mind that after the defeat of France in 1940, the British had no other means of taking the offensive against Germany except by using the bomber. The German blitz of British cities in the six months following the Battle of Britain, killing 21,000 people and causing widespread destruction in London, Bristol, Coventry, Liverpool, Glasgow, and other cities, removed any second thoughts on the British side about bombing. For the British, a policy of doing nothing was not an option. During 1941, President Roosevelt and his military advisers shared the belief that bombing offered the only means to victory. In May 1941, the president ordered the production of five hundred heavy bombers a month—British production was slightly less for the entire year.

In the early stages of World War II, the promise of bombing as virtually a war-winning weapon by itself was an illusion. British daylight bombing raids were massacred by German fighters. With the Germans having the upper hand, the British bombers were compelled to fly at night, but with no radio navigation aids, no radar, and no effective bombsights, it was difficult to locate the area of the target, let alone a specific target. After February 1942, under Air Chief Marshal Arthur "Bomber" Harris, Bomber Command waged war on Germany's major industrial cities. There would be no blitzkrieg air war, just a brutal war of attrition fought by bomber crews in uncomfortable, noisy, subzero temperatures against massive concentrations of antiaircraft guns, enemy fighters, and weather.

When the American B-17 Flying Fortress joined the air war, it was expected that its thirteen .50-caliber machine guns, and its ability to fly seven miles high and still be able to hit a target with precision thanks to the top-secret Norden bombsight, would protect the Flying Fortress from German fighters and antiaircraft guns and flak. In practice, the bombers were like unescorted merchant ships; they needed to be convoyed. Unescorted daylight raids were almost suicidal: in October 1943, the U.S. Eighth Air Force lost sixty-five bombers, with over 600 men, in the daylight bombing raid of the ball-bearing plants at Schweinfurt. By the end of 1943, when the P-38 Lightning and the P-47 Thunderbolt were fitted with extra fuel tanks under the wings, their escort range was increased from 500 miles to 2,000 miles. In March 1944 there appeared a new long-range fighter with the performance of a short-range interceptor; an Anglo-American hybrid, the P-51 Mustang possessed an American airframe with the famous Merlin engine. The P-51 flew with the bombers all the way to Berlin and back. In the words of air historian Richard Overy, the "long-range escort fighter transformed the air war overnight."[8] In the first five months of 1944, the Luftwaffe lost 2,262 fighter pilots out of the 2,395 pilots available on January 1. By D-Day, the German air force had been defeated and could offer only token resistance to the greatest amphibious operation in history.

For hundreds of thousands of Germans, the Allied bombing campaign was the central traumatic experience of World War II. Between 300,000 and 600,000 German civilians lost their lives in the bombing. For American and British airmen, the human cost was 140,000 killed, and 21,000 bombers were lost.

Under day and night attack by the "Mighty Eighth" and Bomber Command, each deploying 1,000 aircraft, German economic life was paralyzed by strategic bombing. The German economy was diverted from offensive production to defensive: antiaircraft guns, searchlights, radar sets, and fighters were built for the defense of Germany. The "second front" in the air drained much of the Luftwaffe from the main combat fronts to protect Germany. German air power declined steadily on the Eastern Front as two-thirds of German fighters were sucked into the battle over the Reich. The German forces on the Eastern Front were drained of equipment and manpower held at home. An estimated two million Germans worked in antiaircraft defense, and over fourteen thousand heavy guns were aimed toward the battlefield in the sky. But under the hail of bombs (2.5 million tons) the Nazi economy creaked to a halt; by late 1944 German antiaircraft guns were forced to fire rock salt at the enemy planes. Bombing had created a nitrogen shortage that in turn reduced the production of explosives; hence 20 percent of ammunition was filled with rock salt.

By June 1944, 2,876,000 Allied soldiers, sailors, and airmen were ready to launch the long-awaited Second Front. It was jokingly reported that only the barrage balloons kept the British Isles afloat under the weight of men and supplies. Allied Supreme Commander General Dwight D. Eisenhower made the momentous decision to launch the invasion on June 5 with a storm raging outside his headquarters, since a break in the weather was expected in the next twenty-four hours. If the invasion succeeded, it would mark the beginning of the end of Hitler's Third Reich; if the invasion failed, then Hitler would be safe in the west for some time to come—time to build more new submarines, more jet fighters, and more missile weapons. Politically, most of Europe, and not just the eastern half of it, would have fallen under Soviet communism.

The vast armada of Allied ships created the impression that one could walk across the Channel to Normandy; the sky contained endless formations of Allied planes heading for the invasion area. The unprecedented numbers of ships, planes, and men created the myth that the outcome of D-Day was a sure thing, a foregone conclusion. The Allied preparations for D-Day were astounding, but the Germans on the other side of the Channel had been busy, particularly after Hitler appointed Field Marshal Rommel commander of the forces facing the invasion threat. The number of German divisions in the west grew from fifty-three to fifty-eight divisions, and the additions were panzer units. D-Day would be nothing less than a frontal assault on a heavily fortified coastline, and everyone, on both sides, knew that the invasion was coming soon and that on its success or failure depended the outcome of World War II. Neither the Allies nor Hitler had any illusions about what was at stake: defeat of the Allied invasion would be a turning point in the war and would dramatically change Nazi prospects on the Eastern Front.

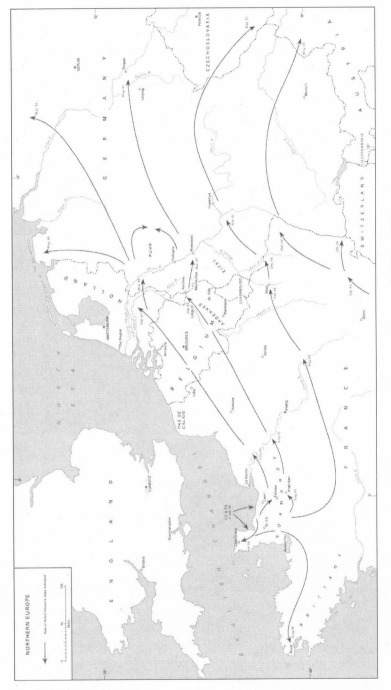

Northwest Europe (U.S. Army Center of Military History)

The Allied deception plan known as Fortitude played an important role in the success of the Anglo-American invasion since Fortitude reinforced and fed German preconceptions that the main invasion would come by the shortest route, to provide better air cover, and would cross toward Calais. The creation of an imaginary army, the First U.S. Army Group (FUSAG), commanded by General George S. Patton, helped to keep an entire Germany army tied up along the Calais coast, ready to fight thirty nonexistent divisions. Dummy camps and supply depots, tanks and planes made of rubber, and a host of other steps were taken to maintain the existence of the phantom FUSAG army.

On June 6, Operation Overlord, the cross-Channel invasion of France, began. Two hundred thousand men, of the American 82nd and 101st Airborne Divisions, British Sixth Airborne Division, U.S. Fourth Division (Utah Beach), U.S. First Division (Omaha Beach), British Fiftieth Division (Gold Beach), Canadian Third Division (Juno Beach), and British Third Division (Sword Beach), with all their vehicles and equipment, had to be landed during the first forty-eight hours. The infantry were told that air and naval bombardment would have destroyed the beach defenses. In the event, nothing went according to plan.

In the film *Saving Private Ryan*, director Steven Spielberg valiantly attempts to create the hell that existed on Omaha Beach (Vierville): the landing craft touching the sand, the ramps dropping, and the men facing a hail of machine-gun bullets as "all hell broke loose." The first waves were all but wiped out by machine-gun fire before the men could get across the beach. Company A of the 116th Regiment, 29th Infantry Division, lost 96 percent of its men before it had fired even one shot. Every inch of the all-but-impregnable beach was covered by pre-sighted flanking crossfire. German defenders of the 352nd Infantry Division were on the cliffs overlooking Omaha and in a trench system connected by tunnels that climbed up the bluffs—almost a Maginot Line. The first fifteen minutes on "Dog Green" sector, Omaha Beach, was "an unmitigated disaster" for the small Virginia town of Bedford, which lost nineteen men on D-Day.[9] The living staggered up against the seawall, while bodies washed ashore, many having been blown to pieces. Hesitant and confused, the German higher command, believing that the landing was a disaster, failed to launch a counterattack. American casualties were over 2,000 out of 34,000 at Omaha Beach. On the extreme right flank of the Allied landings, Rudder's Rangers carried out the amazing exploit of scaling the sheer cliffs of the Pointe-du-Hoc even as German soldiers came to the edge and rolled hand grenades or fired down on the climbing Rangers. On Utah Beach, losses were light. By a stroke of good luck, the landing took place more than a mile south of the original beach. General Theodore Roosevelt of the Fourth Infantry Division, son of the former president, decided to remain where they were and "start the war from here."

In the British sector, a few minutes after midnight, British glider-borne troops seized "Pegasus" Bridge over the Caen Canal to secure the left flank of the invasion. Despite near disaster and plans that went wrong, the Allied invasion had been a stunning success. In the days immediately following the invasion, counterattacks by the Twenty-first Panzer Division and the Twelfth SS (Hitler Youth) Division failed to throw the Allies back into the sea.

Seven weeks after the invasion of Normandy, however, the battle gave every appearance of a stalemate since the Allies had taken only as much ground as the invasion planners had expected to take in the first five days. Critics contrasted the slowness of the Allied advance with the spectacular ground gains made by the Russians in their 1944 summer offensive, in which 140 Soviet divisions destroyed twenty-five German divisions in twelve days along a 350-mile front.

General Bernard Montgomery, commander of Allied ground forces during the Battle of Normandy, became the lightning rod for the criticism. During the planning for Overlord, Montgomery had emphasized the need for aggressive action to push armored thrusts deep inland, and quickly on D-Day. But there would be no Allied blitzkrieg in Normandy: the terrain was not suited for mobile warfare, the Allies fought on a narrow front with little room for maneuver, and if some German units consisted of old men, boys, and nonconscripted Germans, there were also first-class panzer divisions equipped with Panther and Tiger tanks, led by men who had fought on almost every battlefield from Alamein to Moscow.

The Battle of Normandy settled down to a slow, grim war of attrition, with thirty-four Allied divisions fighting twenty-six German divisions. As the Allies were on the offensive, their superiority on the ground was far from overwhelming, and the desperate German defenders, fighting in ideal defensive terrain, followed the Führer's order to hold every inch of ground. Allied soldiers would have agreed with Rommel's description of the battle as "one terrible blood-letting."

Fearing a breakout toward Paris, the Germans concentrated seven and a half panzer divisions, with 700 tanks, on the eastern flank to contain the

British and Canadians. On the western flank, American troops were forced to fight their way yard by yard through the *bocage* or hedgerow countryside of Normandy: small fields bordered by hedgerows so high and thick that a Sherman tank was forced to climb almost vertically, thus becoming easy prey to an antitank weapon. The American ordeal in the *bocage* was reminiscent both of Grant's Civil War Wilderness campaign and the more recent Pacific battle on Guadalcanal. After D-Day, an American division could expect about 85 percent casualties among its riflemen for every six weeks of combat. To overcome what Russell Weigley called "the best defensive country in France, the hedgerows," an American sergeant named Curtis G. Culin, of the Second Division, invented a simple device to break through the barriers that hamstrung and depressed the American army. Culin's "Rhino" consisted of steel tusklike blades or prongs welded to the front of a Sherman that allowed the tank to drive straight through the infamous hedgerows. General Omar Bradley was so impressed that he ordered German steel obstacles from the beaches used to mass-produce the tusks, which would be welded onto as many tanks as possible in preparation for the coming breakout battle. Allied Supreme Commander Dwight Eisenhower would write that American soldiers derived "gleeful satisfaction" from the fact that obstacles intended to prevent their landing on the beaches were now put to use against the enemy.

Finally, on July 25, Bradley concentrated his First U.S. Army on a narrow front and launched a powerful attack to punch a hole in the German line, which was stretched to the breaking point. Operation Cobra was preceded by a tremendous "carpet-bombing attack" by the Eighth and Ninth U.S. Air Forces on almost every square yard of the German positions around Saint Lô. Unfortunately, bombing errors caused 500 American casualties, including the death of Lieutenant General Lesley J. McNair, the highest-ranking American officer killed in Europe. In the days that following the "carpet bombing," General J. Lawton ("Lightning Joe") Collins's VII Corps broke through the gap made in the enemy line. On the German side, what had once been the most powerful armored division in the Wehrmacht, Panzer Lehr, had been reduced by weeks of combat to only fourteen tanks.

Five days before Operation Cobra, on July 20, a group of German army officers attempted to assassinate Hitler at his Rastenburg headquarters. Colonel Claus von Stauffenberg placed a bomb under the conference table that exploded and wounded Hitler but did not kill him. The failure of the coup served only to deepen Hitler's hatred of the traditional officer class, which was watched even more closely by Nazis. Hitler's personal popularity had grown during the war, and the July 20 bomb plot seemed to be an act of betrayal against the Fatherland's fight for survival.

On August 1, General George Patton's Third Army was brought into the battle and began its race to the east. Meanwhile, the British and Canadians had kept German armor pinned down on the eastern flank. Sooner than anyone had imagined possible, the German line finally cracked. The Führer, faced with the choice of a strategic withdrawal or launching a counterattack, decided on the latter, a disastrous mistake that only added to the scale of the coming Allied victory in Normandy. The counterattack began on August 7 at the town of Mortain with the aim of cutting off the American columns that were pouring deep into the German rear.

Blocking the path of the panzer divisions was the U.S. Thirtieth Infantry Division. The mystique of blitzkrieg had passed, and the veterans of the Old Hickory Division, though tired and weary, showed no panic at the sight of tanks. The counterattack failed on the first day; although the German attack isolated the Second Battalion, 120th Infantry Regiment, on Hill 317, the Americans called down massive artillery fire on the enemy columns. At midday, after the morning mist had cleared, German armor was subjected to an intense air attack from Allied fighter-bombers, including RAF rocket-firing Typhoons.

Attention now shifted hurriedly from the Battle of Mortain to the Battle of the Falaise Gap as the Germans found themselves in a closing trap between the British driving from the north and the Americans from the south. With the jaws of the Falaise pocket closing hourly, exhausted Germans ran the gauntlet through the ever-narrowing gap, the retreat turning into a rout. Allied artillery fire and fighter-bombers wreaked havoc on the German forces. Fifty thousand Germans managed to escape the carnage; 45,000 were taken prisoner, and 10,000 lay in heaps among dead horses and wrecked equipment. The battlefield at Falaise was one of the greatest "killing grounds" of World War II.

During the defeat in Normandy and the long rout eastwards, the Wehrmacht lost some sixty divisions; 265,000 men were killed or wounded, and 350,000 were taken prisoner. If many German officers escaped to live and fight another day, Normandy was a crushing defeat for the Wehrmacht. Altogether, 637,000 Allied and German casualties occurred during the eighty-five-day Normandy campaign. Between June and August 1944, the Allies had fought and won the decisive battle in the west.

Besides the Normandy disaster, on August 15, the Germans suffered another blow in France when American and French troops landed in southern France. They proceeded to capture the great port of Marseilles, which proved a logistic windfall to the supply of U.S. forces fighting on the German frontier in hard fighting to come. On August 25, ten days *earlier* than originally planned, Paris was liberated by the Allies. The following day General Charles de Gaulle, leader of the Free French forces, entered Paris and marched in triumph down the famous Champs Élysées.

To the east, in Poland, an early sign of the coming Cold War between the West and the Soviet Union was to be seen in the fate of the Warsaw Rising that began on August 1 when the people of Warsaw rose up against the Nazis. They fought heroically for two months before being crushed. Stalin refused to allow American and British aircraft to land in the Soviet Union after dropping supplies on Warsaw.

With the destruction of the bulk of the German army in the west, from mid-August until the end of the war, disagreements increased over what exactly the Allied armies ought to be doing and where.[10] As remnants of the German army rushed for the Seine and beyond, Montgomery, promoted to field marshal on September 1, proposed a single, concentrated "full-blooded" drive toward the Ruhr, the industrial heartland of Germany, followed finally by Berlin: his Twenty-first Army Group and Bradley's First Army would advance side by side. With the size of his British army shrinking in size (divisions were broken up to find replacements for casualties), Montgomery wanted to end the war quickly. Unless there was a single thrust, he argued, the war would last another six months. The advance would also enable the Allies to capture quickly the deadly weapon sites in Belgium and the Netherlands from which V-1 flying-bombs and V-2 rockets were being fired at London and Antwerp, killing thousands of civilians.

Eisenhower assumed command of the Allied land forces on September 1, 1944. He envisioned a Cannae-like battle involving a double envelopment of the industrial Ruhr region of Germany. Montgomery would advance north of the Ardennes, while Bradley's armies would advance south of the Ardennes and then swing north to complete the double envelopment. This broad-front strategy called for both the American and British armies to move forward more or less simultaneously. Eisenhower's decision was based on intelligence estimates that the Germans were simply too weak to stop a broad-front advance toward the Rhine.

Eisenhower's differences were not limited to Montgomery. Both Bradley and Patton, the Third Army commander, lobbied hard for their own particular war-winning plan. The patient Eisenhower was beset by unhappy, prima donna commanders fighting for an equal, if not a greater, share of the logistical pie. But the very speed of the Allied armies after Normandy caused serious problems. By September Eisenhower had outrun his supplies. Trucks bringing gasoline and ammunition to Patton's army, for example, had to travel 360 miles back to the Normandy beaches. With three-quarters of Allied supplies still arriving over the D-Day beaches, "Ike" turned down Montgomery's proposed single thrust because it could not be supplied. The broad-front advance to the Rhine would continue.

In early September, Eisenhower did authorize Montgomery to mount the largest airborne and glider operation of the war. Code-named Operation Market-Garden, the bold thrust, Montgomery hoped, would outflank Hitler's heavily defended line along the German border called the West Wall or Siegfried Line. The First Allied Airborne Army, composed of the U.S. 82nd and 101st divisions and the British First Airborne Division, were to seize five bridges and canals that led to the lower Rhine, while British land forces would drive sixty-four miles northward to link up with the British First Airborne, or "Red Devils," at Arnhem. Whether or not the bridge at Arnhem was a "a bridge too far," the Red Devils were dropped too far from the Arnhem bridge. Even more serious, the Ninth and Tenth SS Panzer Divisions were re-equipping near Arnhem. Despite the heroic stand of Lieutenant Colonel John Frost's Second Parachute Battalion at Arnhem bridge, Operation Market-Garden was a disaster. Only 2,400 of the original 9,000 Red Devils managed to escape back to Allied lines; 1,400 had been killed and more than six thousand were captured. German military power had recovered, which meant the war would not end that year.

In the autumn and early winter of 1944–1945, the Allies fought bloody, World War I–type infantry battles along the German border in a war of attrition. Besides the winter weather of mud, rain, snow, and bone-chilling damp cold, Allied troops confronted the famed Siegfried Line defenses consisting of interlocking pillboxes and "dragon's teeth" and other anti-tank obstacles. One of the most brutal battles was fought in the well-fortified, dense Hürtgen Forest. It presented Americans with the toughest defense situation that they had encountered since Normandy. The result would be 33,000 American casualties. American superiority in tactical air support and armor were checkmated by the dense tree cover and terrain of the Hürtgen Forest. German artillery projectiles burst in the tops of trees, hurling shell fragments on Americans below. Ernest Hemingway called it "Passchendaele [the World War I battle] with tree bursts." The slightest activity in the American lines brought down a rain of German mortars and artillery. One division after another was flung into the death trap that was Hürtgen in November 1944. Rear support units were stripped to the bone in order to supply replacements to units in the front line, and often the replacements became casualties before anyone had time to learn their names.

In his dire need for replacements, Patton turned to black troops. The demand of African Americans that they be given the "right to fight," a demand denied in the segregated "Jim Crow" army of separate units, mess halls, barracks, and bars, was a least partially granted as the war became one of grinding attrition. At the end of October the 761st Tank Battalion became the first Negro unit committed to combat. Patton declared, "I don't care what color you are, so long as you go up there and kill those Kraut sonsabitches." The 761st did just that with a distinguished record of 183 days in action.

By mid-December, largely because of the weather, there was somewhat of a lull in the grim warfare along the German frontier. In the rugged, heavily wooded Ardennes, with its poor road system, General Bradley had taken what he later described as "a calculated risk" by defending that part of the American line with only four divisions. Unconcerned and dismissive about any possible attack on his sector of the front, Bradley declared, "Let them come." With Hitler's Germany on the verge of invasion from both east and west, everyone in the Allied camp was thinking offensively, about what they would do to the enemy, and not about what Hitler might decide to do.

Under the cover of mist and snow, what would become the greatest American battle in Europe began at dawn on December 16. Some 200,000 Germans attacked 83,000 Americans who were holding an eighty-five-mile stretch of the rugged, heavily forested Ardennes along the Belgium and Luxembourg borders with Germany—for only a brief moment, the ghost of the 1940 German attack returned. Hitler gambled that his surprise offensive would split the Allied front in half, cross the Meuse River, and then drive on to capture Antwerp. The strongest German force struck in the

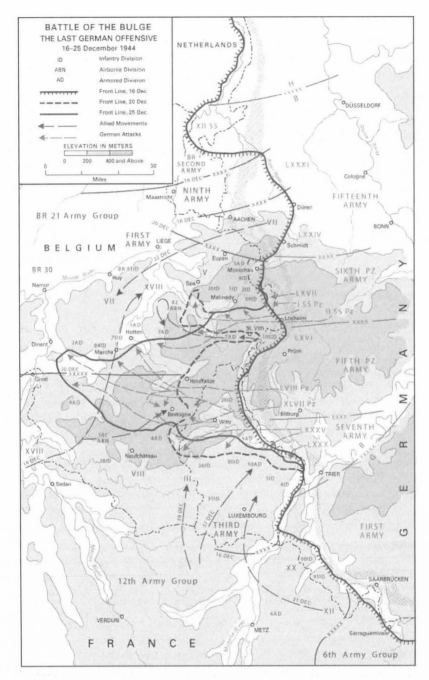

Battle of the Bulge (U.S. Army Center of Military History)

north, and the Elsenborn Ridge became the Little Round Top of the Battle of the Bulge. There, the Ninety-ninth and Second Infantry Divisions would hold the northern shoulder in the face of ferocious German attacks. The stand at Elsenborn Ridge confined the German offensive to a corridor in which it would eventually be stopped and defeated.

Farther south, the front collapsed, and the Germans captured nearly 8,000 Americans on December 19. As the German penetration deepened, it became a "bulge," hence the nickname given to the Battle of the Ardennes. Displaying his greatness as an *Allied* commander, on December 20, Eisenhower placed all American forces north of the Bulge under Montgomery's temporary command, much to the dismay of Bradley. Unlike Bradley, who had not visited First Army headquarters during the crisis, Montgomery did, and arrived like "Christ come to cleanse the temple."

At the two vital crossroad towns of Saint-Vith and Bastogne, American soldiers—airborne, infantry, cooks, clerks, and mechanics—blunted the German drive. On the first day of the offensive, Eisenhower had ordered the Seventh Armored Division to Saint-Vith, where it held on for five days, obstructing one of the two main German supply lines. At Bastogne, the other vital crossroads town, the acting commander of the 101st Airborne Division at Bastogne, General Anthony C. McAuliffe, rejected the German demand to surrender with a single word: "Nuts!" The heroic defense of Bastogne has come to symbolize one of the finest hours of the U.S. Army. In one of Patton's own finest hours of the war, he promised to relieve Bastogne by taking three of his Third Army divisions out of the line, having them make a ninety-degree turn north, moving them over icy roads, and attacking in less than seventy-two hours.

In the final analysis, however, the victory in the Battle of the Bulge belonged to the U.S. soldiers who had withstood the Wehrmacht's fury; the "Krauts," "American"-speaking German troops wearing U.S. uniforms who infiltrated American lines and misdirected American vehicles, turned signposts the wrong way, and otherwise attempted to aid the counteroffensive; the grotesque shape of frozen bodies with arms and legs reaching out of the snow; gun barrels frozen solid; the Malmédy massacre where SS troops massacred eighty-six American prisoners; and the bitter cold, blizzards, and fog. On December 23 and 24 the skies cleared, and Allied planes grounded because of the weather proceeded to destroy enemy tanks and vehicles silhouetted against the snow. The Battle of the Bulge was over by the end of January 1945.

American casualties in the Battle of the Bulge numbered 81,000, with 19,000 of them killed, 15,000 captured, and 47,000 wounded. For those who were captured, the trip from Belgium to the prison camps in eastern Germany would be purgatory as the POWs, some with severe dysentery, were crammed into small railroad cars where there was no room to lie down. GIs who weighed 135 pounds when captured in the Battle of the Bulge weighed 95 pounds when liberated. They faced slow starvation on a daily diet that consisted of a cup of thin potato soup and black bread.

As for the Germans, who had suffered approximately 100,000 casualties and lost vast amounts of military equipment that could not be replaced, they could only wonder why Hitler had decided to attack in the west, thus making it easier for the Soviets to penetrate Germany.

The Red Army pushed closer and closer toward Germany. Stalin, having had already occupied the Baltic states of Latvia, Estonia, and Lithuania, prepared Polish, Romanian, Hungarian, Bulgarian, and German communists to take power once the Red Army reached their respective capital cities. By the beginning of February, the Red Army had "liberated" (established a puppet communist regime in) Warsaw and advanced beyond the Oder River, well into Germany. Only forty miles from Berlin, the Soviet advance stopped because of supply problems after an advance of 300 miles.

As American troops pushed the Germans out of the Ardennes at the end of January, the Allies renewed their advance to the Rhine River. On March 7, a platoon of the Ninth Armored Division found intact a bridge over the Rhine at Remagen and seized the prized possession before it could be destroyed. The unexpected good fortune eventually led Eisenhower to shift his main thrust southeast toward the Leipzig-Dresden area, not Berlin. He informed Stalin of his decision before consulting Washington or London, where Churchill was stunned by Eisenhower's action. From a military perspective, the Red Army was much closer to Berlin—only thirty-three miles away—than Eisenhower's forces: a spearhead of the U.S. Ninth Army, 50,000 men and some artillery, had reached to within fifty miles of Berlin, but most of the American forces were still far to the west. Stalin had 1,250,000 men and 22,000 artillery pieces aimed at Berlin. Eisenhower also knew that at the Yalta Conference in February, Roosevelt, Churchill, and Stalin had agreed to divide Germany into occupation zones such that Berlin would lie within the Soviet zone. The Big Three had also agreed to divide Berlin into occupation zones. To the south, Eisenhower, at the request of the Soviets, also stopped Patton's Third Army from liberating

Prague, the Czech capital. The Red Army gained the honor of liberating Prague. By May 1945, 25 percent of the German population were refugees; tens of thousands of civilians fled from the vengeance of the oncoming Russians.

As Allied armies converged on Hitler's doomed Third Reich, they began to uncover the horror of the concentration camps—Buchenwald, Belsen, Dachau, and, most notoriously, Auschwitz—where six million Jews were murdered: crematoriums, huge piles of corpses, and living skeletons of human beings testified to the utter depravity of the Nazi regime.

On April 26, 1945, in Berlin, deep in his gloomy underground bunker underneath the Reich Chancellery, a physically wrecked Hitler celebrated his fifty-sixth birthday, married his mistress Eva Braun, and wrote his last testament blaming the Jews and the weakness of the German people for the total defeat of the Third Reich. The news of Roosevelt's death on April 12, 1945, caused a flicker of optimism in the bunker. But above ground, Berlin was in ruins, a *Götterdämmerung* (twilight of the gods), as the Russians closed in on the Chancellery. The German garrison fought with fanaticism; deserters or those unwilling to fight for the Nazi regime were hanged from lampposts. On April 30, 1945, Hitler killed himself. In the United States and Britain, victory in Europe, or V-E Day, was celebrated on May 8, and in the Soviet Union on May 9.

The Grand Alliance had prevented a new Dark Age in the form of Nazism from descending on the world. Freedom came to western Europe in 1945, but not to all of Europe, including Russia, until the collapse of Soviet communism decades later. The victory of the Grand Alliance against Nazism saved millions of lives but came too late for the victims of the Holocaust or the life of a young Jewish girl named Anne Frank. The loss of friends, fathers, husbands, sons, and brothers in the cause of freedom seared forever the lives of a generation of Americans.

Notes

1. Gerhard L. Weinberg, *A World at Arms: A Global History of World War II* (New York: Cambridge University Press, 1998), 264.

2. Rick Atkinson, *An Army at Dawn: The War in North Africa, 1942–1943* (New York: Henry Holt, 2002), 5.

3. Joseph W. Stilwell, *The Stilwell Papers* (New York: MacDonald, 1949), 90.

4. Dwight D. Eisenhower, *Crusade in Europe* (New York: Doubleday, 1948), 4.

5. Atkinson, *An Army at Dawn*, 28.

6. Ernie Pyle, *Brave Men* (New York: Henry Holt, 1944), 141.

7. John Keegan, *The Second World War* (New York: Penguin Books, 1989), 122.

8. Richard Overy, *Why The Allies Won* (New York: W. W. Norton, 1996), 123.

9. Stephen E. Ambrose, *D-Day, June 6, 1944: The Climactic Battle of World War II* (New York: Simon & Schuster, 1994), 328.

10. Carlo D'Este, *Eisenhower: A Soldier's Life* (New York: Henry Holt, 2002), 598.

Suggested Readings

Blumenson, Martin. *Breakout and Pursuit*. Washington, D.C., 1961.

Churchill, Winston S. *The Second World War*. 6 vols. Boston: Houghton Mifflin, 1948-1953.

D'Este, Carlo. *Bitter Victory: The Battle for Sicily, 1943*. New York: E. P. Dutton, 1988.

———. *Eisenhower: A Soldier's Life*. New York: Henry Holt, 2002.

———. *Patton: A Genius for War*. New York: HarperCollins, 1995.

Eisenhower, Dwight D. *Crusade in Europe*. Garden City, N.Y.: Doubleday, 1948.

Gavin, James M. *On to Berlin: Battles of an Airborne Commander, 1943–1946*. New York: Viking, 1978.

Williamson, Murray, and Allan Millett. *A Ware to Be Won: Fighting the Second World War, 1937–1945*. Cambridge: Harvard University Press, 2000.

Films

Band of Brothers (DVD), HBO 10-part series, 2001
Memphis Belle (1990)
To Hell and Back (1955)
The Longest Day (1962)
Patton (1970)
Schindler's List (1993)

CHAPTER EIGHT

The Second World War: The War against Japan

H. P. WILLMOTT

A S A RESULT of a naval building program initiated in 1916 by President Woodrow Wilson before America entered the Great War and its continued expansion in 1917–1918, the U.S. Navy challenged Britain as the world's number-one sea power after the Armistice. In the early 1920s the economy-conscious Harding administration, prodded by peace activists, entered into disarmament negotiations with leading naval powers. In the resulting Washington Conference (1921–1922), the United States, under the leadership of Secretary of State Charles Evans Hughes, agreed to naval parity with Britain in capital ships and to a ten-year moratorium on construction of these types of vessels by all major powers. Japan was assigned the lesser tonnage in capital ships in a 5-to-5-to-3 ratio with America and Britain. At the same conference, the United States agreed not to strengthen its bases and fortifications in the western Pacific, thus giving Japan an advantage if a war broke out involving the two powers in the area. The Washington Conference treaties mainly shaped America's naval strategy in the interwar era.

Despite the fact that Japan was a signatory of the Washington agreements, the U.S. military considered the island nation the most likely foe in a future war and continued to develop War Plan Orange, a strategy for a conflict with Japan. Because of the Washington treaties, American naval experts

183

were pessimistic about the possibility of holding U.S. bases in the western Pacific if war broke out. The advent of a militant and expansionist government in Tokyo in the 1930s only heightened the U.S. Navy's concern about a Pacific war. During the late 1920s and early 1930s, as War Plan Orange was being continuously updated, most naval experts anticipated that a Pacific conflict would feature a Jutland-type clash with battleships being the mainstays of the American and Japanese fleets.

When the ten-year moratorium on construction of capital ships expired in the 1930s and the major powers failed to agree to alternative limitations, America and Japan began an arms race in capital-class ships. A few naval experts in both nations doubted the battleships would bear the brunt of fighting in the next war and foresaw that the aircraft carrier would be the most important vessel in a future Pacific conflict. Despite some setbacks at the hands of old-line battleship advocates, Adm. Isorokku Yamamoto was mainly responsible for providing Japan with a substantial number of carriers as well as modern planes and trained pilots as war approached. In the United States, air service proponents, many of whom were Great War veterans such as Gen. Billy Mitchell, championed the cause of air power and the carrier. By the end of the 1920s, some farsighted admirals became convinced of the offensive potential of the carrier and saw to it that the navy had a number of battle-ready flattops by the beginning of the war.

Beginning with its aggressive action in Manchuria in 1931, as H. P. Willmott points out, Japan became engaged in a conflict with China. By 1937, the island nation was involved in a full-scale war with the Kuomintang regime. With relations between America and Japan becoming increasingly strained because of these actions, U.S. Navy planners became more alarmed about the nation's inability to provide an adequate defense for its western Pacific bases. They feared, in the event of war with Japan, that the outlying bases would be easily seized and that America's Pacific Fleet might be limited to operations in a area between California and the waters just to the west of Hawaii. If Japan overran America's western Pacific bases, how could the navy launch offensive strikes to counter Japanese expansion and gain ascendancy in the far Pacific? Although many "battleship admirals" failed to recognize it at the time, the development of new weapons and strategy would provide some solutions to the problem. The use of the aircraft carrier as an offensive weapon provided one answer. The development of long-range submarines also would give the United States an advanced strike force against Japan's naval and marine fleets.

From another quarter, the U.S. Marine Corps developed a strategy to dislodge the Japanese from island bases in the western Pacific if war came. During the 1920s under the leadership of Commandant Maj. Gen. John A. Lejeune, the marines devised plans, acquired equipment, and trained personnel to launch amphibious assaults on enemy-held islands and bases. Although most naval experts considered such assaults against heavily defended positions impossible, Maj. Earl H. Ellis and other marine officers readied the Corps for the task. H. P. Willmott provides a detailed explanation of the origins and expansion of the war in the Pacific and describes and analyzes how the U.S. Navy, with aid from the marine and the army, mobilized their skills and resources to win the Pacific war. Despite errors in judgment and interservice rivalries that led to serious setbacks at the beginning of the conflict, the American military quickly adapted itself to the Pacific war and overwhelmed the Japanese with its strategy and resources. The story is all the more remarkable because until May 1945 the ocean war was given second priority to the struggle to defeat Adolf Hitler's legions in Europe.

For Europeans the Second World War is given very precise dates: it began in September 1939 with the German attack on Poland and the declaration of war by Britain and France on Germany as a consequence, and it ended in May 1945 with the total, comprehensive defeat of Germany. For the United States this conflict also has very precise dates, but the dates are different from those of Europeans. It began in December 1941 with the Japanese attack on the U.S. Pacific Fleet at its Pearl Harbor base and it ended, three months after Germany's defeat, with the surrender of Japan in August–September 1945. When this war began for Japan, and for China, is quite another matter.

What is so often called the Pacific war was, more properly, one part of a war between Japan and her various enemies. The Japanese official histories, of which there are no fewer than 102 volumes, date this conflict from September 1931, when the Japanese army in Manchuria undertook a campaign that resulted in its overrunning three of Manchuria's four provinces by spring 1932. The next four years saw the Japanese conquer Jehol, the last of the provinces, and undertake successive encroachments upon the northern provinces with the result that by the end of 1936 the Kuomintang (Chinese High Command) regime in Nanking had been obliged to withdraw all Chinese military forces from eastern Inner Mongolia and the

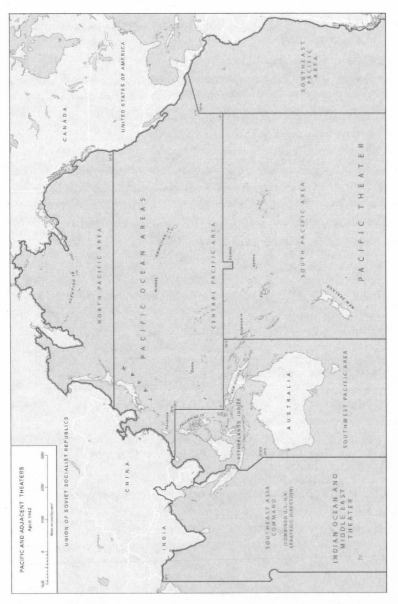

Pacific Theater (U.S. Army Center of Military History)

whole of area north of the Great Wall. With the Japanese holding the power of decision in terms of appointments of personnel to positions of administration, these areas very quickly fell to Japanese forces after July 1937 and the start of Japan's "special undeclared war" in China.

The explanation of the process whereby Japan found itself involved in full-scale war on the Asian mainland after August–September 1937 is very difficult to determine. At work were a series of factors ranging from the very special place that Japan assigned for itself in terms of Asia and Asians, the disastrous impact of the Great Depression, Japan's perceived need for assured markets, sources of food and raw materials, and areas of settlement for a country considered to be overpopulated. Japan reserved for itself a position of privilege in Manchuria and northern China, and in part the war in which Japan found itself after July 1937 was the result of clear indication that China, in the aftermath of the Sian Incident of December 1936, was seeking to halt the series of civil wars that had wracked the area for the best part of two decades in order to present a united front in dealing with Japanese aggression. Japan's existing position in China, and its various mainland ambitions, were dependent upon China's division and weakness, and in the aftermath of the Lukouchiao or Marco Polo Bridge Incident, on July 7, 1937, when a Japanese night patrol and Chinese garrison troops engaged one another just outside Peking, the immediate Japanese attitude was that this was merely one more in a line of incidents that had taken place and had been used to browbeat the Chinese authorities into a series of local, but substantial, concessions. Initially this pattern of events seemed likely to repeat itself because both sides were reluctant to escalate the affair, but in the event three matters came together to ensure that the Lukouchiao Incident could not be contained. The first was the determination of elements within the Japanese army in Manchuria to press the Inner Mongolia issue, and the second was the massacre of Japanese soldiers, police, and civilians at Tungchow in late July. Either of these might have resulted in a widening of Japanese ambition and intention, and together they probably would have led to such an eventuality, but in the final analysis it was the third matter that brought about conflict. Japanese army formations occupied Tientsin on July 30 and Peking on August 8 and established themselves on the Suiyuan-Peking-Linghai line but made no real attempt to move beyond it. But as a direct result of provocation on the part of the Imperial Navy (the *Kaigun*), fighting broke out at Shanghai on August 13, and, as in 1932, the navy was unable to win the battle it had induced. The army (the *Rikugun*) had to send reinforcements to help the navy, and this necessarily involved having to mobilize. This was the decisive act in the sense that, once ordered on August 17, mobilization ensured full-scale, general war in China, and, significantly, not just northern China: by the end of September no fewer than fifteen divisions had been sent from the home islands to China.

As the Japanese commitment in northern China and the lower Yangtze increased, so ambition widened: within weeks of the start of general war the effort was being justified in terms of the establishment of an exclusive Japanese sphere of influence north of the Hwang Ho (Yellow River). In the event, Japanese operations in northern China and eastern Inner Mongolia encountered little in the way of serious or sustained opposition. In front of Shanghai, however, the Japanese position was more difficult. The Nationalist regime of Chiang Kai-shek made a major effort in defense of the city that ultimately cost its army an estimated 270,000 killed and wounded, and it was the extent of these losses that resulted in the collapse of Chinese resistance in the first two weeks of November: Shanghai fell in mid-month, and the Japanese then developed an offensive across four main axes of advance that resulted in the fall of Nanking on December 13 amid scenes of mass murder, torture, rape, and pillage that were to become the hallmarks of Japanese army operations in China over the next five years. An estimated 200,000 Chinese were killed in the two months after the fall of the city.

In the immediate aftermath of the fall of Nanking there took place the episode that really set the terms of reference on the Asian mainland for the next eight years. Chiang Kai-shek's regime, reduced for the moment to a nomadic existence, stated its adoption of a policy of protracted resistance and made clear its refusal to recognize defeat and loss: the Japanese, in response, stated their refusal to deal with Chiang and his regime, and the two sides recalled their ambassadors in the third week of January 1938. In these and subsequent weeks the Japanese armies in north and central China came together on May 19, 1938, with the capture of Suchow in northwest Kiangsu. It was the capture of this city that brought the Japanese into possession of secured overland communications between Peking and Shanghai, but just as the capture of Suchow represented the coming together of two separate offensive efforts, so it also represented their divergence: in the immediate aftermath of convergence the Japanese effort divided between the middle Hwang Ho and the middle Yangtze and

Wuhan cities. On the Hwang Ho sector Japanese forces were able to secure Kaifeng on June 7 and Chengchow three days later. At this point the Japanese had the choice to continue to move to the west, against Loyang, Tungkwan, and Sian, and perhaps even Paochi, or to move across Honan province on the middle Yangtze valley. By this time Chinese forces that had been wrong-footed with the fall of Yungcheng and Suchow had compensation in the fact that the Japanese were too thinly spread to complete battles of encirclement and annihilation properly, and thus were able to withdraw into the interior: against this, however, was the speed of the Japanese offensives after the fall of Yungcheng and Suchow. With virtually no forces with which to try to even slow the enemy, the Chinese opened the Yellow River dikes above Kaifeng, diverting it hundreds of miles until it ran into the Hwai at Pengpu. An unknown number of fellow countrymen were killed and vast areas were devastated, but this desperate measure forestalled the Japanese capture of Chengchow and halted operations along the Chengchow-Hankow railway until 1944. On the middle Yangtze sector the Japanese forces advanced astride the river, and with other forces taking Canton on October 21, on the north bank of the Yangtze, the first of the Wuhan cities, Hankow, was taken on October 25, and on the south bank Hanyang and Wuchang were taken on October 26; Sienning was taken two days later. Japanese success in the area was completed with the capture of Tungshan on November 9 and Yoyang on the eleventh.

Few things are more difficult to explain than an inevitable defeat, and if there is anything more difficult to explain than an inevitable defeat, then it is an inevitable defeat incurred by a nation that initiated the conflict in which it was defeated. To understand Japan's defeat in the Second World War, to understand the process whereby Japan conjured into existence an alliance against itself that ultimately consisted of the world's most populous country, China; the world's greatest empire, Britain; the world's greatest industrial, economic, and naval power, the United States; and the world's largest and greatest military country, the Soviet Union, is impossible: westerners, at this length of time from these events, cannot readily comprehend what was at work, and the achievement on part of Japan, however unintentional, is made all the more remarkable by the fact that the Japanese government in summer 1941 was given a report that predicted national defeat. This report stated that Japan could never win a war with the United States and predicted that in a war with the United States the position of Japan, in terms of shipping, would become extremely difficult after late 1943 and that by the end of 1944 Japan would have reached the point at which it would no longer be able to wage war effectively. What the report could not predict, of course, was the American development and use of atomic bombs, but it did predict a Soviet entry into war against Japan, and, very interestingly, it predicted that the Japanese economy and manpower could not sustain the burden of the China war should that conflict continue for another five or ten years.

Very seldom are states given such notice of their own mortality—if the reader is kind enough to allow mixed metaphors—but the points of immediate relevance herein are three matters relating to both the Second World War overall and the China war. First, the Second World War is something of a misnomer in the sense that it was two wars largely separated from one another: there was an European war and there was a Japanese war, and they were linked by the fact that certain states were common to both and their separate outcomes were related. But the Japanese war was, in its turn, a number of conflicts—one in east Asia and another in southeast Asia—and a political war, fought in terms of the loyalty and commitment of the peoples of these areas. At war's end there was a campaign fought by the Soviet Union in Manchuria, northern China, and the northern islands. There was also not one but two wars fought in the Pacific, one involving fleets, battles, and amphibious landings and the other the war against Japanese shipping and trade. Herein is the basic point of understanding in the sense that it is clear that the Japanese high command never properly understood the situation in which it found itself, and never understood the nature of the war in China. Here—the second point of understanding—was handed to Japan at the end of 1938 proof of the Clausewitzian dictum that it is easy to conquer, hard to occupy. Japan found itself involved in a war that it could not win, neither politically nor militarily. Even with the capture of the Wuhan cities and reduction of the Chiang Kai-shek regime to a position approaching impotent irrelevance in southwest China by the end of 1938, there was no military victory that could be won that would end what was a disastrous, prohibitively expensive commitment in China, and there was no other means by which Japan could either destroy the Kuomintang regime or bring it to the conference table and an acknowledgement of defeat. Japan was to undertake the first strategic bombing campaign in history in an attempt to destroy the Chinese will to resist, but in Operations 100 and 101 Japan lacked the numbers of aircraft needed to carry through such an effort, and in any case it might and did level cities, but that fact of life had no political and moral impact: the Chinese dug into hills, and tried to keep going. The great irony of Operations 100 and 101 was that with the air arm of the *Rikugun* committed to close air-support operations and equipped with short-range aircraft with relatively light payloads, the main cutting edge of this effort had to be provided by the *Kaigun*, which alone had long-range fighters that could protect bombers against Chinese fighters, most of which were Soviet-supplied.

The strategic air offensive proved incapable of bringing the Chinese war to a close: it represented no advance over the land campaigns. The 101 offensive likewise proved no more effective than the earlier Operation 100, and the attempt to mount a third offensive—Operation 102—in 1941 fell foul of the *Kaigun's* withdrawal of formations in anticipation of a "real" war in the Pacific, but there is no indication that this third offensive would have represented any real advance over its two predecessors. Japanese efforts were interesting in that they included, in August 1941, the first— and unsuccessful—attempt to kill an enemy head of state by the use of airpower, but the basic point was that Japan lacked the military means, whether on the ground or in the air, to win a war in China, while the very nature of Japan itself and the effort it made in China precluded Japan's coming into possession of the means whereby it might be able to achieve politically what was beyond its abilities on the battlefield. Japan overran Manchuria, Inner Mongolia, northern China and much of central (and ultimately southern) China and sponsored various local administrations, but with very clear ideas of which people constituted leaders and which people they led. Yet the Japanese effort throughout China was bedeviled by one basic problem. Japan sought resources and markets in eastern Asia, and was never prepared to sponsor Chinese regimes that, on the evidence of past performance, represented a formidable combination of incompetence and corruption. Japan feared, and rightly, to pass to sponsored regimes real power lest that power be used against Japan—in this respect the Tungchow massacre was salutary because it was conducted by what were supposedly local troops under Japanese control—but unless Japan passed such power to client regimes there was not the least possibility that such regimes could secure credibility for themselves, and certainly they could never present themselves, whether internationally or domestically, as real alternatives to Chiang Kai-shek's dictatorship.

The third of the three points relates directly to the situation in which Japan found itself within the context of the war in China and, more generally, the international situation after the capture of the Wuhan cities in the fourth quarter of 1938. The main Japanese effort in China passed with the occupation of the Wuhan cities, Japan being left with more than 1,000,000 troops in China. But with the deterioration of the situation and then, in September 1939, the outbreak of general war in Europe, Japan's position gave rise to a certain caution on the part of Tokyo. The fact that Britain and France chose to go to war with Hitler's Germany was cause for a certain Japanese respect for the two democracies, and there was the small matter that with the outbreak of war in Europe credit and shipping all but disappeared and Japan needed both. No less importantly, in the course of the thirties Japan, as a revisionist power, had associated itself with Germany and Italy, and had been party to the Anti-Comintern Pact of November 25, 1936. In 1938 Japanese and Soviet forces had clashed in the ill-defined border area of what is now North Korea, Manchuria, and Russia's maritime provinces, in the area of Changkufeng. Soviet forces prevailed in this clash (July 11–August 10, 1938), but while a local truce ended this particular fight, the Japanese military was left with a determination not to be upstaged a second time. Unfortunately for the Japanese military, the second time emerged in May 1939, on the other side of Manchuria, between Nomonhan and the river Halha. Beginning in July the Japanese army mounted two major offensives, and then in August it was subjected to a massive attack that literally shredded its formations. As this Soviet counteroffensive materialized, and defeat, if local, became very real and humiliating, Germany chose to sign a nonaggression treaty with the Soviet Union.

Japan's sense of betrayal was very real, and the reaction against Germany, plus the other factors to which reference has been made, made for a certain caution at this stage of proceedings. In the event, however, a number of strands were to come together that made for general war in December 1941. These were the campaign in northwest Europe in spring 1940 that resulted in France's defeat and partial occupation, the German attack on the Soviet Union in June 1941, the increasingly difficult situation in which Japan found itself relative to the United States after January 1940, and, specifically, the series of American decisions and actions that closed down Japan's options in the second half of 1941.

The defeat of France was arguably the most important of these since, in a very obvious sense, so much of what was to follow did so in the wake of an event that rendered the British, Dutch, and French empires in southeast Asia defenseless. Even as France went down in defeat there were Japanese demands for a closing of British and French communications with Chiang Kai-shek's regime, but if there remained a certain caution at this stage, with the replacement of the Yonai administration by one headed by Konoye, a political lightweight who was allowed to become prime minister (for a second time) only after he had acceded to various service demands of a somewhat wide-ranging nature, this was swept aside after June 1941 when, as a direct result of the German attack on the Soviet Union, the *Kaigun* demanded a forward policy in southeast Asia. It did so because it feared that its sister service would seek to reverse the verdicts of 1938 and 1939 by joining in an attack on the Soviet Union: the *Kaigun* sought a commitment in southeast Asia that its real enemy—the *Rikugun*— could not evade. But this development was in no small measure the result of two matters, the fact that by this time—and as a result of the *Automedon* incident—the Japanese knew that Britain could not send a fleet to the Far East and could not undertake to provide for the proper defense of Malaya and Singapore, and the American dimension.

Trade relations between Japan and the United States were governed by treaty until January 1940 when it lapsed, without replacement; thereafter, Japan found itself denied trade in certain goods, raw materials, and foodstuffs. The measures were piecemeal and applied slowly, but together they amounted to something approaching an embargo by mid-1941. This, obviously, made for difficulty in the relationship between the two countries, but what drew the various pieces of the jigsaw together was the United States' passing of the Two-Ocean Naval Expansion Act in July 1940. In a very real sense France had been the first line of defense not simply of the French empire and Britain but also the United States, and with France's defeat, and the seeming inevitability of Britain's defeat, the United States was obliged to provide for its own defense in a way that the nation had been able to avoid since 1814. The act provided for a fleet able to fight simultaneously in both the Atlantic and the Pacific, but in a sense that was not realized in Washington; however, the passing of this act set the clock ticking. Japan had ended naval-limitation arrangements, arrangements that had limited American building and had provided Japan with a measure of security relative to the United States that it could never have commanded in an unrestricted naval race, but now the *Kaigun* was confronted with the consequences of its demand to end limitation: belatedly it saw that American building would result in the acquisition of massive, overwhelming American superiority of numbers by 1944–1948, a superiority that would destroy Japan's capacity to defend itself and even maintain itself as a great power. As a direct result of the passing of this act, the *Kaigun* was brought face to face with the reality that it faced a go-now-or-never dilemma, and herein two points were immediately significant. Its immediate construction programs were to be completed around the end of 1941, and at this time, in mid-1940, the *Kaigun* began to mobilize, and this process was to take some eighteen months. By the winter–spring of 1941–1942, therefore, the *Kaigun* would stand relative to the U.S. Navy at a level of strength and readiness that was without precedent but was certain to ebb thereafter as American building reversed the balance of relative advantage.

To this there was added another matter, namely that naval mobilization necessarily involved the taking of shipping from trade for service needs, but by this time, mid-1940, Japan needed some ten million tons of shipping in order to meet import needs. Japan had, however, but some 6,250,000 tons of shipping under its own flag, and with the outbreak of war in Europe Japan basically could not cover the shortfall. No less importantly, service mobilization meant the requisition of some three million tons of shipping, so Japan was left with just about half a merchant fleet with which to meet its needs. How Japan was to survive beyond winter–spring 1941–1942 is not altogether clear, but that is not the only matter that confounds understanding: what the Imperial Navy in mid-1940 envisaged happening when it began its mobilization is also not clear, the point being that it could not remain mobilized but not at war. But herein the reader is returned to the third and last matter to which reference was made some time ago, but only two were cited. The third matter relates to the nature of the war that the *Kaigun* planned to fight in the Pacific, the importance of this matter resting upon its fundamental misunderstanding of the nature and conduct of the war that it was to initiate.

The *Kaigun* was to go to war in December 1941 with a threefold intention, to neutralize the U.S. Pacific Fleet by means of a carrier strike, to conduct a series of landings throughout southeast Asia and the western and southwest Pacific, and to cast around these conquests a perimeter defense on which the Americans would be fought to a standstill until such time that they came to terms with failure and defeat, the result being a negotiated settlement that would confirm Japan in the possession of its conquests. Japan's defeat in the Second World War can be identified in precisely these terms although, inevitably, two riders have to be added. The first, simply, was the fact that the Japanese, correctly, saw war in political terms, that war was and is essentially political in its character and its determinants likewise are political. The Japanese accordingly placed reliance upon superior will as the means of ensuring victory, and herein were all the elements of national mythology that relate to the divine origins of Yamato, the protection offered by the gods, the impossibility of failure when divinely protected and charged with the liberation of Asia from white rule. With a Tenno who was a god, there could be no question of the Japanese not prevailing in wars with decadent capitalist societies that could not hope to match a Japanese willingness to die. The final manifestation of this was, of course, Japanese recourse to kamikaze attack, but the point was that Allied seamen who fought to live were more than a match for Japanese airmen who died in order to fight. The simple fact was that moral advantage could only apply in a condition of material balance, and it could not offset the material advantage that the Allies had at their disposal by 1944–1945.

The second rider is more difficult to define, but what had happened in the interwar period was that the Imperial Navy had planned for a defensive war, but by the end of the thirties its basic idea, while still defensive in its nature, had reached into the central Pacific. It planned to use submarines forward, in scouting lines astride the Hawaiian Islands, with submarines that had seaplanes for reconnaissance. The task of these submarines was to find an American fleet coming west and then to subject it to successive attacks: likewise, bombers based in the Marshall Islands were expected to continue this process, the *Kaigun* estimating—though perhaps it might be better described as "hoping"—that the submarines and aircraft might each account for a tenth of the enemy force. As the enemy continued to come forward it would be engaged by carrier forces that would be deployed forward of a Japanese battle force, these carrier forces being dispersed and consisting of one or perhaps two carriers: in this way, if discovered, losses might be minimized, but the basic Japanese intention was that their carriers would neutralize those of the enemy and thus deny the enemy formations reconnaissance capability and warning. Then battle would be joined, with the Japanese building small submarines that might be launched for submarine carriers across the line of the enemy advance. More importantly, the main effort at this stage would fall upon light cruisers and destroyers. In a series of massed night attacks, and with perhaps as many as 120 torpedoes being launched in any single scissors attack, the enemy formation was expected to take major losses—perhaps on the order of 30 percent—and to lose its cohesion and order, the battle then being joined, and won, by the battle force.

Such doctrine explains certain matters about Japanese construction and, perhaps more tellingly, reconstruction, programs in the thirties. Light cruisers and destroyers were built primarily around a torpedo armament that, it must be admitted, was superior to anything the Americans possessed until the 1970s: the Long Lance torpedo—which was not carried by aircraft and submarines—was perhaps forty years ahead of its time. Battleships were rebuilt with extra armor, an extra knot or two, and increased elevation and hence range for the main armament. Without the means to meet an American enemy on the basis of equal numbers, the *Kaigun* sought qualitative superiority in any number of material aspects, and it sought qualitative advantage in terms of professionalism, specifically in the night action. But in a manner that is very elusive, herein were all the ingredients of defeat.

The fundamental flaw that reached to the very core of Japanese intent was contained within the name: the *zengen sakusen* was "the Great All-Out Battle Strategy." What the *Kaigun* had here was a tactical plan for the conduct of battle that, by some mysterious process that was akin to transubstantiation, became a plan of campaign and thence the basis of a national war plan. The confusion of the three revealed that the *Kaigun* never properly understood the difference between war and a war, between a war and a campaign, and between a campaign and a battle. It saw them as one and the same and, very significantly, the name itself was revealing: national strategy was to be geared to fighting a battle. Battle is but a paving stone in an operational path marked by signposts that are called strategy. All three are related and interdependent, and the path is two-way, not one-way. But the basic point is that the basic battle plan was intellectually flawed, and was in any case overtaken by time: by 1940–1941 the basic tactical formation was no longer the line but the task group, which the Japanese had espoused even as they planned for battle against it. Moreover, the idea of a perimeter defense was no less flawed on any number of counts. The perimeter in fact consisted mostly of gaps held apart by the occasional island, and whether alone or in a group, no island had the depth or the number of aircraft that would enable it to withstand attack by the force that the Americans were certain to possess as and when they moved onto the offensive. There was, in addition, no guarantee that the Japanese fleet, which necessarily had to be there to support any threatened base, would always be available, while in any case a defensive perimeter necessarily pointed to a dispersal of force, and hence weakness, that was compounded by the fact that Japan simply did not have the construction battalions, equipment, and shipping needed to build the network of bases and feeder routes that were crucial to rapid reaction and defensive success. In a very obvious sense, and to use an analogy, the *zengen sakusen* was like a De Dondi timepiece, a majestic clockwork of wheels-within-wheels that represented the medieval European view of the universe: ingenious, imaginative, beautifully crafted, and hopelessly wrong. Misdirected and obsolescent even as it was put together, the *zengen sakusen* had implications that were disastrous: the *Kaigun* could only fight the battle it intended to win and could only win the battle it planned to fight, but the battles it had to fight were not the ones it could win. That may not be 100 percent true, and for obvious reason, but the basic point is correct: the bitter irony was that even the battles that did more or less conform to Japanese expectation proved to be battles that the *Kaigun* could not win primarily because the antidote of radar gave the Americans an advantage to which it had no counter.

Only two other matters need be cited in order to complete the recounting of the terms of reference for the war in which Japan found itself in terms of understanding the basis of Japan's defeat. The first is the fact that all the matters discussed herein relate to fleet action, and there was virtually no provision for Japan's defense of shipping. It was not until 1941 that the *Kaigun* undertook its first examination of shipping problems, specifically the question of what losses it might expect to incur. By an amazing coincidence, the calculation that American submarines might be able to inflict losses of perhaps 75,000 tons of shipping in any month went alongside the calculation that Japanese yards were good for 900,000 tons of production in any year, the latter figure being roughly twice the maximum output of Japanese yards in any single year between 1937 and 1941. Herein is the second matter, which in its immediate context is simply stated: from the time that Japan went to war, its yards had to build fleet units, build escorts, and build merchantmen, and at the same time had to provide the fleet units and merchantmen with routine refit and repair. On December 7, 1941, just one destroyer was not in service, and this meant that while routine refit and modernization programs for fleet units were not immediately important, they would become so by 1943–1944, and the simple fact was that Japanese yards could not undertake all five tasks simultaneously. In fact, by a prodigious effort Japanese yards were able to undertake new construction of warships, escorts, and merchantmen at least into 1944, but the fact was that in the same period there was no appreciable reduction in the aggregate tonnage of merchant shipping under or awaiting repair and refit. At war's end some 677,000 tons of shipping was thus detailed, and this indeed did represent the lowest total of the war, but the fact was that by this stage what had been perhaps an eighth of Japan's shipping in 1941 was at this stage more than two-fifths of Japan's remaining shipping, and this reduction was obviously related to the fact that warship construction had ended.

The second matter that need be cited in order to complete the recounting of the terms of reference for the war in which Japan found itself relates to the United States and the nature of the war that was fought and its outcome. Reference has been made to the view that Japan fundamentally erred in its view of war and the nature of the war—or more accurately wars—in which it found itself after 1941, but in part this stemmed from the obvious: a basic error in terms of the understanding of American society. This is a matter on which a certain care need be exercised, and for obvious reason: the phenomenal achievement of American industry in the course of the Second World War could not have been anticipated in 1940–1941. The world has become very familiar over the last sixty years with the reality of American power, but that power was not reality in 1940–1941, and Japan was not alone in wholly underestimating American industrial stamina. Herein, of course, is the reverse side of the coin in terms of so much that has been written thus far in this chapter, but the simple fact was that in 1945 the United States produced something akin to three-quarters of the entire industrial output of the world. American factories were responsible for almost two-fifths of all aircraft and more than half of all aircraft engines and airframes produced between 1939 and 1945, while American yards built 32,056,140 tons of shipping between 1942 and 1945, a level of production that must be measured against the fact that the world's largest merchant navy—that of Britain—in 1939 mustered some 21,000,000 tons. The United States raised about a hundred divisions in the course of the war, but the total value of all forms of supply provided to its allies was equivalent to the sum needed for it to have raised 2,000 infantry or 555 armored divisions. But here is additional cause for caution: the victory that was won in the Second World War was not an American victory. The victory that was won was an Allied victory, and it need be noted, as a rough rule of thumb, that nations that fight alone usually lose.

The American contribution to that victory was massively important, but the limits of that achievement and contribution need be noted: the defeat of Germany was primarily a military defeat registered on the Eastern Front by the Soviet Union: the Anglo-American campaign in northwest Europe contributed to the completion of that Allied victory, but no more. In the Japanese war, however, the situation was very different; the nature of that victory is elusive. The Japanese defeat was primarily a naval defeat, and that is historically very unusual: very seldom have polities been defeated by sea, and even more rare have been the defeat of powers across oceans. People live on land, and armies are infinitely more important in the registering of victory than navies, and for this very simple reason: navies and seaborne trade might be the means by which a nation survives and fights, but in the final analysis armies and land power invariably possess a strategic importance and significance that permits no real argument. The credit for Japan's defeat was not an American national monopoly. China provided a dimension in terms of the exhaustion of Japanese resources and distraction of effort, an effort across time and distance that cannot be quantified but was real nonetheless. The European imperial powers, and Australia, Canada, and New Zealand, all made the greatest contribution that was within their ability to command, though even together this remained small—the "nice-to-have" and not "need-to-have" dimension. The Soviet contribution is not to be underestimated, not least in terms of the final Japanese deliberations and the desire on the part of Japan's national leadership to avoid any prospect of Soviet occupation for fear of the social revolution that might follow in its wake: the Soviet victory in Manchuria and northern China in August 1945 was comprehensive and most impressive, and certainly not to be gainsaid or demeaned, but the real Soviet contribution was this added—albeit unintended—dimension, and Japan's defeat had already taken shape, was already a reality, by the time that the Soviet Union came to this war. The real achievement in terms of victory in this war was American, and it was the American effort across the Pacific and in its two forms—the fleet, battle, and landings and the complementary campaign against shipping—that decided the outcome of this conflict.

The basis of this victory can perhaps best be explained to an American readership by reference to the fact that the Pacific war was not the first such war that the United States had been obliged to fight. Between 1941 and 1945 Japan was to the United States what the Confederacy had been exactly eighty years before: starting with the opening attacks upon U.S. military bases, the parallels between the American Civil War and the Pacific war are striking. Both wars saw the United States opposed by enemies that relied upon allegedly superior martial qualities to overcome demographic, industrial, and positional inferiority, and in both wars the United States' superior material resources and ability to mount debilitating blockades proved decisive to the outcome. In both wars the United States was able to use the advantages of a secure base and exterior lines of communication to bring overwhelming strength against enemies that were plagued by divided counsels and that were committed to defensive strategies that involved their trying to hold widely separated positions along an extended perimeter that were not mutually supporting and that could not be properly supplied for want of an adequate transportation infrastructure. In both wars the enemies of the United States, intent upon forcing it to recognize the reality of their existence or conquests, sought to wage wars of attrition and exhaustion against a much superior enemy and in the process were divided and conquered. The Union drive down the Mississippi that resulted in the capture of Vicksburg in July 1863 has its parallel in the drive to the Philippines that separated Japan from the southern resources area: both efforts, for the United States, were characterized by maneuver. The battles in eastern Tennessee and the march to the sea have as their counterpart the central Pacific offensive that, in the form of blockade and the strategic bombing offensive, took the war to the enemy homeland: both efforts, for the United States, were characterized by mass, firepower, and shock action, though on this point a certain caution need be exercised because the parallels are not exact. Stretching the point, one could assert that the battles in the southwest Pacific in 1942 and 1943 were equivalent to the battles in Maryland and Virginia in 1862 in that the outcome of these battles ensured that the enemies of the United States could not prevail in the wars that they had initiated: both the Confederacy and Japan had to win quickly or not at all. Moreover, in both conflicts Europe loomed large. In the American

Civil War the Confederacy looked to European intervention to ensure its victory, and in the Second World War Japan tied itself to the German cause in the hope that Germany's victory would ensure the neutralization of the United States: neither eventuality occurred.

Any competent military historian, given a judicious selection of material and slick presentation, can make one war look like another, and perhaps in thus presenting the American Civil War and the Pacific war this account is guilty of thoroughly mendacious treatment of Clio. One trusts not, but in any case by portraying events thus one is permitted to make one point before setting out an account of proceedings. The point is very simple, and it lies in bringing together all the various aspects of victory and defeat and the reduction of the same to a rendition of the cause of Japan's defeat to single-causation status: the basis of Japan's defeat lay in the fact that the Americans were a pack of cheating bastards. It was not that the *Kaigun*'s intention to fight the U.S. Navy to a draw was flawed. The *Kaigun*'s problem was not that it faced a U.S. Navy but that it faced two U.S. Navies. It fought the first U.S. Navy to a standstill, but the problem was that in the process it exhausted itself as well—and the United States built another navy in the meantime. In 1943 alone six fleet, nine light and nineteen escort carriers, two battleships, four heavy and seven light cruisers, 126 destroyers, 221 destroyer escorts, and fifty-six submarines entered service with the U.S. Navy, the equivalent in tonnage terms of the whole of the Japanese navy in 1941. The U.S. Navy, the prewar navy, met and defeated the *Kaigun* on the perimeter defense, and by spring 1943 was spent. It was spent not so much because of the heaviness of losses, which in fact were remarkably light: the loss was in terms of balance, time, and the need to secure replacement aircrew and air formations on scales that were previously unthinkable. By war's end the U.S. Navy had some 90,000 trained aircrew and numbered 99 fleet, light, and escort carriers, 1,246 fleet units, and 5,250 major combat units, and 67,952 units of each and every size and description with the fleet, amphibious forces, logistics organization, and shore establishments. Herein is the basis of the questioning of American honesty and legitimacy: this navy, overwhelmingly, was a wartime creation. From the time of Grant, the United States waged war on the basis of demographic, industrial, economic, and financial superiority over all enemies, which meant that the American way of war, for a hundred years, stressed superiority of numbers, concentration of massed firepower, and the seeking of battle as the means of ensuring the defeat of an enemy. This formula lacked subtlety and possessed little in the way of finesse, but the yardstick by which it must be measured was effectiveness and success, and it stood the United States in good stead until it fundamentally failed to understand the nature of the war it fought and of the enemy it faced in southeast Asia in the 1960s. But if the American way of war was very basic, one can argue that in terms of subtlety, of elegance and sophistication, there are few examples in warfare in the twentieth century to rival the opening Japanese moves, across nine time zones and 7,000 miles, that brought war to southeast Asia and the Pacific in December 1941. The Japanese put together a plan involving successive attacks by forces operating behind a front secured by land-based air power and then penetrated to the Malay Barrier with an effort remarkable in terms of economy of effort and lack of any overall superiority of numbers but that commanded massive local superiority over enemies defensively dispersed and unable to cooperate to any real effect. And, of course, the war that Japan thus initiated was a war that it lost.

In setting out an account of the war, the narrative of events, one would begin with the statement of the obvious. The war divides into a number of constituent parts, the first of which is the period of Japanese conquest, between December 1941 and April 1942. Thereafter there remained further Japanese acquisitions, most obviously in southern China in the course of 1944 when Japanese formations undertook a series of offensives designed to deny the American bases from which B-29 Superfortresses could bomb the home islands. The process of Burma's conquest was not completed by April 1942, and there remained certain areas—in the Solomon and Aleutian Islands as well as on Nauru and Ocean Island in the central Pacific—but for the most part the period of Japanese conquest had run its course by April 1942: the rampage of the Japanese carrier fleet in the Indian Ocean inadvertently provided the finale to this process in the sense that in this operation Japanese success was singularly impressive and wholly irrelevant. The second phase of the war lasted from May 1942 to February 1943 and was notable for the series of battles that together saw the initiative change hands. This is a period cursed by poor historiographical treatment. In the public mind there must always be "the decisive battle" and "the turning point," just as there must be national heroes, the individuals raised to the status of the people's gladiator but also raised to a status in the pantheon of heroes *"sans peur et sans reproche."* Wars of many years' duration are never decided in a single battle, and there are no battles when assured victory switches sides. It is possible to argue that the outcome of this war was decided in one single episode—the Japanese attack on the U.S. Pacific Fleet constituted such an event in terms of ensuring Japan's national defeat—and that Japan's subsequent waging of war amounted to no more than a national kamikaze effort. That point left aside, the outcome of this war was not decided at Midway, and the passing of the initiative from Japanese hands was not the result of a single defeat. Between May 1942 and February 1943 there were fought no fewer than four fleet battles—Coral Sea in May, Midway in June, Eastern Solomons in August, and Santa Cruz in October—and more than fifty actions involving warships and aircraft on either one or both sides in the waters that washed the lower Solomons and in the skies over them. The latter—which involved the major Allied defeat off Savo Island in August and a very narrow escape from a comparable defeat off Tassafaronga (November 30–December 1)—were ultimately decided by three matters: the American possession of the airfield on Guadalcanal, which ultimately provided a measure of air control over and off the island that the Japanese could not reverse; American possession of radar and slow acquisition of combat experience that enabled them to meet and defeat Japanese battle formations at night; and the prohibitive losses incurred by Japanese shipping in theater, a point that has to be allied to the fact that at this stage of proceedings Japan as a nation and the services could not afford a commitment involving some 750,000 tons of shipping in what was one of the most distant sectors of the perimeter defense. The great irony about these proceedings—and one that seems to have been quite beyond the *Kaigun* to realize, still less appreciate—is that, in effect, in the campaign for Guadalcanal the Americans fought the *zengen sakusen* and made it work against its original authors: the *Kaigun* had forgotten to take out the patent.

The third phase of the war extended from February to October 1943 and was, in a sense, the period when "nothing happened." That, of course, was not the case, but in terms of territories or islands changing hands very little of importance manifested itself. The Aleutian Islands that Japan had taken in June 1943 were returned to their owners; in the Solomon chain the Americans and their allies took the tide of war into the central and northern islands; there was a series of minor Allied gains in eastern New Guinea; and on the border between India and Burma, in the Arakan, there was a British offensive in which the Japanese comprehensively outfought their enemy. But in real terms the lines on the map showed very little in terms of change: the more important events at this time were in Europe, where the German army was outfought in front of Kursk and where the British and Americans, after the victory in Tunisia that marked the end of the campaign in north Africa, staged landings first in Sicily in July and then in southern Italy in September. In the Pacific this was a period of preparation for the Japanese in preparing defensive positions and readying carrier air groups for the next phase of operations. For the Americans and their allies there were a number of small actions in the Solomons and, more significantly, the comprehensive defeat of a series of Japanese air offensives in the Solomons and eastern New Guinea after April, but the real effort was in terms of preparations for the start of the central Pacific offensive. This, the fourth phase of the war, was to open in November 1943 with the attacks on Rabaul, which represented a telling defeat for the Japanese warships and air formations concentrated there: these were followed by the landings in the Gilbert Islands. The latter were to take their place in American national lore because of the ferocity of the fighting and the alleged heavy losses. This, the first major assault, saw the Japanese sink an escort carrier, but the fact was that Operation Galvanic was the overture to Operation Flintlock, the assault on the Marshalls in January 1944. At the same time as these operations, Allied forces advanced into the upper Solomons and landed in western New Britain, and these operations in effect marked the neutralization of Rabaul as a base: the landings on Manus in March 1944 completed the process whereby Rabaul was bypassed.

The reduction of certain Japanese bases in the Marshalls, and the bypassing of others, went hand in hand with a double carrier effort, the first in February 1944 seeing the neutralization of Truk as a base, the withdrawal of Japanese battle and carrier formations from Truk first to the Palaus and then, when that base was threatened, to Singapore, and perhaps the most destructive single day in history in terms of the destruction of shipping (February 17). The second carrier effort, in March and April, saw the American carriers reach as far to the west as the Palau islands, turn back to the east, and then direct their attention to Japanese bases in the Mariana Islands and Caroline Islands. The process continued with the carriers then supporting the first major moves in the southwest Pacific theater, directed against Aitape and Hollandia in April 1944, this fourth period being brought to an end with the American landings on Saipan in June 1944 that set in train the events that led to the battle of the Philippine Sea.

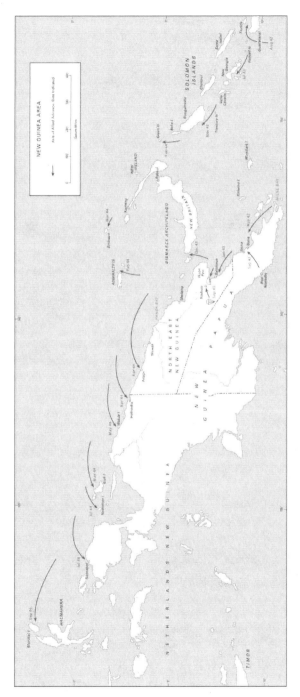

New Guinea Area (U.S. Army Center of Military History)

The point about all these operations was that in a very real sense they came after the decision of the war had been reached. It may not have been apparent at the time, at least not to any non-American observer, but in November 1943 the Americans moved in such strength that the outcome of the offensive to which they were committed was assured: the questions that remained concerned themselves with the cost that would be exacted and the time that would be lost, but the outcome of each and every American offensive operation from this time was assured. No American offensive from this time was on the Guadalcanal level, where the relative slenderness of initial commitment could have cost the Americans dear: from November 1943 each and every American offensive was invested with such carrier strength that the target could be wholly isolated from outside support while massive superiority of manpower and firepower meant that no isolated and unsupported Japanese garrison could withstand assault. At the Philippine Sea the Americans fought and won perhaps the greatest carrier battle in history—if numbers are counted and solely on the basis of fleet and light fleet carriers[1]—and it was a victory that bared the way into the western Pacific. Moreover, it was a victory that, by ensuring the subsequent reduction of Saipan, Guam, and Tinian, provided the bases from which the United States could mount a strategic air offensive against the home islands. This allowed the United States to abandon its previous intention to mount such a campaign from bases in China. The first such raid was conducted in June 1944, but the growing American air threat had already provoked a Japanese offensive throughout southern China in April–May that had revealed the weakness of the initial American intention. The Chiang Kai-shek regime was prepared to sanction an American strategic air offensive from bases in China as the means of avoiding any major, long-term military commitment, but without such a commitment, and without the necessary divisions in order to provide for the defense of these bases, the intention to mount an air offensive induced the one Japanese effort to which there was no answer.

The Japanese offensive opened a crisis in Sino-American relations that came to its climax in October and that led to a major American diplomatic and political defeat: unwilling to consider any alternative to Chiang and his regime, Washington found itself caught in a Kuomintang embrace from which it was not to escape for the best part of three decades. But the October crisis came at a time when the United States was poised to win the naval battle for the Philippines, usually called the Battle of Leyte Gulf. This was a series of actions, none of which were fought in Leyte Gulf, that was the greatest naval battle in modern history in terms of the number of warships engaged and the area of battle, across the whole of the Philippines, and it resulted in a comprehensive Japanese defeat. But the real significance of this battle, the real losses for the Japanese, came not so much in this battle but in the month that followed, because in that time the Americans moved into possession of overwhelming superiority in the air over the Philippines and were thus able to strike at Japanese shipping now stripped of escorts and overhead cover. Herein was the significance of this fifth period of the war. Between July 1944 and March 1945 the Americans carried the tide of war across the Pacific and in this period severed Japanese lines of communication with the southern resources area, and without the wherewithal from the south Japan faced certain defeat. It was recognition of this reality that prompted the Imperial Navy to give battle in defense of the Philippines: it realized that defeat in the Philippines was tantamount to defeat on home soil. Thus it fought and lost a battle that was most unusual in the sense that it was the largest naval battle of the war, and it was a battle fought after the outcome of the war had been decided: no Japanese victory at Leyte was ever going to overturn the imbalance of advantages that then existed.

This period, between July 1944 and March 1945, was notable for two developments and for a host of operations. The first development was the fact that between November 1943 and June 1944 the Americans undertook what was a genuine combined offensive involving land, air, and naval forces operating in support of one another: arguably it was the first tri-service offensive, or would have been if the Americans had possessed three services at this time. Land-based airpower struck at targets that were then subjected to attack and neutralization by carrier and fleet formations; amphibious assault then secured islands or bases from which land-based aircraft could pave the way for the next operation. This technique saw continued employment in western New Guinea and on the approaches to Mindanao between May and September 1944 and was at work in the landings on Leyte, in the central Philippines, in October, but the latter effort was very different from previous American efforts: past efforts had seen American forces overwhelm isolated and individual bases and garrisons, but here, in Formosa and the Philippines, the American carrier forces took on and defeated an enemy that was possessed of what amounted to a contiguous land mass. Obviously the islands were islands, and the Philippines did not represent a continental land mass, but the nearness of islands, the extensive network of feeder routes, and the

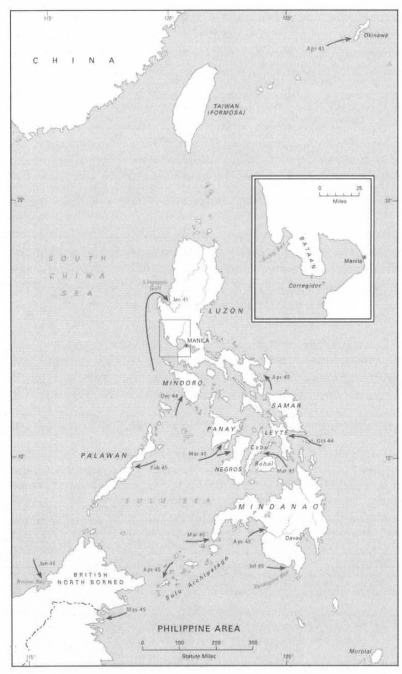

The Philippine Area (U.S. Army Center of Military History)

availability of air formations for battle in effect meant that the American carriers had to take on an enemy with strategic depth and possessed of what should have been marked, indeed potentially decisive, superiority of numbers. By any standard, the Americans were sailing somewhat close to the wind, but in the battles that unfolded, their carrier air formations broke Japanese air power in the Philippines: they totally outfought the Japanese to the extent that the latter's recourse to kamikaze attacks represented nothing more than a minimal tactical response to a lost strategic cause.

No less significantly, the severing of Japan's lines of communication in this phase of the war, as a result of the Americans' establishing themselves in bases throughout the Philippines after October 1944 and then, in March 1945, moving into position for the assault on Okinawa, really represented a development crucial in the unfolding of the campaign against Japanese shipping. In the first two years of war, before November 1943, this campaign was undertaken primarily by submarines, and the returns were modest: the Americans had relatively few submarines, torpedoes were not wholly reliable, and transit times were extensive. Crucially, in this period, before November 1943, the submarine effort was barely supported: between December 1941 and October 1943 carrier aircraft accounted for just one naval and two army transports, and in the third phase of the war, between March and October 1943, they did not sink a single ship, whether warship, service ship, or merchantman. In the fourth phase of war, as the Americans moved against Rabaul and Truk and the Japanese bases throughout the western Pacific, the toll exacted by carrier aircraft was significant, nearly eighty ships of more than 420,000 tons. Virtually all of these were service ships of varying descriptions, and the significance was obvious: the service ships had to operate in waters dominated by American carrier aircraft and increasingly patrolled by submarines detailed to operate in support of carrier and amphibious forces. Now, in this fifth phase of the war, between July 1944 and March 1945, carrier aircraft accounted for over ninety service transports of more than 380,000 tons and some 112 merchantmen of 327,000 tons. Put another way, in the twenty-three months of the period December 1941–October 1943, the Japanese incurred average monthly losses of 8.75 warships of 27,556 tons, 6.55 naval auxiliaries of 34,729 tons, 7.78 military transports of 31,873 tons, and 9.41 merchantman of 34,849 tons: overall shipping losses, excluding warships, totaled 540 ships of 2,308,012 tons, an average of 23.74 ships of 101,451 tons per month. In the eight-month period November 1943–June 1944, average monthly losses amounted to 24.50 warships of 41,881 tons, 28.19 naval auxiliaries of 139,424 tons, 21.75 military transports of 83,417 tons, and 19.31 merchantman of 64,898 tons: overall shipping losses, excluding warships, totaled 554 ships of 2,301,909 tons, an average of 69.25 ships of 287,739 tons per month. Then, in the next phase of war, Japanese average monthly losses in a nine-month period amounted to 46.56 warships of 98,561 tons, 18.67 naval auxiliaries of 77,590 tons, 20.11 military transports of 80,716 tons, and 45.67 merchantman of 148,609 tons: overall shipping losses, excluding warships, came to 760 ships of 2,762,234 tons, an average of 84.44 ships of 306,915 tons per month. No further comment is necessary, but the reader may be reminded of the 75,000-tons calculation.

The landings on Okinawa in April 1945, following those on Iwo Jima in February, represented the closing of the ring around Japan, and this final period of the war, between April and August 15, 1945, possessed a number of significant features. It was the period that saw the systematic mining of Japanese and Korean waters that simply overwhelmed defenses: in this period mines accounted for 174 service and merchant ships of 303,000 tons, and this represented the largest single cause of Japanese losses. No less significantly, this period witnessed the imposition of close blockade with Allied warships undertaking a series of bombardments: for a war that opened with the Japanese sinking of four American battleships at Pearl Harbor and two British capital ships in the South China Sea, the significance of this development demands little in the way of elaboration, but perhaps one of the telling facts about this process whereby Allied carrier and fleet formations came to operate to within distances of sixty miles of the Japanese coast was the fact that of the 117 warships in the American carrier groups that raided Tokyo in February 1945, just six had not been in service on December 7, 1941. No less telling, after March 1945 the American strategic air offensive changed fundamentally, the Americans abandoning any thought of precision attacks in favor of low-level firestorm raids. The first such raid against Tokyo resulted in more than a million people being killed, injured, or rendered homeless, and by war's end 43 percent of sixty-three of Japan's major cities had been laid waste, 42 percent of her industrial capacity had been destroyed, and no fewer than 22,000,000 of her people had been killed, wounded, or rendered homeless as a direct result of the American bombing offensive.

Such results inevitably are overshadowed by "the manner in which the war ended," that is, the attacks on Hiroshima and Nagasaki, but a number of points need be noted to place this in proper perspective. By August 1945

Japanese industry was in end-stage production: the lack of raw materials ensured that work then in hand would be the last. Moreover, it has been suggested that with the disastrous fall of food imports and the prospect of poor harvest, Japan could not have come through the winter of 1945–1946 without perhaps as many as seven million deaths, primarily from disease rather than starvation but obviously directly related to malnutrition. In July 1945 American carriers put 1,747 sorties together on one raid of raids over the Inland Sea, and American carrier aircraft were flying defensive combat air patrols over Japanese airfields. In addition, the greater part of the Japanese army formations in the home islands were poorly trained and equipped, and in any case, they faced an impossible tactical dilemma in the prospect of invasion: held forward on bases they were certain to be subjected to overwhelming direct fire, but held in rear areas they lacked the radios and vehicles to move rapidly and en masse to forward positions and would have been subjected to pulverizing air attacks had they been called upon to do so. All sorts of nightmare scenarios have been painted about what resistance might have been encountered had things come to an invasion of the home islands, but given the Japanese army's lack of armor and firepower, it is difficult to believe that it could have achieved results and inflicted losses that proved beyond German arms in Normandy. As it was, it was the pieces coming together—political; economic, industrial, and financial; military, naval, and in the air—that made for Japan's overall defeat and the victory of the United States in this part of the worst war in human history.

Notes

1. At the Philippine Sea the Americans had eight fleet and seven light fleet carriers and the Japanese had five fleet and four light fleet carriers; at Leyte Gulf the totals were nine and eight plus one and three.

Sources and Suggested Readings

Barnhart, Michael. *Japan Prepares for Total War: The Search for Economic Security, 1919–1941*. Ithaca, N.Y., 1987.

Buell, Thomas B. *The Quiet Warrior: A Biography of Admiral Raymond A. Spruance*. Boston, 1974.

Byrd, Martha. *Chennault: Giving Wings to the Tiger*. Tuscaloosa, Ala., 1987.

Carter, Worall Reed. *Beans, Bullets and Black Oil: The Story of Fleet Logistics Afloat in the Pacific during World War II*. Washington, D.C., 1953.

Cohen, Jerome B. *Japan's Economy in War and Reconstruction*. Westport, Conn., 1949.

Cook, Haruko Taya, and Theodore F. Cook. *Japan at War: An Oral History*. New York, 1992.

Drea, Edward J. *MacArthur's ULTRA: Codebreaking and the War against Japan, 1942–1945*. Lawrence, Kans., 1992.

Duus, Peter, Ramon H. Myers, and Mark R. Peattie, eds. *The Japanese Wartime Empire, 1931–1945*. Princeton, N.J., 1996.

Evans, David C., and Mark R. Peattie. *Kaigun: Strategy, Tactics and Technology in the Imperial Japanese Navy, 1887–1941*. Annapolis, Md., 1997.

Fairbanks, John K., and Albert Feuerwerker, eds. *The Cambridge History of China, vol. 13, Republican China 1912–1949*, part 2. Cambridge, UK, 1986.

Frank, Richard. *Guadalcanal: The Definitive Account of the Landmark Battle*. New York, 1990.

Hall, John W, et. al. *The Cambridge History of Japan*, vol. 6, *The Twentieth Century*. Cambridge, UK, 1988.

Hayes, Grace Pearson. *The History of the Joint Chiefs of Staff in World War II: The War against Japan*. Annapolis, Md., 1982.

Holmes, Wilfred J. *Double-Edged Secrets: U.S. Naval Intelligence Operations in the Pacific during World War II*. Annapolis, Md., 1979.

Lundstrom, John B. *The First South Pacific Campaign: Pacific Fleet Strategy, December 1941–June 1942*. Annapolis, Md., 1976.

Morley, James William, ed. *Japan's Road to the Pacific War. The China Quagmire. Japan's Expansion on the Asian Continent, 1933–1941. Selected translations from Taiheiyo Senso No Michi: Kaisen Gaikko Shi*. New York, 1983.

Peattie, Mark R. *Ishiwara Kanji and Japan's Confrontation with the West*. Princeton, N.J., 1975.

———. *Sunburst: The Rise of Japanese Naval Air Power, 1909–1941*. Annapolis, Md., 2001.

Pelz, Stephen E. *Race to Pearl Harbor: The Failure of the Second London Naval Conference and the Onset of World War II*. Cambridge, Mass., 1974.

Potter, E. B. *Nimitz*. Annapolis, Md., 1976.

Prados, John. *Combined Fleet Decoded: The Secret History of American Intelligence and the Japanese Navy in World War II*. New York, 1995.

Skates, John Ray. *The Invasion of Japan: The Alternative to the Bomb*. Columbia, S.C., 1997.

Y'Blood, William T. *Red Sun Setting: The Battle of the Philippine Sea*. Annapolis, Md., 1981.

The Korean Conflict
and the Cold War

Pierce C. Mullen

A MERICA'S VICTORY over Japan in 1945 was hastened by the dropping of two atomic bombs on the Japanese home islands. The dawn of the atomic age also ushered in a new era of warfare and global military strategy. The post–World War II years were expected to be a time of peace and reconciliation, but instead they became a period of increasing international danger and anxiety as tension grew between the two major wartime allies, the United States and the Soviet Union. By the late 1940s, Communist Russia and capitalist America became implacable enemies as a result of a series of disputes involving the occupation of Germany and the future of Eastern Europe. Within five years after the end of World War II, both powers formed alliance systems—the North Atlantic Treaty Organization (NATO) and the Warsaw Pact—that divided Europe into two armed camps along a line from Stettin in the Baltic to Trieste in the Adriatic, a line that Winston Churchill called the Iron Curtain. The Cold War became a conflict of maneuver, propaganda, and threats that divided nations on the basis of pro-Communist and prodemocratic-capitalist allegiances.

The struggle began in Europe but quickly spread to other parts of the globe. In 1949 the victory of Mao Tse-tung's Communist forces over the Nationalists in a long civil war in China led to the creation of the People's Republic and the expansion of President Harry S. Truman's "containment policy" against communism to Asia. In the same year the Soviet Union, which the United States regarded as the leader of an international Communist conspiracy bent on world domination, successfully tested an atomic bomb and broke the American monopoly in nuclear weapons. These two troubling events of 1949 intensified Cold War tensions and led to a period of political hysteria in Washington that was heightened by allegations that Communist spies had infiltrated the U.S. power structure.

From the end of World War II to 1950, most Americans believed that any conflict with the Soviet Union would begin in Europe. Berlin, which had just experienced a Soviet blockade and a magnificent Anglo-American airlift to sustain the city, would likely be the flashpoint. The United States held a monopoly franchise on atomic weapons for a scant four years—early in 1949 the USSR exploded one over central Asia. The apocalypse scenario imagined a nuclear war, the ultimate war, World War III. Americans were unaware of the huge research program the USSR had begun during the last months of World War II and rightly suspected that internal spies in the United States had given the Russians atomic secrets.

So from its inception, the Cold War fostered the growth of a witch-hunting mentality that sought out anyone who might be suspected of being a spy for the Communists. This initial political paranoia later spawned a search for those who "lost China" and then for anyone who might disagree strongly with the political views of these ultrarightist legislators. Accusations against Secretary of State George Marshall—a hero to most Americans and one of the premier military minds in our history—and subsequent attacks upon the army brought this hysteria before the bar of public opinion, but deeply held worries about Communist influences in government poisoned American politics for decades.

Americans wanted a return to a normalcy that they had not experienced since before the great economic depression: jobs, families, education, and housing dominated their thinking. Veterans, many of whom had never enjoyed any economic security and who had survived the ordeals of World War II, sought a better future for themselves and their children. They supported the rebuilding of Europe, even the rebuilding of their former enemy Germany if that were necessary for European security. But mostly they wanted to be left alone.

President Truman, who had personal combat experience as an artillery officer in World War I, reflected that view. He presided over severe cutbacks in the once huge and immensely powerful American military establishment. Simultaneously the president reorganized the intelligence functions of the federal government and created the Central Intelligence Agency (CIA). A new National Security Council arose to guide leaders in their approaches to the major diplomatic, economic, and military policies they would adopt. The army and navy lost a portion of their independence and were merged into a joint establishment under the Department of Defense. It was an unwieldy structure that now included a new player in the struggle for appropriations and prestige, the United States Air Force. Airmen claimed the military high ground by gaining control over strategic (i.e., atomic and later thermonuclear) weapons.

Because the United States, with its Marshall Plan for rebuilding European democracies and its series of mutual defense alliances like NATO (North Atlantic Treaty Organization), was so centered upon the Soviet threat to western and central Europe, it propounded fuzzy and sometimes misleading projections of interest in Asian affairs. Containing communism in Europe was one problem; how could the nation contain communism in East Asia after the defeat of Chinese Nationalist forces and their virtual internment in Formosa? Japan, still devastated by air and naval strikes, then became the linchpin of an American Pacific strategy. Korea was on the periphery, and was hardly worth defending except as a distant outpost to protect Japan.

Korea was hardly known in the United States. Shortly after the opening of Japan by the American navy in the 1850s, Korea was forced to accept an American presence too. President Theodore Roosevelt sacrificed the country to the Japanese as a means to ending the war between Russia and Japan in 1905. From 1905 to the end of World War II, it had been dominated and brutalized by the Japanese. When the Soviets entered the war against Japan in August of 1945, their armies swept through Manchuria, and a small force occupied the northern half of Korea by the time the Japanese surrendered in September. The Americans agreed to a joint occupation, and a token force claimed control of the south, with its capital at Seoul.

In North Korea a truculent, charismatic Kim Il Sung led a brutal and nationalistic Soviet-style government. In South Korea, the American-trained Syngman Rhee led a similar nationalist government dominated by his cronies. Both sides waged a civil war of varying intensities from 1948 onward. Both governments were determined to enlist the assistance of proxies, Chinese-Russian in the north and American in the south, to seek unification. When the United States radiated vague signals that Korea was not of central importance to American national interest, Kim Il Sung, Mao Tse-tung, and Joseph Stalin hammered out a series of agreements that would encourage a powerful North Korean Peoples' Army invasion of the south. In war-weary Russia, Stalin was wary, and offered only tentative promises of assistance. The Chinese, having won their internal war against the Nationalists, offered strong commitments of supplies, training, technical support, and, if absolutely necessary, armed intervention. After vigorous discussions right after the declaration of the People's Republic of China in October 1949, Mao Tse-tung, the Communist head of government, decided that China would enter a war on the Korean peninsula even though a high casualty figure was the price it would have to pay.

At a time when most expected a nuclear World War III, the United States fought a frustrating and successful limited war. Today it is the "Forgotten War." The Chinese never forgot it because that country became a major player on the great power scene because of it. The Korean conflict, so called because it was not an officially declared war by the United States, is the pivot point of the West's successful challenge to world communism. It is the harbinger of the end of the Cold War.

Pierce Mullen describes and analyzes the Korean conflict within the context of Cold War attitudes and presumptions. He concludes that the United States was ill prepared to fight a limited war of this kind because of its rapid demobilization after World War II and its overwhelming fixation on security in western Europe. American commanders were indeed fortunate eventually to bring to bear the massive firepower, tested in Europe during World War II, against the enormous Communist Chinese forces that intervened on the isolated Asian peninsula in late 1950. Even at that, American conventional forces and their allies could do no better than stalemate their Asian foes. The Korean War, fought under the authority of the United Nations, revealed many weaknesses in America's military preparedness in the nuclear age. Surprisingly, many of these deficiencies were not remedied before U.S. forces would become engaged in another limited war in Asia a little more than one decade later. The war also dramatized the long-standing potential for conflict between the president as commander in chief and his generals as well as the frustrations and tensions entailed in conducting an undeclared war in which the final objective was less than total victory.

Just before a rainy dawn on Sunday, June 25, 1950, heavy guns and mortars of the North Korean People's Army (NKPA) bombarded South Korean positions along the 38th parallel. War had come to Korea. For sev-

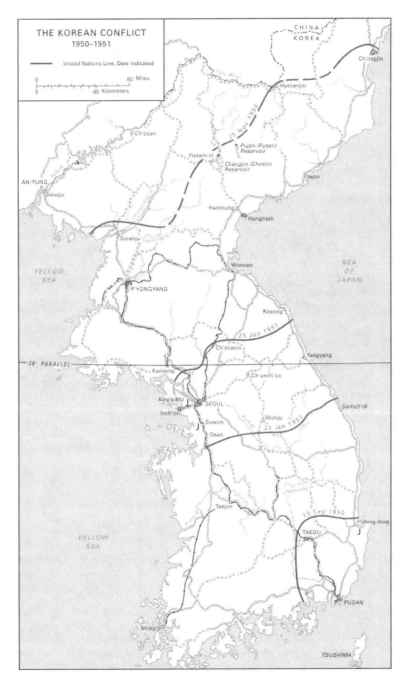

The Korean Conflict, 1950–1951 (U.S. Army Center of Military History)

eral weeks previously, bitter firefights had broken out along this dividing line, so it was some hours before the realization sunk in that this was no drill. At 11:00 that morning North Korean radio announced that the nation was at war with its southern neighbor. North Korean armored spearheads moved south toward the vital bridges over the Han River. Thousands of terrified civilians and scattered elements of the army of the Republic of Korea (ROK) fled before the tanks. Americans on the scene and elsewhere thought that they were experiencing another Pearl Harbor.

In the United States there had been considerable debate over policy toward Korea. Some officials had written off the peninsula as indefensible and undesirable, while others, determined to halt the march of communism, would draw a line there. It was a symbol of the last Western lodgment in northeast Asia, and the peninsula pointed like a dagger at southern Japan. For critics of the Truman administration, Korea was a litmus test of attitudes and resolve in the Cold War.

The Korean conflict breaks down naturally into five major periods: the initial offensive by the North Korean People's Army stalled and fell apart in mid-September 1949. The second major period is the pursuit north of the 38th parallel to the Yalu river following the amphibious landing at Inchon in September 1949. The third period covers the intervention of the Chinese and a UN retreat back across the 38th parallel. Gen. Matthew Ridgway's arrival and his strategy of limited UN offensives then drove the Chinese/North Korean forces into a mountainous defensive position north of Seoul. Following this fourth phase, both sides maneuvered for advantage at the negotiating table. Bitter battles for a chunk of territory important for moving the talks along characterized this fifth and last period.

The Korean conflict thus became the key event in the ideological struggle between godless communism and the American way of life. It destroyed any hope that Soviet expansionism could be contained without strong military action. That meant a massive rearmament program, which would retard economic development and any concept of a return to normalcy after World War II. Most immediately it forced Harry S. Truman to confront the most vital of national security issues: should his administration deploy scarce military assets in the Far East and so invite Soviet aggression in western Europe?

Cold War rhetoric already had led world figures to frame the struggle between Soviet and Chinese communism and Western democratic values in absolute terms. It is ironic, then, that the Korean conflict was a sharply limited action. Neither President Truman nor his chief advisers ever referred to it as a war—in his phrase, it was a "police action." (For many today it is a forgotten war.) Limits placed upon Gen. Douglas MacArthur, who was the overall theater commander, elicited strong protest and led to his recall. In testimony before a congressional committee in the late spring of 1951, Gen. Omar Bradley, representing the Joint Chiefs of Staff, called any effort to enlarge the conflict a strategy that "would involve us in the wrong war, at the wrong place, at the wrong time, and with the wrong enemy."

Because Korea lay west of the international date line, Washington received reports of the invasion on Saturday afternoon, June 24. The president was visiting his home in Independence, Missouri. He immediately boarded his aircraft and returned to Washington, to Blair House (the White House was being rebuilt at this time). That evening he convened his advisers. His secretary of state warned against being paralyzed militarily in Europe by allocating forces to the Far East but agreed that some strong response was needed. There was no doubt, however, that the administration would have to respond quickly and effectively. Our allies would receive our call for assistance, and early the next morning the secretary general of the United Nations was alerted to the emergency.

Truman and his group discussed South Korean capabilities and believed that with U.S. naval and air assistance, ROK forces might repel the invasion. Because the United States and its Western allies had just successfully defended Berlin against strong Russian pressure through a massive airlift campaign, it was thought that logistical support coupled with a show of force might well decide the issue. In their thinking, as in that of their countrymen, Berlin was still the flash point: it was the city of the Cold War. A vicious and paranoid Joseph Stalin glared at the West through his strong forces in East Germany and East Berlin and sought every opportunity to tighten his hold on eastern and central Europe. He had supported national liberation movements elsewhere, but the Communist experiment in Russia had been threatened seriously only from western Europe, and he was determined never to let that happen again. In the East he had found a strong ally in Mao Tse-tung, whose forces had finally taken all of continental China from the American ally, Chiang Kai-shek. Thus, most of the Eurasian land mass north of India was under the control of state socialism of one kind or another. Korea was just a peninsular appendage, unimportant per se but useful as an advertisement to the cause.

Pondering the situation, President Truman could count upon British goodwill because this staunch wartime ally was critically concerned with keeping western Europe free from Communist hegemony. Strong Communist parties in France and Italy supported Stalinism, and it was important that they be kept in check through a combination of democratic toleration and military presence. Germany, as always in modern history, was the key, but it was prostrate. Its terrible wartime occupation policies had alienated all Europeans, and now it lay economically ruined and an outcast. If the United States committed a significant portion of its own offensive capability to a war in far-off Korea, it might prove to be an irresistible invitation to Soviet intervention in western Europe. The Korean crisis made it clear to Washington that nothing in the Cold War would be isolated from anything else: the Soviet menace was everywhere.

How was it, then, that the greatest power on earth in 1945, the United States, had disarmed so completely as to appear helpless? Truman's well-known scorn for brass hats and military thinking went back to his childhood roots and his World War I experiences. Typically, after the great victory over the Axis powers and Japan, the American people wanted no more to do with the great world of evil off our shores. An additional factor was the hunt for internal enemies. A rabid faction of the Republican party led by a senator from Wisconsin, Joseph McCarthy, resuscitated the worst in the American political tradition by looking for spies and Communists in every aspect of public life. (It is interesting to note that he was ruined and disgraced later by his unwarranted attack upon the U.S. Army.) At the time of the Korean crisis he was riding high. He had put the fear of godless communism into the hearts of the Truman administration, and he and his cronies would make great, if temporary, capital of the president's handling of the Korean War.

Truman and his advisers were concerned that whatever Stalin's intentions might be—and they knew that he approved of the North Korean intervention and would support it—they also had to be wary of the new, powerful Communist government in China. And they also were aware that most of their domestic critics attributed the "loss" of China to inept Truman policy following 1945. Communism was seen to be monolithic, and so the Korean crisis was interpreted as a well-planned move designed, perhaps with "oriental cunning," to screen some further offensive thrust elsewhere.

In 1947 and 1948 the Truman administration had presided over the reshuffling of the military structure. In the name of economy and streamlined unification, the army, navy, and air force were joined in a new Department of Defense. Some of the military's intelligence functions were reallocated, and a new and centralized intelligence-gathering system was set up. Assisting the president in his day-to-day work was the new National Security Council. All this machinery was struggling with internal problems, and most of its managers were concerned with internal subversion. It was in this poisonous atmosphere of interservice rivalry that a former secretary of the navy committed suicide.

Truman was entering his second term as president, having been elected by a narrow margin. He was not then popular, and he was not particularly well served by the new Joint Chiefs of Staff. These officers, all veterans of World War II, faced difficult adjustments to modern military technologies and a real and large Soviet menace. They also had to absorb tremendous budget cuts, new relations with the executive and legislative branches, and great pressure from their own constituencies. They adopted a corporate-model management system that was cumbersome and too often diffused responsibility. Most of these officers were more attuned to western Europe, where they rightly feared Russian mischief. Yet they all faced a unique situation in that the American proconsul in the Far East, General of the Army Douglas MacArthur, had achieved almost mythical powers. From Tokyo, he had a special relationship with important congressional leaders and solid backing from the more hawkish veterans' groups back home. All this adulation could be marshaled at will, in spite of his absence from the United States since well before Pearl Harbor. In his case, distance lent enchantment. The Joint Chiefs handled him with kid gloves during the Korean crisis. After all, this living legend wore five stars, one more than any of them could boast.

The United States had long been fascinated by the Far East. As early as 1876 it had recognized the special status of Korea and through the 1880s had maintained an important link with the government there. President Theodore Roosevelt moved away from this policy of amity toward the Korean monarchy and in 1905 brokered peace between Russia and Japan at Korea's expense. From 1905 to the Allied defeat of Japan in September 1945, Korea was dominated, humiliated, and looted of human and natural resources by Japan. As part of the Far Eastern settlement with the USSR, the United States agreed to divide the Korean peninsula at the 38th parallel.

The Korean peninsula resembles a shorter, fatter Italy. Korea is about 525 miles in length and is widest in the north and narrowest at the waist, which is around 125 miles wide and located roughly at the 38th parallel. It is ringed by numerous islands, and internally it is divided by tangles and ridges of mountains. North Korea borders upon Manchuria for most of its width, and a narrow strip touches Siberia. Mountains there created conditions for industry, mining, and hydropower, some of which fed back into the Manchurian power grid.

South Korea, on the Yellow Sea, possessed more farmland, but its capital, Seoul, was located near the 38th parallel and was thus vulnerable to a sudden attack from the north. The south also held the major port on the peninsula, Pusan. Transportation in both halves of the country was channeled into lower areas that could support rail and some waterborne traffic. The continental climate was extreme: brutally hot and humid in the south in summer and arctic, especially in the north, in winter. In the south around sixty inches of moisture fell; less than half that fell in the northern interior mountains.

This unnatural division split the country in ways that made for future difficulties, and it guaranteed that economic recovery from Japanese domination would be slow. The northern half of this corrugated country was rich in a variety of ways: water-powered electrical generators, mines, and industry. The south was agricultural and had not only better land for that purpose but also the greater part of the population (21 million in the south compared with 9 million in the north) and better port facilities and rail transport. United, the country could maximize its strengths, but fundamental political problems defied Korean nationalists' attempts at unification. In the North, the USSR had with Chinese concurrence installed an orthodox Stalinism in the form of Kim Il Sung's government. The United States had brought from exile Syngman Rhee, a crusty, reactionary Christian who was violently antisocialist. Several attempts at United Nations–sponsored elections designed to lead to unity collapsed because of American or Soviet intransigence.

Korea is a mountainous and irregular country. In the north, a great massif is broken into river valleys that constrict any movement from one watershed to another. Here, among the hydroelectric plants and their reservoirs, is found some of the most difficult terrain. It is bitterly cold in the winter. In the middle center, the Han River basin dominates a broken piedmont, with the capital city of Seoul located at the crossing of main road and rail networks. In the south, areas of the peninsula are still tilled vertically, but larger plains are available for intensive rice culture. All traffic is constricted by paddies, flooded at planting and growing seasons but frozen in the winter, and dominated by commanding hills and heights. The practice of conserving human waste, or nightsoil, and using it for fertilizer lent a noisome aspect to the landscape that many still recall vividly.

The Korean people, north and south, were tough and inured to hardship, and were disciplined workers if properly led. They had suffered greatly at the hands of the Japanese. They had retained their Chinese-Confucian outlook and deferred with great reverence to age and authority. These people suffered most in the war, and hundreds of thousands were killed and maimed fighting for one side or the other—or just trying to survive as invading armies as well as guerrilla and pirate bands moved back and forth across the scarred landscape.

This people and land had been largely ignored in the great scheme of bipolar power politics. The army of North Korea, an invention of the Chinese and the Soviets, included many soldiers who had fought side by side with Mao Tse-tung for victory over the Nationalists. It had been equipped with booty taken from the large Japanese Manchurian army in 1945 and over the years had been supplied with matériel by Stalin. By autumn 1949, Mao's forces controlled all of mainland China and a Democratic People's Republic was established in North Korea. The army was tough and well mounted on good tanks, and it enjoyed total support from both Mao and Stalin. On the other side, from the Truman administration's perspective, it was important to build an indigenous South Korean force capable of defending itself but not liable to become a pliant tool of America's loose cannon in Seoul, President Rhee. U.S. military advisers grappled with the task of building a purely defensive force in South Korea to be officered by rational nationalist leaders who would compel Rhee's corrupt government to decent behavior. The Pentagon's defense policy was ambiguous, however. As budget cuts reduced ground forces to a minimum, western Europe received the bulk of the troops. Thus, the United States pulled out of Korea, leaving only small forces of advisers under State Department authority.

In making policy for Korea, the Truman administration relied upon the National Security Council. That group of civil-military advisers drew up a plan for the containment of communism around the world and published it as NSC-68. Internally, the administration was not clear as to how to interpret important aspects of that plan. The secretary of state, Dean Acheson, early in 1950 in an address to the National Press Club mentioned that the United States had vital interests in the Far East, but, as he drew them out, he omitted Korea. Viewed from Beijing or Moscow (and we will not know until archival material there is available), it may have seemed that his omission was an invitation to the Chinese or the Soviets to step into South Korea.

In the spring of 1950, North Korea received substantial increments of offensive weapons from the Soviet Union, and guerrilla units from the North infiltrated the South in great number and frequency. Students in the South protested against Rhee's corrupt regime with increasing violence, and the threat of civil war hung in the air. MacArthur's Far Eastern Command in Tokyo was then most concerned with settling the remnants of Chiang Kai-shek's Nationalist armies in Formosa and figuring out a way to reclaim the Chinese mainland. While a great quantity of good intelligence was available in May and June of 1950, it was not well used. Therefore, the North Korean invasion in late June caught most by surprise.

Kim had discussed the coming invasion with Mao that spring and had received his support. Stalin likewise thought it a good idea. North Korean thinking saw the invasion as a welcome move that would receive wide support among the dissident South Korean nationalists. Apparently no one viewed it as the coming pivotal event in the Cold War.

At the outset the United States enjoyed a priceless advantage: it received a mandate from the United Nations to intervene, militarily if necessary, to restore the legitimate government of the Republic of South Korea. For the critical first year of conflict, the Americans led a broad coalition supported by Free World opinion. Many problems connected with going to war with a committee would emerge, but Korea forged the tough links in the alliance systems that eventually brought on the collapse of Stalinism.

At news of the invasion, the UN Security Council, in an emergency meeting, quickly passed a series of resolutions denouncing North Korean aggression. The Soviet representative was boycotting sessions in protest over the seating of the People's Republic of China—he had wanted Chiang's representative expelled—and business proceeded rapidly. Truman returned quickly from Independence to Blair House; the Pentagon swung into gear; scratch forces in Japan were airlifted to Korea; and the Twenty-fourth Division mobilized for embarkation to Pusan. The United States would defend South Korea with whatever it had at hand. The Seventh Fleet took up positions covering any possible Chinese approach to either Japan or Formosa. There was wide concern that the Korean attack was a feint designed to get the United States committed and then strike elsewhere. South Korean forces in some cases fought valiantly and struck a strategic blow when their navy sank a North Korean transport loaded with troops aiming to cut off Pusan.

The initial fighting was confused, and only here and there could ROK forces slow the North's advance. (Near Taejon, the commander of the Twenty-fourth Division, William F. Dean, fought tanks with his service pistol and was isolated and eventually captured. He endured a rough captivity and won the Congressional Medal of Honor for his bravery.) By late July the Americans were slowly building up the shoulders of the high ground overlooking the Naktong River, which guarded the approaches to the vital port of Pusan. During August the Communists struck repeatedly and hard against this line but were unable to break through. The new ground commander, Gen. Walton H. Walker (he had been with Gen. George Patton's Third Army five years earlier), husbanded his artillery and armor and fought brush fires as North Korean thrusts probed for weak points. By now the Communists were at a severe logistical disadvantage. Their ten-day delay in moving supplies forward cost them the race to Pusan. The Pusan perimeter was unbreakable and through the port came a stream of American arms and men. The situation was perilous but rapidly stabilizing.

By the end of August, UN forces numbered about 180,000, one-half of whom were ROK troops. North Korea still fielded over 130,000 men, but many were conscripts and poorly trained. The United States had 500 tanks against 100 Russian-made T-34s. American air superiority over the battlefield was never threatened by the North. In the air force and navy air arms, many World War II veterans called upon their considerable combat skills to punish the North. The story was similar in the naval war. At this stage the weaponry was still World War II–vintage on both sides.

In Tokyo, General MacArthur had already conceived a plan to maximize his air and naval flexibility. He had gained much experience in the South Pacific with amphibious landings and sought to apply the lessons to the present crisis. Seoul's port, Inchon, lay in a series of mudflats at low tide, in a swelling tide at high; these were difficult waters, tricky and dangerous to navigate. The North Koreans sensed little danger there and defended the area lightly. During favorable lunar periods, MacArthur figured that he could land troops, flank the North Korean armies down south, and cut off and annihilate them. His plan was risky, and the Joint Chiefs protested vigorously. In a reference to the English victory over the French at Quebec in 1759, MacArthur responded that "like Montcalm, the North Koreans would regard an Inchon landing as impossible. Like Wolfe, I could take them by surprise." In a masterful selling job, MacArthur overcame objections. He directed Walker to tie down maximum numbers of enemy forces before Pusan and break out, and then, in mid-September, Inchon would fall.

Following a predawn bombardment of the guardian islands in the bay, the X Corps, consisting mainly of the First Marines and Seventh Army, landed at Inchon early on September 15, 1950. In spite of sporadically fierce resistance, the invasion moved inland, taking the best airfields at Kimpo and then, in two weeks, linking up with Walker's Eighth Army. Because of U.S. logistical problems and hasty staff work, important elements of the North Korean army escaped northward, but these were remnants. About 100,000 prisoners, many of them South Korean conscripts, were taken, but sizable forces escaped north. It was a magnificent victory. All eyes now turned north in spite of some cautious discussion about the nature of the UN mandate and the sanctity of the 38th parallel. MacArthur and his staff, however, had no intention of tethering the now-victorious UN Command. Indeed, MacArthur argued that, no matter what he did or did not desire, President Rhee had already ordered his ROK forces north because he saw in the UN victory a glorious opportunity to unite the country.

In Washington there was uneasiness. While this was an opportunity, the Chinese were making it clear that they would not tolerate a march to their border with North Korea. Nothing in the UN resolutions addressed the question of unification, and some allies, particularly Britain, were concerned about making substantial commitments to a theater so far from western Europe. To them, it just did not make good strategic sense to move precipitously without considering other Cold War problems. Truman himself reflected the ambiguity of the situation. His standing in public opinion polls was poor, while MacArthur's was excellent. More importantly, the two represented polar opposites on the political spectrum and neither had made the acquaintance of the other. In October the president—not the proconsul—journeyed to Wake Island in the North Pacific for a meeting rich in symbolism. The conversation was jointly deemed a success. Later it was seen by critics on both sides as at least a missed opportunity, at most posturing. Truman wanted to know: Would China enter the war? MacArthur replied that it would not, or, if it did, with only small volunteer units. The president wanted the general to know that he should not make the Soviets nervous with a trans–Yalu River bombing campaign.

Within the UN Command in Korea there were opportunities and problems. The opportunities lay with pursuing U.S. forces who, almost at will, took major North Korean objectives: Pyongyang, the capital; Hungnam, a major port; and the approaches to the Yalu boundary with Manchuria. Among the problems was declining UN morale as frontline troops realized that they did not want to be the last to die in a foreign war—"our boys will be home for Christmas" was one refrain. A major command problem also began to emerge as the X Corps and the Eighth Army moved north. The mountainous knots increasingly divided and isolated them, and the command center in Tokyo proved less able to coordinate resources. Narrow thinking led high-ranking officers to discount Chinese intervention and to trust in technical superiority over peasant endurance and drive if the Chinese did enter the war. Moreover, great numbers of bypassed North Korean units had been formed into piratical partisan bands that constantly harassed and interrupted the lengthening supply columns. Trust in aerial reconnaissance, naval interdiction, and the belief that the war was won all combined to blind the UN Command to Chinese intentions and capabilities. Washington could counsel caution, but the president's advisers were confronted by MacArthur's claque in Congress. The general said that he sought no major war in Asia but gave the impression that he did. If terrain features divided the ground forces, doctrine the air and naval commanders, then politics erected a barrier of confusion between Dai Ichi (MacArthur's Tokyo headquarters) and Blair House.

After initial confusion in the war production program in the United States, the country had gotten serious. Now, in the autumn of 1950, industrial output, shipping allocations, and manpower mobilization were reaching 1945 levels. The government called up National Guard reservists (of whom the most famous was Boston Red Sox slugger Ted Williams, a marine pilot) and generally geared up for a long, tough fight. Japan, just a few years earlier a pariah among nations, was the chief financial beneficiary of this mobilization. Its civilian mariners, factory managers and workers, and mills and docks all thrived as a result of American military expenditures. Indeed, with its economic isolation broken, Japan was given a sharp push toward prosperity by the Korean War.

In the early weeks of victory, American forces in particular had begun to attend to the needs of ROK soldiers. Better equipment, some training, and on occasion a sense of camaraderie with Anglo-American troops came to characterize ROK battlefield commanders and their men. All combatants relied heavily upon Korean civilians as porters on the battlefield. These men and women literally took the place of mules in more traditional orders of battle. They provisioned men and guns with stoic patience and great fortitude.

By October 27 the Eighth Army had two Chinese deserters in custody. Within a week there were many more available for intelligence purposes. Tokyo thought that the Chinese represented no problem; they were just a handful of volunteers. But nights grew longer and colder, and a premonitory air hung over the high mountains of the north. MacArthur wanted rapid pursuit to the Yalu and consolidation from a position of strength there. The army itself, ragged and without flank support, also was in a pursuing mood. A major dissenter was the commander of the First Marine Division, Gen. Oliver P. Smith. Ordered to proceed to the hydroelectric plant on the Chosen reservoirs, he procrastinated and worried about eventualities. MacArthur, too, began to sense a dangerous situation; units closing on the Yalu were cautioned, and the UN offensive began to slow. He restrained General Walker, but by mid-November heavy engagements with the Chinese were common along the ROK fronts. On November 28, MacArthur reported: "Enemy reactions developed in the course of our assault operations of the past four days disclose that a major segment of the Chinese continental armed forces of an aggregate strength of over 200,000 men is now arrayed against the United Nations forces in Korea."

The massive infiltration had been undetected. When the Chinese struck hard, nerve failed in the UN Command from the top on down. Previously, MacArthur had considered that the Chinese might slap the UN forces with small units to buy time for the NKPA. General Walker and his staff lost confidence in their troops. Stiff holding actions on the Chongchon and Imjin rivers slowed but could not stop the Chinese–North Korean juggernaut. What later was called the Big Bugout saw many UN troops retreat from the far north to 100 miles south of Seoul in one great, gasping leap. Newly built bridges, rail facilities, harbors, dikes, airfields, and the like were abandoned or destroyed. Ironically, it began to look as if the troops would be home for Christmas—with their tails between their legs.

MacArthur wanted to bomb staging areas and bridges in Manchuria to stop the flow. If the Chinese were truly in the war, then they should be compelled to recognize the consequences of their actions. They should be punished on their own turf. The Joint Chiefs worried that Chinese intervention in Korea presaged Soviet intentions in central Europe. The UN allies were concerned that the United States was incompetent politically to wage this sort of war. The French already faced severe difficulties in Algeria and Indochina, and the British were hesitant because they feared MacArthur wanted nuclear war with China and that Washington was too weak to stop him.

On the ground, frontline soldiers received a hot Thanksgiving dinner. However, confusion clouded every command decision. UN intelligence failed to identify Marshal Peng Duhei as the Chinese commander. From Tokyo MacArthur issued unrealistic orders, and his corps commanders, especially General Almond of the X Corps, followed blindly. Leadership faltered, and many frontline troops were rattled by the blare of midnight bugle calls, bells, whistles, and strange noises. The Chinese soldier was going to be a formidable foe. He was tough and disciplined, lived on only a few rations, and occasionally entered combat armed only with a grenade. If he survived long enough, he could scavenge arms from someone less fortunate. Moreover, it was impossible to tell officer from trooper: the ubiquitous padded cotton jacket simply buttoned differently. The People's Army did not flaunt rank; no insignia, no mark of esteem graced the dull uniform. It was indeed a peasant army possessing initially only light infantry weapons: mortars, machine guns, rifles, and grenades. The Chinese infantrymen moved like goats over the mountainous landscape or lay silent and unmoving as UN air forces searched out their hiding holes.

In spite of its precipitous retreat, the UN Command was a powerful force. Lost and abandoned equipment could always be replaced, and it was, often with better matériel. A significant number of officers were replaced and unit pride reasserted itself. At this time General Walker was killed in a road accident; a ROK truck pulled out and sideswiped his Jeep (strangely like the collision that had killed his former superior, General Patton). Walker's replacement, Matthew B. Ridgway, arrived in Korea shortly after Christmas 1950 and immediately began to rebuild morale, improve intelligence, and instill an attitude of grim determination to win the war. He was in a good bargaining position vis-à-vis the Joint Chiefs and had the respect of General MacArthur, who also had been rattled by the great retreat of his armies.

In early 1951, Ridgway began a series of phased offensives with limited objectives and supported by tremendous firepower. UN troops employed minefields, barbed wire, thousands of gallons of napalm, deeply echeloned artillery, and automatic weapons to counter local Chinese-NKPA manpower superiority. Before a nervous public relations group in Washington and Tokyo objected, Ridgway named these offensives "Killer," "Ripper," and the like. He wanted to make clear to the world that he and his troops were prepared to slaughter as many of the enemy as possible and that he would continue that course indefinitely.

The bitter attacks graduated into larger actions as the Communist forces were pushed back beyond the Han River, then beyond the parallel and finally into the so-called Iron Triangle of Pyonggyang (not the capital but a town with a similar name), Chorwon, and Kumwha. This area was a choke point for Communist supplies; it guarded the approaches to the reservoir system supplying water to Seoul, and it provided substantial benefits to the UN defense system. Altogether, UN forces in the first six months of 1951 enjoyed great success. They had taken the measure of Chinese capabilities and were crushing their manpower at a great rate. By May the numbers of Chinese surrendering in unit-sized contingents dramatically increased. Some front officers in the UN Command forecast the breakup of the Chinese army if these losses continued through the summer. The military smelled victory. It lay within their grasp.

Against the United Nations, however, the Chinese had more than manpower to deploy. They raised propaganda issues that became important to their ultimate aim and that served them well. First, they gained worldwide attention by agreeing to a Soviet agenda for truce discussions. Many allies in the UN alliance were anxious to limit the war and their individual commitments to it. They had not wanted it to spread to the Chinese people, and they were anxious to begin talks because they feared Soviet intentions in central Europe—as did political leaders in Washington. Second, the Chinese and North Koreans raised the frightening issue of germ warfare, asserting that UN troops had employed chemical-biological agents.

Moreover, the Chinese–North Korean governments accused the United Nations of abusing prisoners—and there were tens of thousands in UN stockades. Most of these prisoners not held specifically by the ROK government were located on islands just off the peninsula. As Communist leaders realized the potential for mischief in laxly administered prison compounds, they instructed trained cadres of dedicated Communist subalterns to allow themselves to be captured so that they could indoctrinate and actually take over the day-to-day management of these camps. This clever ploy paid big dividends later in the war when an orchestrated uprising on Koje Island succeeded in capturing the senior American officer. He then, under duress, announced that the UN authority had treated prisoners in contravention to the Geneva Accords.

There was still more to the prisoner issue for UN authorities. American leaders found to their horror that many of the young men captured by the NKPA and Chinese soldiers did not know what they were fighting for. Many of these young Americans were ignorant of U.S. history, of their government's war aims, and even of any unit connections that would bind them to their fellows. As statistics became available it appeared—and there was some truth in this—that American boys gave themselves up more easily, coped badly or would not help their buddies in captivity, and died more easily of disease and neglect. A number chose not to return to the West, and a few made propaganda statements for their captors. The U.S. military responded with indoctrination sessions, a new code of conduct for its armed forces, and a much greater emphasis upon training and unit identification.

As General Ridgway's troops continued to pound away at the Communist forces, another, and very important, action took place. It had an impact upon the war effort, but it is still difficult to assess: for Americans it was either one of the major constitutional issues of our history or a political smoke screen designed to impugn the reputation of a great leader who faced up to political timidity and incompetence. In March 1951, General MacArthur rocked the nation with a letter that he wrote to House Minority Leader Joe Martin. The general was disgusted with the administration's lack of leadership and with President Truman personally, and he knew that opinion polls combined with Democratic losses in elections that previous fall signaled a change in the American mood. "It seems strangely difficult," MacArthur wrote, "for some to realize that here in Asia is where the Communist conspirators have elected to make their play for global conquest. In Asia we fight Europe's war. Lose the war in Asia, and Europe is doomed. . . . If we are not in this war to win, then, this Truman administration should be indicted for the murder of thousands of American troops."

Martin was a well-known Red baiter, a bitter enemy of Truman, and he took delight in reading this letter publicly into the record. The president had been urged by both civilian and military advisers to ease out MacArthur well before this affront. For a variety of reasons Truman refused. But this open attack—of blatant insubordination to the commander in chief—when added to other, more serious reservations by the Joint Chiefs about the general's grip on the war, forced Truman's hand. Amid confusion in Washington about the appropriate means of informing MacArthur, word leaked out that he was fired. In this poisonous atmosphere the general made a gracious exit and returned home, first to San Francisco to a hero's welcome. MacArthur's moving address to both houses of Congress, concluding with "Old soldiers never die; they just fade away," confirmed in many the opinion that the president was incompetent and vindictive. Critics of the administration even threatened impeachment proceedings against Truman.

In Korea, under Ridgway, who replaced MacArthur in Tokyo, and Gen. James Van Fleet, the UN Command consolidated its defensive positions just north of the parallel. The Soviet Union interpreted events that spring as leading to U.S. aggression against China, even to the point of using nuclear weapons, and began to send out dual signals: Red armies in the Far East might intervene to stabilize the crumbling Chinese-NKPA front and pressure the new NATO forces in Europe so as to prevent any reinforcement in Korea, and Russia called for cease-fire discussions. This carrot-and-stick approach reflected Stalin's concern that the whole situation might well explode in his face. The USSR now had a limited nuclear arsenal, but Soviet experts believed that even the World War II plutonium weapons developed by the United States were superior to Soviet bombs and, moreover, that the Americans probably had made dramatic improvements in these bombs in the meantime. Soviet pilots had been involved in fighting in the skies above the western Yalu River area. Their MiG-15s were initially better than any planes that the UN Command had at its disposal, but a hasty shipment of the new Sabrejets (F-86s) did match them. On the whole, American pilots were superior. Thus, in the air as well as on the sea, UN troops fought with immense advantages.

American naval forces were instrumental in preventing initial NKPA successes in the summer of 1950. By the end of that year, now reinforced by other UN shipping and a rapid demothballing program, UN naval forces were very powerful. In the landing at Inchon, in the evacuation of tremendous tonnages and people at Hungnam during the first-phase Chinese offensive, and in many other instances, naval superiority offered strategic benefits to the UN Command. The ROK navy was expanded and generally undertook special insertion missions, counterinfiltration missions, and many ferrying tasks. Communist mining of waters was particularly dangerous as minesweeping was initially neglected, but no serious threat of any substantial nature could be marshaled against UN naval forces. As the war settled into a pounding match, UN military tonnages approached and in some cases exceeded those of 1945. The supply pipeline ensured that there would not be a deficit of required matériel.

After the war, there would be vigorous debate concerning the quality and availability of close-air support for UN troops. Marine units had trained for and enjoyed first-class tactical air support from their attached air units, either land or carrier based. The air force had melded tactical air into a complex management structure with centralized allocation so as to ensure close support capability to the much more numerous army units. Some observers questioned whether the air force control and communication system really was adequate for the task. In particular, critics could point to a deckload of naval-marine aircraft arriving on the scene and having to attack secondary targets because the air- and ground-based air force–army tactical controllers were unable to deal with the traffic. At the level of interservice doctrinal differences, these issues remained unresolved at the end of the Korean War. With this in mind, it was still apparent that Communist forces were pounded hard by air force and naval air. The workhorses initially were the World War II naval bombers and the venerable P-51s (in the new nomenclature the F-51s). Swifter jet aircraft soon proved their usefulness and were employed increasingly as they came on line.

Interdiction missions were always necessary in order to hamper the flow of men and equipment to the front. Whether an appropriate emphasis upon interdiction campaigns—at the expense of more tactical support—was forthcoming was yet another debate. For example, B-29 raids on Communist facilities near the Yalu River would force an air response; UN pilots, mainly but not exclusively American, could then whittle away at Communist air resources. Most air commanders were unhappy with the sharp restrictions on their deployments because bomb runs became canalized and more vulnerable to a variety of antiaircraft defenses; furthermore, because they could not destroy enemy aircraft and facilities on the ground on the other side of the border, there was always a safe haven for enemy airmen should the contest become too difficult.

Air and naval superiority positively contributed to fewer UN ground casualties and to greater losses for Communist forces. Naval superiority was established early and never seriously threatened. There were losses due to enemy action—gunfire and mining mainly—but they were not serious. The usual operational hazards were multiplied in Korea because of the inhospitable climate, uncharted waters, and the usual dangers of high-octane aviation gasoline, explosives, rough seas, and fatigue.

Air superiority was not a state but a process. The air force had sound reasons for demanding manpower and technical capability for achieving superiority in any theater. In Korea, the air force, with navy and marine air alongside, gained initial superiority over the battlefields only to see it threatened as Soviet MiGs entered the war. Chinese, North Korean, and Russian pilots flew a variety of aircraft, but only the newest-model MiGs were a true threat. In the screaming attacks over "MiG Alley," both U.S. and Communist pilots contested for local air control. As B-29 losses in the bombing campaign against the bridges over the Yalu mounted, escort missions by fighters were necessary. For air force leaders, as for MacArthur and Ridgway, the greatest problem was the limit placed upon pursuit across the boundary into Manchuria—a limit that one American general called "an albatross around the neck of U.S. airpower." Air enthusiasts had little stomach for limited war in the skies, and Korea was a war of limits.

Recently new archival materials from China and the USSR show that the joint air force–navy interdiction programs were far more successful than generally believed at the time. Each major North Korean Peoples' Army and Chinese offensive collapsed after six to eight days because of their logistics problems. By July 1951 both of their armies were suffering deep logistic deficits, and huge casualties were the result. As the Chinese matured in their understanding, planning, and provision for supplying their men, they markedly improved their systems. Even with the help of dozens of frontline pilots and aircraft from the USSR and the enlargement of their own Chinese air forces, any serious offensive from the north was bound to meet formidable UN challenges to their logistics. By 1953 it was crystal clear to the Chinese that stalemate was the only possibility and that an armistice with prisoner exchange was the only way out of a devastating war. They came of age as a military to be reckoned with and were willing to settle for that international reputation.

In the 1970s the popular television series *M*A*S*H* ensured that Americans would identify the helicopter with the Korean War. Choppers were not that ubiquitous but were used increasingly in a variety of roles, most spectacularly as rescue craft for downed pilots and for medical evacuation. Much of the equipment for the war, especially in the first year, was scrounged from Pacific battlefields. After it was collected, most was shipped to Japan for refurbishing and then sent on to Korea. There were newer models of various radars, radios, self-propelled guns, planes, and so on, but generally the Korean War, as noted earlier, was fought with World War II technology. Much more firepower was given to line units, and especially heavy concentrations of large-caliber artillery pieces were allocated. A division of heavy infantry might have a far greater volume of fire at a given time than its comparable World War II unit.

At this time, one of the goals of the newly unified U.S. military services was racial integration. There had been some progress earlier, but the Korean War cemented the process even though the majority of African American men and women in the service were found in supply, motor pool, kitchen, and service areas such as entertainment, facilities management, and recreation. In spite of latent bigotry, frontline units saw more black troops in integrated situations. The Korean War accelerated the momentum of integration, and civil rights gains in the decade following the conflict owed much to the contributions of African American servicemen and women in the Korean War.

As for relations between ROK troops and other UN units, they often depended upon purely local and almost accidental circumstances. For example, South Korean divisions possessed considerably less firepower than other UN units. However, officers and soldiers in elite units such as the Capital Division were held in high regard. At the outset and for some time thereafter, ROK troops, as individuals, were placed in U.S. units and fought there. Although cultural and linguistic problems plagued both sides during the war, several ROK units received special recognition from their UN comrades. Although both NKPA and ROK officers could be brutal, even murderous, toward their own men and the civilian population, it was clear from the first day of the war that more Koreans would rather live under the ROK regime than under Kim Il Sung. South Korean troops attached to UN forces were absolutely necessary to control crowds of civilian refugees who were used by infiltrators to cause trouble behind UN lines. Indeed, one of the great tragedies of the war was the destruction and loss of life and limb incurred by the civilians of both sides. A legacy of mistrust and resentment between ROK and UN officers and men survived the war, although mutual admiration and respect connected many individuals in the UN effort. One certain result of the war was that ROK military strength was substantial and enduring. Whether that was good for the democratic movement in South Korea is another story.

As peace talks fizzled in August 1951, renewed heavy fighting erupted in the Iron Triangle–Punch Bowl areas. Given the respite, the Communists changed their tactics. They burrowed deep into substantial fortifications, brought up heavy weapons—particularly artillery, which they previously had lacked—and coordinated more carefully their political propaganda with battlefield schemes and rear-area guerrilla attacks. From the UN Command's point of view, the truce talks at Kaesong had only allowed the Communist side a necessary respite and a golden opportunity, not wasted, to reinforce the Iron Triangle.

In September, Ridgway moved the peace talks to Panmunjom, where for nearly two years each side faced the other across a table covered with green felt. These interminable discussions, often conducted at childish levels because of Communist intransigence and strategy, became a symbol of the fruitless war itself. The political maneuvering mirrored the fighting. The X Corps along with the ROK I Corps battered away at the enemy positions north and east of the Hwachon Reservoir in the Punch Bowl. In the nearby Heartbreak Ridge–Bloody Ridge complex, equally punishing fighting erupted. In this bitterly contested terrain, Van Fleet's troops secured control of a strong defensive position north of the parallel.

The UN Command's problem now was how to coordinate battlefield pressure with peace overtures. The administration eased pressure on the Communist front, hoping to encourage a climate of moderation so that a real bargain could be struck. The gamble failed. Once military pressure tapered off, the Chinese tunneled deep into the mountains and brought up more and more big guns. Mao's policy of talking and fighting and fighting and talking paid dividends. His troops burrowed into bunkers and tunnels so solid that they could resist even nuclear weapons. For the final twenty months of the war this area in particular resembled the lunar aspect of World War I battlefields. From then on operations were conducted as if the areas were a siege field. Limits upon Van Fleet's authority were so restrictive that he could employ no units larger than a battalion without permission.

This stage of the conflict destroyed the electoral basis of the Democratic party's hold on the presidency. People in the United States were fed up with a war that they could not win and from which they could not disengage. Truman's reputation reached bottom. Even the initial enthusiasm for the triumphant MacArthur waned. Gen. Dwight D. Eisenhower, the hero of World War II, won the 1952 Republican nomination. In his presidential campaign he promised to end the war and threatened to use nuclear weapons to redeem that promise. That got the attention of Communist leaders.

Stalemated on the battlefield, the Communists launched a successful propaganda assault. In Stockholm, Sweden, the World Peace Committee rallied along lines laid out by Chinese and Soviet policies. The conference endorsed nuclear disarmament and basically identified U.S.-British capitalism as evil. The dove of peace, borrowed from Pablo Picasso, became a symbol of this propaganda success. In a further effort to discredit the United Nations that merged with the nuclear theme, the Communists stepped up their shrewd campaign that accused UN forces of using germ warfare. A few U.S. prisoners in North Korea "confessed" to having released agents into the air, and some evidence was introduced that indicated that UN forces were using forbidden chemicals. As the United Nations teams tried to discover the nature of these false charges, the propaganda barrage continued.

An effective counter to this verbal offensive was the attitude of prisoners of war in UN hands. About 175,000 Chinese and North Koreans were held in a complex of camps by UN authority. The facts were clear to neutral observers: one-third of these men would not return to their homelands. Some of the Chinese had been taken into captivity earlier from their Nationalist units by the Communists. They had been given the option of fighting or dying—thus, many had no home on the mainland to which to return. The prisoner issue became a major sticking point in the peace negotiations. Communist officials would not admit that many in their armies wanted to remain under Western control and so insisted upon forced repatriation. Also, the returning prisoners would have to be sealed off from the remainder of the population in order to prevent rumors that might damage the regime. Prisoners in Communist camps were denied visits by the Red Cross or other neutral bodies, so it was important to the Communists to pursue the prisoner issue forcefully to deflect world attention from the high death rate in their compounds. (Finally, during the latter part of the truce talks, President Rhee took over, ordering prisoners held in ROK camps turned loose. They melted into the local South Korean population, and that helped settle the issue.) The exchange of prisoners of war would become a characteristic problem for limited wars in the second half of the twentieth century.

Meanwhile, Eisenhower had judged before his election that China needed peace and would bargain seriously for it. China's Russian ally,

Stalin, died in March 1953. Reaction in the USSR against Stalinism could be predicted. As a result of war costs and immense human losses, the Chinese economy was in a serious condition. The nation had been ravaged by a half century of political division, foreign invasions, and civil wars. However, China was in no mood to make peace because it had garnered considerable world attention with its intervention in Korea. Its leaders knew that Eisenhower's electoral victory in the United States was directly tied to the unpopularity there of the Korean War, but they could not be certain that he would resist calling in Chiang's army from Formosa or refrain from using nuclear weapons.

Events in the Soviet Union were probably as important as any other factor in ending the bloodshed. At the time of Stalin's death, the hard-line military controlled the government. Georgi Malenkov succeeded Stalin as premier and faced a series of challenges from East Germany, Poland, and Hungary. When the Eisenhower administration agreed to a truce near the 38th parallel, the UN mandate upholding the conflict had been fulfilled. Jacob Malik, the Soviet delegate to the United Nations, quickly agreed to a serious truce agreement. (President Rhee desperately strove to delay a truce because his goal all along had been to unify the country under his government; now, it might be divided permanently. Rhee had misjudged American enthusiasm for the war; when he urged the use of nuclear weapons in an address to Congress, he could evoke no positive response.) The Soviets knew full well that the early American containment effort had, by spring 1953, snowballed into a full-fledged Cold War military confrontation. Moscow concluded that it was useless to continue to fuel anti-Communist sentiment in western Europe and the United States. Soviet interests would be better served by ending the most visible East-West conflict quickly.

The prisoner-of-war issue remained the major point of disagreement. In March 1953 sick and wounded prisoners were exchanged, although haggling over repatriation continued. Meanwhile, the Chinese reopened a ground offensive on Pork Chop Hill, west of the Iron Triangle, and took it. On July 27 a truce agreement was signed. Some 77,000 Communist prisoners returned north, and 3,597 Americans and other UN soldiers came south. There was some consolation. The UN Command won a major concession in selecting the final line of demarcation, which, unlike the 38th parallel, was defensible. The demilitarized zone has bristled with weaponry ever since.

The Korean War has much to teach us today. The UN support for the American initiative established a solid moral basis for further military actions. In subsequent military operations, the United States in general has not enjoyed initial support, and it has been difficult to rally either the American people or the world community behind it (the Persian Gulf War being an exception). The decoupling of political and military aims had serious consequences also. Brig. Gen. Roy K. Flint, former chairman of the History Department at West Point, summarizes the significance of this aspect of the war:

> The decision to cross the 38th Parallel offers a fundamental lesson about waging war. Throughout the months of October and November (1950), Washington relinquished direction of the war to MacArthur, contrasting sharply with the carefully coordinated steps taken by the administration to strengthen its position of leadership in the international community. . . . What was missing was close coordination between coalition goals on the battlefield and coalition goals world wide.

The war was neither popular nor well understood in the United States. Veterans returning home met with indifference. (Civilians, however, were not hostile as they would be in the Vietnam War some fifteen years later.) World War II veterans, who had no Korean experience, were often unwilling to acknowledge that this was a tough fight. They compared it unfavorably to their own days of glory and gore. For most of its history, the United States has fought limited wars, but in the popular mind all-out war and unconditional surrender seemed the only conceivable policies. The Truman administration was discredited by its handling of the conflict, and the internal balance of political power began to shift toward a harder anti-Communist posture.

War in Korea was costly. The Chinese sustained 1,010,700 casualties, including 152,000 dead and 383,000 wounded. The Soviets lost far fewer but never admitted to having lost men in this war. Nearly 150,000 Americans were casualties; about 34,000 died in combat. The UN Command lost 118,000 killed, 264,000 wounded, and 100,000 captured; most of this last group died in captivity. Chinese and North Korean losses totaled over 1,600,000; their numbers of wounded and sick were likely also very high. But the Korean people, the civilians, paid the highest price; over 3,000,000 perished because of the war. And physically the country was devastated from end to end.

Some of the lessons of obvious importance stemming from the Korean War are clear and probably still applicable. First, mobilization, rotation, logistics, and overall resource allocation were areas that demanded improvement. Planners for 1945–1950 were projecting an all-out war with the Soviet Union and estimated that a two-year period would be available to mobilize the resources of their country and coalition. Thus, in 1945 the National Guard was demobilized, as were other regular units of the armed forces. By 1946 there literally was only a shell of a National Guard force. Budget cuts severely restricted equipment acquisition and manpower programs. That situation was changing slowly by 1949. About 330,000 men were in one or another National Guard program, and about one-third of these were mobilized during the Korean War. Four divisions and two combat regimental teams represented the bulk of National Guard participation in the war. A heavy burden fell upon the inactive reservists, mostly veterans who had not expected to be called up. Indeed, many men were called up not because they volunteered (they did not) but because they possessed manpower skills critical to survival in Korea. These specialties often were in naval and air operations and were crucial to the prosecution of the war. Problems existed in the munitions, shipping, and distribution systems critical to the war effort, although most of the equipment and doctrines were World War II vintage and much had already been learned.

Second, some of the bitter fighting in places such as Heartbreak Ridge during the truce talks depleted rifle companies so much that de facto racial integration was instituted. Generally, on a ratio of one African American soldier to ten of the other troops, blacks were simply integrated into combat units. It would be another decade before anything like true integration occurred, but the Korean War undoubtedly contributed to the growing civil rights movement and attendant military integration effort. Similarly, women were recruited to work in jobs where other manpower might be released. Generally, these were service and clerical tasks, but they did continue the previous war's efforts to involve the other half of the human race in military activity. In this sense, war was a leveler favoring democratic practices.

Third, limited war was extremely unpopular politically, and it led to an orgy of internal recriminations, witch-hunting, and vindictiveness. The level of political dialogue was lowered, and national policy suffered. However, the concept of war as containment has endured to the present day. Whatever the result of this limited war, the policy of the United States and its allies was to contain communism and revolutionary expansionism, and to accomplish that within a framework excluding total war. From a military point of view, then, improving or adopting military equipment that would inflict massive casualties without resort to nuclear weapons was important. This meant tooling up a new set of factories for the production of improved or new models of everything from machine guns to artillery, guided bombs, and missiles.

Fourth, in the short run, both the Soviets and the Chinese could represent themselves as liberators. They alone, they said, had the will and means to resist U.S. imperialism. (In fact, the Soviets wound up constructing a massive and ugly reminder of their economic and social incompetence in the form of the Berlin Wall in 1961.) The most important international outcomes were the rebuilding of Japan in such a manner that it left the traditional pillars of corporate and family dominance intact and the arrival of the People's Republic of China as a great power on the world stage. Without the aid of Japanese leaders, industry, and workers, the Korean War could not have been fought. In 1954 a peace agreement with the United States and its World War II allies signaled that Japan was back in the comity of nations. China emerged as a communist nation independent in its own right and increasingly a rival to the USSR. This was a fact that the United States neglected to factor in when it decided to pick up the pieces of the French empire in Indochina later in the decade.

And fifth, the Korean War was the crystalizing event in the Cold War. From June 1950 to the present day, the United States has been determined never to be caught napping again. For Americans, the self-congratulatory euphoria attendant upon success over Germany and Japan in 1945 was short-lived. After only five years of peace, the country was enraged when it had to return to the mud and blood of war. The distortions induced by shifting to a mobilization that would last for nearly a half century affected the economy as well as the trust between citizen and government, and it cheapened the political process. Investment flowed away from schools and education and the needs of cities and farms and into the massive and growing defense industry. Even the most peaceful of projects, such as the walk on the surface of the moon, now would have ominous military applications. The president, as leader of the Cold War coalition, enjoyed vastly enhanced power that in time would lead to Watergate and constitutional crisis. Secrecy became an obsession and ultimately a source of deep national division.

Diplomatically, the country was faced with the dilemma of containing communism even when it appeared in the guise of nationalism, as in Indochina, or in anticolonialism, as in Nicaragua. Two interesting outcomes might be considered here: by 1954 the United States would be supporting up to 75 percent of all expenditures in the French effort to retain Indochina; and by 1955 the former number-one enemy, Germany, would be rearmed by its former foes and established as the centerpiece of NATO. In Europe two massive coalitions glared at one another across a wall, minefields, and barbed wire; in Asia the United States maintained huge force structures in Japan, Okinawa, and the Philippines.

The Cold War would proceed with its ups and downs, its détentes and démarches. The Cuban Missile Crisis of 1962 would bring the threat of nuclear death to America; in Berlin a similar threat would face East Germany. Stalin's successor, Nikita Khrushchev, would even threaten to bury us. His successor, Leonid Brezhnev, would take a more pragmatic attitude, trusting to historical forces to lay capitalism low. Talks on limiting nuclear weapons and on human rights would begin, and the Nixon administration would open dialogue with China, which helped ease the country out of the Vietnam War and isolated the Soviets. They in turn would become bogged down in their own Vietnam, Afghanistan. Like a weary heavyweight after the fourteenth round, the Soviets finally would slip to the canvas, exhausted.

China took its place as a world power following this conflict. The United States sought to contain communism everywhere, and the political issue of which candidate would do it best animated all domestic politics. The twentieth-century creation of a draftee army gave way to a technically trained, but much smaller, voluntary force—a professional military. The Korean conflict, from the perspective of fifty years later, appears to have been a far more important event than contemporaries might have judged it. Although the atomic genie remained in the bottle, military research and development brought the machinery of death to new levels of lethality. Only a sound historical understanding will enable the United States or any possessor of military might to employ it justly.

Sources and Suggested Readings

Acheson, Dean. *Present at the Creation: My Years in the State Department.* New York, 1969.

Appleman, Roy E. *Disaster in Korea: The Chinese Confront MacArthur.* College Station, Tex., 1989.

———. *South to the Naktong, North to the Yalu.* Washington, D.C., 1961.

Cagle, Malcolm W., and Frank A. Munson. *The Sea War in Korea.* Annapolis, Md., 1957.

Condit, Doris M. *The Test of War, 1950–53,* vol. 2, *History of the Office of the Secretary of Defense.* Washington, D.C., 1988.

Cumings, Bruce, ed. *Child of Conflict: The Korean-American Relationship, 1945–1953.* Seattle, Wash., 1983.

Dean, William F. *General Dean's Story.* New York, 1956.

Flint, Roy K. *The Tragic Flaw: MacArthur, the Joint Chiefs, and the Korean War.* Washington, D.C., 1974.

Futrell, George F. *The United States Air Force in the Korean War.* Washington, D.C., 1983.

Hermes, Walter G. *Truce Tent and Fighting Front.* Washington, D.C., 1966.

Li, Xiobing, Allen R. Millett, and Bin Yu. *Mao's Generals Remember Korea.* Lawrence, Kans., 2000.

MacArthur, Douglas. *Reminiscences.* New York, 1964.

Oberdorfer, Don. *The Two Koreas: A Contemporary History.* New York, 1999.

Ridgway, Matthew B. *The Korean War.* Garden City, N.Y., 1967.

Shrader, Charles R. *Communist Logistics in the Korean War.* Westport, Conn., 1995.

Stueck, William. *The Korean War: An International History.* Princeton, N.J., 1995.

Weintraub, Stanley. *MacArthur's War: Korea and the Undoing of an American Hero.* New York, 2000.

Zhang, Shu Gang. *Mao's Military Romanticism: China and the Korean War, 1950–1953.* Lawrence, Kans., 1995.

Zhang, Xiaoming. *Red Wings over the Yalu: China, the Soviet Union, and the Air War in Korea.* College Station, Tex., 2002.

Electronic Archives

Cold War International History Project, Woodrow Wilson International Center for Scholars. cwihp.si.edu/.

MacArthur Archives. www.history.navy.mil/sources/.

National Archives and Records Administration (NARA). www.archives.gov/research/korea/.

Truman Library and Museum. www.trumanlibrary.org/.

U.S. Army Center of Military History. www.army.mil/cmh/.

TEN

America in Vietnam

JOHN M. CARROLL

BOUT SIX MONTHS before American forces intervened on the Korean peninsula, policy planners within the Truman administration conducted a reassessment of the military meaning of "containment." The resulting document, which was issued three months later in April 1950, was known as National Security Council memorandum 68 (NSC-68). It presented several alternatives to the president but recommended a massive military buildup by the United States and its allies to counter Soviet expansionism and war. Harry S. Truman took no action on the suggestion at the time, but once the Korean War began he authorized an enormous expansion of American military power along the lines recommended by NSC-68. The Cold War, which had been confined largely to Europe and surrounding areas until 1950, began to evolve into a global arms race between the United States and Russia and their respective allies.

Even while American forces were engaged in the bloody and frustrating conflict in Korea, Truman and many of his advisers remained convinced that the Communist invasion in Northeast Asia was a ploy to bog down Western forces there while the Soviets prepared for a massive attack in Western Europe. For this reason, the U.S. military buildup gave priority to increasing the conventional forces and nuclear weapons that might be needed to deter Soviet aggression in Europe. Between June 1950 and mid-1953 the United States nearly tripled the size of its land forces and more than doubled the strength of its air power. A sizable portion of the rearmament funding was aimed at bolstering North Atlantic Treaty Organization (NATO) forces and increasing America's deterrent capacity in Europe.

During the early stages of the Korean War, Truman sent military aid to French Southeast Asian forces who were fighting a war against a Communist insurgency in the French colonial area called Indochina. Previously, the administration had been reluctant to support the French colonial war, but now it viewed the conflict as part of a larger Communist plan for expansion in Asia. The Joint Chiefs of Staff feared at the time that if Indochina fell to the Communist Vietminh, then neighboring non-Communist states would be similarly overwhelmed in a kind of domino effect. Despite American aid, the war went badly for the French in the early 1950s. President Dwight D. Eisenhower, who took office in 1953, ascribed to the "domino theory" but refused to commit American arms in an attempt to prevent a disastrous French defeat at Dien Bien Phu (1954). The French negotiated a settlement of the First Indochina War at the Geneva Conference (1954), which temporarily divided Vietnam at the 17th parallel into pro- and anti-Communist regions. The United States quickly intervened in southern Vietnam to supplant French influence and to build and support an anti-Communist nation, the Republic of Vietnam.

During the 1950s, Eisenhower, concerned about the fiscal impact of Truman's military buildup, instituted a "New Look" defense policy that substantially reduced conventional forces and put more reliance on nuclear weapons. He continued to support President Ngo Dinh Diem's Republic of Vietnam as a model anti-Communist state. By the end of the decade, however, the South Vietnamese pro-Communist National Liberation Front rose up to oppose Diem in what would evolve into another war in Vietnam. The Democratic Republic of Vietnam in the north quickly supported the Communist insurgency below the 17th parallel.

When John F. Kennedy became president in 1961, the United States had nine hundred military advisers in South Vietnam. With the war going poorly for Diem's forces, Kennedy gradually increased America's military commitment in the south in the early 1960s. He also built up the nation's conventional forces in response to Soviet Premier Nikita Khrushchev's threats concerning West Berlin and his pledge to ignite "wars of national liberation" around the globe. For Kennedy, the intensifying struggle in Vietnam became a test case of America's will to resist Soviet subversion of Third World "democratic" nations.

Although Kennedy believed that Communist guerrilla-style wars such as the one in Vietnam could be won by a counterinsurgency strategy like the one the British had used in Malaya, John Carroll points out that the U.S. Army was trained and equipped to fight a conventional land war in Europe. Senior army officers paid lip service to the president's support for and fascination with the elite, counterinsurgency Special Forces, some of whom saw action in Vietnam, but trained and equipped Diem's Army of the Republic of Vietnam (ARVN) with high-tech weapons to fight a conventional land war. When the U.S. Military Assistance Command, Vietnam, was established in 1962, its advisers urged ARVN officers to make use of American-supplied helicopters, fighters, and firepower. Despite this aid and the increasing number of U.S. personnel in Vietnam, the war continued to go against the South Vietnamese forces. After Kennedy was assassinated in Dallas in November 1963, just a few weeks after Diem was overthrown and assassinated during a coup by South Vietnamese generals in Saigon, the new American president, Lyndon B. Johnson, prepared to send U.S. ground forces into Southeast Asia to fight America's longest war.

Marine Col. Al Bowser, who served in both the Korean and Vietnam wars, remarked that "it was amazing that so many of the mistakes we made in Korea, we repeated in Vietnam." By that, Bowser meant errors in military tactics and strategy as well as in the larger area of political decisions. In the latter category, the U.S. intervened in two wars in which, given the limitations imposed by our government, the military had little chance of winning a decisive victory. In both conflicts, America was attempting to support a corrupt and unstable government. Neither the South Korean army nor the South Vietnamese army (ARVN), moreover, had the will or motivation to fight effectively, although South Korean forces improved noticeably toward the end of the conflict. Most of our allies were reluctant to provide sustained support for the American military commitment to either South Korea or South Vietnam despite the fact that both wars ostensibly were being fought against international communism. These are just a few of the similarities between the two conflicts. There is also some irony in the fact that the American political and military commitment in Vietnam was the result, at least in part, of the outbreak of the Korean War in 1950.

When North Korean troops moved across the 38th parallel in June 1950, President Harry S. Truman responded quickly by sending U.S. forces to support the beleaguered South Korean army. Many miles to the south in Indochina, France, America's Cold War ally against the Soviet Union, was engaged in a conflict against the Vietminh, a Communist-led, nationalist army that was attempting to drive the French from Southeast Asia. France had begun its colonial rule in Indochina—the present-day nations of Vietnam, Cambodia, and Laos—in the mid-nineteenth century. Two world wars in the next century undermined French dominance and nurtured an anticolonial movement that was led in the 1940s by the Communist-trained Vietnamese nationalist Ho Chi Minh. During World War II, the Vietminh cooperated with the Allies in opposing the Japanese occupation army in Indochina. After the war, Ho proclaimed his country's independence and established the Democratic Republic of Vietnam (DRV).

During the turmoil that followed the war, Truman acquiesced in a British initiative to reestablish French control in Indochina, despite the fact that his predecessor, Franklin Roosevelt, had been a strong opponent of French colonial rule. In 1946 French forces bombarded Haiphong, thus beginning the First Indochina War, which lasted until 1954. The Vietminh, under the military direction of Vo Nguyen Giap, mainly conducted a guerrilla war against the conventional French forces, and by 1950, the Vietminh controlled about two-thirds of the countryside, while the French retained tenuous control in the cities. Up until 1950, the United States maintained a policy of pro-French "neutrality," providing some covert support for its European ally but remaining reluctant to openly champion colonialism.

With the Communist victory over the Nationalists in China in 1949 followed closely by the outbreak of the Korean War, American leaders became convinced that the war in Indochina was part of a grand Soviet design to expand world communism. The United States decided to openly support the French in Indochina, the first step toward direct American involvement in Vietnam. By 1954 it had a small number of military advisers in Vietnam but was underwriting 78 percent of the French war costs. The First Indochina War reached a climax in the spring of the same year when the French attempted to bait Vietminh forces into a set-piece battle in the remote village of Dien Bien Phu in northwestern Vietnam. In one of the most dramatic battles of the twentieth century, General Giap moved his army of four divisions and supporting artillery through seemingly impenetrable terrain and surrounded a French force of 15,000. Using well-directed artillery fire, mining, and finally human wave assaults, the Vietminh overwhelmed the isolated French garrison on May 7, 1954. Only

73 of the 15,000-man army escaped. It was a stinging military and psychological defeat for the French.

At this point, all seemed lost for both French and American interests in Vietnam. But at the 1954 Geneva Conference, Soviet and Chinese diplomats, hoping for a thaw in Cold War tensions in the wake of Joseph Stalin's death, failed to fully support the DRV, and an agreement much more favorable to Western interests than could have been reasonably expected was signed. The Geneva Accords temporarily divided Vietnam at the 17th parallel, with the understanding that reunification would take place by 1956 through national elections. The DRV controlled the North, and a government under Emperor Bao Dai was established in the South. Laos and Cambodia became separate neutral states. By 1955, the American-supported Premier Ngo Dinh Diem became the first president of the Republic of Vietnam (RV). It would not be an exaggeration to say that both Diem and the RV were a creation of the United States, most particularly of its foreign aid. In the mid-1950s, American foreign-policy specialists were committed to experiments in "nation building" in Third World areas, and South Vietnam became a showcase in that initiative. The experiment could hardly have been attempted in a more chaotic environment.

Like President Syngman Rhee in South Korea, Diem was a harsh, autocratic, and corrupt leader who often ignored American advice concerning needed reforms in the South. He was, however, militantly anticommunist and adamantly opposed to holding the national elections mandated by the Geneva Accords. It was largely as a result of his reactionary land policies and campaign of terror against Communists in the South that the Second Vietnamese War broke out in the late 1950s. Communist forces, who Diem called the Viet Cong, used guerrilla and terrorist tactics to strike back against his government. At first, the Viet Cong and its political organization, the National Liberation Front (NLF), acted alone, but by the early 1960s they had received considerable military aid and direction from the North. To help meet the threat of Communist insurgency in the South, Presidents Eisenhower and Kennedy sent more military aid to Diem and increased the number of American advisers supporting the Army of the Republic of Vietnam (ARVN). By the end of 1962 the United States had more than 9,000 military advisers in South Vietnam.

Under the Military Assistance Command, Vietnam (MAVC), the advisers served, built, trained, and advised the ARVN to fight a conventional war. This was the case because the U.S. Army, itself, was trained and organized to fight in a mobile, high-intensity conflict such as that which took place in Europe at the end of World War II. The advisers put great emphasis on the use of heavy firepower and such new "high-tech" weapons as helicopters and defoliants. This military orientation was unfortunate because, as Andrew F. Krepinevich points out, the basis for a successful guerrilla warfare operation "is a primary support system anchored on the population." Almost from the beginning, the use of these high-tech weapons alienated the very population whom the United States was in Vietnam to protect. This was ironic because President Kennedy was an ardent supporter of counterinsurgency forces, such as the Green Berets, and their use in Vietnam. Kennedy believed that such forces, stationed in the midst of the South Vietnamese population, would provide an effective means of undermining the insurgency. Although the army occasionally paid lip service to Kennedy's push for the training and use of the Special Forces, high-ranking officers were determined to conduct in Vietnam the kind of war they had been trained and organized to fight.

The U.S. Army would soon get its chance because in the early 1960s the military and political situation rapidly deteriorated in South Vietnam. The Viet Cong mainly controlled the countryside, especially at night, and conventional military operations conducted by the ARVN were largely ineffective. Facing heavy firepower and sophisticated weapons, the enemy simply fled unless presented with a favorable situation in which to fight. In late 1963, Diem was assassinated during a successful coup by a group of South Vietnamese generals. American officials had encouraged the generals and took no action to prevent the coup. A short time later Kennedy was gunned down by an assassin in Dallas. South Vietnam teetered on the brink of disaster as a succession of Vietnamese military leaders attempted to govern.

Despite the increasingly pessimistic reports from Vietnam, the new U.S. president, Lyndon Johnson, bided his time during 1964, awaiting the fall elections and what he hoped might be a mandate from the electorate. During the election campaign, a naval encounter between U.S. and North Vietnamese vessels in the Tonkin Gulf provided the opportunity for Johnson to ask for nearly unlimited authority to conduct military operations in Southeast Asia. In early August the Senate and House approved, nearly unanimously, Johnson's request with the passage of the Tonkin Gulf Resolution. Three months later Johnson won an overwhelming victory over the Republican challenger, Senator Barry Goldwater. The stage was set for a major escalation of U.S. military involvement in Vietnam.

Since the early 1960s, American advisers in South Vietnam had coordinated a series of commando raids against the North. Although the insurgency in the South had begun without significant support from North Vietnam, it became clear by 1959–1960 that Ho was sending substantial aid to the NLF. As political and military conditions in South Vietnam continued to deteriorate into the fall of 1964, President Johnson was anxious to strike at what he thought was the source of the problem, North Vietnam. In doing so, he hoped to raise morale in the South, shut off material support for the insurgency from the North, and bring about a peace settlement. After a Viet Cong mortar attack against U.S. barracks at Pleiku in early February 1965, which resulted in more than twenty American casualties, Johnson ordered several reprisal air raids against targets in the North. By mid-March, these raids became a regular program of attacks (codenamed Rolling Thunder) and were continued until November 1968, when peace talks began in Paris.

Operation Rolling Thunder, which was eventually launched from bases in South Vietnam, Thailand, and Guam and from aircraft carriers in the South China Sea, became almost a separate war in Southeast Asia. In the beginning, Johnson authorized raids against only certain targets in North Vietnam and expanded the list as time went on. This strategy of gradual escalation, or as Johnson more graphically put it, creeping up Ho's leg an inch at a time, was designed to force the DRV into peace negotiations. During the early Rolling Thunder raids, U.S. pilots were forbidden to attack Hanoi (North Vietnam's capital), the harbor at Haiphong, or areas along the DRV border with China. Attacks against petroleum storage facilities, so-called POL strikes, were not authorized until mid-1966. Johnson was clearly concerned about the possibility of Soviet and Chinese intervention and an expanded land war in Asia similar to that in Korea.

A number of former military commanders and some academic writers maintain that the target restrictions as well as the policy of gradual escalation allowed North Vietnam to escape the full impact of U.S. air power. The DRV, they argue, was given time to disperse its resources of war and build a formidable defense perimeter around the Hanoi/Haiphong area utilizing Soviet-made surface-to-air missiles as well as Russian antiaircraft crews and support troops from China. There was also time to repair damage to roads, bridges, and the like and for the civilian population to become accustomed to the bombing. These critics maintain that U.S. air commanders were operating with one hand tied behind their backs, and a few of the more extreme critics advocated bombing North Vietnam back to the Stone Age regardless of the consequences.

Other critics of Rolling Thunder have viewed it as a costly waste of resources, energy, and lives. Although the initial raids did raise morale in the South, they soon became commonplace and, as the South Vietnamese became "addicted" to the attacks, morale returned to a low level. What was worse, they argue, Rolling Thunder had minimal impact on the primitive North Vietnamese economy. According to these critics, the concept of strategic bombing was designed to destroy the heavily industrialized fabric of a war economy, which simply did not exist in the DRV. The North Vietnamese army, moreover, did not have a huge supply tail like that of Western nations. At the beginning of the war, it relied on a primitive transport system of coolies, sampans, and some trucks, which U.S. pilots found difficult to destroy. In a recent book on the Korean War, Max Hastings notes that it was astonishing that after the failure of strategic air power in Korea to interdict Chinese supply lines, American commanders ten year later "were allowed to mount a campaign under almost identical circumstances to those in Korea, with identical promises of potential and delusions of achievement, and with exactly repeated lack of success."

The beginning of Operation Rolling Thunder was one reason for the introduction of American combat forces into Vietnam in March 1965. Marines, who first went ashore at Da Nang, were given the task of protecting bases from which air operations against the North originated. Viet Cong sapper and mortar attacks posed a real threat to the security of these bases. For a brief period in 1965, there was a debate in Washington concerning the role of American combat forces in Vietnam. The U.S. ambassador to South Vietnam, Maxwell Taylor, advocated the enclave idea, which would restrict these combat forces to within fifty miles of their base areas. The theory was that this would limit U.S. participation in the war, deny the enemy a knockout blow, and allow time for an ARVN buildup while the bombing of the North began to take effect. By the summer, however, with the situation in Vietnam becoming worse, President Johnson authorized Gen. William Westmoreland, the commander of U.S. forces in Vietnam, to use his troops in any way he saw fit. The arrival of additional American forces marked the beginning of a buildup that would peak at more than 500,000 by mid-1968. Some of Johnson's critics, such as Col. Harry G. Summers, have faulted him at this point for failing to mobilize the American people through a declaration of war against North Vietnam and for not calling up the reserves. But Johnson hoped to settle the issue without cutting back on his domestic reform program, the Great Society. He was convinced, as were most of the first combat troops in Vietnam, that the enemy would soon collapse under the weight of America's military might.

In late 1965 American combat forces got their first real test when General Giap, employing three North Vietnamese divisions, attempted to divide South Vietnam in half along a line from Pleiku in the Central Highlands to the coast. Westmoreland sent the First Cavalry Division into the rugged Ia Drang Valley to counter the Communist move. Using helicopters to provide mobility in the dense and mountainous area, the First Cavalry established powerful firebases and inflicted heavy casualties on the enemy when he chose to attack. During October and November, American forces killed more than 1,200 North Vietnamese while suffering a loss of 200 men. The American initiative in the Ia Drang Valley thwarted Giap's plan to divide and seal off part of South Vietnam and put Westmoreland on *Time* magazine's cover as the 1965 "Man of the Year" for saving the day.

The victory at Ia Drang also revealed certain weaknesses in the Johnson administration's conduct of the war. American troops relied almost exclusively on helicopters for their mobility, and once on the ground remained immobile near firebases where heavy firepower was available. The North Vietnamese, on the other hand, maneuvered, attacked, broke contact, sidestepped, and continued their march. Westmoreland would later call this lack of mobility on the ground "firebase psychosis," but in late 1965 he was impressed by his army's ability to punish the enemy. From 1965 to 1969, as Andrew Krepinevich has noted, the army was convinced "that the essence of the conflict was military, not political" and thus downplayed the pacification program in favor of an all-out effort to destroy the enemy. The strategy of attrition that Westmoreland embraced in 1965 was a product of the American philosophy of war in the 1960s: extravagant use of munitions, matériel, and technology to save lives. Remembering the tragedy of Verdun in World War I, some commentators have charged that the strategy of attrition was no strategy at all.

The search-and-destroy operations that had begun in the summer of 1965 relied heavily on helicopters to bring American forces into contact with the enemy. Once contact was made, these troops usually backed off as air power rained tons of munitions on enemy positions. As former marine officer Philip Caputo has cynically suggested, the GIs, or grunts as they were known in Vietnam, were used as bait for the enemy. In many cases the Communist forces withdrew before the tactical air strikes were delivered. Occasionally, enemy units clung close to their American counterparts to shield themselves from the air attacks. With U.S. forces remaining close to their firebases and landing zones, the enemy was more mobile and held the initiative. He could stand and fight if he chose, or withdraw. This type of fighting largely neutralized the traditional strengths of U.S. soldiers, who performed best when on the offense and with a clear objective in sight.

The helicopter, which was the workhorse of the army in Vietnam, became, at least in part, its Achilles' heel. As guerrilla warfare expert Sir Robert Thompson has noted, "it is probable that without the helicopters 'search and destroy' would not have been possible and, in this sense, the helicopter was one of the major contributions to the failure of strategy." Search-and-destroy was attractive to Westmoreland and his fellow officers, however, because it was the type of combat the army was organizationally ready and able to conduct. It also had great appeal because it did not involve the South Vietnamese, whom the Americans found unreliable.

In addition to the search-and-destroy operations that were generally conducted in more sparsely populated areas of South Vietnam, the army also attempted a number of big-unit assaults. These operations—such as Attleboro (September–November 1966), Cedar Falls (January 1967), and Junction City (February–May 1967)—were carefully planned, utilized several U.S. divisions, and employed tanks and other heavy equipment. A favorite target for the Americans was the Iron Triangle, a Viet Cong stronghold northwest of Saigon and directly adjacent to the Cambodian border.

The Iron Triangle, which had been a refuge for the Vietminh during the Japanese occupation, was catacombed with hundreds of miles of tunnels and was only a few miles away from sanctuary in Cambodia. In operation Cedar Falls, Westmoreland sent 30,000 troops into the area. After B-52s pounded the Iron Triangle for days, specially trained combat troops were landed in the villages and thoroughly swept the region. The remaining population was then removed, and giant Rome plows with huge spikes attached to them leveled what remained. The Iron Triangle was then burned and bombed again in an attempt to destroy the miles of underground tunnels. Westmoreland deemed the operation a success, but, in fact, the enemy returned to the area within a matter of months.

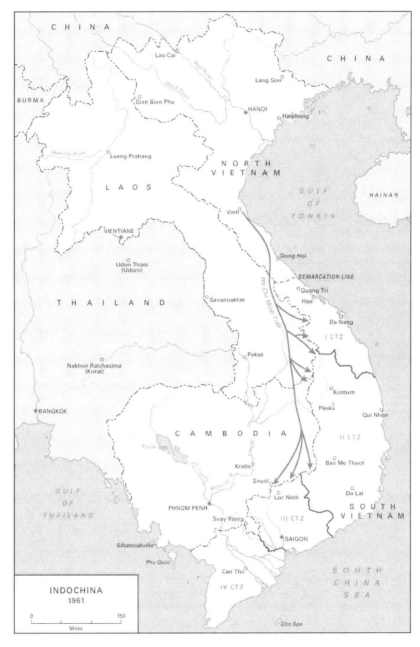

Indochina, 1961 (U.S. Army Center of Military History)

There were several major drawbacks to big-unit operations of this nature. Large-scale assaults such as Cedar Falls tied up great numbers of American troops because the heavy equipment required substantial logistical support. Meanwhile, enemy operations elsewhere, as well as the American and RV pacification efforts, were neglected. In the Iron Triangle, in particular, U.S. forces found it difficult to close the back door on the enemy before he fled across the border to Cambodia. This was in part because of the massive buildup and heavy bombing that preceded this type of operation. The Viet Cong and North Vietnamese, moreover, generally put up only token opposition against such heavy American firepower. As Maj. Gen. William Depuy remarked after operation Attleboro, "they metered out their casualties, and when the casualties were getting too high . . . they just backed off and waited." It sometimes took several tons of ordnance to kill just one of the enemy. Finally, the Americans vastly underestimated the extensiveness and complexity of the Viet Cong tunnel complex that ringed Saigon. In his memoirs, Westmoreland remarked that "no one has ever demonstrated more ability to hide his installations than the Viet Cong; they were human moles." It was not until the advent of the specially trained American unit known as "tunnel rats" that even a part of the underground network was neutralized.

By mid-1967 it was becoming increasing clear that Westmoreland's attrition strategy was not paying dividends. Although he continued to send encouraging data to Washington indicating that the enemy was sustaining heavy casualties, there was no evidence that either the Viet Cong or the North Vietnamese were having difficulty replacing their losses. More importantly, the search-and-destroy operations resulted in a large number of American casualties that some administration officials deemed prohibitive, given the mounting antiwar sentiment in the United States. In an effort to prove that their forces were succeeding in "attriting the enemy," army officers regularly reported "body count" statistics to Washington. These ghoulish reports were regularly inflated by as much as 30 percent. According to former officers who served in combat, the rule of thumb in the field was that a dead Vietnamese was automatically a Viet Cong.

The army's rotation system for officers was an additional obstacle to the effective conduct of the war. American officers generally served in Vietnam on a one-year cycle with only six months of combat duty. This policy came about, in part, because the army wanted to test its career officers in combat, and those men were anxious to fight, perform well, and gain advancement in the ranks. Career officers, therefore, were extremely aggressive in their approach to the war and in some cases inspired their subordinates to inflate the body-count reports. To further complicate the situation, GIs served in Vietnam for a 365-day period. American forces were regular army with a number of marine divisions in support. The soldiers were either volunteers or draftees, and only one or two National Guard units were called up. Of the 2.5 million Americans who served in Vietnam, a disproportionate number were poor, undereducated, and black. During the U.S. escalation, black casualties accounted for nearly one-quarter of the American total, but by 1973 the black casualty rate stood at 13 percent for the war, a little above the African American share of the U.S. population as a whole. But, as Gabriel Kolko points out, about one-half of the average company was made up of blacks and Hispanics. Moreover, between 7,500 and 11,000 women were on active military service in Vietnam. In addition, 30,000 to 40,000 women worked for the Red Cross or other voluntary services in Vietnam during the war.

Although the American soldier performed well in combat until the latter stages of the war, some troops who were nearing the end of their tour in Vietnam, or were "short," were reluctant to conduct the kind of aggressive operations mandated by the career officers. This situation created a certain tension between the higher-ranking officers and combat soldiers that became extreme toward the end of the war. Beyond this, the rotation system worked counter to two of the prime objectives in antiguerilla warfare: for soldiers to understand the nature of the war and win the confidence of the people.

In fairness to Westmoreland, his attrition strategy was hampered by the geographical difficulties that the war in Vietnam presented. South Vietnam was a long, narrow country with a width of between 50 and 150 miles and a 1,400-mile coastline. It also had a 900-mile land border with the neutral countries of Cambodia and Laos. In addition, its one major railway and most important roads ran north-south and could easily be cut by the enemy. Thus, the Americans could not establish one major supply base but had to build several along the coast. Unlike Korea, where U.S. forces used heavy firepower to punish the enemy along the 38th parallel, Westmoreland had to seek out and engage the Communist forces where he found them. There was no set front or battle line on which to bring to bear the army's enormous firepower. Although American forces performed well in combat, and in the view of Colonel Summers won nearly every battle, the enemy remained elusive. The Viet Cong and North Vietnamese used Laos and Cambodia as safe havens from American forces and established supply bases and infiltration routes along the border with South Vietnam.

Both during the war and afterward, many critics of President Johnson have suggested that he should have allowed Westmoreland to invade the Communist sanctuaries in Laos and Cambodia. In the spring of 1967, Westmoreland presented a grim assessment of the war to Johnson, stating that unless North Vietnamese infiltration could be stopped, the war could go on indefinitely. After careful consideration, Johnson rejected Westmoreland's advice to invade Cambodia and Laos and intensify the air war against the North. The president, who was continuing with his Great Society reforms at home, was motivated in part by the fear of a larger war that might cause the intervention of Chinese Communist forces, as happened in Korea. He was also aware of a 1966 Central Intelligence Agency (CIA) report that indicated that the vast majority of Communist supplies were generated within South Vietnam rather than through the infiltration routes.

During 1967, Westmoreland gave more emphasis to the pacification program and to the training of the ARVN so that one day the South Vietnamese might fight the war on their own. The general recognized for the first time that "military success alone will not achieve the United States objectives in Vietnam." But he also continued to support the bombing of the North and conducted aggressive search-and-destroy missions against the enemy. American forces persisted in raining heavy firepower on Communist troops and on suspected enemy positions, with air power delivering one-half of the explosives. By 1972 the United States had used fifteen million tons of munitions in Southeast Asia, which was more than double the amount it expended in World War II. In addition to inflicting heavy casualties on the enemy, the lavish use of firepower by American forces created havoc in the countryside of South Vietnam. Somewhere between 200,000 and 400,000 South Vietnamese civilians were killed, the landscape was devastated, and in some places the peasantry was forced off the land and into refugee camps or urban areas. The social and economic costs for the RV were enormous.

By early 1968 many officials in Washington, including the president, remained publicly optimistic about the war but in private concurred with a CIA report that a stalemate had developed. The pacification program was proceeding slowly, and efforts to upgrade the combat effectiveness of the ARVN had been disappointing. On the ground, U.S. forces were winning tactical victories, but the enemy was showing few signs of weakening or being ready to seek a negotiated settlement. Westmoreland was one of the few who believed that an American victory and the end of the war was in sight.

In late 1967, North Vietnamese regulars began a series of attacks against American-held outposts scattered around South Vietnam. By early the next year they had besieged Khe Sanh, a marine base near the Laotian border. These attacks were a prelude to the Tet Offensive, which most experts consider the turning point of the war. The Communist plan was to draw off American and ARVN troops from the cities to defend these isolated outposts and then deliver a devastating attack against hundreds of urban areas all across South Vietnam. According to Kolko, North Vietnamese officials believed that the offensive might totally succeed and bring the war to a quick end, or simply protract the war, or cause a major American escalation. In any case, it would shock the United States out of complacency and force Washington to make some political decisions.

Remembering General Giap's spectacular victory in 1954 at Dien Bien Phu, Westmoreland rushed reinforcements and air support to the beleaguered marines at Khe Sanh. Westmoreland apparently believed that he could bring about a reversal of the results of the earlier battle at Dien Bien Phu and deliver a crushing blow to the enemy. He inadvertently played into the hands of the North Vietnamese by dispersing American troops and leaving the urban areas vulnerable. On January 31, 1968, coinciding with the Lunar New Year celebrations, Viet Cong forces, who had slipped into cities and towns all over Vietnam, began an attack against all major cities and a large number of provincial capitals and towns. Despite a CIA warning about an impending attack against the cities, officials in Washington were so riveted on the battle at Khe Sanh that they were totally surprised by the scope and magnitude of the Communist offensive.

Although caught off balance, American and ARVN forces quickly recovered and inflicted crushing defeats on the Viet Cong and, to a lesser extent, the North Vietnamese. With the exception of Hue, where furious fighting continued for three weeks, the main thrust of the Tet Offensive was smashed within ten days. During the spring and summer the Communists renewed the offensive but with limited results. In the process, American and ARVN forces virtually demolished cities and parts of cities throughout Vietnam. As an American colonel said in reference to the city of Ben Tre, "We had to destroy the town to save it." In the aftermath of the offensive, the U.S. Army maintained that it had scored a major victory over the enemy and had practically wiped out the Viet Cong infrastructure in South Vietnam.

One of the enduring controversies relating to the Tet Offensive is the role of the print and television media in covering the war. Critics of the media, such as Robert Elegant, charge that reporters overreacted at the outbreak of Tet, as in other instances during the Vietnam War, and helped turn the public against the war. Elegant and others maintain that while television reporters focused their attention on such dramatic scenes as Viet Cong sappers penetrating the U.S. embassy compound in Saigon, they failed to adequately convey to the public the fact that it was American and ARVN forces that were victorious in the Tet Offensive. Some critics have blamed the media for stimulating antiwar sentiment in the United States, and ultimately for losing the war. Other journalists, such as Peter Arnett, have defended the media's role in Vietnam and have charged that the government and editors alike were responsible for concealing much of what the public should have known about the war.

Despite the controversy over Tet, it is clear that the Communist offensive caused leaders in Washington to make a number of important decisions about the war. As Gen. Dave Richard Palmer later recalled, "The Tet offensive was the most disastrous defeat North Vietnam suffered in the long war. Paradoxically, it was also the North's most resounding victory during the years of American military presence." Faced with a worldwide monetary crisis, domestic turbulence (including race riots), and a serious challenge to his bid to be the Democratic nominee for president in 1968, Johnson announced to the nation on March 31 that he would not run for reelection, urged the DRV to begin peace negotiations, and talked in general terms about a bombing halt north of the 20th parallel. Lost among the president's more sensational pronouncements was the one that the United States was "taking the first steps to deescalate the conflict. We are reducing—substantially reducing—the present level of hostilities." In a vague statement at the time, Johnson hinted that America would limit its commitment to South Vietnam and begin to turn over the combat role in the war to its Vietnamese allies. Hence, the Tet Offensive can be seen as a turning point in the war to the degree that the United States tentatively mentioned a policy of disengagement that presaged President Richard Nixon's Vietnamization program the following year.

In the fall of 1968, after a turbulent and hotly contested campaign, Nixon was elected president. Nixon had assured the voters that he had a "secret plan" to end the war. After taking office in early 1969, he announced that his administration would begin a gradual withdrawal of American troops from Vietnam and at the same time attempt to build the ARVN into an effective fighting force. During that year more than 100,000 American troops were pulled out. To a large extent the Johnson-Nixon decision to begin disengagement from Vietnam was dictated by the strain that the cost of the war was putting on the domestic economy and on the county's capacity to fulfill other military commitments abroad. By 1969, for example, almost 40 percent of the U.S. military budget was devoted to the war.

Although Nixon did not reveal a secret plan in 1969, the public was patient with the new president. Not only was Nixon withdrawing troops, but the intensity of the fighting tapered off in Vietnam during 1969 and with it the number of U.S. casualties. The large number of casualties incurred by Communist forces during the Tet Offensive helped account for the decline in enemy combat activity during the year. In the interim, Nixon embarked on a strategy of "big power" diplomacy in an effort to end the war. National Security Adviser Henry Kissinger conducted extensive negotiations with both the Soviet Union and China in the hope that they might influence the DRV to seek "peace with honor" with the United States. Meanwhile in Vietnam, Gen. Creighton W. Abrams, who had replaced Westmoreland, continued to stalk the enemy but also placed greater emphasis on controlling the countryside and implementing various pacification programs that had been underfunded and generally neglected by the army in the past.

By the spring of 1970, with more American troops departing from Vietnam, the training of RV forces proceeding slowly, and the enemy gradually recovering from the effects of the Tet Offensive, Nixon was determined to protect the remaining U.S. forces and gain additional time for his big-power diplomacy to work. The overthrow of Prince Norodom Sihanouk's neutralist regime in Cambodia and his replacement by the pro-American Lon Nol raised the possibility of a strike against Communist sanctuaries and supply bases in Cambodia near the South Vietnamese border. In early May, Nixon announced to a nationwide television audience that U.S. and ARVN troops had invaded the border areas in Cambodia to clear the sanctuaries, destroy enemy supplies, and, if possible, capture the central headquarters for all Communist operations in South Vietnam, which was thought to be located in the area. The Cambodian incursion was deemed a success by military officials despite the failure to find the enemy's central command post, but it sparked widespread antiwar demonstrations throughout the United States, especially on college campuses. Four students were killed at Kent State University in Ohio and two at Jackson State College in Mississippi as a result of angry confrontations with National Guardsmen and police. Ostensibly unshaken by the violent demonstrations, Nixon reaffirmed his commitment to "peace with honor" in Vietnam, although his military options now were limited by the domestic reaction to the Cambodian invasion.

As larger numbers of U.S. military personnel were being withdrawn from Vietnam by 1970, the armed services, and especially the army, experienced one of the most severe crises in their history. Military discipline and morale began to break down in units all over Vietnam. Many combat soldiers, realizing that American participation in the war was winding down and possibly affected by the antiwar movement back home, often rebelled against what they considered the overly aggressive orders issued by career officers. Not wanting to be among the last Americans killed in Vietnam, many GIs preferred search-and-evade tactics to the more aggressive order of search and destroy. Symptoms of the breakdown in morale and discipline included a large number of "fragging" incidents (that is, soldiers throwing live grenades into their officers' tents), a high incidence of drug use, and increasing racial conflict in many units. There were also a number of instances of mutiny in the field and sabotage against military property, including a major fire aboard the aircraft carrier USS *Forrestal*. While the continued withdrawal of U.S. forces and the resulting decrease in casualties seemed to have a calming effect on the American public by 1971, the reliability of these forces to carry on the war much longer was in serious doubt.

In February 1971, Nixon attempted once again to buy time for his Vietnamization program by ordering an invasion into Laos with the objective of dislodging the enemy and destroying supply bases in the sanctuary area. This time only ARVN units were employed on the ground, but they were supported with ample air cover by the Americans. After some initial success, the ARVN was battered by several North Vietnamese divisions that General Giap had rushed into the area. The South Vietnamese forces, who suffered a 50 percent casualty rate, retreated hastily and raggedly out of Laos. Although the Laos incursion did not spark the kind of domestic turbulence that the earlier Cambodian invasion had, it did not portend well for the ARVN's ability to contend with the enemy once all U.S. combat forces were withdrawn.

During the next year, Nixon and Kissinger continued to engage in triangular diplomacy with both the Soviet Union and China in an effort to bring pressure on North Vietnam to sign an honorable peace. The DRV was convinced, however, that a complete and immediate victory in the South was still within its grasp. In March 1972, North Vietnam launched a massive conventional invasion of the South. At the time there were fewer than 100,000 American soldiers in Vietnam and only about 6,000 combat troops. Taken by surprise, American and ARVN forces reeled before the DRV attack as North Vietnamese divisions drove deep into South Vietnam. Convinced that China and Russia would not intervene, but also aware that the American public would not permit a reintroduction of more combat forces, Nixon ordered a massive air attack against enemy targets in both North and South Vietnam. In addition, the harbor at Haiphong was mined and a naval blockade imposed on the DRV. The American response to the spring offensive represented the greatest escalation in the war since 1968. To a degree, at least, the massive use of American air power worked. By late summer 1972 the North Vietnamese attack stalled, and in a few instances ARVN forces launched counterattacks. North Vietnamese forces were badly bloodied by the American air assaults, and their source of supplies in the North had been severely bombed and seriously depleted. But DRV troops continued to occupy significant areas in South Vietnam.

The stage was now set for serious peace talks between Hanoi and Washington. In the early fall, Kissinger and North Vietnam's delegate, Le Duc Tho, worked frantically to end the long and costly war. Just before the November election in which Nixon was running for a second term, Kissinger announced that "peace was at hand." The announcement proved to be premature; the United States and its South Vietnamese ally as well as the DRV continued to wrangle over the details of the peace agreement into the winter months. Nixon threatened and cajoled South Vietnamese President Nguyen Van Thieu into accepting the basic settlement, even promising further support in the event of a DRV attack on the South. In December, Nixon ordered a massive and devastating bombing attack on North Vietnam, which he hoped would impel the DRV to sign an agreement. The so-called Christmas Bombings resulted in a wave of criticism against Nixon from Russia and China as well as from domestic sources. Finally, in early January 1973, the United States and North Vietnam signed a peace agreement. The remaining U.S. forces would leave Vietnam, and the Americans would have their prisoners of war returned. North Vietnamese troops would remain in place where they were in the South. As George Herring has stated, "Only by the most narrow definition can the agreement be said to have constituted 'peace with honor.'" The political future of South Vietnam—the major reason why the United States fought in Vietnam—remained in doubt.

During the course of the war, more than 58,000 Americans died in Vietnam. The nation spent more than $150 billion in the Southeast Asian conflict. For the Vietnamese people, the cost of the conflict in terms of war dead, devastation, and social welfare was far worse. The final chapter of the Second Vietnamese War came in early 1975 when a second North Vietnamese invasion of the South brought about the collapse of the South Vietnamese army and government. As the remaining American personnel were evacuated by helicopters to aircraft carriers waiting in the South China Sea, DRV troops marched victoriously into Saigon, soon to be renamed Ho Chi Minh City. Since that time Americans from all walks of life have asked: What went wrong in Vietnam?

Some, like Col. Harry Summers, maintain that American forces won every battle in Vietnam and, had they not been restricted and restrained by political leaders, would have won a clear victory over the North. Others, like Kolko, insist that the war was unwinnable: that Communist forces had momentum and endurance based on years of revolutionary struggle and that the U.S. or any other western power could not have indefinitely propped up the corrupt, unstable, and artificial South Vietnamese government. Other historians have staked out positions somewhere in between these two interpretations.

From a military perspective, most observers agree that American forces fought well in Vietnam, at least until the early 1970s. The army, however, has been criticized by Krepinevich and others for being unprepared to fight a limited war and being inflexible in its response to the crisis in Southeast Asia. Most critics now agree that Westmoreland's attrition strategy was futile and that the army could have better used its resources by protecting South Vietnamese civilians, as many marine battalions did, and focusing on the pacification program. The U.S. Navy and Air Force made many of the same mistakes that they had made in Korea, believing that strategic air power could totally destroy the economy of even a primitive nation. Soon after the war, the United States ended the draft and instituted an all-volunteer professional army, which has performed well in small engagements in the Caribbean, Southeastern Europe, and the Middle East. Today, the armed services have regained most of their reputation that had been tarnished in Vietnam. But the question remains: Have they learned the right lessons from the Vietnam experience?

More than thirty years after the end of the Vietnam War, issues surrounding the conflict continue to influence American diplomatic and military policy. Since the end of the Cold War in the early 1990s, some politicians and scholars have argued that Vietnam was a necessary war in maintaining U.S. credibility in its attempt to contain communism throughout the world. Michael Lind maintains that there really was an international communist conspiracy and America's military intervention in Vietnam was needed to prevent "a dramatic pro-Soviet realignment in world politics." According to Lind, the war was fought with the wrong strategy and the U.S. should have withdrawn after 1968 in order to preserve the domestic commitment to oppose international communism.

The 1991 Iraq war put to rest the idea that a large U.S. force again would become bogged down in a full-scale conflict halfway around the globe. One reason for the rapid withdrawal of American forces after the defeat of the Iraqi army, however, had to do with public anxiety about U.S. troops becoming entangled in a Middle East country for an extended period. The second Iraq war of 2003 again raised the specter of Vietnam as U.S. troops, after a rapid and complete victory over Saddam Hussein's armed forces, faced a perplexing guerrilla-style resistance. Once again, American politicians as well as citizens were discussing such issues as reasons for intervention, winning the hearts and minds of Iraqis, and an exit strategy. The Vietnam War remains a reference point by which Americans weigh and evaluate overseas military intervention.

Sources and Suggested Readings

Brigham, Robert. *Guerrilla Diplomacy: The NLF's Foreign Relations and the Vietnam War*. Ithaca, N.Y., 1999.

Caputo, Philip. *A Rumor of War*. New York, 1977.

Duiker, William J. *U.S. Containment Policy and the Conflict in Indochina*. Stanford, Calif., 1994.

Gardner, Lloyd C. *Pay Any Price: Lyndon Johnson and the Wars for Vietnam*. Chicago, 1995.

Hastings, Max. *The Korean War*. New York, 1987.

Herring, George C. *America's Longest War: The United States and Vietnam, 1950–1975*. New York, 1996.

———. *LBJ and Vietnam: A Different Kind of War*. Austin, Tex., 1994.

Kolko, Gabriel. *Anatomy of a War: Vietnam, the United States, and the Modern Historical Experience*. New York, 1985.

Krepinevich, Andrew F., Jr. *The Army and Vietnam*. Baltimore, 1986.

Lind, Michael. *Vietnam—The Necessary War: A Reinterpretation of America's Most Disastrous Military Conflict*. New York, 2000.

Mangold, Tom, and John Penycate. *The Tunnels of Cu Chi: An Untold Story of Vietnam*. New York, 1985.

McNamara, Robert S., James G. Bright, and Robert Brigham. *Argument Without End: In Search of Answers to the Vietnam Tragedy*. New York, 2000.

Mersky, Peter B., and Norman Palmer. *The Naval Air War in Vietnam*. Annapolis, Md., 1981.

Palmer, Dave Richard. *Summons of the Trumpet: U.S.-Vietnam in Perspective*. San Rafael, Calif., 1978.

Salisbury, Harrison, ed. *Vietnam Reconsidered*. New York, 1984.

Sheehan, Neil. *A Bright and Shining Lie: John Paul Vann and America in Vietnam*. New York, 1988.

Small, Melvin. *Covering Dissent: The Media and the Anti-Vietnam War Movement*. New Brunswick, N.J., 1994.

Summers, Harry G., Jr. *On Strategy: A Critical Analysis of the Vietnam War*. Novato, Calif., 1982.

Thompson, James Clay. *Rolling Thunder: Understanding Policy and Program Failure*. Chapel Hill, N.C., 1980.

Westmoreland, William C. *A Soldier Reports*. Garden City, N.Y., 1976.

Williams, William Appleman, et al. *America in Vietnam: A Documentary History*. New York, 1984.

Websites

Vietnam Online. www.pbs.org/wgbh/amex/vietnam/index.html.

Vietnam War Bibliography. tigger.uic.edu/~rjensen/vietnam.html.

The Wars of Vietnam: An Overview. vietnam.vassar.edu/overview.html.

Proliferation:
The United States and
the Nuclear Arms Race

WALTER L. HIXSON

I N JULY 1945 a brilliant flash of light and an immense explosion in the New Mexico desert near Alamogordo signaled the beginning of the atomic age. A group of U.S. scientists had successfully tested a nuclear device with a force equal to nineteen kilotons of TNT, or about nineteen thousand tons of conventional explosives. It would have taken hundreds of World War II–vintage bombers to deliver a comparable blow to the enemy. In the following month President Harry S. Truman authorized the dropping of two atomic bombs on the Japanese cities of Hiroshima and Nagasaki to hasten the end of the Pacific War. Japan quickly surrendered, and the world entered a new era in the history of warfare and diplomacy. The viability of Karl von Clausewitz's idea on "the use of combats" as a definition of strategy was seemingly at an end. A strategy of annihilation that included the use of atomic weapons could no longer serve as a useful purpose of war, unless the object was complete destruction of an enemy and his territory.

Because of the potential destructive power of atomic weapons, there was a debate about the use of the bomb in World War II and its use as a diplomatic weapon in the postwar period. Both issues continue to interest historians today. After the war, President Truman considered Americans the "trustees of this new force" and committed the nation to a policy of nonproliferation. In 1946 he appointed financier Bernard Baruch to develop and present a plan to the United Nations for the international control of atomic energy. The Baruch Plan was based on an earlier proposal by David Lilienthal, then chairman of the Tennessee Valley Authority, and Undersecretary of State Dean Acheson, but it included a clause, approved by Truman, to eliminate the UN Security Council's veto power on atomic energy matters. Soviet delegate Andrei Gromyko flatly objected to tampering with the veto power, effectively killing the plan. Some historians argue that the clause was designed to elicit such a response from the Soviets. In the same year Congress passed the Atomic Energy Act (1946), which, among other points, was designed to protect America's nuclear monopoly. It prompted Britain, France, and the Soviet Union to accelerate their own programs of atomic weapons research and production, thus triggering a nuclear arms race.

As the Cold War intensified in the postwar years, U.S. diplomats used the threat of the atomic bomb in an effort to moderate what Americans came to view as Soviet expansionism. The tactic—atomic diplomacy—was not successful. In 1949 the Soviet Union surprised many political leaders in Washington when it successfully tested its first atomic bomb. Despite predictions by American scientists to the contrary, government officials had not expected the Soviets to develop nuclear weapons so quickly. The Soviet achievement heightened Cold War tensions and led to an era of proliferation in the atomic arms race.

In early 1950, President Truman responded by initiating a crash program to develop a much more powerful thermonuclear, or hydrogen, bomb. His decision significantly increased the defense budget and raised the stakes in the nuclear arms race. On November 1, 1952, the Atomic Energy Commission detonated an experimental device with a force equivalent to over seven hundred times the power of the Hiroshima bomb. Less than a year and a half later, the United States tested an "air-supportable" thermonuclear bomb that had the force of five times the explosive power of all the conventional bombs dropped on Germany by the Allies during World War II. The Soviet Union accelerated the pace of its hydrogen bomb program and once again surprised many Americans by testing a thermonuclear weapon in August 1953. Although the United States still led in the nuclear arms race, Americans realized that Russia would soon have enough nuclear weapons to devastate large portions of their country.

The nuclear arms race also put pressure on the military services, especially the air force, to develop the delivery capability for the new weapons. The Strategic Air Command formulated plans for a rapid nuclear strike in time of war and urged the development of new long-range bombers. At the same time, both Washington and Moscow proceeded with the development of missile technology that promised to increase the speed and accuracy of a nuclear attack. Both sides employed the services of former German rocket scientists, who had developed the V-1 and V-2 missiles during World War II. Walter Hixson describes and analyzes the development of America's nuclear weapons policy from the late 1940s to the present. While he is cautiously optimistic about the prospect for a substantial reduction in the size of nuclear arsenals in the wake of the conclusion of the Cold War, Hixson points out the many obstacles that impede full nuclear disarmament.

World War II (1941–1945) marked the arrival of the United States as the preeminent world power. Although the Soviet Union and its allies contested U.S. power until the end of the Cold War (1989–1991), American economic, cultural, and military strength proved supreme. However, as a result of waging World War II and the Cold War the United States became deeply militarized—a nation that not only ceaselessly prepared for war but also fought major wars in Korea, Vietnam, Afghanistan, and Iraq, as well as myriad smaller conflicts and interventions across the globe. While Washington employed a vast array of conventional weapons in warfare, neither the United States nor any other nation used nuclear weapons following the two atomic bombs dropped on Japan in August 1945. However, collusion among the Pentagon, private defense industries, and universities and think tanks fueled the growth of a "military-industrial complex" devoted to research, development, and deployment of new nuclear as well as conventional weapons systems. The United States thus took the lead in fueling an arms race in nuclear weapons research, development, and deployment throughout the postwar era. As the Soviet Union struggled to keep up, the accumulation of weapons of mass destruction spread fear and uncertainty across the globe, even as the failure to contain nuclear proliferation spurred a growing number of nations to seek to become nuclear weapons states themselves.

During the Cold War, both the United States and the USSR embraced deterrence through mutual assured destruction (MAD). Each would maintain nuclear forces sufficient to absorb an atomic attack and launch a massive retaliatory strike. MAD thus would deter any use of the weapons of mass destruction. MAD could have been achieved on a basis of "finite deterrence" by maintaining only enough invulnerable nuclear weapons to ensure the capacity for a devastating retaliatory strike. Instead, however, Washington led an arms race of seemingly boundless escalation, wasting resources, heightening the danger of nuclear war, and setting a poor example for the world. The excesses of this race contributed to the economic collapse of the former Soviet Union but did not bring about the end of the Cold War.

Atomic weapons had first appeared not during the Cold War but in World War II. Fearing that Nazi Germany, which had harnessed its scientific establishment to Adolf Hitler's aggressive course, would develop and use atomic weapons, President Franklin D. Roosevelt authorized a crash course to ensure that the United States would be first to build the bomb. The Manhattan Project, as the top-secret research effort was known, began in August 1942. The $2 billion program, by far the most expensive research undertaking during the war, involved some 150,000 people operating primarily in the three "atom bomb cities" of Hanford, Washington; Oak Ridge, Tennessee; and Los Alamos, New Mexico. By relying on oral rather than written communication, the Manhattan Project remained unknown to most of the public, although Soviet spies did penetrate the program.

Before dawn on July 16, 1945, the Manhattan Project culminated in a brilliant flash of light over the New Mexico desert. The first successful test of an atomic weapon came at the very time that Harry S. Truman, Roosevelt's successor as president, British prime minister Winston Churchill, and Soviet premier Joseph Stalin were meeting at Potsdam, Germany, to make final plans to secure the unconditional surrender of Japan. After some debate, American officials resolved to employ the bomb as soon as it became available. Since Nazi Germany had been defeated by means of the Allied conventional war effort, Japan remained the only potential target of American atomic bombing. The British had been kept apprised of the Manhattan Project, but Roosevelt and Churchill decided not to inform their Soviet allies about the progress of the bomb. Finally, in the wake of the successful test blast, Truman casually informed Stalin at Potsdam that the United States had developed a powerful new weapon. The Soviet premier just as casually encouraged Truman to use it against the Japanese.

President Truman assumed responsibility for the subsequent bombing of Hiroshima and Nagasaki on August 6 and 9, but he was merely following through on a course that already had gathered momentum: a government committee charged with planning for the bomb had approved targets in Japan. Truman would have had to reverse American policy to stop the attack. In the context of the most brutal war in human history, one in which Allied bombing had already obliterated German and Japanese cities, the decision to use the new weapon did not seem out of context. Racism ran high against the "treacherous Japs" who had bombed Pearl Harbor in a "sneak attack" in 1941 and thus had unleashed a brutal imperial war, replete with atrocities and kamikaze raids, across Asia and the Pacific. The horrific destruction beneath the giant mushroom cloud over Hiroshima left some 130,000 dead and buildings leveled in Japan's eighth-largest city. The gruesome effects of radiation also attested to the destructive potential of nuclear weapons. An incomparably destructive age had begun in the history of warfare.

Was the atomic bombing necessary to secure the surrender of Japan? Were there alternatives, such as a demonstration blast on some remote Pacific atoll, that Americans rejected in favor of the awesome display of military technology? Scholars and citizens have long debated these questions. President Truman and defenders of his decision argued that the use of the bomb was necessary to prevent the thousands of American casualties that would result from an invasion of the Japanese home islands. In retrospect, however, it is clear that Tokyo faced certain defeat and that forces were at work in Japanese society to compel the emperor to accept that reality. The United States and its allies probably could have succeeded through diplomacy in securing Japan's defeat without using the bomb or invading the home islands—especially with the Soviet Union poised to join the United States in attacks on Japanese positions. Even after using the two atomic weapons, Washington had to agree to allow the emperor to remain in power as a symbolic figurehead before the country agreed to surrender. The policy of unconditional surrender, racism, and four years of bloody war made the decision to use the bomb expedient and popular.

The destruction evident at Hiroshima and Nagasaki made it clear, at least, that world leaders would have to find ways to prevent the use of such weapons in the future. American scientists such as J. Robert Oppenheimer, the "father" of the atomic bomb, had nurtured gnawing doubts about the development and use of nuclear weapons, and they advocated international agreements forbidding their use. American efforts to promote a system of international controls before the new United Nations fell victim to Cold War tensions. The Soviet Union, increasingly seen not as a wartime ally but as an aggressive global rival driven by Communist ideology, would not accept a 1946 American proposal (the Baruch Plan) that would have maintained the U.S. monopoly until all other nations turned over their atomic energy programs and matériel to the United Nations. Even a more equitable plan probably would have been ignored by the USSR, which was committed to its own program of atomic research and development.

By the time of the successful Soviet test of an atomic weapon in September 1949, Cold War tensions had escalated dramatically. Europe had been divided into spheres of influence, and both the United States and the USSR had begun to compete for influence in the developing world. Washington and its European allies had formed the North Atlantic Treaty Organization (NATO) to "contain" putative Soviet expansionism. Both superpowers had inaugurated a military buildup. When China "fell" to communism in 1949 and Communist and non-Communist forces went to war in Korea the next year, the Truman administration put the United States on a war footing. The decisions codified in the National Security Council's paper (NSC-68) in the spring of 1950 envisioned massive increases in military spending, which could not help but fuel the burgeoning nuclear arms race.

By 1950 both American and Soviet scientists were at work on more powerful fusion bombs. Despite the opposition of Oppenheimer and several other scientists, Truman authorized the development and testing of a thermonuclear, or hydrogen, bomb that was one thousand times more powerful than the weapons that had devastated Hiroshima and Nagasaki. The H-bomb test succeeded in November 1952, followed nine months later by another successful test that culminated in a furious Soviet effort to match American nuclear advances. Both nations began stockpiling weapons of incalculable destructive force.

Despite the potentially suicidal nature of nuclear war, the United States, especially under the Eisenhower administration, made the weapons a central component of Cold War strategy. President Dwight D. Eisenhower, a Republican and fiscal conservative, argued that nuclear weapons provided "more bang for the buck" than maintaining sprawling military bases and occupation forces overseas. Washington would contain the Soviets by threatening to unleash what Secretary of State John Foster Dulles called "massive retaliation" against either the USSR or China in the event of Communist aggression anywhere in the world. This implicit nuclear threat may have contributed to the willingness of the Communist powers to help bring about an armistice in Korea in July 1953. American officials discussed the possibility of using the bomb to aid the French, who were on the verge of defeat in Vietnam in 1954, but no such plans came close to being operational.

Rather than actually using nuclear weapons, the Eisenhower administration continued to employ the bomb as a tool of psychological warfare. Implied threats to use the weapons of mass destruction, especially when offered by outspoken anti-Communists such as Dulles, would serve to restrain presumed Soviet and Chinese expansionism and keep the Communist powers off balance. Efforts to exploit the bomb for propaganda purposes succeeded only in heightening Soviet insecurities and fueling the arms race. Both superpowers conducted research and development on intercontinental ballistic missiles (ICBMs) that could deliver nuclear warheads from land or sea, thousands of miles from their target. The recognition of American vulnerability to Soviet rockets accounts for the high level of anxiety in this country that greeted the Soviet launching of *Sputnik*, the first Earth satellite, in October 1957. Although the achievement electrified world opinion and sent tremors through the American political landscape, the 184-pound *Sputnik* actually was technologically crude and of no military significance. It became obvious, however, that if the Soviets could launch a satellite into space, they also could deliver nuclear-tipped warheads over American shores.

Sputnik precipitated a panic that gave rise to the myth of a "missile gap," which held that the Soviets had gained the strategic superiority that would allow them to launch a crippling first strike. The arms race had entered its most dangerous phase. Democrats and critics within his own party condemned Eisenhower and his administration for allowing the supposed gap to occur. Money flowed into national defense think tanks, into nuclear research and development, into public schools for scientific education, and into the political coffers of advocates of nuclear escalation. Ignoring muted calls to rein in the weapons race, the United States continued to take the lead by placing nuclear missiles targeting the Soviet Union on European territory.

Hysteria over the missile gap drowned out Eisenhower's pleas for calm. The president himself knew that there was indeed a missile gap—

one weighted heavily in favor of the United States, which maintained a substantial lead in both bombers and missiles. American submarine technology was also far superior to the Soviets'. As Premier Nikita S. Khrushchev recalled in his memoirs, the men in the Kremlin plainly understood that Washington's strategic superiority—and their own vulnerability—could not be challenged for at least another decade. Unable to check the momentum for escalation in the wake of the missile gap controversy, Eisenhower warned his listeners in his 1961 farewell address to "guard against the acquisition of unwarranted influence . . . by the military-industrial complex." The existence of a vast public and private "complex" devoted to research and development of the instruments of Armageddon fueled the arms race even after new satellite reconnaissance photographs in 1961 belied reports of massive Soviet ICBM deployment.

Under pressure from the more militant Chinese as well as from his own Communist party hard-liners to respond to the American escalation, Khrushchev decided in 1962 to place Soviet nuclear missiles secretly in Cuba. This decision must be seen in the context of the breakdown of early efforts toward détente and of Soviet frustration over the inability to eliminate the Western enclave in Berlin. Efforts to ease tensions began with the "spirit of Geneva," dating from a 1955 summit in that city, and continued through Khrushchev's 1959 tour of the United States and the opening of an American cultural exhibition in Moscow that same year. Both superpowers had observed an informal moratorium on nuclear testing since 1958 and were within reach of a formal agreement until the shooting down of an American U-2 spy plane, which had penetrated 1,200 miles into restricted Soviet airspace, propelled Washington-Moscow relations into a downward spiral. Eisenhower had authorized Central Intelligence Agency (CIA) overflights in the ultralightweight spy planes, packed with photographic equipment, in order to monitor Soviet nuclear development. Following the downing of Francis Gary Powers's U-2 on May 1, 1960, Khrushchev denounced the United States and abruptly ended a summit conference in Paris two weeks later.

The Soviet decision to place nuclear weapons in Cuba thus came in the midst of heightened East-West tensions over the missile gap and the U-2 incident. Newly elected president John F. Kennedy had made no progress at a tense meeting with Khrushchev in Vienna in June 1961. Moreover, two months earlier the United States had failed miserably in an attempt to topple Communist leader Fidel Castro by landing CIA-trained

Cuban exiles at the Bay of Pigs. CIA assassination plots against the Cuban president continued. The Kremlin had already broken the informal moratorium on nuclear testing and now made secret plans to build the missile sites. By placing nuclear missiles targeting the United States in Cuba, Khrushchev intended to enhance Castro's ability to defend the Cuban Revolution as well as to give Americans "a little of their own medicine"— to teach them "just what it feels like to have enemy missiles pointing at you," which the Soviets knew very well from the deployment of NATO missiles in Europe and across the Black Sea in Turkey.

The Soviet action was legal under international law but dishonest, since the Kremlin had denied that the USSR intended to place nuclear missiles in Cuba. Khrushchev clearly hoped to confront the United States with a fait accompli that would strengthen his standing with the Chinese and his own Politburo hard-liners. Instead, Kennedy, having learned of the missile sites through a U-2 overflight, went on national television on October 22, 1962, to demand that the Soviets dismantle them. He established a naval blockade of Cuba to interfere with Soviet freighters but avoided calls for bombing the missile sites. The tense international crisis carried a palpable threat of a Washington-Moscow confrontation that might easily escalate to nuclear war.

Khrushchev stopped Soviet ships that were steaming toward Cuba and agreed to dismantle the missile sites, but only after Kennedy pledged publicly to respect Cuba's territorial integrity and privately to withdraw Jupiter missiles from Turkey. The crisis had the salutary effect of sobering both leaders about the real dangers of nuclear war, and it also broke the impasse in the ongoing test-ban negotiations. In 1963 the two superpowers established a hotline for instant communication in the midst of any future crisis and signed the Limited Test Ban Treaty terminating above-ground nuclear tests. A new era of détente had begun, but research, construction, and deployment of nuclear weapons and various delivery systems continued unchecked.

The Soviets embarked on a concerted effort to build large-scale ICBMs that, while less accurate, were far more powerful than the Pentagon's Minuteman missiles. The overthrow of Khrushchev in 1964 signaled the triumph of hard-liners, led by Leonid Brezhnev, who eventually would pursue détente but only while striving simultaneously to achieve strategic parity. The United States continued to assemble a massive nuclear force on the European continent, emplacing 7,200 nuclear weapons there by 1966—an absurd exercise in overkill that, as Secretary of Defense Robert S. McNamara admitted, served no rational purpose. Despite the accumulation of overkill, the appropriately named system of MAD perpetuated stable, but not finite, deterrence.

Washington, backed as always by the quest for profit and influence on the part of the military-industrial complex, continued to take the lead in expanding the arms race. An exception to this role was the Soviet decision to install an antiballistic missile (ABM) system around Moscow. The weak defensive system hardly could have stopped a nuclear onslaught against the capital, but it strengthened the case of American proponents not only of ABMs but also of the new, far-reaching innovation of multiple independently targetable reentry vehicles (MIRVs). Under this technology, individual nuclear warheads could be released from a missile at various times and angles with the ability to reach multiple targets.

The Soviets, previously reluctant to sacrifice their primitive ABM system, were willing to negotiate to head off an explosive arms race in both offensive and defensive weapons against a technologically superior adversary. Washington announced and then canceled the Strategic Arms Limitation Talks (SALT), set to begin in late 1968, in response to the Warsaw Pact invasion of Czechoslovakia in August of that year. At the same time the United States had become deeply embroiled in a fruitless war in Southeast Asia. While détente lagged, the arms race, now centered around the research and development of multiple warhead missiles, gained momentum.

President Richard M. Nixon, little interested in arms control on its own merits, sought to revive negotiations in an effort to gain Soviet assistance in finding an acceptable basis for U.S. withdrawal from Vietnam. Simultaneously, he and his national security adviser, Henry Kissinger, sought to pit the now bitterly divided Soviets and Chinese against each other. Nixon and Kissinger agreed to limit ABMs in the historic 1972 SALT I treaty, whose essence was mutual recognition of the futility of defensive systems, which could always be penetrated by an array of offensive weapons. Nixon and Kissinger threw away a golden opportunity to limit offensive MIRVs, which the Soviets soon developed in response to the American initiative and placed on their mammoth ICBMs. Similarly, Washington proceeded with the development of the Trident nuclear submarine, thus furthering its distinct advantage at sea.

With both superpowers amassing thousands of warheads within their strategic triad (land-, air-, and sea-based weapons), any international crisis carried with it the threat of a devastating nuclear holocaust. At least since the 1967 Six-Day War, the Middle East had been considered a likely site for the escalation of a regional conflict into a superpower confrontation. With the outbreak there of war in 1973, and with Washington's client Israel poised to deliver a humiliating defeat to Egypt, Brezhnev pointedly threatened Soviet intervention. Nixon, then in the midst of the Watergate scandal that later would force his resignation, ordered Defense Condition III, which put American military forces just short of full readiness for war for the first time since the Cuban missile crisis in 1962. The Middle East crisis quickly abated, however, when Egyptian president Anwar Sadat withdrew his request for Soviet support in favor of an international peacekeeping force.

Détente helped resolve the crisis in the Middle East, but the relaxation of Soviet-American relations proved short-lived. Détente broke down over a whole host of issues—East-West trade, human rights (including Jewish emigration from the USSR), and Soviet support for Marxist revolutionaries across the globe—and arms control was a casualty of this collapse. A summit meeting between President Gerald R. Ford and Brezhnev at Vladivostok in 1974 established ceilings on the number of delivery vehicles and MIRVs. Since the ceilings were actually higher than the numbers in existence, the agreement did not represent arms reductions at all, but both leaders planned a more comprehensive accord in a subsequent SALT II treaty. However, vocal critics of détente misrepresented the arms control process, arguing that it offered the Soviets a strategic advantage. Détente thereafter became a dirty word, and Ford held off on SALT II until after the 1976 presidential election, which he lost.

By the time Jimmy Carter came to the White House in 1977, the escalatory spiral continued. Pentagon planners had already authorized a new B-1 bomber, and cruise missiles that could be launched from land, air, or sea. These low-flying missiles were small, relatively cheap, and easy to hide, all of which made them destabilizing and an impediment to arms control. As was often the case, the United States initiated a new weapons system that contributed nothing to deterrence and therefore represented a pointless escalation that the Soviets were sure to match. Once the Pentagon and private defense contractors—the military-industrial complex—committed to a new system, however, its momentum could scarcely be stopped.

Criticism of détente and arms control mounted under Carter, whose focus on human rights abuses angered the Soviets as much as his cancellation of the B-1 bomber infuriated American hawks. He did go ahead with the cruise missile program while shelving SALT in the first half of his presidency. By the time Carter signed a SALT II treaty with the Soviets, he had already spent most of his political capital in the Senate to gain approval for the 1978 Panama Canal Treaty. To restore a consensus for arms control, he had to appease the critics who argued that the latest Soviet ICBM, the more accurate and heavyweight SS-18, could serve as a first-strike weapon. The fictional "window of vulnerability," reminiscent of the missile gap, held that the Soviets might wipe out the Minuteman force in a first strike, thus subjecting the United States to blackmail or nuclear devastation before it could react. This absurd scenario, aside from viewing the Soviets as suicidal, ignored some 7,000 American warheads at sea as well as bombers that might respond from scores of U.S. bases. The Kremlin leaders were hardly in a position to ignore those weapons even if they had been as demonic as Washington's hawks liked to picture them. But as arms-race historian John Newhouse has noted, "Common sense was no match for the minatory bolt from the blue; it had become the fashionable anxiety."

To appease his critics and build consensus, Carter authorized the MX, or experimental missile, which the Congressional Budget Office estimated would cost $60 billion. In 1979, NATO approved the deployment of 464 ground-launched cruise missiles and 108 Pershing II missiles throughout western Europe, including West Germany. In that year the American political atmosphere turned sharply to the right. While hawks made an issue of the existence of a fictional Soviet "combat brigade" in Cuba, moderates withdrew their support for the SALT II treaty. Giving up on détente, the Soviets lent credence to worst-case scenarios in the West by invading Afghanistan in December 1979. A month earlier, Iranian militants had taken Americans hostage at the U.S. embassy in Tehran, initiating an agonizing crisis that strengthened the appeal of those who argued that the United States had become weak in defending its national interests. Carter's presidency collapsed in an overwhelming reelection defeat at the hands of Republican conservative Ronald Reagan.

Long considered too far to the right to gain the presidency, Reagan not only won two landslide elections but also became one of the most popular chief executives in American history. In a nation wounded by defeat in Vietnam, humiliated by the Iranian hostage crisis, and no longer the dominant superpower, Reagan's optimistic appeal to traditional values, including military supremacy, enjoyed broad support. The California Republican labeled the USSR an "evil empire" whose machinations were at the root of "all the unrest that is going on" in the world. Openly declaring that the United States would not settle for parity with the USSR, Reagan set off a paroxysm of military spending that threatened to destabilize the arms race. Like his hawkish subordinates Alexander Haig (State), Caspar Weinberger (Defense), and William Casey (CIA), Reagan believed in the "window of vulnerability" as well as that the Soviets were preparing to fight and win a nuclear war. Shunning all negotiations, the president committed the United States to a massive rearmament campaign reminiscent of NSC-68 in the Truman years.

The Reagan military buildup received much popular support, but it also alarmed many Americans and NATO allies. Antinuclear demonstrations erupted throughout the West, while the nuclear freeze movement—advocating an immediate halt to the rampaging arms race—gained momentum. Under public pressure, Reagan initiated the Strategic Arms Reduction Talks (START) and opened negotiations on intermediate-range nuclear forces (INF) in Europe in the midst of American plans to deploy new Pershing missiles. Negotiator Paul Nitze, a veteran Cold Warrior who had written NSC-68 more than thirty years before, came to terms with his Soviet counterpart during the famous "walk in the woods" in 1982, but Secretary Weinberger and his aides sabotaged what would have been a significant agreement requiring the Soviets to remove 80 percent of their midrange missiles targeting Europe.

Brilliant as the "Great Communicator" but often out of touch on specific issues, Reagan took the lead on nuclear weapons only when some particular aspect struck his fancy. Such was the case with the Strategic Defense Initiative (SDI), promptly dubbed Star Wars after a popular science-fiction movie, which proposed to employ lasers, particle beams, and interceptors to shoot down incoming Soviet missiles, thus rendering nuclear weapons, as the president put it, "impotent and obsolete." Reagan stunned the public with his glib, but entirely sincere, announcement of the program in March 1983. The problem with SDI, besides its inherent impracticality, was that the ABM Treaty—probably the most successful U.S.-Soviet agreement in arms control—forbade testing and deployment of the type of defensive systems envisioned by Reagan. SDI would replace deterrence with an unworkable defensive system whose costs would far exceed any other program in the history of the weapons race. Soviet leader Yuri Andropov reacted sharply in *Pravda* four days after Reagan's speech, declaring that SDI would "open the floodgates of a runaway race of all types of strategic arms, both offensive and defensive. . . . Engaging in this is not just irresponsible, it is insane."

If SDI was one nail in the arms control coffin, then the shooting down of Korean Airlines Flight 007, which had strayed hundreds of miles into Soviet airspace on September 1, 1983, was another. The Soviets apparently mistook the jetliner for an American RC-135 spy plane, but the Reagan administration wasted no time in asserting that the Kremlin knowingly had shot down the civilian plane, killing all 269 passengers on board. Reagan used the incident to bolster his "evil empire" thesis and to lobby Congress for MX funding. Two months later the United States began deploying Pershing II missiles in the NATO countries, prompting bitter denunciations from Moscow and mass demonstrations in western Europe. The USSR suspended all arms control talks. At this time, the popularity of the ABC television movie *The Day After*, which depicted the devastation of nuclear war, and books such as Jonathan Schell's *The Fate of the Earth* attested to mounting anxieties. Veteran Cold Warriors Robert McNamara, George Kennan, McGeorge Bundy, and Gerard Smith—dubbed the Gang of Four by critics—launched a campaign against the NATO policy of "first use," which envisioned using nuclear weapons in a conventional war. The Soviets had previously renounced first use.

Following his overwhelming reelection in 1984, Reagan took the advice of moderates such as Secretary of State George Shultz as well as his wife Nancy to soften his hard line and leave a more peaceful legacy. British prime minister Margaret Thatcher, herself a staunch conservative, also urged Reagan to pursue arms control. By far the most important development in the revival of a consensus for arms control, however, was the rise to power of a new Soviet leader, Mikhail Gorbachev. Committed to revolutionary changes in world politics, he displayed an openness to accommodation with the West and a flair for public relations that shattered all stereotypes about the succession of dour Kremlin leaders. Gorbachev hoped to forge a peaceful relationship with the West in order to devote Soviet resources to deep-seated economic and political problems.

Gorbachev urged massive reductions in military forces, including, above all, the superpowers' nuclear arsenals. He proved his sincerity with concrete actions that could not be dismissed as typical Communist machinations. The Soviet leader denounced the war in Afghanistan as a "bleeding wound" and initiated the withdrawal of the Red Army from that country. He made dramatic unilateral cuts in Soviet Warsaw Pact forces while allowing the Baltic republics and Eastern European satellites to go their own way. Deemphasizing class struggle against capitalism, Gorbachev withdrew support from Third World revolutionaries, including longtime clients such as Cuba's Castro, and championed the United Nations as a forum in which to settle international conflicts.

In no area did Gorbachev move more swiftly or decisively than in his calls for reining in the nuclear arms race, which he denounced as dangerous and excessive. Soon after taking power in 1985, he unilaterally suspended nuclear testing, halted deployment of middle-range weapons in Europe, and proposed mutual on-site inspections of each superpower's weapons installations, a move long resisted by previous Kremlin leaders. Gorbachev made a favorable impression on Reagan, as he had on Thatcher, in meetings at Geneva in 1985 and at Reykjavik in 1986. America's *Challenger* space shuttle and two rockets had exploded shortly after takeoff that year, which also included the worst nuclear disaster in history at Chernobyl, in the Ukraine. Such technological failures soured world opinion even further on nuclear devices and made a mockery of the concept of perfecting a space-based defense system.

These developments argued powerfully for a breakthrough in the arms control impasse, but Reagan's commitment to Star Wars remained the chief obstacle. Much to the chagrin of his advisers, the president was actually a radical who favored absolute solutions on arms control. The former actor sought a happy ending to the arms race saga. To Reagan, the ideal solution was either a perfect defense (which he promised to share with Moscow) through SDI, or an abolition of nuclear weapons. He and Gorbachev nearly agreed to the latter during fifteen hours of conversations at the Reykjavik summit, but the abolition option collapsed over Gorbachev's insistence on reaffirmation of the ABM Treaty and Reagan's refusal to refrain from SDI testing.

American hawks and European allies made it clear that abolition was going too far and that deterrence through MAD, the foundation of postwar defense, had to be maintained. As Secretary Shultz put it, "Reykjavik was too bold for the world." Although they failed to agree at Reykjavik, Reagan and Gorbachev now trusted one another sufficiently to take a small step forward in 1987 with the INF Treaty on forces in Europe. The agreement, signed in Washington in December 1987, included unprecedented Soviet accommodation on verification, allowing for the inspection of more than eighty Eastern Bloc nuclear facilities compared with some thirty in western Europe.

The INF Treaty brought actual dismantlement of missiles in Europe by both sides rather than merely setting ceilings on future escalation.

By the end of the Reagan administration, Gorbachev withdrew his opposition to SDI testing, perhaps realizing that the cost and impracticality of the program would eventually cause its own quiet death. Indeed, such has been the case. In the meantime, stunning political events—the Eastern European revolutions of 1989, German reunification in 1990, and the collapse of the Soviet Union in 1991—overshadowed arms control efforts. Following the disintegration of the USSR, Washington's policy focused on supporting Russian democracy and promoting solutions that would allow for stable command and control of the former Soviet Union's nuclear arsenal. Russian President Boris Yeltsin assured the West that he had established such control, but in a nation desperate for hard currency and riven by corruption, a real danger existed of Russia's nuclear weapons technology being sold abroad.

The collapse of the Soviet Union gave rise to an interpretation vindicating American nuclear weapons policy, particularly during the Reagan years, and including most especially SDI. According to this interpretation, the arms race had forced the Soviets to spend themselves into oblivion, thus leading to the collapse of the USSR and the end of the Cold War. The Soviet economic collapse stemmed from an emphasis on heavy industry, armaments, and a large standing army. Not only the nuclear arms race but also the Cold War as a whole asked too much of the Soviet Union—hardly an "Upper Volta with rockets," as one wag once put it, yet in certain fundamental respects still a developing country.

More than the pressures of the Cold War, the collapse of the Soviet Union stemmed from the unworkability of, and inability to reform, a command economy that dated to Stalin's "revolution from above" in the 1920s and 1930s. That system produced an unwieldy, corrupt bureaucracy, offering little incentive or individual reward. Defense spending amounted to as much as one-quarter of annual disposable income over the course of the Communist regime's history. The East-West conflict placed heavy demands on the Soviet system, but the system itself was flawed. Gorbachev's efforts to reform the Stalinist structure and revivify socialism encountered insuperable economic, ethnic, and political obstacles, leading to his own fall from power. Nevertheless, his statesmanlike pursuit of accommodation with the West, including a series of unilateral concessions and the repudiation of class struggle, led to the end of the Cold War.

Even as the collapse of the Soviet Union fulfilled a long-standing U.S. foreign policy goal, uncertainty prevailed with respect to nuclear arms control. Gorbachev's ouster eliminated the single figure most responsible for reining in the strategic arms race. On July 31, 1991, Gorbachev and President George Bush, Reagan's successor, signed the first START agreement in Moscow, but the coup unleashed only days later by Soviet hard-liners, though ultimately repulsed, marked the end of Gorbachev's leadership. Boris Yeltsin, the new president of Russia, allied himself with the United States and pledged continuing cooperation in the arms control process. However, serious issues immediately surfaced over the efficacy of post-Soviet command and control operations as well as the fate of nuclear missiles emplaced in the suddenly independent republics of Belarus, Kazakhstan, and Ukraine. Moreover, as massive fraud and corruption came to characterize the transition to capitalism, serious doubts surfaced over whether fissionable material had been spirited out of Russia and sold abroad.

A post–Cold War commitment to finding diplomatic solutions enabled significant arms control measures to continue to be effected. First, substantial U.S. financial assistance and a concerted diplomatic effort helped persuade the newly independent republics to dismantle their missiles and send them to Russia for disposal. In 1992 Bush and Yeltsin agreed to another round of massive cuts in START II, under which they reduced the number of strategic weapons on both sides to the lowest levels since 1969. Even more importantly, they agreed to eliminate the land-based MIRVs, long a destabilizing factor in the arms race, carrying the potential of hair-trigger employment in the event of the outbreak, or perceived outbreak, of hostilities. Yeltsin appeared before a joint session of the U.S. Congress and Russian and American negotiators affirmed the existence of a new relationship by drafting and signing a declaration of "American-Russian partnership and friendship." However, START II did not achieve Senate approval in the United States until 1996, and the Russian *duma* never did ratify the accord. For some time both sides adhered to the basic agreement, as arms control talks continued to progress during the presidency of Bill Clinton, notably at a 1997 summit in Helsinki with Yeltsin.

Despite the dramatic progress of bilateral arms reductions, Russian command and control, as well as Moscow's inability to account for all fissionable materials, raised disturbing questions. Command and control weaknesses hit home in 1995 when the Russian strategic command mistook a joint U.S.-Norwegian test rocket as a multiple-warhead missile launch.

Russia went on high alert and Yeltsin summoned the nuclear weapons "suit-case" through which he could order a retaliatory strike. Joint communica-tion quickly exposed the false alarm, which nevertheless left both sides shaken. In 1998 Washington essentially funded a revamped Russian early warning system. While Russia continued to make unilateral cuts in its arse-nal, the United States continued to encourage the warmer relationship by bringing Russia in on the evolution of the international space station.

The status of fissionable materials remained a grave concern, however, amid the weakened security, corruption, and rise of organized crime that characterized post-Soviet Russia. The state prosecuted several cases of attempted theft and sale of fissionable materials. Russia next moved to cen-tralize and reduce the number of storage facilities to ensure better control of weapons-grade materials. Both Yeltsin and his successor, former secret police chief Vladimir Putin, insisted that the problem had been solved. Still, with myriad dissatisfied political and "terrorist" groups as potential buy-ers, the risks associated with the availability of even tiny amounts of fis-sionable material remained frightening to contemplate.

While so-called "vertical" arms control—conducted between the two superpowers—had achieved a breakthrough, efforts to limit "horizontal" proliferation—involving third parties—proved far more problematic. Washington had looked the other way while its ally Pakistan had responded to India's possession of the bomb by actively pursuing mem-bership in the nuclear weapons club (which it proclaimed in 1998). Indeed, Washington regularly equipped both Pakistan and Israel with massive con-ventional weapons packages, even as the two allies flouted the 1968 Nuclear Nonproliferation Treaty to become nuclear weapons powers. The Russians, meanwhile, sold nuclear technology to both Iran and Iraq before sharp U.S. protests brought an end to the trade. Meanwhile, China continued to invest heavily in advancing its military and strategic capabilities and in launching nuclear weapons tests. France continued testing as well. Throughout the 1990s and to the present, North Korea defied U.S. containment efforts by becoming a threshold nuclear power. That situation remained unresolved in 2004, by which time President George W. Bush had branded North Korea (along with Iran and Iraq) part of an "axis of evil."

U.S. efforts to contain nuclear proliferation suffered from the poor example set by fueling the arms race from its inception in 1945 and engag-ing in absurd accumulations of missile overkill throughout the Cold War. Subsequently, well after the breakthrough with Russia, the United States continued to escalate the arms race through continued research and development of space-based and other defensive systems. Even though Reagan's fantastic vision of an absolute shield rendering nuclear weapons "impotent and obsolete" scarcely could be taken seriously, research and development of defensive systems remained at the forefront of the military-industrial complex agenda. Washington's obsession with space-based defense remained a sore point in Russia, China, and in other nuclear-armed and nuclear want-to-be states. Under George W. Bush, Congress continued its lavish funding of space-based defense. Despite well more than $100 billion spent on the project in the twenty years since Reagan's initial Star Wars address, little real progress had been made in developing an effective defensive system. Moreover, even if developed, such a system could not combat a small-scale terrorist operation of the type depicted in Tom Clancy's novel *The Sum of All Fears* and the film based on it, which featured the quite plausible scenario of a smuggled nuclear device emplaced in a soft drink machine and detonated in Washington.

Nothing brought home—literally—the threat of "low-tech" terrorist operations like the September 11, 2001, passenger jet hijackings and successful suicide assault on the World Trade Center twin towers and the Pentagon. Amid the angry post-9/11 atmosphere in the United States, the Bush administration justified its invasion of Iraq, launched over UN and allied opposition in March 2003, as an effort to contain the threat posed by weapons of mass destruction (WMD) allegedly in the possession of Iraqi dictator Saddam Hussein. The invasion sacked Hussein, but no such weapons, or much-vaunted weapons laboratories, were found. More than a year later, Washington remained mired in war in Iraq as part of the Bush administration's universal "war on terror," a struggle that had alienated much of the Muslim world and many other nations as well. Angered by U.S. militarism, as well as unqualified American support for Israel against the Palestinians, a whole host of organizations, including Al Qaeda, which perpetrated the 9/11 attack, might welcome an opportunity to use a nuclear device, or other form of WMD, against the world's dominant superpower.

The militarist Bush administration also reversed the momentum of post–Cold War arms control by authorizing a new wave of nuclear escalation. First, in 2002, the administration negotiated the Strategic Offensive Reduction Treaty (SORT) with the Russians. Despite the term "reduction," the treaty actually enabled the two powers, as Secretary of State Colin Powell admitted, "to have as many warheads as you want." SORT reduced the number of *deployed* warheads but allowed the two powers to store rather than destroy the bombs, which could be cultivated and redeployed on missiles and bombers at short notice. The treaty also sanctioned MIRVs, reversing the most significant accomplishment under START II, and allowed for increased numbers of warheads under storage in Russia, where security of such facilities had long been a major concern.

The Bush administration's doctrine of preemptive war, and its refusal to rule out a first strike with nuclear weapons, encouraged proliferation rather than containment. Iran, North Korea, and other potential adversaries might well conclude from the Iraq war that Hussein's mistake had been his failure to become a nuclear power as a deterrent against U.S. invasion. As part of the turn away from international control in favor of unilateral force, the Bush administration pursued a dramatic escalatory step by seeking funding to build a war-fighting "bunker-buster" tactical nuclear weapon. The administration requested initial funding of $500 million in the 2005 budget for the proposed "Nuclear Earth Penetrator," which could bore deep to root out underground installations with a nuclear explosion. The proposal represented the most dramatic escalatory step in the arms race since the introduction of MIRVs and SDI.

The Republican-dominated Congress under Clinton, and then Bush, rejected the most effective means of containing proliferation—the Comprehensive Test Ban Treaty (CTBT). The CTBT would discourage escalation by bringing to a halt efforts to test new weapons systems. The Clinton administration helped to negotiate and then signed the multilateral CTBT in 1996, but Congress refuses to ratify the agreement and the Bush administration does not want to preclude testing of its escalatory program of defensive and bunker-buster weapons. Like the United States, China signed but has not ratified the treaty. India, Pakistan, and North Korea refused to sign the CTBT. As long as this international treaty remains in limbo, nuclear escalation can be expected to continue.

Thus, despite the ephemeral breakthrough in post–Cold War Russian-American arms control, the world did not appear any less dangerous than during the height of superpower conflict. Heavily militarized since World War II, the United States itself occupied regions, launched foreign invasions, and continued unilateral escalation of the arms race through stockpiling of warheads, refusing to rule out first use, failing to ratify the CTBT, and pursuing the new "bunker-buster" as well as the dubious quest for a space-based defense system. None of these actions produced stability or a world order conducive to containing nuclear proliferation. While militarized violence and bitter rivalries offered little cause for optimism, the need for dramatic diplomatic efforts to contain nuclear weapons—and all manner of WMD—had never been more apparent.

Note

Reprinted with minor revisions from *Modern American Diplomacy* (Lanham, Md.: SR Books, 1996).

Sources and Suggested Readings

Allison, Graham T., et al., eds. *Avoiding Nuclear Anarchy: Containing the Threat of Loose Russian Nuclear Weapons and Missile Material*. New York, 1996.

Alperovitz, Gar. *Atomic Diplomacy: Hiroshima and Potsdam*, rev. ed. London, 1994.

Arkin, William M., and Robert Norris. *The Internet and the Bomb: A Research Guide to Policy and Information about Nuclear Weapons*. New York, 1997.

Bundy, McGeorge. *Danger and Survival: Choices about the Bomb in the First Fifty Years*. New York, 1988.

Fitzgerald, Frances. *Way Out There in the Blue: Reagan, Star Wars, and the End of the Cold War*. New York, 2001.

Freedman, Lawrence. *The Evolution of Nuclear Strategy*. New York, 1989.

Gardner, Gary T. *Nuclear Non-Proliferation: A Primer*. Boulder, Colo., 1994.

Garthoff, Raymond L. *Détente and Confrontation: American-Soviet Relations from Nixon to Reagan*. Washington, D.C., 1985.

———. *The Great Transition: American-Soviet Relations and the End of the Cold War*. Washington, D.C., 1994.

Gorbachev, Mikhail. *Perestroika*. New York, 1985.

Herken, Gregg. *Cardinal Choices: Presidential Science Advising from the Atomic Bomb to SDI*. New York, 1992.

Hersey, John. *Hiroshima*. New York, 1946.

Holloway, David. *Stalin and the Bomb: The Soviet Union and Atomic Energy, 1939–1956*. New Haven, Conn., 1994.

Kaplan, Fred. *The Wizards of Armageddon*. New York, 1983.

Kennan, George F. *The Nuclear Delusion: Soviet-American Relations in the Atomic Age*. New York, 1983.

Newhouse, John. *War and Peace in the Nuclear Age*. New York, 1990.

Paul, T.V., Richard J. Harknett, and James J. Wirtz, eds. *The Absolute Weapon Revisited: Nuclear Arms and the Emerging International Order*. Ann Arbor, Mich., 1998.

Powaski, Ronald E. *Return to Armageddon: The United States and the Nuclear Arms Race, 1981–1999.* Oxford, 2000.

Schell, Jonathan. *The Fate of the Earth.* New York, 1983.

Sherry, Michael. *In the Shadow of War: The United States Since the 1930s.* New Haven, Conn., 1997.

———. *The Rise of American Air Power: The Creation of Armageddon.* New Haven, Conn., 1987.

Sherwin, Martin A. *A World Destroyed: Hiroshima and the Origins of the Arms Race,* rev. ed. New York, 2000.

Shultz, George. *Turmoil and Triumph: My Years as Secretary of State.* New York, 1993.

Union of Concerned Scientists. *The Fallacy of Star Wars.* New York, 1983.

Internet Sources

See also Arkin and Norris, The Internet and the Bomb, *cited above.*

The Acronym Institute for Disarmament Diplomacy. www.acronym.org.uk/.

Arms Control Association. www.armscontrol.org/.

Bulletin of Atomic Scientists. www.thebulletin.org/index.htm.

Global Beat Syndicate: The Center for War, Peace, and the News Media at New York University. www.nyu.edu/globalbeat.

TWELVE

Counterterrorism and the U.S. Military after 9/11

CHRISTOPHER C. HARMON

HE TERM "terrorism" dates from the era of the French Revolution in the late eighteenth century. More than seventeen thousand prisoners were executed by revolutionary leaders on the guillotine, which became a symbol of the so-called Reign of Terror. Street mobs supporting the revolution also killed thousands of other alleged pro-monarchists throughout France. Acts of terrorism, however, began many centuries before the French Revolution. In the first century A.D., a group of radical Jews called Zealots used assassination and the taking of hostages in an attempt to end Roman control over Judea, a mainly Jewish area in the Middle East. Another premodern terrorist group was the Assassins, a minority Islamic sect driven by a combination of political and religious discontent. The aim of the Assassins was to spread their style of Islamic theology throughout the Muslim world. Operating in the Middle East from 1080 to the end of the 1200s, the group specialized in suicide missions, which their leader promised would reward the perpetrators with a glorious afterlife in paradise.

When a series of abortive European revolutions in the late 1840s failed to restore republican governments of the type promised by the French Revolution, the result was the rise of a political philosophy called anarchism. Anarchists believed that the state was responsible for inequality and injustice and defended the interests of the elite class. Their view was that the state must be overthrown by any means necessary including violence. Beginning in the late 1850s, anarchists targeted political leaders in assassination attempts. Terrorism in the recent era can be traced from the failed assassination attempt on French emperor Napoleon III in 1858. In the latter part of the nineteenth century and early twentieth century, anarchists assassinated the president of France, the empress of Austria, the prime minister of Spain, the king of Italy, and the U.S. president William McKinley. The most famous terrorist attack before September 11, 2001, was the assassination of Archduke Franz Ferdinand of Austria in 1914, which created a crisis leading to the outbreak of World War I.

Although the revolutionary Communist philosophy of Karl Marx (1818–1883) repudiated terrorism, many terrorist groups of the nineteenth and twentieth centuries have claimed allegiance to Marxism. In the aftermath of World War I, Marxist-inspired groups in the United States and elsewhere engaged in terrorist acts. During the Red Scare in America (1919–1921), terrorists exploded a bomb outside banker J. P. Morgan's offices on Wall Street in New York and sent mail bombs to members of President Woodrow Wilson's administration. Between the First and Second World Wars, however, most terrorism by individuals and small groups was part of the anticolonial movement around the globe. In the Middle East, Jews and Arabs battled one another over who would control the British-owned area of Palestine. Closer to home, Britain confronted Irish militants of the Irish Republican Army (IRA), who demanded complete independence for all of Ireland. During the interwar years, terrorism in the traditional sense was eclipsed by repressive state terrorism of massive proportions practiced in Nazi Germany and Stalinist Russia.

After World War II, the movement for independence by colonial peoples escalated and led to a significant increase in terrorism. In some mainly agricultural areas, for example Asia, nationalist groups pursued independence mainly through guerrilla warfare. Elsewhere, terrorism was a major part of the independence movements, as in the cases of Israel and Algeria. Another element of the anticolonial movement was separatism. In Spain, Canada, and Palestine, for example, national groups demanded autonomy and used terrorism as a major weapon in the struggle. During the 1960s and 1970s, left-wing groups such as the Baader-Meinhof Gang (Red Army Faction) in Germany and the Red Brigades in Italy committed terrorist acts in protest against capitalism and/or imperialism. In more recent decades, the methods of terrorists have become more sophisticated in the areas of hostage taking (1972 Olympic Games in Munich) and gaining maximum publicity for their actions (airline hijackings and bombings). Christopher Harmon focuses on this recent era of terrorism and especially the United States' response to international terrorism and the September 11, 2001, attacks on the nation. This chapter was written in April 2004, and some parts were updated in 2005.

———————

In the long view, the United States' military has only rarely had a direct and focused role in counterterrorism campaigns. One must stretch to include it, but the first of a few cases was President Thomas Jefferson's famous deployment of the new U.S. Navy against the Barbary pirates. While their hostage taking, extortion, and threats to lives of American citizens can be called terrorism, the difference was that greed, more than political aspirations, drove the pirates. Jefferson's combination of force with other measures over several years proved sufficient to quiet the area.

Coincidentally, the most notable modern example of deployment of the military in a counterterrorist role came in the same region, Libya. Stirred toward action after many years of flagrant Libyan support for international terrorism, and then provoked by the bloody bombing of a West Berlin nightclub in which Americans and many Germans were injured or killed, President Ronald Reagan delivered a strike that was both punitive and defensive vis-à-vis future Libyan acts. It was again the U.S. Navy—now in tandem with the U.S. Air Force—that carried out the April 1986 military acts against the strategic and operational leaders of Libyan transnational terrorism.

There are many reasons why American military force has not often been deployed against terrorism, which has been well defined as the deliberate use or threat of violence against the innocent to inspire fear for political ends. First, terrorism usually appears most forcefully in peacetime, or at least in circumstances in which there is no open state of war. Second, terrorism deals in ambiguities, cutouts, and "bite and flee" tactics, meaning that the hammer of Mars often has no suitable place to strike. Third, terrorism is frequently carried out by individual attackers or very small groups—even when they work for far larger organizations or networks or even states. When this is true, policemen and federal marshals may be more appropriate than battalions or brigades. Fourth, terrorism is by definition political, meaning that usually a military response would be asymmetric. Asymmetric replies are less commonly considered by American statesmen, who are likely to think in terms of "proportionality." And, even when full military force is justified, it may be difficult to explain in foreign ministries and in the wide realms of public opinion. Fifth, the political causes of terrorism, and its explicit grievances, delivered in rich moralistic speeches and communiqués, tend to persuade, deter, or baffle, influencing enough of those in government to make them withhold military force. That is, terrorism has often spawned appeasement.

Americans have preferred to see embarrassed self-searching, confusion, and forms of weakness in other countries: the French government is alleged to have made deals with terrorists in the 1980s to keep them from attacking France; the Spanish, after the hideous train bombings of March 2004, sacked their government and then changed foreign policy too. But 9/11 required many Americans to recognize that, here too, terrorism had lulled and even stupefied some sectors of opinion and some of our senior representatives. Just as post–World War II insurgency often proved a means of slowly gaining power without triggering a full military response, terrorists of recent decades have frequently been able to advance their cause without ever being confronted by overwhelming military force. It is one of history's grim lessons that terrorism often works—or works well enough to keep terrorists trying.

It is therefore a most unusual feature of world politics that the world's greatest state begins this new millennium with a deadly serious focus on what in the past has been a secondary or tertiary problem of foreign policy. The U.S. response to Al Qaeda, and more largely to what may be called the militant Muslim international, is now war.

The "global war on terrorism" began in reply to Osama Bin Laden's masterstroke on September 11, 2001. That attack killed about as many as died at Pearl Harbor. It devastated Manhattan, left a giant hole that was still smoking on Thanksgiving Day, and ran up property losses of between 70 and 100 billion dollars. An enemy without a state and without a serious conventional army had struck at the only superpower, the victor over Soviet Communism, the centerpiece of the NATO alliance, the leading military authority worldwide. A few dared to argue that Al Qaeda had overplayed a short hand; almost no one in the West doubted that Al Qaeda would take a fierce beating. But a change in grand strategy would be required. It was too evident that this enemy was not the usual terrorist band: it was tactically innovative, wealthy, and multinational and possessed unprecedented international operating powers, compared with traditional terrorism. With adroitness it deploys guerrillas against military forces, clusters of terrorists against "soft" targets, and suicide bombers and aims at targets both soft and hard. Were that not enough, Al Qaeda displays interest in weapons of mass destruction (WMD).

In the first hours after the catastrophe, the U.S. resumed the defense of its skies. The air defense presence had dwindled over the decades, so that on the tenth of September 2001 a mere twenty fighters were assigned to this once-enormous mission. There is another reason the Air National Guard's combat air patrols over American urban areas are remarkable: only a few years earlier, citizens of several cities had been scandalized by the discovery that specialized police forces were practicing airborne nighttime operations in urban areas. Now it seemed appropriate that the Guard flew 13,000 missions over the territory of the United States in only three months.

The U.S. Coast Guard responded as quickly, refocusing its multifaceted efforts. Narcotics and illegal fishing would be somewhat neglected, as greater attention turned to port security, incoming foreign ships, and the accuracy of cargo manifests on break-bulk shipping. Fast, shallow-draft "Cyclone" class ships were acquired from the navy and proved valuable for work on the coasts. Many other organizations sharing responsibility for border security, such as Customs, redoubled their efforts. The Federal Bureau of Investigation, which had already been transferring hundreds of agents into counterterrorism work over recent years, now began operating at a hot pitch.

The first call for reservists was another dimension of the new homeland defense, "Operation Noble Eagle." Active-duty personnel, also, were on special alerts in many places, domestic and foreign. By early 2004 these demands would remain, and their effects would show in full-page press stories about families neglected, employers' despair for absent reservists, the fears over loved ones long gone abroad, and the tragedies of small-town military funerals. The U.S. Army alone had a third of a million men and women deployed in some 120 countries.

After the disaster, during September, President George W. Bush delivered perhaps the best speech of his life to a joint session of Congress and launched a new "National Security Strategy." It demonstrated that a man elected for his interests in education and other domestic issues was irrevocably turning to face an intense outside threat. The point was then underscored by the first-ever "National Strategy for Combating Terrorism" (February 2003). The effort was to be national in scope: terror "color alerts," military deaths abroad each month, grave Pentagon briefings.

Secretary of Defense Donald Rumsfeld quickly became the cabinet's leading officer and a man of prestige in America—whereas the summer of
2001 had shown him struggling with procurement and transportation issues
and quarreling with Congress and the military hierarchy. An entire new
cabinet-level institution came into being as 2003 began: the Department of
Homeland Security, which absorbed large swaths of twenty-two existing
bureaucracies. Government insiders confessed that they hoped the reor-
ganization would be more effective than disruptive, but that three to five
years would be required before one might judge. If that was a diversion,
there was also a drain upon the national treasury; coin spent on national
security, and the red ink of deficits and planned deficits, ran steadily. Even
political party traditions were compromised: Democrats came to attack
Republicans for deficit spending.

The war on terrorism has had four direct effects on the U.S. armed
forces. The trend that began in the late 1990s (after attacks on Khobar
Towers and the USS *Cole*) toward more attention to force protection has
been strongly advanced. Second has been the pattern of deployments,
extended deployments, and redeployments, leading to considerable human
strain. Third, there has been restructuring. This is especially evident in dramatic and pervasive use of special operations forces, which had been as
marvelously trained as they were little used. Restructuring is also evident in
the more direct engagement of the intelligence community in military
operations against terrorists and guerrillas. Fourth, and a point deserving
much elaboration: the military engaged in several campaigns directly tied
to the war on terrorism.

The initial and most conclusive of the military campaigns subordinate
to the overall war on global terror opened only four weeks after 9/11. From
four carriers, and airfields nearby—as in Diego Garcia—navy and air force
cruise missiles, strike aircraft of all kinds, and bombers pounded air
defenses and other military targets in Afghanistan. Some bombers literally
made the round trip from Missouri in the continental U.S. The marines
made the longest insertion inland in their history, from the Arabian Sea,
and took up combat and patrolling and occupation on the Afghan ground.
The U.S. Army, which had been occasionally criticized for moving too
slowly in the first Iraq war and in a later peacekeeping deployment, was
the first to emplace ground units inside Afghanistan, and throughout the
war won much prestige. The army provided the Central Command chief,

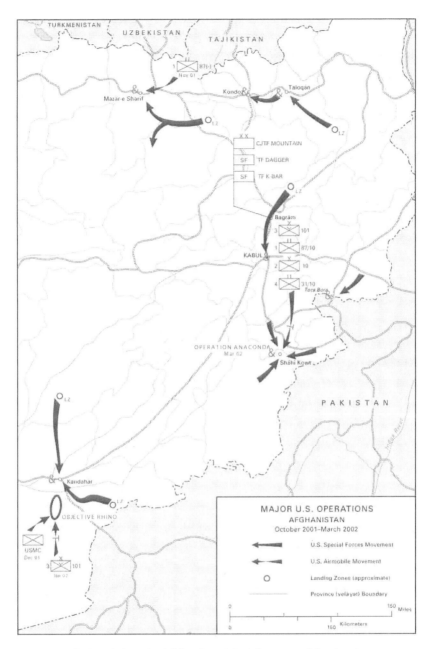

U.S. Operations in Afghanistan, October 2001–March 2002
(U.S. Army Center of Military History)

Tommy Franks, who guided forces into the theater until overall U.S. man-power reached 50,000. Only 10 percent of this was needed on the ground in Afghanistan, where battlefields were witness to skillful deployments of U.S. Army attack helicopters, Green Berets, and Rangers.

The war was as well a coalition war, as nearly all NATO-country con-flicts have been since the Falkland Islands in 1982. France speedily deployed two thousand personnel to the region. The British sent a submarine, sur-face ships, and air forces. Other contingents—many very small—eventually came from fifty-three other countries. Relations with Pakistan were altered in a positive way by the conflict. Scores of countries granted the coalition overflight rights, and seventy-six gave landing rights as well. The most impressive and unexpected aspect of coalition war was inside Afghanistan, where allies may be "won" yet not necessarily trusted. Al Qaeda had used a rigged television camera to assassinate "The Lion of the Panshir Valley," Ahmed Shah Massoud, two days before attacking U.S. cities; now it fell to the United States to locate other anti-Taliban leaders of credibility and fighting force. The results were mixed, but Massoud's prepared Northern Alliance worked in impressive partnership to find and fix and kill Taliban and foreign Arab forces.

According to many, the history of Afghanistan proved that no outsider could win. By December 6, 2001, the Taliban was fleeing from its last urban center, and the conventional wisdom required refinement: with internal aid, money, and outside power, Afghanistan could be conquered. But could it be held? Washington's answer was that it did not intend to hold the coun-try, only liberate it. In 2004 only ten thousand American troops remained deployed there. A salutary number, from a Pentagon perspective, it would prove too low to assure full security during the rebuilding phase.

Operation Enduring Freedom, with its subordinate efforts such as "Anaconda," succeeded in two months. One of modernity's most primi-tive and destructive regimes was replaced. The training camps that had readied tens of thousands of foreign fighters over a decade were swept up. Organized Taliban resistance was first decimated and then destroyed, yield-ing some 5,000 prisoners (both indigenous and foreign Arab). There was, however, no catching the three principals who made 9/11 possible: Sheik Mohammad Omar, who had ruled Afghanistan for the Taliban; his close partner Osama Bin Laden; and Bin Laden's closest partner, the Egyptian doctor and terrorist Ayman Al Zawahiri. All three were at least put on the run. Terrorism in Afghanistan was suppressed, and remained so for two years. It reemerged in the opening months of 2004, embodying a new archetype of evil: calculatedly brutal attacks on outside aid workers and humanitarians trying to help the Afghan people.

The second military campaign was against Abu Sayyaf, the strongest Al Qaeda ally in the Republic of the Philippines. For Washington, this was war of a radically different character; it gave supplies, intelligence, advice, and exhortation. The U.S. carefully kept its hands limited to those duties. The Pacific Command's Admiral Thomas Fargo had the lead in the theater, and his work was supported and scrutinized from the Pentagon by the office of the secretary of defense, its assistant secretary of defense for special operations and low-intensity conflict, and the military's powerful Joint Staff. Other players included the military advisors resident in the State Department's office of the coordinator for counterterrorism; these are specialists in unobtrusively aiding foreign allies in counterterrorism work— the kind of discreet help that would have been admired by Edward Lansdale, Air Force brigadier and CIA hero of the Filipinos' success against the Huks a half century ago.

Month after month during 2002, the armed forces of the Philippines, many with U.S. training behind them, hunted the Muslim gunmen through the heavy vegetation and bogs of the southern, largely Muslim territories. One pursuit in the Zamboanga del Norte will be long remembered in turn-of-the-century guerrilla wars. Attrition bled the group and killed a notorious Abu Sayyaf leader, thirty-nine-year old Abu Sabaya. April 2004 would bring the combat death of another Abu Sayyaf leader, Hamsiraji Sali, in southern Basilan island, the southwesternmost land mass in the archipelago. This campaign has punctured the pride of a cocky Al Qaeda ally and repressed what had become active training grounds for Al Qaeda allies in the region. During the last century there has rarely been complete quiet in the Philippine Islands, but the recent military operations have earned an important respite. Other Muslim groups that had earlier made peace deals with Manila will also feel encouraged in their choice.

Modern terrorism's dangers have become intertwined with the threats implicit in weapons of mass destruction (WMD). Many worthy books testified to this by the late 1990s. It was this feared combination, more than the hunt for Bin Laden, which provoked the third martial campaign: in Iraq.

About late 1992, Al Qaeda completed and disseminated on paper and CD-ROM a five-thousand-page *Encyclopedia of the Afghan Jihad*. The terrorists were also using another training manual, discovered in 2000 in Manchester,

England, and used against Al Qaeda at trial. Both of these publications discussed the use of WMD. There were as well the reports and observations of neutral parties, including a powerful series of *New York Times* articles in January 2001. The world became increasingly aware that Al Qaeda was not only calling for development of WMD but trying to procure and experiment. In the wreckage of Al Qaeda camps after 2001, as well, were documents related to producing and using nerve gases and ricin. Ricin was later found in several camps and European safe houses maintained by militant Muslims. Nor could one discount two separate Bin Laden declarations of war on America, in August 1996 and February 1998. Finally, there were emerging indicators of Al Qaeda contacts with Iraq's Saddam Hussein, whose earlier years of emphasis upon WMD development were well known—and not even renounced by Baghdad. Thus the White House began to focus hard upon Iraq. And when diplomacy and United Nations coercion failed, the United States and Britain moved toward war. In a campaign lasting four weeks, Australia, Great Britain, and the United States swept aside or crushed organized conventional Iraqi forces and drove the Hussein leadership into an underground of basements, hideaways, hovels, and spider holes.

Operation Iraqi Freedom failed famously as a hunt for WMD, but it concluded as a limited counterterrorist success. Realistically, this is all it could be, since as was noted, counterterrorism had been markedly low on the rankings of concern: a senior Air Force general listed six overriding coalition political/military objectives of the war, and in sixth place was "Destroy terrorist networks in Iraq. Gather intelligence on global terrorism; detain terrorists and war criminals . . . ." But if this objective was limited, it was legitimate and it was ultimately well-served. Abu Nidal (Sabri al Banna), the most infamous terrorist since "Carlos the Jackal," was killed in Baghdad just before the invasion, probably by an Iraqi government eager to take down such a lightning rod. The Palestine Liberation Front's chief Abu Abbas (Mohammed Abbas), another veteran leader of attacks on the innocent to advance the conception of a Palestinian homeland, was captured during the war (but has since died). Soldiers found a depot with 350 suicide vests, half of them already rigged with ball bearings—human shrapnel. Also found were innumerable arms caches (most doubtless government-owned). As such dominoes fell, so too did the prospect of keeping Iraq as a safe base for future international terrorist operations, as it so long had been. Now, after more than three decades, the country will be removed from the State Department's list of state sponsors of terrorism.

Clausewitz has warned that war is interactive, and he warned as well that no defeat is really final until the will of the adversary is beaten. Both axioms came true after "major combat operations" ended in mid-April 2003. Outside guerrillas and terrorists entered Iraq: from Iran, Jordan, and, above all, Syria. One bus stopped for inspection was carrying two-thirds of a million dollars and fifty-nine military-aged men, some bearing letters promising rewards for killing U.S. soldiers. A prominent Al Qaeda ally named Abu Musab al Zarqawi was identified as the author of a seventeen-page letter circulating in Iraq and exhorting war between Shia and Sunni in Iraq as a method of ruining the coalition victory. This in fact began by April 2004; Shia-Sunni hatreds boiled up; a young Shia cleric much more fiery than holy emerged; and death came to Kurds with ferocious bombings of their two main political party headquarters. All this is part of classic terrorism, by which the lives of the innocent are sacrificed to create a climate of fear in which the perpetrators may fulfill their own political objectives.

During 2003 and 2004 the ambiguities of guerrilla war and the savage terrorist attacks on Iraqi civilians, aid workers, and United Nations personnel were accompanied by continued confusion on the home front over the extent of Al Qaeda involvement with Saddam Hussein's regime. Public commentary and media, domestic and foreign, showed near-total disinterest in Iraqi links to any terrorists *except for* Al Qaeda. Some presidential candidates suggested the Iraqi war undercut that against international terror, as when Senator Bob Graham of Florida essayed a *bon mot* about "Osama Been Forgotten." Critics disparaged the limited evidence of what connections there were between Baghdad and Bin Laden. Many assumed a secular Baathist regime would not traffic with Muslim militants, although Iraq and Syria had done just that for years, if quietly. *The Weekly Standard*, a D.C.-based newsmagazine, finally pronounced "Case Closed" as it reprinted an October 27, 2003, memorandum to congressional intelligence committee chairmen from the Pentagon's undersecretary of defense for policy detailing some fifty instances of contact between the Bin Laden organization and Saddam's regime. The famous and disputed meeting in Prague with suicide hijacker Mohammed Atta is now but one in the formidable litany. But a document that could have had the power of a new "Pentagon Paper" was first disdained by most major media, and then attacked by Daniel Benjamin, formerly of the National Security Council, with predictably dampening effect.

Three years after the 9/11 catastrophe galvanized the American nation, the subsequent war in Iraq came to be perceived by most as having had little positive effect in the global war on terrorism. White House senior officials show only the rarest flashes of skill at public diplomacy, yet casualties in Iraq mount: as of the fall of 2005 nearly two thousand Americans have died in the low-intensity conflict phase following the end of major combat operations. American voters, and foreign allies, show uncertainty. And that illustrates how modern unconventional war may differ from more definitive conventional forms, and in doing so challenge U.S. power and imagination.

The most significant military and psychological dimension of these three campaigns is their offensive character. Mere concern for force protection, and the view of terrorism as primarily a law-enforcement matter, diminished amidst government effort in a strange new war. A Pentagon press release of February 25, 2003, observed that the president had been prompt in recognizing a state of war, and just as prompt in concluding that a solely defensive strategy was no option: "We saw our choice as: Change the way we live or change the way the terrorists live." This accorded with good sense and military wisdom. Clausewitz, having enumerated the natural strengths of the defensive in conventional war, pointedly added that he who is *only* defensive will find that, after some effort, a determined enemy will make a bypass and a successful attack. This enemy had. The U.S. response was to take the offensive on a global scale. New base agreements were explored or agreed to. Military operations began in distant lands. There were arrests and captures in scores of foreign countries. Detainees filed steadily into the U.S. leasehold at Guantanamo Bay, Cuba, and other holding points beyond the normal jurisdiction of American courts.

Again, coalition operations have proven to be a major feature of the counterterrorism war. Initially, and for the first time in its history, NATO invoked its Article Five, pronouncing an attack on one as an attack upon all. Yet that spirit of collective defense was marred by considerable discord between France and Germany, on the one hand, and the United States on the other. And when Spain, relatively new to the NATO structure, was attacked in Madrid in early 2004, its government fell and the succeeding prime minister announced a troop withdrawal from Iraq. Poland—stolid and steady Poland—also then waffled. Others who were U.S. allies of only a limited kind, such as Russia and China, seemed to use the 9/11 attacks as a tool to win American silence while they dealt with violent internal factions, only some of which had links to Al Qaeda.

But as Winston Churchill observed, the only thing worse than fighting with allies is fighting without them. Problems with the militant Muslim enemy easily exceed problems with allies. Ever adaptive, Al Qaeda has replied to the global war on terrorism by hiding its leaders, moving its money, and drawing new fighters out of its popular underground. It peppers the international media with tapes and tracts. It attacks in new theaters where security has never been strong or suspicions have not sufficiently heightened: Casablanca, Morocco; Tunis on the same littoral; Bali, Indonesia; Mombasa, Kenya; housing compounds in Riyadh, Saudi Arabia.

By the second anniversary of the war, in September 2003, President Bush declared that "Al Qaeda has lost nearly two-thirds of its known leaders" to killing or capture. Analysts spent the next months essaying their own judgments. They weigh their best hopes, and the Bush administration's words, against their belated recognition that in the 1990s, tens of thousands went through the group's camps in the Sudan and Afghanistan. Most such "graduates" are still at liberty. Germany's intelligence service chief has used the figure of 70,000 trainees. Others have used similar, or far lower, figures. But no one believes all such trainees are now Al Qaeda members. It is almost impossible to closely estimate the numbers who are Al Qaeda. Even estimates of the senior leadership strength differ. Pessimists may point to the continued at-large status for the top three leaders in Afghanistan on 9/11, as well as the reserve in Iran of a promising son of Bin Laden. Optimists—and there are a few—may argue that the original core Al Qaeda leadership was as small as 180 loyalists who had taken an oath of fealty to the Saudi construction heir and veteran mujahideen. This cadre has been battered by kills and arrests: Mohammed Atef; Khalid Sheik Mohammed; Ramzi Binalshibh; and also Abu Aliu Harithi, the Yemeni who planned the USS *Cole* disaster. Does this attrition at the top leave Al Qaeda's regional arms too unconnected from the brains? Is the body wasting? How fares "the Base" (Al Qaeda) when it has no apparent physical base?

Indeed, what does it mean to read that Al Qaeda is now increasingly decentralized? For this there are precedents and similar patterns in modern international terrorism. While Al Qaeda probably is less hierarchical than in 2000, the Naval Postgraduate School's Dr. David Tucker notes that much the same could be argued about terror networks of the late 1960s and 1970s. Indeed, there were multiple ideologists (Castro, Che, Lenin, Trotsky, Mao); financiers were as diverse as Italian publishing heir Giangiacomo

Feltrinelli and the Eastern Bloc services; there was no predictability about any movement's armorers; remote zones were found for training hijackers and assassins and guerrilla fighters; regionally based groups often honored foreign leaders, and leavened their membership with nonnationals or foreign secret agents.

But it is clear that several key features of Al Qaeda are relatively new. Its extraordinary lust for blood exceeds that of most traditional terror groups; only a few, such as Aum Shinrikyo, are comparable. Terrorism may still be "theater," but it is no longer as modest as placing a pistol to one's temple to attract infinite cameras. Al Qaeda's kind of theater is what Chechens presented in a Moscow suburb in October 2002: hundreds attending a stage production found themselves taken hostage, sealed into the theater like a tomb, and kept there by men and women wearing explosives. Then, stupidly, the hostages were poisoned to death along with the terrorists when Russian security services used "incapacitating" gas. Second, Al Qaeda is more powerful and more international than any previous terror group of modern memory. Third, the gifted analyst Rohan Gunaratna is correct in writing about the thoroughly multiethnic character of Al Qaeda. There have been such blends in teams before, but never so many nationals pressed into one terror organization's world service. This makes it unique. A fourth and lesser point may be marked. Al Qaeda possesses naval forces and conducts naval operations. Reports, and sometimes the searches and seizures of recent years, have yielded evidence such as Al Qaeda–owned vessels; an individual carefully locked inside a shipping container for insertion overseas; many plans for attacks on ports; and a record of assaults on vessels at sea, including a French oil tanker.

The three military campaigns in the global war on terrorism have followed a reasonable grand strategy. Military effort has been but one part of a far larger scheme and has been mainly limited to three countries. Diplomats have sought, and often found, foreign official support for strong efforts: the standouts include Tony Blair of Britain, Pakistan's Musharraf, Hamid Karzai's Afghan coalition, John Howard of Australia, and the new members of NATO. In an echo of the success of international broadcasting during the Cold War, new international media stations have been created and deployed. Terrorism's money, very difficult to find, has been hunted and sometimes sequestered, and the outgoing lead counsel for the Department of the Treasury has made assurances that it is markedly harder for transnational terrorism to move and store money. Within the

United States, too, arrests on charges of funding terror have jumped since 9/11; aliens and citizens alike have been netted in investigations.

On some fronts, results have been slow to emerge, or have faltered. The legal dimension of counterterrorism is a minefield of complicated questions of civil rights, scrutiny of every prosecutorial action, and complex issues with foreign governments whose view of a given suspect always varies somewhat from Washington's. Prominent Al Qaeda suspects have been arrested only to be freed, or convicted in court only then to be freed. American public diplomacy has mostly failed. Some foreign partners have disappointed the United States, showing that bilateral diplomacy, too, has its fallibilities. Syria, under the hand of Hafez al Asad's son Bashar, has angered Israel and frustrated the United States by remaining a major protector of international terrorists, especially Palestinians. Despite rising pressure from Washington, Damascus resisted closing the Syrian-Iraqi border to inspired killers from outside; they still pass through to join in the ongoing violence in post-Saddam Iraq. The Sudan, a past key to Al Qaeda training and logistics, shows more helpful signs of working with the United States and has kept close control over the nation's leading militant Muslim, Hassan al Turabi. Once the grinning power behind the secular throne, he now lives with lesser options—house arrest or incarceration.

Two firm political barriers to victory in the war on terror have been the ongoing crisis in Palestinian territories and wide anti-Americanism in the world. Most foreigners, and some Americans, believe that the U.S. stance in supporting Israel assures continuation of anti-American terrorism. They believe this even though the United States also supports the Palestinian Authority, financially and diplomatically. Unfortunately, even when former president William J. Clinton dwelled ceaselessly upon the problem, he could not solve it. Varying approaches by presidents Bush I and Bush II have also left the Gordian knot uncut. And few to none expect Arab states to do so. Thus the problem of the entire second half of the twentieth century smolders and burns in the early twenty-first. The second major political barrier, anti-Americanism, is based on the Middle East problem as well as many other causes, including rank resentment and jealousy. An acrimonious view of U.S. policy prevails in great swaths of opinion in the Arab world (several hundreds of millions) and among people of the Muslim faith globally (1.2 billion). Only two or three White House spokesmen have the rhetorical talent, credibility, and power to dent such psychological and political defenses. Not only are the world's ideologically militant Muslims not putting down their arms; they will not even open their camps and entertain envoys to parlay.

If, as some analysts argue, Al Qaeda is more a living creed than a discernible human organization, then this terrible war is destined to pass to our daughters and sons, if not to their sons and daughters too. But if Al Qaeda is both a creed and a discernible human organization, as this author believes, then it possesses dual centers of gravity, both of which can and must be attacked. War upon each is necessary and can make progress—even if tactical successes by the coalition of states do not bar similar or offshoot groups from later arising. Hopes for defeating Al Qaeda are best lodged in the intelligent and aggressive practice of grand strategy, and one part of that is clearly capturing or killing enough of its principals to demoralize and disperse the active organized members. After all, governments do not ignore crime networks merely because "if they should be destroyed, their remnants may later re-form"; on the contrary, policy and prudence and the public all dictate a serious effort against crime, and all reasonable observers suspect that even limited successes discourage active and prospective criminals.

And terror groups do end. Some end in success, but not many. The most famous terrorist group of all has been the cult-like "Assassins" of the Middle East of a millennium ago; while they carried on killing for two centuries, even they were defeated. Almost no modern group has shown such resilience; perhaps the Irish Republican Army (IRA) comes closest, and it is blessedly quiescent for now. Peru's Tupac Amaru is wrecked and its remnants are in jail; Sendero Luminoso remains, but as a shadow of itself; the Kurdish Worker's Party is thoroughly demoralized by the jailing of Abdullah Ocalan; two successive generations of the Red Army Faction died away, leaving Germany richly democratic; talk of a Red Brigades revival in Italy has been illusory . . . continuous, but illusory.

Al Qaeda can be beaten with overwhelming effort over the coming years with a good grand strategy. That strategy would be likely to contain these and other elements:

Public diplomacy must reach out in creative and intelligent ways to compete with the terrorists' propaganda for hearts and minds. Currently a major U.S. weakness, this component is essential to long-term prospects for success, against not just Al Qaeda but the other parts of the militant Muslim international. Public diplomacy does not pretend to convert the hardened trainee. It aims instead at the great center, and by moving it a little, does a lot to isolate the violent zealot.

Traditional bilateral and multilateral diplomacy have their own roles to play. The United States must keep counterterrorism high on its list of foreign policy priorities because, sad to say, it is as important as current issues like relations with Russia, and as critical as future threats like that increasingly posed by mainland China. The secretary of state cannot afford to confine the subject to underlings deep within the department but must lead a multifaceted effort to organize friends, partners, and allies. Treaties have to be updated; conference agendas must be swayed; physical security and diplomatic security details must be adequately budgeted. Before the 1998 East Africa embassy bombings one U.S. ambassador fought nobly for better protection; she did not get it, in part because the Department of State has seen niggardliness from Congress in the last decade.

Counterterrorist intelligence is especially the work of human agents and case officers of long expertise, foreign language ability, and courage. This has always been and remains at a premium. Al Qaeda came into being in the late 1980s, declared war on the United States in 1996 and again in 1998, and consistently and successfully drew American blood, and yet, incredibly, retired CIA operative Reuel Marc Gerecht could write publicly, months before 9/11, that his agency had virtually no American expert in Afghanistan, the country where Bin Laden had lived since 1996. For a quarter century, educated Americans have known that the 1970s saw a vast dismissal of veteran Directorate of Operations personnel from the CIA, and for much of the time subsequent to that, terrorism experts have called for a re-creation of this capability and the hiring and training of first-rate spies ("human intelligence"). It is time that the intelligence community delivered. Perhaps it is beginning to do so. Certainly liaison between the CIA and the military services has improved; that closer relationship was spurred by the First Gulf War and is proving important in the ongoing war on terrorism.

Law enforcement is another centerpiece of the grand strategy. The Federal Bureau of Investigation (FBI) has seen nothing but increases in its funding; from fiscal 2000 to fiscal 2004 alone, its budget increased by 50 percent. This has allowed a dramatic high-tech retooling of the old file card–based intelligence system, creation of a new Strategic Information Operations Center in the Washington building, and expansion of the FBI's small "Legat" program of agents abroad, where they work to prepare cases for courts back home. The FBI's performance has been adequate to good, generally; its anticipation, intelligence, and other counterterrorism work are also slightly easier now, given changes in public attitudes and law since 9/11.

Better performance must be hoped for from U.S. immigration authorities. Their egregious failures were already known before 9/11, as when
the number of suspected illegal aliens in the country was often published
and was received like news from Ripley's Believe It or Not. Too few cared.
September 11, 2001, made it very apparent that one could readily lie on
applications and overstay one's visa with little risk of arrest; that aliens
(rather than U.S. citizens of left or right extremes) were a direct threat to
life and limb; that radical Islamicists could move here and blow up New
York's World Trade Center towers—twice if they cared to. Here came a
brutal if unpopular lesson in political realism: there is a difference
between thinking of America as a regime based upon universal principles and imagining that America is a universal regime. The former is true;
the latter is not true. Immigration reform has been a persistent but negli-
gible part of U.S. lawmaking; now it seems likely to be attended to with
seriousness.

The next phase of the global war on terrorism is likely to be more
legal and political than military. The secretary of the new and still-inchoate
Department of Homeland Security, the secretary of the Department of
Justice, and the Secretary of State may be increasingly important in the
near future, for better or for worse, while the Secretary of Defense may
well see less time in the public eye. The war in Afghanistan has receded,
and if troop withdrawals begin as expected, so too will combat operations
in Iraq. It appears unlikely that any U.S. administration of 2005 would take
the war on terror directly to Hezbollah in Lebanon or FARC in Colombia
any time soon. But there are certain to be many more skirmishes, reaction
teams, occasions of covert reconnaissance, military assistance to the State
and Justice departments during renditions of individual killers, work details
to special events like the Olympics, tireless stretches of interrogations of
prisoners, exercises in perimeter security, lectures on force protection, and
concern with the complicated art of threat assessment and publication of
warnings. Most in the military dislike missions in which they function like
policemen, but in the third, fourth, and fifth years after the devastation of
September 11, 2001, those very duties are essential to their own safety, and
to the country they protect.

Several conclusions now suggest themselves.

The current war on terrorism has no American parallel. The closest
might be to the Barbary pirates, a collection more criminal than political,
and restricted to one mere littoral of one continent.

This war is very much one being waged on the offensive. Offensive strategy in the field, in the rooms of diplomats, and in the netherworld of intelligence is clearly dominating the past defensive-mindedness that seemed wise and cautious and proved to be folly.

This has indeed been war, if only of the medium and then low-intensity sorts. Casualty figures, if the ongoing fight in Iraq is included, as it should be, are higher than in quiet years of the Cold War. One may hope that the current war with the militant Muslim international will not require great regional wars, as that one did. One may further hope that this contest will not last a half century, yet it is notable how many analysts are insisting that it will, and a few who disagree say it will go yet longer.

Given the economic, human, and diplomatic costs of this war, its pursuit in any military form cannot be taken for granted. That will be subject to the American electorate and the support of our allies. American withdrawal from Iraq in the near future may lead to a decline in U.S. casualties worldwide. Whether it does or not, the safest bet is that the struggle with militants of Islam will more often be legal and political than conventionally military.

There will be no "unconditional surrender" by the enemy. Its subculture of religious obsession with martyrdom will forbid it, even if its political judgment does evolve. Thus, victory in this war (for the United States and its many partners) will come by slow attrition and will never be complete. Osama Bin Laden, Ayman Al Zawahiri, and the Taliban's mullah Mohammad Omar must all be captured, but a broader effort is necessary to pull in their hundreds of lieutenants and perhaps thousands of footmen. This is not a war of civilizations, but it is a war against numerous voluntary fighters from a range of ethnic groups and religious sects across the globe. Patience and persistence will be paramount. So will the continued insistence upon the difference between the tens of millions who hold Islam dear, on the one hand, and on the other the terrorist bombers and unconventional killers who are the enemy of everyone.

Sources and Suggested Readings

Crenshaw, Martha, ed. *Terrorism in Context*. University Park: Pennsylvania State University Press, 1995.

Department of State. *Patterns of Global Terrorism: 2003*. Washington, D.C.: U.S. Government Printing Office, April 2004 (annual).

Drell, Sidney D., Abraham D. Sofaer, and George D. Wilson, eds. *The New Terror: Facing the Threat of Biological and Chemical Weapons*. Stanford, Calif.: The Hoover Institution Press, 1999.

Emerson, Steven. *Jihad in America*. PBS film, 1994, since reissued.

Gunaratna, Rohan. *Inside Al Qaeda*, 3rd ed. New York: Berkley Books, 2003.

Harmon, Christopher C. *Terrorism Today*. London: Frank Cass, 2000.

Hiro, Dilip. *War Without End: The Rise of Islamist Terrorism and Global Response*. London: Routledge, 2002.

Howard, Russell D., and Reid L. Sawyer. *Terrorism and Counterterrorism: Understanding the New Security Environment: Readings and Interpretations*. Guilford, Conn.: McGraw-Hill, 2002.

Jane's Intelligence Review. London (monthly).

Miller, Judith. *God Has 99 Names: Reporting From a Militant Middle East*. New York: Simon & Schuster, 1996.

Mizell, Louis R., Jr. *Target USA: The Inside Story of the New Terrorist War*. New York: Wiley, 1998.

Stern, Jessica. *Terror in the Name of God*. New York: HarperCollins, 2003.

Tucker, David. *Skirmishes at the Edge of Empire*. Westport, Conn.: Praeger, 1997.

Tucker, Jonathan B. *Toxic Terror: Assessing Terrorist Use of Chemical and Biological Weapons*. Cambridge, Mass.: MIT Press, 2000.

Wilkinson, Paul. *Terrorism Versus Democracy: The Liberal State Response*. London: Frank Cass, 2001.

AFTERWORD

✦❧✦

From the Gulf War of 1990–1991 to the Iraq War

IN THE AFTERMATH of the end of the Cold War and the collapse of the Soviet Union in the late 1980s, extreme optimists predicted that the ideological victory of liberal democracy over Soviet communism marked "The End of History" and the possible arrival of a permanent, peaceful world order. Such dreams were dashed in August 1990 when the Iraqi dictator Saddam Hussein invaded and occupied the oil-rich kingdom of Kuwait, a member state of the United Nations. Saddam, the leader of the Baathist party, had begun his reign of tyranny in 1979, and soon afterward he started the bloody Iran-Iraq War (1980–1988).

Saddam assumed that American people had not recovered from the disaster of the Vietnam War and that they would not support a war to protect a small feudal kingdom half a world away. He clearly miscalculated the reaction of the United States, which, under the leadership of President George H. W. Bush, gained the full support of the United Nations, including the former Soviet Union, as well as Muslim nations, for its effort to reestablish an independent Kuwait.

Prior to Operation Desert Storm, there were dire predictions of another World War I–type war of attrition. Saddam himself promised to wage the "mother of all battles," in which Americans would swim in their own blood. In the event, a relentless air campaign between January and February 1991 broke the back of Saddam's vaunted million-man army. After the thirty-nine-day air bombardment, the allied ground attack delivered the coup de

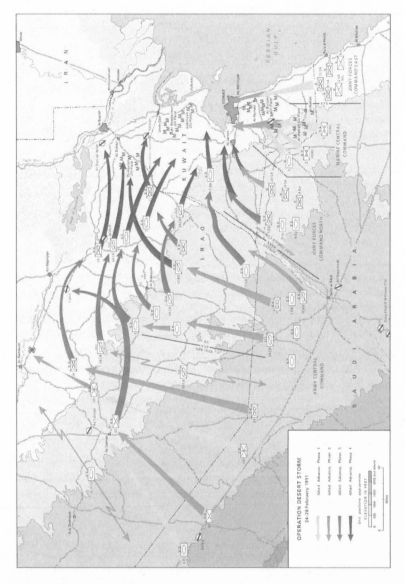

Operation Desert Storm, February 24–28, 1991 (U.S. Army Center of Military History)

grâce. Chief of Staff General Colin Powell declared, "First we're going to cut it off [the Iraqi army], and then we're going to kill it." General Norman Schwarzkopf proceeded to execute the classic military maneuver of pinning down the main enemy forces while launching a massive flanking attack. President Ronald Reagan's large defense increases in the 1980s paid off handsomely as America's high-tech, high-quality volunteer army of specialists, including 30,000 women, brought honor to themselves and their country. Similarly, the British First Armored Division and the French Foreign Legion won the respect of their comrades in arms.

The hundred-hour ground blitz ended with the liberation of Kuwait and the mass surrender of demoralized Iraqi troops. In an act of wanton destruction, the enemy set fire to six hundred oil wells as they retreated back to Iraq. Although in many ways a model military operation in conventional warfare, Operation Desert Storm cost the lives of three hundred Americans and those of thousands of Iraqis. The decision not to march on Baghdad and remove Saddam aroused criticism both then and later. Critics overlooked an unwelcome result of such an offensive: the breakup of the victorious coalition, which had no United Nations mandate to overthrow the Iraqi government. Others did not wish to repeat what happened in 1950 when UN forces crossed the 38th parallel and ultimately expanded the Korean conflict. In hindsight, many would agree that Saddam's Republican Guard divisions should have been further reduced so as to prevent their brutal suppression of Kurd and Shiite uprisings.

On September 11, 2001—forever named 9/11—the world changed when terrorists, under the direction of Osama Bin Laden, flew two civilian airliners into the World Trade Center twin towers in New York City, flew another plane into a section of the Pentagon, and attempted but failed to fly another aircraft toward the nation's capital. Nearly 3,000 were killed in the acts of terrorism. President Bush wrote in his diary the night of September 11, "The Pearl Harbor of the 21st century took place today."

The attacks were organized from Osama Bin Laden's sanctuaries in Afghanistan, where he was protected by the radical Muslim Taliban regime. Acting on a twisted interpretation of one of the world's great religions, Bin Laden sought to rid the world of "Western" liberal values by turning the clock back to the most brutal and inhuman aspects of the seventh century. His Al Qaeda network of terrorists would bring a new age of barbarism into the twenty-first century.

After 9/11, President George W. Bush would lead a united people, with virtually universal worldwide support, in military action to overthrow the Taliban regime giving sanctuary to Bin Laden and Al Qaeda. He received the full support of Prime Minister Tony Blair of Great Britain. American special forces aided the Northern Alliance, the Taliban government's main opposition. By December, the Taliban was overthrown, but Bin Laden had not been captured and Al Qaeda terrorists remained in hiding.

The Bush administration now made a critical decision to launch a controversial preemptive war to topple the government of the brutal dictator Saddam Hussein. Bush's vice president, Dick Cheney, had been secretary of defense during his father's presidency, and Cheney harbored a deep sense of unfinished business regarding Saddam Hussein. Furthermore, since the Gulf War, American and British warplanes had enforced no-fly zones over Iraq in order to protect the minority Kurds and keep watch on the southern half of Iraq.

The administration based its decision for war on three basic grounds: that Saddam was linked to 9/11 and global terrorism; second, that he possessed or would soon have weapons of mass destruction (WMD), that is, biological, chemical, and nuclear weapons; and lastly, that a democratic Iraq would serve as a model for the entire Middle East. Those who disagreed with the administration's analysis of the threat argued that intelligence sources did not tie Saddam to Al Qaeda or the September 11 attacks. The invasion of Iraq was undertaken in the face of international opposition, most notably from France, Germany, and Russia. The decision for war against Saddam would involve an almost go-it-alone strategy.

On March 20, 2003, a much smaller but even higher-quality coalition force prepared once more to invade Iraq. A total of 241,516 U.S. military personnel were in the region (which included 17,000 female soldiers) joined by some 41,000 British, 2,000 from Australia, and 200 from Poland. The ground forces, which numbered 183,000, were ready to move north from Kuwait into Iraq and then cover the 250 miles to Baghdad.

One of the most significant aspects about the opening of the war was what did not happen. Unlike in 1991, there was to be no six-week air attack. The Iraqis expected weeks of air attack, which would provide them ample time to torch the oil fields. Instead, the fields were seized on the first day.

General Tommy Franks, the commander in 2003, rejected a repetition of the 1991 air campaign in favor of a brief air attack and lightning-speed ground offensive that would leave no time for Saddam to use the WMDs that

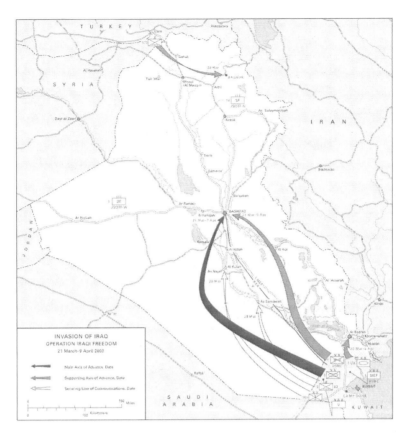

Operation Iraqi Freedom, March 21–April 9, 2003
(U.S. Army Center of Military History)

it was presumed were in his possession. Militarily, Iraqi forces were widely dispersed and did not present a target-rich environment compared to 1991. As a consequence, the scheduled five days of bombing was whittled down to just nine hours of "shock and awe" bombing and missile strikes before the major ground offensive scheduled for the night of March 21. The bombs used were far more accurate than those dropped in 1991, when only 10 percent of the munitions had been "smart" bombs. In the Iraq War, the proportion was 70 percent. Guidance systems were now fitted on the bombs, which were delivered by the B-2 Stealth Bomber, the B-1, and the veteran B-52.

The conventional war between coalition forces and the Iraqi army was quick and decisive. Two enormous columns advanced from Kuwait on Baghdad, 300 miles to the north. The main effort was a sweeping left hook from the west by the Army's V Corps, Third Infantry Division. The second column, the First Marine Expeditionary Force, pushed up from Kuwait along Route 1 between the Euphrates and Tigris Rivers. Troops of the 82nd and 101st Airborne Divisions would secure objectives short of Baghdad. The British First Armored Division was to capture Basra, Iraq's second largest city and home to 400,000 Shiite residents who remembered Saddam's brutal suppression of their 1991 uprising.

As the coalition forces crossed into Iraq, military vehicles stretched for miles from Kuwait into Iraq. It "looked like all of California was driving into Nevada." One division required 8,000 vehicles, which consumed 200,000 gallons of fuel each day. Amidst choking dust, the Third Infantry Division and First Marine Division, wherever possible, bypassed cities and towns as they raced over the featureless, bleak landscape toward Baghdad. An Nasiriyah, a sprawling mud-brick and cinder-block city at a strategic point over the Euphrates River, could not be bypassed. There, Baath party die-hard supporters, fedayeen fighters, and Arab jihad (holy war) volunteers resisted the American advance with rocket-propelled grenades (RPGs), Kalashnikov assault rifles, and explosive charges. A supply unit of the Third Infantry Division, 507th Maintenance Company, after midnight on March 23, missed a turning and drove into an ambush, suffering nine killed and six captured, including Private Jessica Lynch, who was later recovered from captivity.

By April 2, lead elements of the Third Infantry were ten miles from Baghdad. In one of the few episodes of organized resistance staged by the Iraqi conventional forces, the 101st Airborne Division destroyed the Hammurabi Republican Guard Division defending the southern approach to Baghdad. On April 9, U.S. Marines swept into downtown Baghdad and helped a group of Iraqis pull down a twenty-foot statue of Saddam Hussein in Al Ferdous Square as onlookers cheered and waved. Most Iraqis welcomed the fall of one history's most brutal tyrants. The U. S. Army and Marines had occupied Baghdad and overthrown Saddam Hussein's government within an astonishing twenty-one days, at the price of only 117 American lives.

On May 1, on the flight deck of the aircraft carrier USS *Abraham Lincoln*, just off the coast of San Diego, President Bush proclaimed, "Major combat operations in Iraq have ended." In the background, a large banner proclaimed: "MISSION ACCOMPLISHED." The astonishing victory and the swift capture of Baghdad in early spring turned sour by the summer as witnessed by a growing insurgency by die-hard Baathists, Islamic jihadists, and Sunni extremists.

The overthrow of Saddam Hussein had ended the historic dominance of Iraq by Sunni Muslims, who make up about a fifth of the population. Their resentment would fuel the growing insurgency.

During the summer, attacks upon American forces increased in the so-called Sunni Triangle, an area inhabited by six million Sunnis that stretched 80 miles west of Baghdad and 120 miles north. Not even the capture in December 2003 of the sixty-six-year-old Saddam Hussein, hiding in a tiny cellar, a "spider hole," near his hometown of Tikrit, ended the car bombings and other acts of violence. Improvised explosive devices (IEDs), RPGs, and bullets killed hundreds of Americans and thousands of Iraqis who sought only peace and a decent life for their children. It is clear, however, that the effort to create a democratic government in Iraq must include a political element to win the support of all the diverse groups within that society if civil war is to be avoided.

Elections were held in Iraq on January 30, 2005, and a newly elected assembly and political system took power. A constitution is to be drafted by August 15 and approved by referendum in October 2005. The constitution will provide for power sharing between Shiites, Sunnis, Kurds, and other minorities that make up the modern nation of Iraq. Saddam Hussein no longer rules 27 million Iraqis with an iron fist. On the contrary, he awaits his day in the court of justice.

The Iraq War has cost 1,770 American deaths, thousands of wounded, and a financial cost of well over two billion dollars. Twenty-five thousand Iraqis have probably died in the two years of conflict that began in March 2003. For the U.S. Army, the irregular phase of the war has required participation by National Guard combat units on a scale not seen since World War II. National Guard soldiers from every corner of America represent about 40 percent of U.S. ground forces in Iraq, although that percentage is scheduled to be reduced to 11 percent in 2006 as the army deploys two newly expanded active-duty divisions.

There is no cheap and easy solution to the war against global terrorism, religious fanaticism, and the insurgency in Iraq. On the positive side, many of the world's devoutly religious are now fully alive to the metastasized malignancy that, in the name of religion, destroys human life without remorse. Iraq teaches us a twofold lesson: regular armed forces are not an endangered species—our military will sometimes need to wage war on a battlefield and win, but our most severe test may be the battles fought outside the confines of a normal battlefield.

Index

About the Editors
and Contributors

COLIN F. BAXTER is professor of history and chair of the Department of History at East Tennessee State University. A native of Harrow, England, he earned his master's degree and PhD at the University of Georgia in Athens, Georgia. He is the author of *The Normandy Campaign, 1944: A Selected Bibliography* (1992), *The War in North Africa, 1940–1943: A Selected Bibliography* (1996), and *Field Marshal Bernard Law Montgomery, 1887–1976: A Selected Bibliography* (1999). He is presently writing a history of Holston Ordnance Works, Kingsport, Tennessee, and the production of RDX during World War II.

JOHN M. CARROLL is Regents' Professor of History at Lamar University in Beaumont, Texas. He coedited, with George C. Herring, *Modern American Diplomacy*, 2nd ed. (1996). Carroll also has an interest in sport history, and his most recent book is *Red Grange and the Rise of Modern Football* (1999). He is currently working on a life-and-times biography of football great Jim Brown.

OWEN CONNELLY is McKissick Dial Professor of History at the University of South Carolina. He is the author of ten books, including a widely used text, *The French Revolution and Napoleonic Era*, 3rd ed. (2000); *Blundering to Glory: Napoleon's Military Campaigns*, 2nd ed. (1999); and *On War and Leadership* (2002). He was a member of the Institute for Advanced Study, Princeton, in 1989 and 1995. He served in the Korean War and was later executive officer of the Rangers' Jungle and Amphibious Training Camp in Florida.

KEVIN M. GANNON is assistant professor of history and a teaching scholar at Grand View College in Des Moines, Iowa. His research spans the Revolutionary period through the Civil War, and he has recently published essays in the *Journal of the Early Republic*, *The Encyclopedia of the New Nation*, and the Blackwell *Companion to the Civil War and Reconstruction*. He is currently working on a manuscript entitled *Nationalism's Opposite: States' Rights, Nullification, and Secession in the Antebellum North*.

JEROME A. GREENE is a research historian with the National Park Service and is stationed in Denver. He is author of *Nez Perce Summer, 1877: The U.S. Army and the Nee-Me-Poo Crisis* (2000); *Morning Star Dawn: The Powder River Expedition and the Northern Cheyennes, 1876* (2003); *Washita: The U.S. Army and the Southern Cheyennes, 1867–1869* (2004); and, with Douglas D. Scott, *Finding Sand Creek: History, Archaeology, and the 1864 Massacre Site* (2004). His most recent book is *The Guns of Independence: The Siege of Yorktown, 1781* (2005). He is currently completing a study of army veterans of the Indian wars of the nineteenth century.

CHRISTOPHER C. HARMON took a BA in history and French language and attained a doctorate in government and international relations from Claremont Graduate School, where his mentors included Harry V. Jaffa, William B. Allen, and Harold W. Rood. His academic fellowships have been with the Claremont Institute, the Hoover Institution, and the E. B. Earhart Foundation. After service as a congressional aide on foreign affairs, where he often wrote on terrorism, Harmon began a decade and a half of teaching strategy, low-intensity conflict, and other subjects to military officers and civilians at the Naval War College, the Marines' Command and Staff College, and other graduate schools, including the Institute of World Politics in Washington, D.C. Dr. Harmon's second book, *Terrorism Today*, appeared in 2000 with advice for a grand strategy that would include greater use of force in counterterrorism. The *London Times Literary Supplement* called the volume "a masterly survey of the big picture of world violence." The author's appreciation is due to Randy Bowdich and Len Rosanoff for their critical reviews of the draft.

WALTER L. HIXSON is the author of numerous studies on U.S. foreign policy, including *Parting the Curtain: Propaganda, Culture, and the Cold War* (1997) and *George F. Kennan: Cold War Iconoclast* (1989). Hixson, professor of history at the University of Akron, is completing work on a new book, *Myth to Power: Identity, History, and the Crisis of U.S.-American Power*, to be published by Yale University Press.

PIERCE C. MULLEN completed graduate work at the University of Nebraska, Lincoln, and earned his doctorate at the University of California, Berkeley, in 1964. He is professor emeritus at Montana State University in the history of science and technology. He participated in the army history program at U.S. Military Academy via the Army ROTC program in the summers of 1984 and 1985 and subsequent Army War College activities.

DAVID H. OVERY was professor and chair of the history department at Saint Cloud State University, Minnesota.

WILLIAM GARRETT PISTON received his BA and MA from Vanderbilt University and his PhD from the University of South Carolina. Author of a biography of Confederate general James Longstreet and coauthor of *Wilson's Creek: The Second Battle of the Civil War and the Men Who Fought It*, he is currently working on a photographic history of the war in Missouri. He teaches military and Civil War history at Missouri State University in Springfield, Missouri.

J. DAVID VALAIK is professor emeritus of history at Canisius College in Buffalo, New York. His published work has been in the area of American Catholicism and the Spanish Civil War. The subject of Theodore Roosevelt has also received the attention of Dr. Valaik. He was awarded the Bene Marenti Medal (meaning "well deserved") from Canisius. Dr. Valaik is currently writing a memoir of his forty-four-year career.

H. P. WILLMOTT currently is the director of the online MA program in military history at Norwich University in Northfield, Vermont, and is a research fellow with Greenwich Maritime Institute, University of Greenwich. A fellow of the Royal Historical Society, he has served on the faculties of Temple University, the University of Memphis, and the Department of Military Strategy and Operations at the National War College. He has written extensively on modern naval and military subjects including *Empires in the Balance*, *The Barrier and the Javelin*, and *Grave of a Dozen Schemes* and the critically acclaimed *The Great Crusade*. His latest book is *The Battle of Leyte Gulf* (2005).

David R. Woodward is professor of history at Marshall University. He has been a student of the First World War for some forty years. His books include *Lloyd George and the Generals*; *Trial by Friendship: Anglo-American Relations, 1917–1918*; *Field Marshal Sir William Robertson: Chief of the Imperial General Staff in the Great War*; and *The Military Correspondence of Field Marshal Sir William Robertson, Chief of the Imperial General Staff in the Great War*.